to Ming

from Masayoshi

24 August 2001

FINANCIAL BIG BANG IN ASIA

Financial Big Bang in Asia

Edited by
MASAYOSHI TSURUMI
Hosei University, Tokyo

Ashgate

Aldershot • Burlington USA • Singapore • Sydney

Published by
Ashgate Publishing Limited
Gower House
Croft Road
Aldershot
Hants GU11 3HR
England

Ashgate Publishing Company
131 Main Street
Burlington, VT 05401-5600 USA

Ashgate website: http://www.ashgate.com

British Library Cataloguing in Publication Data
Financial big bang in asia
    1.Financial crises - Asia 2.Asia - Economic conditions -
    1945-
    I.Tsurumi, Masayoshi
    332'.095

Library of Congress Control Number: 2001086243

ISBN 0 7546 1691 6

Printed and bound by Athenaeum Press, Ltd.,
Gateshead, Tyne & Wear.

Contents

List of Figures and Tables

Figures

Tables

List of Contributors

Prakarn Arphasil

Assistant Professor and the Director of Graduate Program, Faculty of Economics, Thammasat University, Bangkok

Kok Fay Chin

Lecturer in Economics, Faculty of Development Science, Universiti Kebangsaan, Selangor

K.S. Jomo

Professor, Faculty of Economics and Administration, University of Malaya, Kuala Lumpur

Dong Won Kim

Editorial Writer, Maeil Business Newspaper, Seoul

Tsun-Siou Lee

Professor, Department of Finance, National Taiwan University, Taipei

Joseph Y. Lim

Professor, School of Economics, University of the Philippines, Manila

Shi Jin Liu

Researcher, Development Research Center, The State Council of P. R. China, Beijing

Yim Fai Luk

Lecturer, School of Economics and Finance, University of Hong Kong, Hong Kong

Anwar Nasution

Dean, Professor, Faculty of Economics, University of Indonesia, Jakarta; Senior Deputy Governor, Bank Indonesia

Inn Won Park

Associate Professor, Graduate School of International Studies, Korea University, Seoul

Takao Saga

Senior Researcher, Financial and Securities Markets, Tokyo

Partha Sen

Professor, Delhi School of Economics, Delhi

Masayoshi Tsurumi

Professor, Faculty of Economics, Hosei University, Tokyo

Chen Ghui Zhang

Researcher, Development Research Center, Beijing

List of Japanese Version's Contributors

The Japanese Version is entitled *Financial Crisis and System Reform in Asia* (in Japanese), Hosei University Press, Tokyo, 2000.

Hideki Esho — Professor, Faculty of Economics, Hosei University, Tokyo

Masanao Ito — Professor, Graduate School of Economics, University of Tokyo, Tokyo

Won-Jung Kim — Professor, Faculty of Humanities, Niigata Sangyo University, Niigata

Fumiharu Mieno — Assistant Professor, Faculty of Economics, Hosei University, Tokyo

Sumimaru Odano — Professor, Faculty of Economics, Shiga University, Shiga

Hidenobu Okuda — Professor, Faculty of Economics, Hitotsubashi University, Tokyo

Megumi Suto — Professor, Faculty of Economics, Chuo University, Tokyo

Masayoshi Tsurumi — Professor, Faculty of Economics, Hosei University, Tokyo

Mariko Watanabe — Researcher, Institute of Developing Economies, Chiba

Dong-Ho Yeom — Lecturer, Faculty of Economics, Hosei University, Tokyo

Preface

The East Asian economies enjoyed "miraculous" economic growth in the 1990s, and were expected to prosper in the twenty-first century. However, the scenery suddenly darkened in the summer of 1997. People were terrorized by the prospect of falling straight from heaven to hell. The currency crisis spread quickly from Thailand to the ASEAN economies, and then in the fall to the Northeast Asian economies. The crisis badly shook all of the East Asian economies. Few scholars or researchers expected that the crisis would deepen and spread from a currency crisis into a banking crisis, and finally into an economic crisis. Discussions of the causes of the crisis have elicited a great variety of opinions on the culprits: hedge funds, foreign exchange policy, dependence on foreign capital, bubble economies, corporate governance, undeveloped financial markets, and so on. The variety may be attributed perhaps to the compound nature of the financial crisis. This book focuses on the Asian financial crisis from the long-term perspective of the development of financial reform in Asia.

It may be that the Asian financial crisis was merely one (large, however) event along the long road of financial reform in the East Asian economies. The characteristics of the road are as follows. First, it was a result of financial reform up to then. Second, the defects of the financial systems in these economies caused the crisis. Third, financial system reform has developed rapidly since the outbreak of the crisis.

The outbreak of the financial crisis pushed the Asian economies, including not only Japan and Korea but also the ASEAN countries, toward much more radical financial system reform. The financial systems in the East Asian countries are making revolutionary changes toward more efficient, robust, and transparent systems, with great dependence on market mechanisms. These reforms include not only programs for financial liberalization but also programs for the restructuring of financial and economic systems. The East Asian countries have been pushed strongly to radically transform their out-of-date financial systems. Their financial markets have been opened to the world and their financial structures changed toward more market-based ones. We term this new wave of radial financial reforms in Asia the "financial big bang in Asia". The purpose of this book is to analyze and assess the financial crisis in the different Asian economies by comparing them from the point of view of long-run financial system reform, and to consider the future prospect of financial reform in Asia.

This book is one of the results of the international research project "Financial Big Bang in Asia" at the Institute of Comparative Economic Studies. The project, which was designed in the fall of 1996, was organized as one of the institute's international research projects of the spring of 1997. More than twenty representative, distinguished Asian scholars participate in this project. Their activities were carried out mainly in two groups: the Japanese and the overseas participants. At the beginning, the aim of the project was to analyze and assess financial reforms in Asia countries from the point of view of balanced development between banking systems and capital markets. In the summer of 1997, however, the financial crisis broke out in East Asia. We therefore found ourselves compelled to also analyze the causes of the crisis. Therefore we slightly modified the main issue of the project to analyzing and assessing the Asian crisis from the point of view of the development of financial reform in each Asian economy.

This project on the "Financial Big Bang in Asia" has been carried out over three years, from 1997 to 2000. In September 2000, we published the other result, a book with the title *Financial Crisis and System Reform in Asia* (in Japanese; Hosei University Press, Tokyo) written by the Japanese group members. The current book's contributors consist of ten prominent scholars representing nine Asian economies: Japan, Korea, China, Hong Kong, the Philippines, Thailand, Indonesia, Malaysia, and India.

This book consists of eleven chapters which analyze the financial crisis and reform in nine Asian economies. The first chapter is an introduction which gives an overview of the financial crisis and financial reform in the nine economies. The five chapters that follow it consist of an analysis of five Northeastern Asian economies: Japan, Korea, Taiwan, Hong Kong, and China. The seventh to tenth chapters focus on four Southeast Asian economies: Thailand, Malaysia, Indonesia, and the Philippines. The last chapter concerns India. These economies can be generally divided into three groups from the point of view of the depth of the crisis and how it influenced the economy. First, there was a group of severely shaken economies, including Japan, Korea, Thailand, and Indonesia. Second, Malaysia, China, Hong Kong and the Philippines belong to a group that were moderately or weakly affected. Finally, India suffered very little at all. The differences in the effects of the crisis between these ten economies depend mainly on their differing developments in terms of financial liberalization. This book has some advantages compared to other works on the Asian financial crisis in terms of the area it covers.

First, it places greater emphasis on the five economies of Northeast Asia than on those of Southeast Asia. It has been typical for these groups to be discussed separately, or through the use of representative economies, such as Thailand, Korea, and Indonesia. The second advantage of this work is that it includes Japan, an advanced economy, in addition to the developing economies of East Asia. Although it played a key role in the Asian financial crisis, Japan has often been discussed apart from the developing economies of East Asia. It is necessary, however, to analyze Japan as one part of the development of financial reform and crisis in the East Asian economy. The third advantage it that this work includes Hong Kong, Taiwan, and India, which managed to avoid the financial crisis. Singapore, which was originally to be included as one chapter, has been dropped from this book, as it is not important enough economically to trigger a third wave of the financial big bang in Asia.

The editor would like to acknowledge the financial support provided for this project by the Institute of Comparative Economic Studies, Hosei University and the Zengin Foundation for Studies on Economics and Finance (Tokyo).

In addition, I have received intellectual assistance of various sorts from a number of people and institutions. I wish to thank in particular: Hugh T. Patrick of Columbia University, Lawrence J. White of New York University, Wan-Suk Koh of the Korean Stock Exchange, Andrew L. T. Scheng, formally of the Hong Kong Monetary Authority, Mathew Harrison of the Hong Kong Stock Exchange, Jyuro Teranishi of Hitotsubashi University, Konosuke Odaka of Hosei University, Masahiro Kawai of the World Bank, and Kichiji Oritani of the Bank of Japan.

Finally, I wish to thank Dong-Ho Yeom, Guo Fu Min, Takeshi Uesaka, Hiroshi Gunji, Yuko Nikaido, all graduate students of Hosei University, who gave me tremendous and enthusiastic help in organizing this project and editing this book.

Masayoshi Tsurumi
Professor, Faculty of Economics
Former Director, The Institute of Comparative Economic Studies
Hosei University, Tokyo

1 Introduction: Financial Crisis and System Reform in Asia

MASAYOSHI TSURUMI

The Financial Big Bang in Asia

During the past few years, Asian countries suffered from a host of financial and economic crises. What were the main causes of the financial crises? Did the Asian countries have serious defects in their financial or economic systems? If so, these troubles might at least be indications that the financial systems of these countries, which in the recent past were efficient enough, have somehow come to a standstill. These countries are now being pushed to reform their financial systems so as to reach the so-called international standards, enabling their economies to survive in the future.

Many Asian economies have carried out financial reforms, either rapidly or gradually, since the 1980s. In the middle of the 1990s, just before the outbreak of the Asian financial crisis, the Japanese and Korean governments each announced major action plans involving drastic financial reforms toward more efficient and robust financial systems. They termed these reforms "Financial Big Bangs" in accordance with the precedent in the UK. The financial "Big Bangs" in Japan and Korea would actually cover larger areas than the original model which was carried earlier out in England: they would involve financial opening, capital markets, banking, the supervision system, and so on.

The outbreak of the financial crisis pushed the Asian economies, not only Japan and Korea but many of the ASEAN countries, toward unprecedentedly radical financial system reforms. Many Asian countries are tackling their financial system reform with the help of or in consultation with the IMF and leading developed countries. The financial systems in the Asian countries are changing drastically toward much more efficient, robust, and transparent ones, with great dependence on market mechanisms. The reforms include not only financial liberalization but also programs for restructuring financial and economic systems. The Asian countries have been pushed to radically transform their out-of-date, weak financial

1

systems. Their financial markets had been opened to the world and their financial structures have changed toward more market-based ones. We term this wave of radical restructuring of the financial system the "Financial Big Bang in Asia".

It is the purpose of this chapter to clarify how financial system reform has been implemented in the Asian countries, comparing cases in order to find a preferable financial system for economic development. I will try to cast light on the structural problems or defects of the financial systems in Asian countries by analyzing the causes of the Asian financial crisis. The first section clarifies that the Asian financial crisis was a regional liquidity crisis driven by overseas capital movements which were induced by an increasing macroeconomic imbalance related to private capital activities such as an asset bubble or an over-investment. The next section focuses on the crisis that was caused by disorder of a financial system following to liberalization. The last section is conclusion in this chapter.

The Liquidity Crisis in Asia

Characteristics of Modern Financial Crises

The Asian financial crisis was the most serious in recent history in terms of its depth and regional extent. The European currency crisis in 1992 and the Mexican crisis in 1994 may have been immature precedents. Some have called it "a 21st century type" financial crisis. What were the new phenomena in the recent modern financial crisis? The remarkable characteristics were that it was: (1) a *compound crisis*, (2) a *regional* crisis, (3) a *liquidity* crisis, and (4) a *private capital-driven* crisis.

The first conspicuous feature of the Asian financial crisis is that it was not a simple phenomenon but a combined one: a currency crisis, an asset deflation, a banking crisis, and an economic crisis. The first feature, the currency crisis, involved a sudden fall in the exchange rates to the US dollar, and a critical shortage of foreign reserves. The Asian currencies, from the Thai baht to the Indonesia rupiah to the Korean won, fell sharply one after another, to less than half of their value in the pre-crisis six months. Interestingly enough, this currency crisis was accompanied by sharp slumps in the stock markets. Asset deflations in stock and real-estate markets occurred before or after an outbreak of the currency crisis in many of the Asian economies. The slumps in foreign exchange markets were accompanied not only by asset deflation but also by the banking crisis. Many banks suffered from the liquidity crisis due to the sudden increase of non-performing loans and large amounts of deposits withdrawn. While the banking crisis in Thailand, Korea, and Japan occurred before the outbreak of the currency crisis, the banking crisis followed the currency crisis in Malaysia and Indonesia.

The second characteristic is that it was a regional crisis, where contagion spread easily from country to country, similar to a domestic run with exchange at par. Sudden capital outflows from a domestic market represent an attack not only against the country's domestic financial markets, but also against its foreign reserves. This causes a liquidity crisis. It was this kind of regional liquidity crisis that caused the "contagion" in the Asian financial crisis. In a regional collapse of financial confidence, foreign "runs" affect not only economies with bad economic fundamentals, but occasionally also well-performed like a contagion from Thailand to the other Asian countries through sudden, huge capital outflows. Foreign and domestic investors, seeing the collapse of financial confidence in the Asian economies, rushed to be the first to withdraw their financial assets or claims from the domestic markets. While a domestic "run" is an exchange of deposits for cash, a foreign "run" is an exchange of domestic assets for foreign assets. The stiffer the setting of the foreign exchange rate, the more a foreign run comes to resemble a domestic run, which is an exchange at par. Sudden capital outflows from a domestic market represent an attack not only against the country's domestic financial markets, but also against its foreign reserves. This causes a liquidity crisis. It was this kind of regional liquidity crisis that caused the "contagion" in the Asian financial crisis. In a regional collapse of financial confidence, foreign "runs" affect not only economies with bad economic fundamentals, but occasionally also well-performing economies.

The fourth characteristic is that the crisis was driven by private capital movements. While the foreign debt crisis in the 1980s was a default problem caused by public institutions in developing countries, the Asian financial crisis was caused by financial trading among private capital; not only suppliers but also seekers of capital overseas.

In short, the Asian financial crisis was a *compound, regional, liquidity, private capital-driven* crisis.

The Liquidity Crisis in Asia

Many scholars, during the first phase of the Asian financial crisis, understood the crisis simply as "a currency crisis", using Krugman's (1979) model. Krugman, on the basis of the currency crises in Latin America in the 1970s, analyzed the problem as speculative attacks, resulting in a currency crisis, within a process of the deterioration of economic fundamentals. He focused on government budget deficits, increases in money supply(M2), and inflation as the main economic fundamentals. On the basis of the Krugman model, the first generation model, Obstfeld (1996) described a self-fulfilling speculation model based on new experiences of currency crises in the 1990s, such as those in Europe and Mexico. Obstfeld insisted that a currency crisis could occur through a self-fulfilling speculative attack rather than because of economic fundamentals, meaning that there were multiple equilibria. It belongs still to a category of a currency crisis as the second generation model. Both models analyze the occurrence of currency crises in a fixed foreign rate exchange system, although they assign a different role to economic fundamentals in the currency crisis.

The occurrence of the Asian financial crisis has opened new fields in financial crisis theory beyond the Krugman and Obstfeld models. Both models may have some theoretical limitations in analyzing the Asian financial crisis. The first issue involves the fixed foreign exchange rate system, which both models assume in their arguments on the balance-of-payment crisis. Before the outbreak of the Asian financial crisis, many of the Asian economies had not formally adopted a fixed foreign exchange rate system. According to IMF (1996), Asian countries were using four types of foreign exchange rate systems: (1) a float system (Japan, India, Philippines) (2) a managed float system (Singapore, Indonesia, Korea, Malaysia), (3) a currency basket pegging system (Thailand), and (4) a currency board fixed system (Hong Kong). However many of these economies managed their foreign exchange rates more stiffly in practice than would appear formally, because they used the foreign exchange rate as an anchor in their macro-economic policies. Thus many scholars insist on the validity of the models based on fixed foreign exchange rate systems, calling the systems in Asian countries at the time "*de-facto* dollar pegging systems". Although the "*de-facto*" approach might be useful, we must not neglect the differences between Thailand, with its "*de-facto* dollar pegging system", and Korea, Malaysia, and Indonesia, which had more flexible managed float systems.

The second issue is related to whether the Asian financial crisis came from economic fundamentals or from self-fulfilling speculation. Many of the pre-crisis Asian economies had successfully held down their budget deficits and inflation to a low level, and thus would have been seen as models of good performance from the point of view of the Krugman' first generation model. Krugman (1999) in fact admitted that the Obstfeld self-fulfilling speculation model was superior to his model for analyzing the Asian financial crisis. It is certain that self-fulfilling speculation played a considerable role in the Asian financial crisis. However, where one finds smoke there is always fire. Have people, influenced by the Krugman model, overlooked signals of imbalances of economic fundamentals. Sachs *et al.* (1999) cited a rapid increase of bank credit, an appreciation of the real foreign exchange rate, and insufficient foreign reserves for foreign capital outflows as main causes of the Asian financial crisis. Some factors driven by private capitals in the economic fundamentals deteriorated while the public sector-driven fundamentals ameliorated in many of the Asian economies in the latter 1990s.

Thus, the Asian financial crisis was caused by self-fulfilling speculation based on the deterioration of private-driven fundamentals, such as over-investment, excessive bank credit, mini-bubbles, current account deficits, excess capital inflows, lacks of foreign reserves and so on. New theoretical trials based on this deterioration of the private-driven fundamentals have emerged since the outbreak of the Asian financial crisis. The representative model is a "twin crises" model, which is now called a "third generation" model against Krugman's first-generation and Obstfeld's second-generation models.

Kaminsky and Reinhart (1996, 1999) found a trend of co-occurrences of currency crises and banking crises through analyzing twenty financial crises from 1970 to the middle of 1995 around the world. Currency crises followed banking crises, which followed financial liberalization. In other words, a financial liberalization would cause a "twin crises", of a currency and banking crisis.

The next question is why or how currency and banking crises tend to occur at the same time. In this regard Calvo *et al.* (1993) and McKinnon and Pill (1996) pointed to a cycle of boom-bust or bubble-burst. Calvo *et al.* (1993) focused on the relationship between international capital movements and bubble-burst cycles. Immense foreign capital inflows bring about a rapid expansion of domestic bank credit, pushing regional economies into a bubble. Sudden capital outflows cause the burst of this bubble. This link between foreign capital flows and bank credit causes not only currency crises but also, simultaneously, banking crises. On the other hand, Goldfajn and Valdes (1997), Chang and Velasco (1998), and Miller (1998a, b) cast light on the occurrence of twin crises from the point of view of a liquidity crisis. They extended the depositor's run model built by Diamond and Dybvig (1983) from a closed economy to an open one where there is no longer any clear distinction between an overseas drain of funds from foreign reserves and a domestic drain from bank reserves. These studies argue that in an open economy, these twin crises are an issue of a regional liquidity crisis or a regional bank run, without distinction between the internal and external economies. This paper, by analyzing the elements of a regional liquidity crisis, develops the twin crises hypothesis further to a triple crises hypothesis.

In general a bank run or a panic withdrawal by depositors causes a banking crisis. If many of the funds drained from banks flow overseas, rather than staying in the local market, there is a sharp decrease not only in bank reserves but in foreign reserves as well. In this case twin crises erupt: a currency crisis and a banking crisis. In contrast, a crisis can also arise due to an external factor. A sudden huge repatriation of foreign funds, for whatever reason, gives rise to sharp decreases in both bank reserves and foreign reserves, causing simultaneous internal and external liquidity crises. These types of twin crises have tended to occur more and more frequently under the recent financial globalization which has blurred distinctions between internal and external drains.

A huge drain of deposits from banks causes not only a banking crisis or liquidity crisis for domestic banks, but also simultaneously a currency crisis or liquidity crisis for the central bank. This sudden drain of deposits brings about a financial panic both in the domestic and regional markets. In the recent financial crises, it was clear that such a regional *liquidity* crisis caused a regional *contagion* effect. In a financial panic, a bank run can affect not only unhealthy banks or economies but also coincidentally healthy banks or economies, due to incomplete information about banking activities.

The Asian financial crisis was a combined phenomenon: a drain of enormous deposits from banks simultaneously became a fatal drain from the central bank's foreign reserves. A "twin crises" approach is much better than the "currency crisis" approach at grasping the real aspects of the Asian financial crisis. The "twin crises" approach should be highly evaluated for theorizing a new phenomenon, namely the regional liquidity crisis of the 1990s. However the "twin crises" approach is still insufficient as a theory of the modern financial crisis. This is because it potentially underestimates the aspect of asset deflation that has become more and more pronounced in financial crises in the 1990s. Asset prices, especially those of stocks and real estate, collapsed in the most seriously affected Asian economies in parallel with the fall of the foreign exchange rates. The asset deflation deepened the financial crisis by negatively influencing currencies, banking, and the real economy in Asia. The movement of asset prices played a critical role in the bubble-burst cycle. Therefore the Asian financial crisis should be understood as "triple crises" consisting of a currency crisis, asset deflation, and a banking crisis. In order to incorporate this point, we need to analyze depositors' or investors' behavior in greater detail, as follows.

Many of the twin crises hypotheses assume that all deposits in a local market have the potential to flee overseas. For example Sachs *et al.* (1996) adopted M2 as a denominator for a ratio of foreign reserves, which is one of the crisis signals. From the point of view of a liquidity crisis, it seems a very unique idea to adopt M2 rather than imports or exports as the denominator. Is it really, however, common for all depositors, whether they use demand accounts or saving accounts, and whether they are residents or non-residents, to freely transfer their deposits from local to overseas markets? At present this assumption seems unrealistic, although its reality may be increasing along with financial globalization. Table 1.4 shows changes in the foreign reserves/M2 ratio in the main Asian economies throughout the 1990s. Nearly all the economies maintained ratios around the level of 10-20% with the exception of Singapore, for which the level was nearly equal. These numbers hardly reflect the degree or the depth of the 1997 financial crisis for the different economies; Thailand and Malaysia should have been more stable than China and Taiwan. Why did not this ratio play a signaling role for the financial crisis? It is because the deposits which fled overseas were only a small part of all deposits. At present, it is likely not realistic for all depositors to freely access both local and overseas markets. Some countries still maintain various kinds of capital controls and many small depositors have little access to the overseas markets. In order to solve this problem, we need to re-examine the characteristics of depositor behavior and focus on the group of depositors who have high propensity toward capital flight.

Who moves their capital overseas? As we will see, capital flight may consist of two forms: withdrawals by foreigners, and capital flight by residents.

The first form is withdrawals by foreigners. One of main triggers of financial crisis is that foreign financial institutions suddenly withdraw their investments from a local market. Withdrawals by foreigners consist of repatriations by both foreign lenders and by portfolio investors. In the former case, foreign lenders suddenly refuse a new loan or a loan rollover to a local financial institution, while in the latter case foreign investors suddenly repatriate their portfolio investments from the stock or real estate markets. Whether a cause is internal or external, this repatriation of capital by foreigners triggers a liquidity crisis both in the domestic banking system and the foreign exchange rate system.

The second form is capital flight by residents. The capital flight begins when residents lose confidence in their own financial or economic system due to soaring inflation, a banking crisis, or a political crisis. Again, there are two types of actors: wholesalers and retailers. Financial institutions and major firms, in the early stage of capital flight, begin to transfer their local currency assets to overseas currency markets in order to hedge the risk of a sharp depreciation of the local currency. As the confidence breaks down severely, the capital flight comes to involve not only wholesalers but also common people in the retail market. At that stage, the nation's currency system comes to the brink of collapse due to the internal and external drain.

Huge sums of foreign capital which had accumulated in the Asian local markets in the last decade began suddenly to flow out in the summer of 1997. For the main, as mentioned above, there were four main routes of capital outflow: debt repatriation, portfolio repatriation, wholesale flights, and retail flights. Which was the main route of the capital outflows in the Asian financial crisis? First, I would like to address the issue of the balance between bank debts and portfolio investments.

Table 1.1 Gross Capital Outflows in Asian Crisis

(Unit: US$ millions)

		Thailand			Korea			Indonesia		
		Portfolio Investment	Other Capital	Bank	Portfolio Investment	Other Capital	Bank	Portfolio Investment	Other Capital	Bank
1997	I	169	1723	2543	2903	3499	1220	1009	636	-244
	II	1630	-5971	245	6107	3985	1664	1103	-119	-99
	III	2533	-8889	-3022	5364	-2087	-1179	646	-231	709
	IV	466	-9045	-3288	-2086	-13714	-11490	-5390	-2756	-642
1998	I	251	-7793	-2176	2657	-7172	-3343	-3548	-2147	-840
	II	4	-4266	-2393	1746	-2622	-662	1840	-1990	-1064
	III	-309	-3306	-2831	-3766	-3323	-2020	-	-	-

		Philippines			Taiwan			India		
		Portfolio Investment	Other Capital	Bank	Portfolio Investment	Other Capital	Bank	Portfolio Investment	Other Capital	Bank
1997	I	1205	1547	1323	1333	1825	1688	791	2092	1078
	II	514	2528	2243	-369	3830	3010	735	3531	817
	III	-442	958	-359	-2287	1131	192	508	1602	-587
	IV	-677	-637	-1539	-231	-1179	-1690	509	2053	-210
1998	I	-182	974	-24	734	133	193	87	4313	913
	II	319	96	683	-201	445	590	-423	1030	5
	III	-483	-219	-687	-193	-328	-947	-117	3580	-393

Source: IMF, *International Financial Statistics*, June 1999.

Table 1.1 indicates quarterly changes in amount of capital outflows divided by bank debts and portfolio investments in the main Asian economies around the time of the outbreak of the crisis. These figures demonstrate that indeed, bank debts and portfolio investments were the two main routes of capital outflows during the Asian financial crisis. For Thailand and Korea, bank debts were the main route of capital outflows; portfolio investments did not play a major role. On the other hand, in Malaysia, Indonesia, the Philippines, and Taiwan, portfolio investments, who carried as heavy a weight as bank debts, became the trigger for the outbreak of the crisis. Looking upon Thailand and Korea as typical cases of crisis, many scholars emphasize the aspect of debt crisis in the Asian financial crisis. Certainly, Korea and Thailand played a critical role in the outbreak of the Asian crisis. However Malaysia, the Philippines, and Taiwan played their own parts. If they had not been involved, the crisis would have ended as merely a local crisis in Thailand or Korea. The Asian financial crisis was a regional crisis which worked through the effects of both types of capital movements, i.e. bank debts and portfolio investments. The influence of portfolio investments on national economies and financial crises should not be underestimated.

New trends in capital movements could be seen in the Asian financial crisis. The first conspicuous trend was that the crisis involved international private debts. While the international crisis in the 1980s was one of sovereign debts, that of the 1990s was one of private debt. In the 1997 crisis, neither the lenders nor the borrowers with default problems were state enterprises; rather they were private capital. The second new trend was the increasing development of international portfolio investments. While stock markets developed rapidly in the developing economies of Asia since the end of 1980s, the foreign portfolio investments which were growing in the developed countries flowed into the Asian stock markets in huge amounts.

These two types of capital flows, which mutually affected one another, pushed the crisis into a downward spiral. First, the sudden withdrawal by foreigners of portfolio investments from local stock or real state markets caused sharp falls in currency and assets prices, in turn giving rise to the withdrawal of private loans by foreign banks from the local market. This early development brought about a full-scale currency crisis in the Asian economies. Second, a sharp fall in asset prices or a liquidity crisis in regional capital markets such as Tokyo, Hong Kong, and Singapore forced already-suffering large financial institutions to drastically readjust their balance sheets downwards. This downwards readjustment caused a large scale withdrawal from local markets, bringing a severe credit crunch not only to the domestic market but to overseas local markets as well. Miller (1998a) pointed out this contagion effect through the readjustment of balance sheets by big banks in her "twin crises" model.

Capital flights is a second issue involving the relationships between capital outflows and a financial crisis. Did capital flight by residents, in addition to withdrawals by non-residents, play an important role in exacerbating the Asian crisis? I do not yet have sufficient detailed data about capital flight by residents in the Asian economies. At present it is only possible to get information on monthly changes of outstanding deposits of commercial bank depositors in some economies.

Table 1.2 Changes of Demand Deposit Outstanding by Ownership in Indonesian Commercial Banks

(Unit: A= Rupiah billions, a~d= %)

denominated	A Total Bank Deposit rupiah	foreign	a State Enterprises rupiah	foreign	b Private Enterprises rupiah	foreign	c Individual Residents rupiah	foreign	d Non-residents rupiah	foreign
1996 12	44,817	12,675								
1997 1	43,410	13,398	-19.6	1.6	2.0	2.6	1.9	0.7	2.5	4.3
2	44,872	13,344	11.9	-4.5	8.0	4.7	1.3	4.4	-14.5	-14.4
3	42,628	14,375	5.3	9.2	-4.4	3.5	7.0	10.5	12.8	38.5
4	44,320	13,769	8.0	12.4	6.0	6.0	-3.0	1.6	-3.3	-27.2
5	44,546	14,625	-8.2	1.2	-3.3	12.5	-2.0	5.5	0.6	-8.9
6	44,785	14,585	7.0	5.2	10.9	-0.1	3.7	8.7	-11.9	-15.0
7	48,805	16,913	-1.2	15.6	-4.9	14.1	5.6	24.9	97.0	-13.4
8	41,291	20,892	-4.0	-7.1	-17.2	16.9	-15.3	17.6	-29.0	28.1
9	43,482	21,913	10.1	36.6	5.6	10.2	4.3	6.8	24.1	14.0
10	43,327	24,317	-11.8	8.4	4.5	5.1	-4.0	26.9	-40.2	-27.1
11	45,430	23,804	16.1	-27.2	-1.1	3.9	-1.3	-10.3	21.2	-4.6
12	53,103	30,125	-3.5	12.4	23.2	17.1	19.3	27.6	146.6	35.0
1998 1	58,477	59,393	16.9	109.1	13.7	117.9	18.9	50.9	-1.4	161.3
2	61,248	52,522	-3.1	9.4	-1.3	-12.2	4.5	-11.2	51.5	20.9
3	64,074	44,629	39.2	-13.9	8.2	-6.7	14.8	-13.1	16.0	-52.5
4	56,928	40,127	-13.9	-16.7	-7.1	-5.6	-7.2	-9.9	-59.4	-6.2

Source: Bank Indonesia, *Indonesian Financial Statistics*, July 1998, I.31.

The first salient feature of the change in deposit structure during the crisis in Indonesia, Korea, and Malaysia was that the changes in demand deposits were more remarkable than those of saving deposits (time and saving deposits). A second feature is that, looking at different depositors, enterprises and government-related entities were much more sensitive to financial conditions in changing their portfolios than were individuals. There is little data about how much of the withdrawal of deposits originated in capital flight. Table 1.2 shows changes in deposits outstanding denominated in rupiah and in foreign currencies, by depositors. Non-residents changed their deposits much more frequently than did residents, and among residents, state or private enterprises did so more frequently than individuals. There were two stages in these changes. The first involved a combination of decreasing holdings in rupiah and increasing those in foreign currencies. The second was a combination of decreasing holdings in both rupiah and foreign currencies. While the first indicated a transfer from rupiah to foreign currency deposits within the local market, the second consisted partly of capital flight overseas. Both August 1997 and March 1998 were critical periods for the development of the financial crisis in Indonesia. In August 1997, deposits outstanding in rupiah fell by 7.5 billion rupiah, while foreign currency deposits grew by 4 billion rupiah. The main withdrawers were individuals and private enterprises. During February and April 1998, foreign currency deposits outstanding decreased, more than offsetting the increase of local currency deposits by all four categories of depositors. While rupiah deposits decreased by 4.3 billion rupiah, the decrease in holdings in all currencies reached 12.4 billion rupiah during a three-month period. Even for individuals, rupiah deposits decreased by 2.7 billion rupiah, while foreign currency deposit increased by just 0.9 billion rupiah. This suggests that not only non-residents and enterprises, but also many individual depositors must have sent their capital overseas. Residents in other Asian economies might also have moved their capital overseas, but in smaller volumes than in Indonesia. In the spring of 1998, the financial crisis in Indonesia became much deeper than those in the other Asian economies, when not only wholesalers but many retail depositors as well began to send their capital overseas.

To prevent a recurrence of a financial crisis, we should ensure that a regional liquidity crisis does not arise. The amount of foreign reserves plays a critical role in coping with a liquidity crisis. How much foreign reserves do a central bank need to prevent such a crisis? There are four candidates for ratios to measure whether the foreign reserves are sufficient or not: the ratio of foreign reserves to monthly imports (or exports), money supply (M2), short-term foreign debts, or the sum of short-term foreign debts and portfolio investments. The first is a traditional approach which has typically been used to prepare against imbalances in current account payments. However, the regional liquidity crises in 1990s have revealed the inadequacy of this approach. The other candidates were developed to cope with the regional liquidity crisis from the point of view of the capital account. The second and third are based on the "twin crises" (a liquidity crisis and a debt crisis), while the last is based on the "triple crises" hypothesis.

Of the different types of outflows, those of foreign short-term debts and portfolio investments have great potential for threatening a nation's foreign reserves. As accumulated capital flows out at a stroke when a crisis broke out, it may become necessary to measure the desirable, required level of foreign reserves for the national economy not against net capital flows but rather against gross capital outflows. Whether or not a national economy is involved in a currency crisis depends on how much solvency it maintains for an total accumulated volume of short-term foreign debts or/and foreign portfolio investments. The first line prepared to preserve solvency is the foreign reserves. The second is the ability for the national economy as a whole to borrow new foreign debts, while the third is short-term foreign assets which can be quickly liquidated. Among these, the amount of foreign reserves plays a critical role in coping with a liquidity crisis.

What is the best candidate for indicating the degree of fragility or resiliency of a currency to speculative attacks? Tables 1.3, 1.4, 1.5, and 1.6 show the performance of four candidates – imports, M2, short-term foreign debts, and cumulative amount of short-term debts and portfolio investments – in various Asian economies at the time of the Asian crisis. The higher the percentage, the stronger the resiliency of the national currency. First, the ratios of foreign reserves to imports in Table 1.3 fail to reflect differences in the depth of the financial crisis among the Asian economies. According to this ratio, Hong Kong (3.9) and Malaysia (4.6) would have been more vulnerable than Thailand (7.3) or Korea (5.6). Second, the figures in Table 1.4 show that the ratio to M2 must also not be eligible as it may not reflect the different depths of the financial crisis. Thirdly, as shown by Table 1.5, foreign short-term debt is a more eligible candidate than imports or M2. At the end of 1996, the ratio of foreign reserves as a percentage of outstanding short-term debts was remarkably high in Singapore, Taiwan, Hong Kong, China, India, and Malaysia. While the ratio in the Philippines and Thailand were over one 100%, that in Korea and Indonesia were only about 50%, meaning that foreign reserves covered just one half of the outstanding short-term foreign debt. These ratios as a whole give a much better picture of the Asian crisis than the ratio to M2. However, they still leave serious disagreement in the cases of Thailand, Malaysia, and the Philippines. These economies were deeply embroiled in the financial crisis in spite of the fact that their ratios as shown by the table were not bad. This is because the ratio overlooks the influence of portfolio investments on the crisis in those economies. Table 1.6 takes into account the influences of both foreign short-term debts and portfolio investments. The ratios in all economies except China had rapidly deteriorated due to continuous capital inflows since 1993. As a result, some economies were already in an explosive situation at the end of 1996. The economies of Asia could be by and large divided into three groups according to the rate. The first group was the most vulnerable. In this group, including Korea and Indonesia, foreign reserves were far below potential capital outflows, at 29% and 41%, respectively. The second group was vulnerable, with ratios falling far short of 100%. They were the Philippines (67%), Thailand (72%), and Malaysia (85%). The third group was in decent positions, with their economies holding far and away enough foreign reserves to surpass potential capital outflows. They included India (123%), China (291%), Taiwan (293%), and Singapore (817%). These three groupings reflect quite well the differences in the depth of the crisis in the Asian economies: a seriousness of the crisis in Thailand, Korea and Indonesia, the contagion to Malaysia and

Philippines, and the avoidance of the crisis by Taiwan, China, and India. This table shows that the "triple crises" hypothesis might have better explanatory power than the "twin crises" hypothesis. In other words, the Asian financial crisis stemmed not only from an international debt crisis but from an international portfolio crisis as well.

Table 1.3 Foreign Reserve / Imports (months)

(as on year end, Unit: %)

	China	Hong Kong	Taiwan	Korea	Philippines	Indonesia	Malaysia	Thailand	Singapore	India
1990	9.8	3.6	17.8	4.4	2.0	4.8	4.9	5.8	6.0	-
1991	11.5	3.5	17.4	3.8	4.4	5.0	4.3	6.5	6.7	-
1992	4.6	3.4	15.2	4.6	4.4	5.1	6.0	7.0	7.1	-
1993	3.8	3.7	14.6	5.5	4.0	5.3	7.9	7.5	6.7	-
1994	7.3	3.7	14.5	5.7	4.0	4.9	5.8	7.6	7.1	-
1995	8.8	3.5	11.7	5.6	3.5	4.4	4.1	7.0	7.4	-
1996	10.2	3.9	11.4	5.6	4.4	5.3	4.6	7.3	7.9	-

Source: ADB, *Key Indicators of Developing Asia and Pacific Countries* 1999

Table 1.4 Foreign Reserve / M2 Ratios in the Asian Economies

(as on year end, Unit: %)

	China	Hong Kong	Taiwan	Korea	Philippines	Indonesia	Malaysia	Thailand	Singapore	India
1990	10.7	15.9	34.0	15.5	19.3	19.1	31.8	23.6	78.3	3.5
1991	12.9	16.4	30.6	12.5	35.1	20.6	31.2	25.4	80.0	5.5
1992	5.0	18.0	25.3	14.0	35.1	19.7	39.6	25.5	86.6	6.2
1993	3.8	18.8	23.4	14.6	34.5	18.0	52.9	25.9	94.7	9.8
1994	9.6	19.1	22.0	15.2	28.8	16.6	40.8	26.9	90.4	13.6
1995	10.4	18.8	20.4	16.5	27.0	15.3	30.5	28.1	95.3	12.6
1996	11.7	19.5	18.4	16.1	35.3	15.9	28.8	26.6	96.1	12.2
1997	12.9	21.3	19.1	17.8	33.1	22.7	27.8	29.3	96.8	13.1

Sources: IMF, *International Financial Statistics*, June 1999.
   ADB, *Key Indicators of Developing Asia and Pacific Countries* 1999

Table 1.5 Foreign Reserve / Foreign Short-term Debts Outstanding Ratios in the Asian Economies

(as on year end, Unit: %)

	China	Hong Kong	Taiwan	Korea	Philippines	Indonesia	Malaysia	Thailand	Singapore	India
1990	324.2	426.7	499.9	65.1	46.3	76.5	517.9	171.5	3770.1	60.7
1991	411.0	460.5	530.3	54.7	91.5	71.6	530.6	147.4	3738.6	96.1
1992	154.2	545.2	511.0	68.0	101.6	63.1	476.6	143.8	4256.7	136.7
1993	150.4	585.3	452.0	72.9	117.6	68.7	393.7	112.4	4909.7	373.0
1994	306.4	606.9	488.6	63.9	124.6	67.8	412.7	103.8	5720.5	540.6
1995	340.6	706.5	490.8	55.5	147.3	56.9	328.5	89.9	5491.2	427.6
1996	423.8	450.0	498.9	51.9	147.4	59.8	245.1	102.7	3885.1	353.6
1997	455.6	731.1	398.1	39.2	74.1	48.3	139.9	77.2	2578.3	546.3

Source: IMF, *International Financial Statistics*, June 1999

Table 1.6 Foreign Reserve/(Short-term Debt+Portfolio) Ratios in the Asian Economies

(as on year end, Unit: %)

	China	Hong Kong	Taiwan	Korea	Philippines	Indonesia	Malaysia	Thailand	Singapore	India
1990	324.2	-	502.1	55.3	46.8	77.2	517.9	172.3	2497.6	60.7
1991	390.6	-	508.4	43.5	46.0	72.1	805.0	148.8	1834.1	96.1
1992	144.2	-	461.2	46.8	34.6	63.8	286.4	136.4	1214.9	130.8
1993	115.6	-	371.7	40.3	29.3	63.0	145.9	88.0	780.3	256.2
1994	205.9	-	360.2	36.7	26.8	52.9	108.8	79.8	916.9	202.1
1995	240.9	-	325.8	31.9	24.7	41.6	89.6	68.5	983.0	156.6
1996	290.9	-	293.3	26.1	27.9	41.2	80.0	71.5	818.7	122.5
1997	282.3	-	261.3	16.1	15.1	36.1	68.6	48.0	641.5	135.9

Sources: IMF, *International Financial Statistics*, June 1999.

Bank Negara Malaysia, *Monthly Statistics Bulletin*, December 1998.

Financial System and Financial Crisis

The Asian financial crisis occurred in the background of the enormous foreign capital movements of the 1990s. The crisis could not have taken place without these huge foreign capital movements; they were, however, a necessary but not a sufficient condition. Other factors are needed to explain clearly the causes of the crisis. Did the crisis-hit economies exhibit any bad signs in their macro-economic fundamentals just before the outbreak of the crisis? Obstfeld (1996) emphasized the role of self-fulfilling speculation in the currency crisis. It is certain that in recent currency crises the aspect of self-fulfilling speculation has become stronger compared to imbalances in macro-economic fundamentals. However there is never smoke without fire. A currency speculation attack aims at the weakest point in the fundamental macro-economy. Even if sudden speculative attacks are launched, an economy can survive through good economic policy management. Examples of this are Taiwan, Hong Kong, and Singapore, which avoided the contagion of the currency attacks during the Asian crisis. The decisive factor is the strong and weak points of the macro-economic fundamentals in terms of private capital activities. While foreign capital inflows are the main overseas factor, over-investments or economic bubbles driven by private capital are the main domestic factors in financial crises.

Why did many of the Asian economies experience over-investments or bubble economies in the middle of the 1990s? That is the next question we shall investigate.

Fundamentals in the Asian Crisis

Up until the summer of 1997, few could forecast the outbreak of the Asian crisis from the point of view of macro-economic fundamentals. Nevertheless, the crisis happened. Where was the error? It is likely that macro imbalances had already emerged in many of the Asian economies. The error thus may have been taking the wrong slant in analyzing the fundamentals rather than the simple question of whether there were such imbalances. Many economists focused on indices related to the activities of the public sectors, and tended to put little emphasis on indices on the private sectors in the fundamental macro-economic indices.

Table 1.7 shows the development of the macro-economic fundamentals of the nine Asian economies in the 1990s, giving some main indices. There are ten items, which includes both public and private activities. The years 1993 and 1996 (end of year) were chosen because they show well that there was a bubble-burst cycle in the Asian economies in the 1990s. There were two booms, in the first and latter half of the decade, which were stopped respectively by the 1994 Mexican Crisis and the 1997 Asian crisis. The first point that can be drawn from Table 1.7 is that nearly all the economies, with the exception of the Philippines, achieved high real economic growth for five consecutive years. Second, government budgets were balanced or in surplus in almost all the economies. It is conspicuous that for Singapore the surplus was over 16% (as a % to GDP) and that for Taiwan, at worst, there was a deficit around 4% in 1993. Third, increases in the consumer price index was by and large moderate in the eight economies, with the exception of China, in spite of the fact that Indonesia, the Philippines, and Hong Kong were on slow inflation bases. Fourth, by contrast, there was striking growth in money supply (M2), ranging from 10% to 30%. China's rate was remarkably high, between 20 and 40% while Singapore's alone was under 10%. The above-mentioned indices show that these high rates of increase of money supply did not stem from budget deficit problems. Then what caused them? They may have stemmed from private activities in the following ways: an over-lending or over-investment problem.

Fifth, the growth rate of private consumption was high in some economies. The average rate of the nine economies fell from 10% in 1993 to 7% in 1996. The economies which had higher-than-average figures were China (34.4% falling to 12.4%), Indonesia (11.8% to 9.7%) and Singapore (12% to 6.2%), while the Philippines and India maintained low levels. It is obvious that an abnormal consumption booms occurred in China and Indonesia.

Table 1.7 Macroeconomic Indicators in Asian Economies

(Unit: %)

	Singapore		Thailand		Malaysia		Indonesia		Philippines		India	
	1993	1996	1993	1996	1993	1996	1993	1996	1993	1996	1993	1996
Real GDP Growth	12.6	7.5	8.4	5.5	8.3	8.6	7.3	7.8	2.1	5.8	6.2	7.8
Changes of Consumer Prices Index	2.3	1.4	3.4	5.9	3.5	3.5	9.7	7.9	7.0	9.1	6.4	9.0
M2 Growth	8.5	9.8	18.4	12.6	22.1	19.8	22.0	29.6	24.6	15.8	18.4	16.2
Changes of Domestic Credit to Private Activities	13.9	16.2	24.5	14.5	12.9	23.8	22.7	20.8	40.6	50.4	8.0	8.9
Changes of Stock Price Index	-	3.9	88.4	-35.1	98	24.4	114.7	24.1	154.8	22.2	29.4	-2.7
Stock Trading Value/ GDP	142.2	46.7	69.4	24.4	239	175.4	5.8	14.1	12.5	30.8	7.6	6.7
Fiscal Balance/ GDP	15.8	-	1.9	0.9	0.2	0.7	-0.5	1.4	-1.6	0.3	-2.4	-1.5
Gross Domestic Investment/ GDP	38.0	37.0	39.9	41.8	37.8	41.6	29.5	30.7	24.0	24	20.8	23.1
Gross Domestic Saving/ GDP	45.1	49.3	36.1	36.9	37.6	42.6	32.5	30.1	13.8	14.6	21.8	24.4
Changes of Domestic Consumption	12.0	6.2	8.4	6.3	4.6	6.0	11.8	9.7	3.0	4.6	4.7	6.8
Currebt Account/ GDP	7.3	15.8	-4.9	-7.9	-4.8	-4.8	-1.3	-3.4	-5.5	-4.8	-0.7	-13

	Korea		China		Taiwan		Hong Kong		Average	
	1993	1996	1993	1996	1993	1996	1993	1996	1993	1996
Real GDP Growth	5.8	6.7	13.6	9.6	6.3	5.7	6.1	4.5	7.7	7.0
Changes of Consumer Prices Index	4.8	4.9	14.7	8.3	11.7	3.0	8.6	6.3	7.2	5.9
M2 Growth	16.6	15.8	42.8	25.3	14.7	9.1	16.2	10.9	20.4	16.5
Changes of Domestic Credit to Private Activities	12.0	19.5	43.2	24.3	19.5	6.0	-53.7	16.4	14.4	20.1
Changes of Stock Price Index	27.7	-26.2	6.8	65.2	79.8	34.0	-	-	60.0	11.0
Stock Trading Value/ GDP	61.2	34.1	7.3	31.3	155.7	172.7	113.4	108	81.4	64.4
Fiscal Balance/ GDP	0.6	0.4	-0.01	-0.01	-3.9	-1.4	5.2	3.0	1.5	0.4
Gross Domestic Investment/ GDP	35.5	37.9	43.3	39.6	25.2	21.2	27.6	32.1	32.2	32.9
Gross Domestic Saving/ GDP	36.0	34.0	41.7	39.5	27.0	25.1	34.6	30.7	34.1	33.3
Changes of Domestic Consumption	5.7	7.1	34.4	12.4	8.2	6.2	7.5	4.7	10.0	7.0
Currebt Account/ GDP	0.3	-4.4	-1.9	0.9	3.2	4.0	-	-	-0.8	-0.6

Sources: ADB, *Key Indicators of Developing Asian and Pacific Countries*, 1998,1999.
IFC, *Emerging Stock Markets Fact Book*, 1999.

Sixth, domestic private credits soared in almost all the economies. The rates of increase in China and the Philippines were more than 40%, and in Indonesia, Thailand, and Malaysia were in the range of 20%. In Singapore, Korea, Hong Kong, and Taiwan they were on the level of 10%, and in India alone were in the single digits. It was inevitable that this boom of domestic loans in developing economies caused some macro-economic problems in private capital activities: over-investment, over-consumption, or in other words a bubble economy.

Seventh, the ratio of gross domestic investments to GDP was very high in all nine economies. China, Singapore, Thailand, Malaysia, Korea, and Indonesia reached high levels of over 30%, and the Philippines, India, and Taiwan were still over 20%. In general the domestic investments were covered mainly by gross domestic savings. This provides a clue to the "miracle" of high economic growth in the East Asian economies compared to those of Latin America. However, as the investments increased in the midst of the boom, a discrepancy grew between domestic investment and savings. This I-S gap resulted in an expansion of imbalances in the current accounts of quite a few of the economies: Thailand, Malaysia, the

Philippines, Korea, and Indonesia. It is likely that these economies fell into a state of over-investment.

Eighth, asset prices soared sharply with the development of the over-investment or bubble economy. Table 1.7 focuses only on changes in the stock market, because data on the real estate market is not available in many of the economies. It includes the stock price indices and value of stock traded. These indices show that most all the economies enjoyed relative booms in their stock markets during the first or latter half of the 1990s. In some economies such as Thailand and Korea, the asset boom had already burst in the middle of the 1990s while at the end of 1996 Malaysia and the Philippines were still on the verge of the burst. It is probable that the stock market booms caused relative bubbles not only in the economies deeply affected by the Asian crisis, but also in the least affected ones such as Singapore, Taiwan, and Hong Kong.

Table 1.8 Market Structure in Asian Banking Industries

(Unit: %)

Year	Share of Bank Asstes in Total Financial Sector Assets	Concentration of the Five Largest Banks in the Banking Industry	Share of State-Owned Banks	Share of Foreign-Owned Banks	Risk Based Capital Adequacy Ratio	Non-Performing Loan Ratio	Share of Loans to Manufacturing
	1994	1994-96	1994	1994	1995	1994-95	1996
China	-	70	-	0	-	-	-
Hong Kong	-	29	0	72	17.5	3.1	-
Taiwan	80	-	57	5	12.2	2.6	42.8
Korea	38	50	13	5	9.3	1.0	50.5
Philippines	-	60	-	10	-	26.8	31.6
Indonesia	91	-	48	4	11.9	11.2	26.9
Malaysia	64	40	8	21	11.3	8.2	22.0
Singapore	71	39	0	80	18.7	-	9.6
Thailand	75	62	7	6	9.3	7.6	27.1
India	80	42	87	8	9.5	19.5	-
Japan	79	22	0	2	9.1	3.3	14.6

Sources: Goldstein and Turner (1996), table 4, 6, 8.
Monthly Report of the Central Banks in Asia.

Ninth, an asset bubble tends to be accompanied by a misallocation of domestic credit from manufacturing sectors to non-manufacturing sectors, and especially to stock related commodities, real estate, and the financial sector. The right-most column of Table 1.8 shows the ratio of loans to the manufacturing sectors to total bank lending in each Asian economy. These economies fell into two groups. The ratio was greater than 50% in the NIES such as Korea and Taiwan, while it was under 25% in many of the ASEAN economies. It depended, in general, on the level of the nation's economic development. The ratio in the developing economies tended to be far lower than in the developed economies because of the under- development of their manufacturing sectors. Furthermore, contemporary development policies based on foreign direct investments strengthened the misallocation in the domestic credit market, as fund raising for leading manufacturing sectors depended on overseas markets rather than on the domestic market. Financial institutions which had relatively small outlets into manufacturing sectors sent their funds into non-manufacturing sectors.

In short, first, the macro-economic imbalances in the Asian economies grew gradually beginning in the middle of the 1990s. However, as a whole these imbalances were not so large to stop most economists from maintaining an optimistic view of their economic conditions. Second, there were remarkable imbalances on the side of private capital, while those originating from the governments' public activities were small. The high growth policy based on foreign private capital gave rise to the prosperity of the Asian economies in the first half of the 1990s, but led to a major deviation from balanced development, toward over-investment or economic bubbles, in the latter half of the decade. From this, we can see the rapid deterioration of economic fundamentals on the side of the activities of private capital as a cause of the Asian crisis. Foreign speculators attacked the Asian economies in 1997, focusing on these macro-economic imbalances: (1) the swelling of M2, (2) over-investment, (3) asset price inflation, (4) the I-S gap, (5) current account deficits, and (6) the misallocation of bank loans for non-productive sectors.

In this regard, the McKinnon and Pill (1996) boom-burst cycle hypothesis is very interesting because the processes before and after the Asian financial crisis may have been very similar to a boom-bust cycle. According to this hypothesis, huge foreign capital movements caused an expansion of domestic credit, resulting in a boom of domestic consumption and asset inflation. The sudden capital outflow killed the consumption boom, leading to the financial crisis and depression. McKinnon and Pill recommended to the Latin American countries the introduction of short-term capital controls, consumer credit controls, and a public pension fund, ideas which could have successfully prevented the financial crisis from past experiences of the East Asian economies. Ironically enough, their high assessment of the East Asian economies, which were also involved in a boom-bust cycle failed. Why did it fail? The boom-bust cycle hypothesis should be reexamined from this point of view.

The failure originated from the assumption that a rapid decrease of savings was a critical cause of the reversal from boom to bust. Even immediately before the crisis broke out, the saving ratio in the Asian economies kept increasing, contrary to the hypothesis, and the I-S gap did not deteriorate as sharply as the hypothesis would have expected. The

Asian financial crisis showed that a boom-bust cycle could occur without a sharp decline in the savings ratio. An interesting, useful example in this regard would be a comparison between Singapore and Malaysia during the crisis.

According Table 1.7 shows that the ratio of domestic investment to GDP in both Singapore and Malaysia reached very high levels of 40% around the middle of the 1990s. This large volume of domestic investment was nearly covered by domestic savings. From the point of view of the I-S gap, there were few conspicuous signs of unhealthiness in either economy. However a balanced I-S gap does not necessarily mean a healthy macro-economy. This can be seen in the difference between Singapore and Malaysia. While Singapore was healthy from any point of view – inflation, money supply, and current account – Malaysia faced rapidly increasing money supply, asset inflation, and current account deficits. In Malaysia an abnormal expansion of domestic credit promoted a surge of domestic investment, creating an asset bubble in the stock and real estate markets. Therefore more than 40% of Malaysia's domestic investment must have been "over-investment" or "excess-credit," while Singapore's was balanced. The terms "over" and "excess" mean that domestic investment or credit far exceeds a balanced orbit based on the economy's potential growth rate.

The development of the macro-economic fundamentals around the time of the Asian financial crisis differed from the assumption of the Krugman model focused on budget deficits or the McKinnon and Pill model focused on the I-S balance. The macro-economic imbalance in the Asian economies enlarged gradually beginning in the middle of the 1990s, especially on the side of private capital's activities. The imbalance resulted in over-investments, over-consumption, or asset bubbles. Those macro-economic imbalances were caused by huge inflows of foreign capital. Speculators saw this as a weak point to attack. If the financial authorities had succeeded in preventing the development of imbalances in the macro-economy, the financial crisis would have been milder. The depth of the crisis depended on the development of the over-investment and the bubble economy as follows.

The economies involved in the Asian financial crisis can be divided into three groups, in regard to the timing of the bubble-burst cycle, and the outbreak of currency and banking crisis. The front runner was Japan, where the bubble burst in 1990, earlier than in the other Asian economies, and where the crisis deepened from banking difficulties into deflation. In Japan, which had large foreign reserves, attacks by speculators never caused a currency crisis, though there was volatility in the dollar-yen exchange rate. The second group consists of Korea and Thailand. There, hidden banking crisis occurred before the outbreak of currency crisis. The fall of asset prices and the loss of banking confidence began as early as around the time of the 1994 Mexico crisis. Then, when currency speculators launched attacks based on these imbalances in 1997, the financial crisis deepened into full-scale depressions. In the case of the third group, the currency crisis induced the banking crisis in 1997 by bursting their economic bubbles. Malaysia and the Philippines fall into this group. China followed as one of the last runners of this group. From the point of view of macro-economic fundamentals, the financial crisis in Indonesia should have been as mild as in Malaysia or the Philippines. However it fell into a bottomless swamp because of a collapse of confidence among its common people, due to the links with a political crisis.

Why Did the Over-Investment or Bubble Occur in Asia?

Many of the Asian economies fell into economic imbalances of over-investment or bubble economies from the late 1980s into the 1990s. This was an uncommon phenomenon through their long development histories, but became characteristic in the 1990s, when they adopted development policies based on the introduction of foreign capital. The over-investment or bubble economies took place in the midst of a process of financial liberalization under that policy. It is consistent with Kaminsky and Reinhart's research that in recent history, financial liberalization has been followed by a banking crisis in 18 to 25% of cases. That issue has so far been argued as a question of sequencing of financial and economic reforms: good macro-economic conditions, a balanced fiscal budget, prudent liberalization of the capital account, and so on. Financial reform is a structural matter rather than a mere policy option, because it relates deeply to matters of financial institutions or customs formed historically. A mismatch between financial institutions and customs during financial reform can cause disorders in the governance structure of the financial system, from which over-investment or bubbles can arise. The point is the micro-structure, and especially structure and behavior in the banking market.

We can see several features of the financial structures in the eleven Asian economies in Table 1.8 (based on data mainly from 1994). First, the shares of bank assets among overall financial assets were very high in ten economies, with the only exception being Korea. The financial systems in these economies depended significantly on the banking system, as does Japan's. Second, the market shares of the five biggest banks were very high in nine economies, excepting Japan and Hong Kong. In particular in China, Thailand, the Philippines, and Korea, the five largest banks controlled over half of the banking market. Third, the market share of state-banks was much higher in China, India, Taiwan, and Indonesia than in Japan, Hong Kong, Singapore, Thailand, Malaysia, or Korea. The financial market in the former four economies might have been in fact mainly controlled by state-related big banks, including not only state-owned but state-controlled ones. Many of the banks owned by the state in Korea were privatized in the 1980s. Fourth, the market shares of foreign banks were very low in nine of the economies, with the exceptions of Hong Kong and Singapore. Malaysia had the highest ratio among them (21%). Taking into account the fact that Singapore's monetary authorities enforced a strict separation between the local market and the offshore market, foreign banks did not have as high a share of the Singapore local market as the table would seem to indicate. Fifth, the ratio of loans to industrial sectors among all commercial bank loans was low. While the ratio was close to 50% in Japan, Korea, and Taiwan, it was around 25% in Singapore, Malaysia, Indonesia, the Philippines, and Thailand. Sixth, the BIS risk-based capital adequacy ratio was very high, at over 8%, in all eleven economies. Singapore, Hong Kong, Taiwan, Indonesia, and Malaysia were far above 10%, while Japan, Thailand, Korea, and India had ratios just over 9%. Tenth, the ratio of bad loans was high, at over 5%, in India, Indonesia, Malaysia, and Thailand, but low in Japan, Korea, and Hong Kong. Since the ratio of bad loans is influenced by the timing of or by lags in the bubble-burst cycle between these economies, these numbers (in a single year) are not necessarily useful as an indicator of financial structure.

In short, we could draw the following rough picture of the structural characteristics of the Asian financial system. It is a structure that is bank-dominated, oligopolistic, relatively closed to foreign financial institutions, and subject to significant state interventions. These characteristics serve mainly for a government to be able to autonomously regulate the allocation of scarce capital. China, which is in transition from a planned to a market economy, may be a polar case which strongly embodies these characteristics due to strict state regulations. Hong Kong is at the opposite pole; it is the most liberal, and far different from China. The other nine economies more or less share a few of the four characteristics, between the two poles. They can be divided into two types of groups in terms of the degree of state intervention. The first, which is relatively more regulated, and based on an oligopolistic banking system driven mainly by state-owned banks, includes Taiwan, Indonesia, and India. The second, which is less regulated, and based on an oligopolistic banking system regulated by the government, includes Singapore, Korea, Malaysia, Thailand, the Philippines, and Japan.

Financial liberalization has changed their market structures from strictly regulated to liberal ones. Since the financial systems in the nine economies were far more strictly regulated before liberalization than after, we can emphasize that these four characteristics are common features among the ten Asian economies. Such state-intervened regulation itself is not a central problem from the point of view of a financial crisis. It is difficult for bubble-burst cycles to occur in economies where the financial systems are strictly regulated such as China, Singapore, Taiwan, or the pre-liberalization economies. The problem is an institutional mismatch during financial liberalization, which causes disorders in the governance structure of the financial system. The failure of the crisis to occur came from a mismatched combination of well-regulated systems and the rapid financial liberalization in the Asian economies, meaning an institutional, structural mismatch in the financial system.

The first aspect of the institutional mismatch is a transborder one. The Asian economies began carrying out capital account liberalization in 1980. Japan adopted a free capital trade policy in two steps, in 1980 and 1984. This overseas liberalization was followed by many of the other Asian economies in the late 1980s to early 1990s, as they accepted open policies for foreign capital. Although liberalization of the domestic markets was carried out in parallel with the overseas liberalization, domestic changes were delayed because of difficulty in reaching consensus among business groups. It is very hard for developing economies to quickly build up robust domestic financial systems able to withstand the large shock of huge transborder movements of capital.

Establishing market liquidity is another important issue for the robustness of the financial system. The first aspect involves capital markets. The deeper the development of the domestic capital markets, the more shock-resistant the financial system is, because the economy becomes able to absorb the shock from volatile foreign capital flows. All economies in Asia except Japan have such small capital markets that huge inflows or outflows of capital heavily affect asset prices, causing the rise and bursting of asset bubbles. The second aspect is the money market. Foreign capital flows cause volatility in money supply, which tends to cause macro-economic imbalances such as the bubble-burst cycle. Both deep money markets and sophisticated monetary policies are necessary conditions for absorbing the excess liquidity from foreign capital inflows.

The second aspect of the institutional mismatch relates to the division of labor between the banking system and capital markets. The banking system has played a dominant role in the financial markets in many of the Asian economies. Government has preferred the banking system to capital markets as a means to control the allocation of scarce capital. Once the governments embarked on the rapid liberalization of the financial systems, which had suffered from excess intervention, it was inevitable serious structural defects would surface in the transition. The critical one was a lack or weakness of loan examination ability among local financial institutions. Even though banks were given the ability to loan freely, they had accumulated little information about manufacturer's businesses. In the past, loans had not necessarily been decided on a market basis but rather on a credit-rationing scheme for national projects under excess intervention by the government. Second, local financial institutions tended to be isolated from the fund raising of foreign enterprises investing directly into the local market. Furthermore the problem of low loan examination ability was far more serious for newly entering banks or for growing non-bank financial institutions after liberalization. The Asian boom in the 1990s failed to fix the lack of loan examination ability, but rather planted the seeds for bubbles and bad loans in these economies. Bank loans, under conditions of such information difficulty, tended to be given to family, crony, territorial, or political relatives, or to non-manufacturing sectors such as construction, finance, or real estate, following major national projects.

The another mismatch related to the bank-dominated structure involves the term structure. Since the capital markets were underdeveloped in the Asian developing economies, banks were forced to intermediate short-term funds to long-term projects. The banks had to carry the burden of a mismatch of term structure. The banks, without access to major manufacturers, who were dominated by foreign direct investments, provided new funds mainly to long-term investments in infrastructure sectors and privatized enterprises. This burden, which arises from the term structure, makes the banks fragile [Teranishi (1991)]. Strict governmental regulations, however, had long placed firm constraints on the exposure of bank to crisis. However, after liberalization it became hard for banks to contain that fragility from developing into a banking crisis.

Dis-intermediation was the other mismatch that put further pressure on bank profits. With the liberalization of the financial business, big firms changed their fund-raising routes from banks to capital markets or non-bank financial institutions. The more rapid or large the process of dis-intermediation, the more the banks' profits diminished. The banks were pushed to change their portfolios from previously profitable areas into new risky investments such as loans related to real estate, stock shares, or small- and medium-sized firms. This change in bank portfolios might have been one of the causes of the asset bubbles.

The third aspect of the institutional mismatch involved privatization. Among the Asian economies, Malaysia, China, India, Indonesia, and the Philippines actively carried out privatization schemes beginning at the end of 1980s[Lieberman *et al.* (1998)]. While this promoted the rapid development of capital markets through the birth of many big stock companies, it also caused disorder in corporate governance structures.

With privatization, the corporate governance structures changed from unitary structures controlled by the government to pluralistic ones controlled by a mix of government, stockholders, managers, creditors and so on. Much time is required for an economy to establish institutional rules for the governance of corporations between the parties concerned. This disorder was worsened by the vague stance of governments toward privatization. In many countries they retained practical control over the corporate management by holding a majority of stocks or by retaining the power to appoint the main executives of the firm. Under such vague conditions for corporate governance, it was relatively easy for politicians, bureaucrats, or businessmen to influence the privatized firms' management through informal, unfair connections. These have often been criticized as nepotism, cronyism, Chabol capitalism in the Asian economies following the outbreak of the crisis.

Furthermore, the privatization of a bank is likely to have even greater influence than a common company, because banks play a key role in the money supply process. If, with privatization, a bank's governance structure falls into disorder, it makes difficult for banks to constrain increases in bank loans. The allocation of bank credits becomes easily distorted by special interest connections between politicians, bureaucrats, and businessmen. Such distortions can easily result in an easygoing monetary policy which helps not only the fund-raising of the privatized big firms directly, but also indirectly the development of capital markets. This can encourage the rise of a bubble economy.

The fourth aspect of the institutional mismatch is the division of labor between the state and market under the liberalization. Liberalization consists both of a retreat of the state's role and an enlargement of market mechanisms in the whole financial system. Mismatch between the two movements can cause a serious loss in the system's governance structure, giving rise to over-investment or a bubble economy.

A typical case would be an institutional mismatch around a market entry and exit policy under liberalization. Though they implemented liberalization on market entry as well as on interest rates and business areas, the governments in many of the Asian economies, including Japan, maintained restrictions on banks' exiting from the market. This restriction was the one useful means governments had to maintain control over the more competitive markets following liberalization. Nearly all of the Asian economies, with the exception of Hong Kong, long maintained strict restrictions on both entry and exit to the banking market. Japan, Malaysia, and India restricted both entry and exit by banks until the outbreak of the crisis. Although competition in the banking market intensified with the liberalization of bank entry since the end of 1980s, Korea, Taiwan, Indonesia, and the Philippines retained restrictions on bank entry until the crisis. Why were they loath to allow banks to leave the market? First, maintaining employment at big firms is critical from a social security point of view in developing countries such as Korea, India, and Indonesia. Second, the governments or people much preferred market order or stability to market efficiency. A typical example of this may be Japan's banking system, which is called "a Convoy system." Whenever a bank failed, the government would bail it out through an injection of public funds or through a merger with some other sound bank. This was common in many other Asian economies as well. It meant that the state gave an informal, implicit guarantee to banks, especially big banks [Ross (1996)]. As a result, bank managers were not sufficiently sensitive to the increasing risk after liberalization. The government's implicit guarantee must have created the following conspicuous characteristics or serious distortions in the financial system.

First, because of the implicit state guarantees, state deposit insurance schemes played only a small role in the Asian countries. China, Hong Kong, Indonesia, Korea, Malaysia, and Singapore had no such schemes until the crisis. Although such schemes were established much earlier in Japan, India, Taiwan, and the Philippines, they played only minor roles in the system of implicit state guarantees. Whenever a bank failed under the system of implicit state guarantees, nearly all those concerned with the bank, meaning not only small depositors but stockholders and creditors, had their funds protected by government bailouts. Therefore the cost of poor management was not significant for them.

Second, clear rules for bank failures were not necessarily needed in economies with a system of implicit state guarantees. First, there was a lack of effective accounting rules to decide when a bank's balance sheet fell into insolvency. The second was a lack of a clear rule about whether the bank should be bailed out or be forced to exit the market. The third was the lack of an effective bankruptcy act laying down various procedures for bankruptcy or corporate reorganization. Even though such rules were formally legislated in some countries, they were executed in an easygoing manner that usually left the business in the market. Decisions were not made based on clear rules, but mainly at the discretion of the financial authority. Thus, special informal connections between the authority, politician, and banks often influenced the decision.

Third, the system of implicit state guarantees weakened the sensitivity of banks to business risks. Many banks tended to depend on superficial collateral rather than on strict loan examinations. Many bank loans in Asia were based on collateral such as stock shares or real estate. Since the banks' credits were firmly connected to such stocks and real estates, the bank were easily harmed by fluctuations in asset prices. Fluctuations in asset prices influenced the quality of bank loans through collateral, affecting the real economy in a major way: the bubble-burst cycle. Typical examples are bank loans collateralized with real estate in Japan, or with stock shares in Malaysia.

Due to the governments' implicit guarantees, on the other hand, banks set up few institutional shock absorbers against risks, such as regulation of the liquidity ratio or capital adequacy ratio. In developing countries, liquidity ratios have commonly been used as an effective social policy rather than as one of financial prudence. Governments have also failed to introduce other prudential schemes such as a capital adequacy ratios in place of the liquidity ratio. As a result, the Asian economies did not possess effective schemes to curb the development of bubble-burst cycles before the crisis.

Fourth, governments needed to introduce vast interventions or regulations to recover balances lost by the implicit state guarantees. The system of implicit government guarantees tends to weaken the incentive for a bank to voluntarily maintain sound management. *Collateralism* and *discretionism* prevailed throughout the Asian economies under the system of implicit government guarantees. Both strict regulation by the authority and mutual regulations by banker's clubs were indispensable for preventing lax management in the banks.

Fifth, these regulation and intervention systems gave rise to special informal relationships of interests between bureaucrats and business groups. Systems of mutual dependency and monitoring between wise bureaucrats and active business groups created stable economic performance with little moral hazard. Before liberalization, business groups based on family, crony, party, or territorial bonds in Singapore, Korea, Indonesia, the Philippines, and Malaysia contributed to economic development in a delicate balance between such guarantees and government intervention.

The financial and economic liberalization broke this balance between guarantee and intervention. While, on the one hand, financial regulations or intervention were liberalized, the authority also had to keep the government's implicit guarantee for the purpose (or pretext?) of financial stability. The result was a weakening of not only autonomous but also heteronomous discipline for sound banking. When these heteronomous restrictions on the banking business were removed, the governments ought to have filled the gap by reinforcing autonomous incentives. Either the government or private entities continued to behave on the basis of the government's implicit guarantees as they had before, failing to take into account the consequences of this failure.

This loss of systemic balance caused the over-investment or bubble economy during Asia's period of extreme high economic growth starting from the latter half of the 1980s. The process was accompanied in many cases by various kinds of financial scandals involving bureaucrats, politicians, bankers, or businessmen. These should have been taken as bad signs that a crevice had opened in the system of implicit government guarantees.

The deeper the gap between the implicit guarantees and liberalization, the larger was the disorder of the governance structure in the financial system. This systemic gap gave rise to a swelling of bank credits, causing the over-investment or the bubble economy. This defect occurred not only in Japan, Korea, and Thailand but also in Malaysia and Indonesia. On the other hand, Singapore and India were not heavily affected by the financial crisis because of a delay in financial liberalization.

The Financial Crisis and the IMF

The Asian financial crisis may have been a new type of financial crisis. As mentioned earlier, the main characteristics of the Asian financial crisis can be summed up as follows. (1) A regional liquidity crisis broke out in Asia, including Japan, the NIES, and the ASEAN countries. (2) It took place on the basis of worsening economic fundamentals, mainly in the private sectors, caused by an asset bubble and an over-investment. The question here is: what is the best prescription for this new type of crisis? A good prescription must come from an accurate recognition of the symptoms of the crisis. It should consist of two parts in accordance to the above-mentioned characteristics. The first should be countermeasures against a regional liquidity crisis. The second should be countermeasures against the development of bubble economies or over-investment. Did financial authorities, on a local or international basis, take appropriate measures to curb the development of the crisis? Policies against the crisis can been divided into two categories. Thailand, Korea, and Indonesia dealt with the crisis under the control of the IMF, while Japan, Malaysia, Hong Kong, Taiwan, and China managed their problems without IMF help. Were the IMF's policies appropriate for mitigating the crisis?

The IMF's prescription for the crisis consisted of three elements: a high interest rate, prompt banking restructuring, and economic structural reform. These measures seem to correspond to the complexity of the crisis. However many policy makers and scholars have suggested that IMF's policy measures might have greatly aggravated the crisis rather than mitigated it. The IMF may not have sufficient capability to understand comprehensively the new characteristics of the crisis.

The first issue regarding the IMF's prescription is the occurrence of the bubble economy or over-investment. The IMF failed to prevent the outbreak of the crisis in Thailand although it had cautioned that country regarding its foreign exchange rate policy several months before the crisis. The more the crisis fit Obstfeld's model of "self-fulfilling speculation", the more difficult it likely would have been to predict the outbreak. There is, however, no smoke without fire even in a "self-fulfilling speculation" crisis. Some early signs could be found in the worsening of the private sector-driven economic fundamentals related to the bubble economy or over-investment. Few economists have seen these bad signals as important, but rather have looked at the sound public sector-driven fundamentals in their macro-economic analyses of the Asian economies involved in the crisis. Why did this misunderstanding prevail among economists all over the world? The Krugman and McKinnon models, which emphasized the importance of budgetary soundness, had too much influence over economists around the world. McKinnon later admitted that budget balancing had been overused as a signal for investor decisions [in McKinnon and Pill (1996)]. This could be called the evil of the "securitization of a theory".

The second issue about the IMF's prescription is that there was little, and insufficient, understanding on the regional liquidity crisis. The IMF's policy measures toward the financial crisis were counterproductive. At first, it carried out a high interest rate policy to stem both the huge overseas capital drains and the current account deficits. According to one textbook on economics, an increase in domestic interest rates has two effects. Not only does it improve the current account due to a change of competitiveness, but it also helps to balance the foreign capital account thanks to a change in differences of interest rates between the domestic and overseas markets. These mechanisms may work effectively in ordinary economic condition, but not in a severe financial panic. This is because the capital outflow panic no longer arises from rational calculation, i.e. differences of interest rates between the domestic and overseas markets, but rather from abnormal behavior under the breakdown of market confidence. The high interest rates would have needed to be maintained at dangerously high levels for a long period of time (in Hong Kong it was close to 300%) to be effective. Since Thailand or Korea were already on the verge of a banking crisis due to the outbreak of asset bubbles or over-investment, the high interest rate policy made the banking crisis much worse by weakening the liquidity of banks further, causing sharp deflation.

Another policy measure also aggravated the liquidity crisis. Under the IMF's initiatives in Thailand, Korea, and Indonesia, many ailing financial institutions were forced to exit from the market immediately. Fifty-five finance companies in Thailand, five banks in Korea, and sixteen banks in Indonesia were suddenly closed down under the liquidity storm. This sudden closing of so many financial institutions caused a breakdown of market confidence which further aggravated the liquidity crisis.

The third policy measure adopted by the IMF under its structural adjustment policies brought about another adverse result. It called for structural adjustments of the economies in exchange for funds. The purpose was to make the macro-economic structures more stable and sound. The IMF demanded restructuring not only on a system level, involving the budget or money supply, but also at the micro structure.

As the result, the IMF's policy measures against the financial crisis were truly counterproductive. Why was this so? Fundamentally, the IMF made light of the fact that the Asian financial crisis was a regional liquidity crisis. Its policy measures were not designed to ease a liquidity shortage, and in fact only made things worse. Moreover, under financial globalization a local drain is at the same time an overseas drain. The high interest rates, immediate shut-downs, and structural adjustment policies adapted by IMF deepened the liquidity crisis further, not only in the local market but in the region. The best prescription for a regional liquidity crisis is to supply the liquidity that the market demands in a prompt and flexible manner, in order to quickly alleviate the financial panic. The policy should consist of two levels: a supply of sufficient liquidity to local markets and a supply of international liquidity to the regional or global market. The IMF should have worked as the "lender of last resort" in the face of the regional financial crisis.

Bagehot's principle of the "lender of last resort" consists of two factors: elastic liquidity supply, and market selection. W. Bagehot, in the late nineteenth century, established the principle of the "lender of last resort" meaning that in a banking panic the central bank should supply ample liquidity to the market in an elastic manner. Bagehot insisted that the role of the central bank should be limited to providing sufficient liquidity to solvent banks which happened to be thrown into a liquidity shortage due to unreasonable deposit drains in a liquidity crisis. The implication is that the central bank should let insolvent banks exit the market in order to curb the banks' moral hazard. However, it has always proved difficult for central banks to select good banks from bad ones and to control money supply well under the Bagehot principle. It may be that in the past, the issue of market selection may have been neglected compared to that of money supply.

Under the current financial globalization, the Bagehot principle poses difficulties for central banks, since it was established in the nineteenth century, focusing on local banking crisis. The first difficulty involves how to supply liquidity. As mentioned earlier, a liquidity crisis is no longer simply local, but can also be regional or global, since a panicked lack of liquidity can occur simultaneously both in the local market and the regional market. A liquidity crisis can be alleviated solely through the means of an elastic supply of liquidity both into the local and the regional market. The key measure today may be to promptly and elastically supply ample foreign reserves to national economies involved in a regional financial crisis. This can help to ameliorate both the domestic liquidity crisis and the balance-of-payment crisis. In this regard, the IMF not only failed to promptly provide adequate international liquidity to the ailing Asian economies, but also added a great deal of fuel to the liquidity crisis in the local markets through its hard exit policy.

When a debt crisis breaks out, simply supplying sufficient liquidity is not greatly effective without the support of a restructuring of international debts. This is because without a restructuring of international or domestic debts, the liquidity provided in an emergency by the IMF or foreign authorities can be infinitely absorbed by ailing debtors, and will ultimately fail to fundamentally mitigate the liquidity crisis. A restructuring or rescheduling of debts should be carried out by the authorities alongside the emergency supply of liquidity. The IMF should lead concerned institutions to restructure or reschedule international debts toward a much longer-term debt structure while the local authority should take care of domestic debts in the local market. The Paris club scheme has already been established for a sovereign debt crisis where the debtors are governments or public entities. However, there was no effective restructuring scheme for international private debts crisis, in which the concerned institutions are private, before the outbreak of the Asian crisis. The IMF should have tried to quickly establish an international scheme, such as the London scheme, before or during the Asian crisis, and should have promptly supplied sufficient liquidity.

The second difficulty involves the market selection related to the exit of insolvent banks. The Bagehot principle suggests that the exit of insolvent banks should be done through market forces, without the provision of any additional liquidity to them. However, there is an alternative exit policy for monetary authorities, local or international. They can force insolvent banks to exit the market through intervention. It seems that under the IMF conditionalities, local authorities adopted the latter approach, which may be more efficient but might have had worse aftereffects than the former. While the prompt exit of insolvent banks from the market was successfully completed, the IMF's policy measures failed to ameliorate the liquidity shortage crisis.

Another issue regarding the market selection function is that the IMF forced the local authorities to execute the prompt exit policy. Although they had far greater and more accurate detailed information about their local markets than the IMF, the local authorities under the IMF had little autonomy in deciding how to execute bank exits. The IMF seems to have intervened excessively in local exit policies. Why did the IMF carry out this excessive intervention? One reason might be that although authorities can force an insolvent enterprise or financial institution to exit from the domestic market, it is impossible to force an ailing national economy out of the global market.

How should an insolvent bank be exited in a regional liquidity crisis? One possible answer might be to apply Bagehot's idea of market selection in a domestic market to the regional or global sphere. In other words, the IMF should provide sufficient international liquidity to an ailing economy and help to reschedule foreign debts, whether they are sovereign or private. It should let the local authority to decide autonomously how and when to deal with an insolvent bank: whether to force it to exit from the market or bail it out. The problem in this case is whether or not the local authority executes, strictly and fairly, both functions of ample liquidity supply and market selection. It is possible in fact for a local government to misuse funds supplied by the IMF to bail out an insolvent bank or for some other purpose. The IMF should monitor how the local authority uses such funds.

Coping with Regional Liquidity Crisis

The recent financial crisis suddenly pushed the Asian economies into misery. How can we cope with future financial crises?

One key point might be to reduce the domino effects between various parts of the crises, such as currency crises, asset deflation, banking crises, and deflation. One of the striking features of the recent financial crisis was that it was a *compound* crisis. The most effective way to reduce these domino effects is to contain the banking crisis, meaning to cut the connections between the banking crisis and other crises such as the currency crisis, asset deflation, or deflation.

Three policy measures can be used to prevent the occurrence of a banking crisis. The first is to restrain the breakout of currency crises stemming from volatile movements of foreign capital. Another is to maintain a financial system so resilient that the monetary authority and banks can contain the development of an over-investment bubble even in the presence of sudden and huge inflows of foreign capital. The third is to work to strengthen the soundness of the banking industry itself. A banking industry always needs to keep sufficient robustness or soundness to withstand these shocks, even when a currency crisis or asset deflation occurs. I will discuss some of these issues here, from the point of view of containing occurrences of liquidity crises.

The first issue is how to cope with the regional liquidity crisis, which was one of the remarkable features of the recent crisis. A currency crisis can spread by contagion to many of economies in a region, due to a liquidity crisis stemming from the sudden withdrawal of international capital following an inflow. It is this huge foreign capital inflow which lays the foundation of the liquidity crisis. Therefore, the monetary authority must constantly monitor the accumulation of foreign capital inflows. Foreign capital flows into a domestic market through both the debt market (for instance, bank loans) and the asset market (stocks), where players are private enterprises rather than state-related institutions. Therefore the authority needs to monitor movements not only of foreign debts but also of portfolio investments. It must monitor, at the very least, the ratio of short-term foreign debt outstanding as well as the ratio of foreign-owned equity to GDP.

How can a monetary authority control the volatile and huge movements of foreign capital which can cause a liquidity crisis? There are market-based and non-market-based measures that can be adopted. The non-market-based measure is direct regulation, which administratively limits the volumes of foreign capital inflows or outflows; the market-based measures can include indirect controls through a price mechanism such as a tax or an additional deposit reserve. As the sudden adoption of direct regulation can ruin the policymaker's credibility to investors, and thus worsen the financial crisis, it should be limited to emergency situations. The market-based measures are better than the non-market-based ones in terms of such negative policy reactions. However the critical question is the measure's efficacy. It seems apparent that the tax measures introduced in the United States and West Germany during the 1960s did not achieve brilliant results. Regulations against capital outflows must be far more difficult for monetary authorities than regulations against inflows. This is because panic capital outflow stems mainly from a breakdown of confidence rather than the rational behavior of costs and benefits upon which inflows are based. Thus, in a panic, a government may be forced to take both market-based and non-market-based measures. In 1997, the Malaysian monetary authority successfully executed an administrative measure to forbid the repatriation of foreign portfolio investments with a time limit of one year, while in 1994 it had carried out market-based measures, mainly involving additional foreign deposit reserves, to restrain foreign capital inflows.

If a small country imposes such capital regulations alone, without regional or global cooperation, the negative costs of the policy reaction may far exceed the benefits under financial globalisation. If such measures are adopted on a global scale, they will surely have a major effect. This is the idea behind the "Tobin Tax". There are, however, some issues which need to be resolved in practice. First, to be effective the "Tobin Tax" would require that all economies over the world carry it in accord. If its adoption is limited to a regional rather than global scale, a massive capital flight might occur, devastating the economies that adopt it. Second, it is not clear what tax rate, in practice, would be appropriate not only to restrain the demerits but also to maintain the merits of global capital movements in terms of resource allocation. The idea of the "Tobin Tax" is good, but questions remain in terms of feasibility.

The second issue is reforming foreign exchange systems to cope with foreign capital inflows, through a floating or fixed rate system pegged to some foreign currency. In both developed and developing countries, it is not through the current account but rather the capital account that foreign exchange rates are determined. While a fixed rate system is appropriate for an economy based mainly on the current account, a floating system corresponds to an economy based both on the capital account and the current account. The more inflexible the setting of the exchange rate, the more probable it is that a currency crisis will break out as a liquidity crisis. Even developing countries should avoid adopting a fixed rate system to restrain the outbreak of currency crises. While some economies which have reached a level of capital accumulation equivalent to NIES status should adopt a floating rate system, the other Asian economies should shift from a *de-facto* fixed rate system, pegging around the dollar, to a currency basket system using major currencies such as the dollar, yen, euro, and so on. ASEAN countries should at least raise the weight of the yen in their currency baskets in the near future. Foreign capital inflows will surely decrease in proportion to the increase in flexibility of foreign exchange rates. However, these reform measures by themselves cannot constitute a basic resolution, because foreign exchange rates in the Asian economies are unstable by nature, depending deeply on the volatile yen-dollar rate. Above all, we need to stabilize the international currency system itself, which mainly consists of the yen, dollar, and euro, in order to stabilize the exchange rates in the Asian developing economies.

The third issue concerns the establishment of a region-wide liquidity supply system. The recent financial crisis took on the aspect of a regional liquidity crisis. The most important issue for coping with a liquidity crisis is to ensure a swift supply of ample liquidity, as well as the conversion of short-term foreign debts to longer-term instruments. The IMF has not worked well for this purpose. It has few schemes to provide economies with the liquidity to cope with a liquidity crisis. This is because it has emphasized the current account balance rather than paying attention to the condition of the capital account.

Furthermore, the IMF's organization is too global to enable it to closely monitor the macro and micro financial conditions of so many countries around the world. Market mechanisms do not necessarily work in a universal manner but through in local economic systems with regional or individual characteristics. It is likely the IMF lacked sufficient information and recognition on each economy's detailed financial conditions on a micro and macro base just before the breakout of the Asian financial crisis. To maintain close monitoring and carry out swift injections of liquidity at the right time and in the right manner, the IMF should be reformed into a much more pluralistic organization carrying out close cooperation with the emerging Regional Monetary Funds. Regional organizations should be built up independently or subordinately to the IMF on a continental-wide scale, such as Asia, Africa or Latin America. Furthermore the Regional Monetary Fund in Asia must make efforts to coordinate monetary policy among the Asian economies and help to establish a regional payment system or another measures to cope with financial crises.

The fourth issue involves the sequencing of financial reform. We learned the lesson that opening up Asia's financial system to foreigners before robust banking systems had been established contributed to the financial crisis. However, financial opening has already marched on to a further stage, due to the acceleration of financial reform by the financial crisis. It has moved to the new entry of foreign capital and free capital transactions. It may be very hard to return to a system of regulations on foreign capital without global cooperation. It may be possible at least for an authority to monitor and check movements of capital transactions. At the same time, domestic financial systems should be restructured into more efficient and robust ones.

The last issue is how developing economies can build financial systems that are robust enough to be little affected by huge movements of foreign capital. The robustness of a system may be assessed from both the point of views of efficiency and stability. While strengthening the competitiveness of financial markets in terms of efficiency, we should restructure out-of-date financial safety nets. The Asian financial market remains inefficient still today because of the "implicit government guarantees".

References

Asiamoney (1999a), 'Guide to Asian Currency Bond Markets 1999', May.

Asiamoney (1999b), 'Hong Kong's Big Bang: Too Much of a Good Thing', June.

Bank for International Settlement (1996, 1997), 66th, 67th *Annual Report*.

Calvo, Guillermo, Leonard Leiderman and Carmen Reinhart (1993), 'Capital Inflows and Real Exchange Rate Appreciation in Latin America: the Role of External Factors', *IMF Staff Papers*, Vol.40, No.1.

Chang, Roberto and Andres Velasco (1998), 'Financial Crises in Emerging Markets: A Canonical model', *Federal Reserve Bank of Atlanta Working Paper* 98-10, July.

Corsetti, Giancarlo, Paolo Pesenti and Nouriel Roubini (1998), 'Paper Tigers?: A Model of the Asian Crisis', *National Bureau of Economic Research Working Paper*, No.6783, November.

Diamond, Douglas W and Philip H. Dybvig (1983), 'Bank Runs, Deposit Insurance, and Liquidity', *Journal of Political Economy*, Vol.91, No.31.

Eichengreen, Barry, Andrew Rose and Charles Whyplosz (1996), 'Contagious Currency Crises', *National Bureau of Economic Research Working Paper*, 5681, July.

Emery, Robert F (1997), *The Bond Markets of Developing East Asia*, Westview Press, Oxford.

Glick, Reuven and Andrew K Rose (1998), 'Contagion and Trade: Why are Currency Crises Regional?', *National Bureau of Economic Research Working Paper*, 6806, November.

Goldfajn Ilan and Rodrigo O. Valdes (1997), 'Capital Flows and the Twin Crises: the Role of Liquidity', *IMF Working Paper* WP/97/87, July.

Goldstein, Morris (1998), *The Asian Financial Crisis: Causes, Cures and System Implications*, Institute for International Economics, June.

Goldstein, Morris and Philip Turner (1996), 'Banking Crises in Emerging Economies: Origin and Policy Options', *BIS Economic Papers*, No.46, October.

Gorton, Gary (1998), 'Banking Panics and Business Cycles', *Oxford Economic Paper*, Vol.40, No.4.

Hancock, Phil and Greg Tower (1995), 'Accounting Regulation in East Asia', in Ky Cao (ed.), *The Changing Capital Markets of East Asia*, Chapter 9, Routledge.

Haq, ul Mahbub, Kaul, Inge and Grunberg, Isabelle (1996), *The Tobin Tax: Coping with Financial Volatility*, Oxford University Press, Oxford.

Heij, Gitte (1995), 'Tax Regimes in East Asia: A Comparative Review', in Ky Cao (ed.), *The Changing Capital Markets of East Asia*, Chapter 8, Routledge.

Huar, Tan Chwee (2000), *Financial Sourcebook for Southeast Asia and Hong Kong*, Singapore University Press.

IMF (1996), *International Financial Statistics*, December.

Kaminsky, Garcia and Carmen Leinhart (1996), 'The Twin Crises: the Causes of Banking and Balance of Payments Problems', *International Finance Discussion Paper* No.544, Board of Governors of Federal Reserve System, March.

Kaminsky, Garcia and Carmen Leinhart (1999), 'The Twin Crises: the Causes of Banking and Balance of Payments Problems', *The America Economic Review*, Vol.89, No.3, June.

Krugman, Paul (1979), 'A Model of Balance-of-Payments Crises', *Journal of Money, Credit and Banking*, Vol.11, No.3, August.

Krugman, Paul (1999), 'Balance Sheets, the Transfer Problem, and Financial Crises,' http://web.edu/krugman/www/FLOOD.pdf. January.

Levine Ross (1994), 'Government Insurance and Financial Intermediaries: Issues of Regulation, Evaluation and Monitoring', Farugi, Shakil ed, *Financial Sector Reforms, Economic Growth, and Stability*, EDI Seminar Series, World Bank.

Lieberman, Ira W and Christpher D. Kirkness (eds) (1998), *Privatization and Emerging Equity Markets*, World Bank.

McKinnon, Ronald (1991), *The Order of Economic Liberalization: Financial Control in the Transition to a Market Economy*, John Hopkins University Press.

McKinnon, Ronald and Huw Pill (1996), 'Credible Liberalizations and International Capital Flows: the 'Overborrowing Syndrome' ', in Ito, Takatoshi and Anne O. Kruger, eds., *Financial Deregulation and Integration in East Asia,* University of Chicago Press.

Miller, Victoria (1998a), 'Domestic Bank Runs and Speculative Attacks on Foreign Currency', *Journal of International Money and Finance*, No.17.

Miller, Victoria (1998b), 'The Double Drain with a Cross-Border Twist: More on the Relationship between Banking and Currency Crises', *The American Economic Review*, Vol.88, No.2, May.

Montes, Manuel F (1998), *The Currency Crises in Southeast* Asia, Updated Edition, Institute of Southeast Asian Studies.

Obstfeld, Maurice (1994), 'The logic of Currency Crises', *National Bureau of Economic Research Working Paper,* No.4640, February.

Obstfeld, Maurice (1996), 'The Model of Currency Crises with Self-fulfilling Features', *European Economic Review,* Vol.40, No.1, April.

Sachs, Jeffrey D., Aaron Tornell and Andres Velasco (1996), 'Financial Crises in Emerging Markets: the Lessons from 1995', *Brookings Papers on Economic Activity* I.

Singh, Ajit (1997), 'Financial Liberalization, Stockmarkets and Economic Development', *The Economic Journal*, No.107, May.

Teranishi, Juro (1991), *Industrialization and Financial System (Kougyouka to Kinyu –shisutemu in Japanese),* Toyo Keizai Shinpousya.

Tobin, James (1978), 'A Proposal for International Monetary Reform', *Eastern Economic Journal,* Vol. 4, No.3-4.

Tornell, Aaron (1999), 'Common Fundamentals in the Tequila and Asian Crises', *National Bureau of Economic Research Working Paper,* No.7139, May.

Tsurumi, Masayoshi (1998), 'Prewar Financial Crises: Lesson for Today', *Social Science Japan*, The Institute of Social Science, University of Tokyo, August.

Tsurumi, Masayoshi (1999), 'Coping with Regional Liquidity Crisis', presented for the Taegu Round Global Forum in Taegu, October 6-8.

World Bank (1989), *World Development Report 1989: Financial Systems and Development,* Oxford University Press.

World Bank (1993), *The East Asian Miracle: Economic Growth and Public Policy,* A Policy Research Report, Oxford University Press.

World Bank (1995), *The Emerging Asian Bond Market,* The World Bank.

World Bank (1998), *East Asia: The Road to Recovery*, The World Bank.

2 Financial Reform in Japan

TAKAO SAGA

Introduction

The separation between long-term and short-term financing, the separation between the banking and securities sectors, and a system of specialized financial institutions that characterized Japan's financial system in the post-war era have ended their historical roles, giving way to prominent new moves towards a reconstruction of the financial system. However, it has become evident from the experience of the past few years that this is an agenda that involves an extremely difficult process which must be pursued at the same time as resolving the negative legacy of the 'Bubble Economy' – the bad loans problem at Japanese banks. The collapse of Hokkaido Takushoku Bank, a major commercial bank, was followed by the failures of the Long-Term Credit Bank of Japan and the Nippon Credit Bank, which one after the other were temporarily placed under state control. Along with the chain of banking failures, the lack of inadequate disclosure of banks' bad loans have led to various speculation in the financial markets, causing major disturbances throughout the entire banking system. As a result, the banks have accelerated their efforts at loan collection and have become extremely reluctant to provide new lending, thus severely limiting financial procurement by corporations and in turn worsening the economic downturn.

The agenda of Japan's financial reform calls for the creation of a balanced financial intermediary system by correcting the over-emphasis on indirect financing and by strengthening the functions of the securities markets, while at the same time preventing systemic risk from manifesting itself. The purpose of this paper is to offer an overview of aspects that have characterized Japan's post-war financial system, to clarify the process through which the system became incompatible with the real economy, thus making restructuring unavoidable, and to examine the current status of financial reform and issues to be taken up in the future.

Overview of Japan's Post-War Financial System

In the post-war era, Japan created a unique financial system aimed at recovering an economy devastated by war.[1] First of all, the absence of a securities market that normally would have taken on long-term financing functions necessitated the allocation of such functions to the banking system. The aim of the Long-Term Credit Banking Law of 1952 was to create a new long-term credit bank and to allow it to issue bonds as a means for procuring funds, which were to be used as capital for providing industry with long-term financing. The policy of separating trust banks adopted by the Ministry of Finance was also designed to create banks that specialized in trust banking operations in order to give them long-term financing functions. The fact that in recent years it is these banks that were created in the early post-war era that have either collapsed one after another, or are at the center of restructuring, clearly demonstrates that the financial system that had played its historical role between the post-war era and the high-growth period is now showing discrepancies with the real economy.

Secondly, Japan adopted a specialized banking system. Examples include banks that specialize in the provision of finance to small- and medium-sized companies (former Sogo banks and Shinkin banks) and a bank that specializes in foreign exchange (the Bank of Tokyo). While such divisions in operational areas have already been abolished, until recently banks operated within their allotted business areas, and stability in the banking sector was maintained by distributing a set amount of business. Financial administration was geared to the standard of the financial institution with the least effective management structure, which is why the system was commonly referred to as the 'Convoy' system.

Thirdly, Japan separated the banking and securities businesses, with exceptions in some areas of operation. In America, the ban on combined management was said to have had its aims in preventing the risks accompanying securities operations from affecting the banking sector. In fact, true to that purpose, in America that rule is laid out in its banking law. However, in Japan the same piece of regulation is found under Article 65 of the Securities and Exchange Act, and many have observed that the rule is not necessarily aimed at ensuring sound management in the banking sector. In their view, the rule aims rather at stabilizing the management of securities companies by cutting out an area of operation for them. Judging from the actual effects, the separation between the banking and securities businesses seems to have been intended more as a policy to support and nurture the securities companies, which were weak in terms of management compared to the banks, which were first to be provided for with a structure befitting their central role as financial intermediaries.

The fourth characteristic was the preventive administration practiced by the Ministry of Finance. It virtually limited new entry through a licensing system for both banks and securities companies (in fact, no newcomers obtained a license to operate a securities business during the 30 years since the license system was adopted in 1968), and managed to keep monitoring costs low through preventive regulation. On the other hand, such a regulatory policy gave enormous power to the Finance Ministry, with its grip on licensing authority, and at the same time created a backdrop for the introduction of administrative guidance, which lacked transparency and had no clear legal basis. And that has provided cause for scandals concerning collusion with a specific industry in recent years, which in turn blemished the ministry's prestige.

Setting that aside, it was such financial administration that also prevented the collapse of financial institutions. Should such a situation arise, the failed bank was to be absorbed by a healthy bank which was seen to have been making excess profit under the 'Convoy' administration.

Pressures For Financial Reform[2]

The Limits of Specialized Financial Institutions

The financial system centered on banks functioned well until the end of the high economic growth period of the late 1970s. However, large companies that flourished during the period began seeking more favorable terms for capital procurement, and increased the weighting of fund procurement from the securities markets. The trend was especially marked among corporate clients of major commercial banks whose client base consisted of major corporations, and long-term credit banks and trust banks whose main operation was providing long-term capital.

This break away from banks had serious implications for these financial institutions. As their operational foundation – which constituted the very basis for their existence – began to shrink, they were forced to expand into new business areas. As a result, the ratio of lending to small- and medium-sized companies and real estate financing increased, and they actively sought to enter the securities business. Under Article 65 of the Securities and Exchange Act, banks were banned from operating securities businesses. However, while Article 11 of the Anti-Monopoly Law of 1947 prohibited them from acquiring more than 5% of total outstanding stock in any given company, it placed no limitations on banks holding other companies through affiliates. So major commercial banks already owned affiliated securities companies through indirect shareholdings. But as the ratio of capital procurement from the securities markets rose among top corporations, commercial banks which felt threatened by a shrinking operational base played a central role in seeking full-scale involvement in the securities business. That resulted in a heated discussion with the securities industry, which was opposed to the idea, but in the end the Financial Reform Act was enacted in 1993, allowing banks to establish fully-owned securities subsidiaries. Securities companies and trust banks were similarly allowed to set up banking and securities subsidiaries, respectively. However, certain limits were placed on reciprocal entry into each other's business areas, because such moves would have had a significant impact on the operational foundation of either industry.

Despite such deregulation, long-term credit banks and trust banks, whose main clients were the major corporations, and financial institutions catering to small- and medium-sized companies could not avoid a contraction in their basic operations, and were forced to turn to business areas involving higher risk. While it is correct to attribute the direct cause of the current bad loans problem in the banking sector to their speculative investment activities during the 'Bubble Economy' era in later years, the roots of the problem can also be traced to the domino effect that resulted from the confusion in the specialized banking system. In that respect, the continued existence of the specialized banking system, and especially that of the long-term credit banks and trust banks which had out-lived their historical purpose, should have been reconsidered at that time.

Hollowing Out Effect on Financing

Another problem posed by the progress of economic globalization was the financial administration pursued by the Ministry of Finance, which had come to place significant restrictions on the activities of corporations and financial institutions. A typical example was the collateral requirement, where the provision of collateral was an absolute prerequisite for companies that sought to issue bonds. As a result, companies that could not meet the requirement went ahead and began issuing bonds in the Euromarket or the Swiss market, where they could sell their bonds without having to provide collateral. And often enough, Japanese institutional investors turned out to be the buyers of such bonds.

Faced with this pressure, the Finance Ministry began to indicate a significant shift towards abolishing or easing regulations in its financial administration. The epoch-making event occurred in 1984, when the Yen-Dollar Commission Report declared the liberalization of the entire financial markets. Thereafter, Japan was to take the course of deregulation following steps laid out in the Report, as in the liberalization of deposit interest rates.

During the 'Bubble Economy' years, the Tokyo market acquired the weighting that gave it a corner of the world's financial centers on a par with London and New York, and Japanese banks raised their presence to the extent of sweeping the top ranks among global financial institutions in terms of asset value. However, as the 'Bubble' burst, the deterioration of the Tokyo market was again taken up as an issue. The symptoms included the continuing departure of foreign financial institutions, the decline in the number of foreign corporate listings on the Tokyo Stock Exchange, the decrease in foreign exchange transactions in the Tokyo market, and the shift in trading of Nikkei 225 index futures and options to the Singapore market. To a certain extent, these moves were the direct results of the slump in Tokyo's financial markets, but there was a further question concerning the possibility that what regulations that still remained were acting as obstacles to free activity and making Tokyo a cumbersome market to operate in.

Competitive Decline Among Financial Institutions

Financial institutions continued to operate within the divisions allotted under the specialized banking system, and since deposit interest rates were regulated, there was hardly any competition among them in terms of product development. The only competition that existed – if it can be called that – was over obtaining permission from the Ministry of Finance for opening a new branch in the best possible location.

Lacking innovation in operations, product development and marketing channels, banks wasted away in their race to capture deposits, and as a result, their high-cost structures significantly reduced their Return on Equity (ROE). Even in the late 1980s, when they prided in their overwhelming presence in terms of asset size, ROE levels at Japanese banks were not high. More importantly, domestic coexistence based on business allotment took the edge off any efforts to develop new businesses such as derivatives or securitization, and drained their vitality to compete with U.S. and European financial institutions in international financial markets.

Slow and Partial Reform of the Financial System

As we have seen, though discrepancies between Japan's financial system and the real economy, or systemic fatigue, had been pointed out from a relatively early period, no effort was made towards comprehensive reforms until the 1990s. This is due to several reasons.

The first is the Ministry of Finance's experience of successful financial administration, which caused a delay in shifting its stance. Japan's dazzling post-war economic recovery – dubbed the 'Japanese Miracle' – and subsequent economic growth were in effect guided by policy decisions at the Ministry of Finance and the Ministry of International Trade and Industry. While the Ministry of International Trade and Industry saw its powers greatly reduced as core industries gained competitiveness in the global markets, the Ministry of Finance managed to continue exercising its formidable authority by maintaining protective regulatory administration of the financial markets and financial institutions, which were still well behind in terms of global competition. If any one of the financial institutions created cause for concern, all the others cooperated in maintaining the financial system, thus avoiding major rents from appearing. A typical example might be the provision of special loans by the Bank of Japan and the creation of a stock purchasing organ that transpired in 1965 at the time when Yamaichi Securities collapsed. The crisis was overcome by making banks with close relations with Yamaichi, such as the Industrial Bank of Japan, provide support in terms of personnel and financing, and by getting the central bank to extend special emergency loans. Also, in the subsequent sale of government bonds, financial institutions went out of their way to cooperate in the smooth sale by organizing underwriting syndicates. It is not difficult to imagine that the experience of such success delayed the shift in the ministry's stance in financial administration.

What prompted the Ministry of Finance to realize the dead-end of traditional financial administration and the necessity for financial reform as critical issues were probably that the 'infallibility myth of banks' of the past was going to be difficult to maintain in the process of resolving the bad loans problem that worsened after the burst of the 'Bubble', and the increasing criticism that was directed at the ministry. To be precise, it dates back to the collapse of Kizu Credit Cooperative in August 1994, and that of two more credit cooperatives in Tokyo which occurred consecutively in December of that same year, which necessitated not only full-fledged bailout loans by financial institutions, but supportive special loans from the Bank of Japan and the Deposit Insurance Organization as well. From then onwards, it became clear that the 'Convoy administration' could not be maintained. Also, much confusion ensued in providing public funds to clean up the housing loan companies in 1996, increasing mistrust in the Finance Ministry. That mistrust reached its peak with the subsequent revelation that officials of the Finance Ministry and Bank of Japan had been entertained by the companies.

Secondly, the specialized banking system and rigid administrative structure gave rise to powerful interest groups, which acted as obstacles in structure gave rise to powerful interest groups, which acted as obstacles in promoting fundamental reforms of the financial system. As we can understand from the previously-mentioned domino effect that accompanied structural changes in corporate fund procurement, major commercial banks were eager to expand their operations. But small- and mid-sized financial institutions, whose own operational niches could be eroded, rejected such moves as the 'stronger man's logic'. As a result, Japan's financial reform had to take the shape of mutual entry into each others' business areas, making fundamental reform based on sound principles difficult.

Thirdly, the 'Bubble Economy' of the late 1980s also had its share in delaying the start of financial reform. Following the accord reached by the Japan-U.S. Yen-Dollar Commission, liberalization of the Tokyo financial markets began to show some progress, raising asset values such as stock prices, and money began to flow in from abroad. As a result, the Tokyo financial market was recognized as a global financial center on par with New York and London, and raised the presence of Japanese financial institutions in European and U.S. markets. These were likely to have led to over-confidence in global competitiveness by the Finance Ministry and the financial institutions, delaying any efforts to reform the financial system.

Due to these reasons, while the need for financial reform had been pointed out much earlier, such reform remained slow and partial up to this stage.

Comprehensive Financial Reform

The Purpose and Structure of 'Japan's Big Bang'

In November 1996, Japanese Prime Minister Mr. Hashimoto announced plans for an acceleration in and broadening of financial reform in Japan. The purpose was to reform the state of the Tokyo market – which had deteriorated significantly to the point that, far from being a global financial center, its status as Asia's central market was being challenged by Hong Kong and Singapore - and to develop it into a financial market that could rival New York and London by 2001. To that end, the following principles were adopted.[3]

1. Free (a free market governed by market principles) – liberalization of entry, products, pricing;
2. Fair (a transparent and reliable market) – clear and transparent rules, investor protection;

3. Global (a global market at the cutting edge) – a legal structure that responds to globalization, creation of a monitoring system, accounting system.

In response, the Financial System Research Council, the Securities and Exchange Council and the Insurance Council began their deliberations, which culminated in their reports on May 21, 1997. These reports differed considerably in terms of their zeal for reform, but laid out a time schedule for reforming the financial markets and financial services sector. With regard to the securities market, which was to undergo the most wide-ranging reforms, the Securities and Exchange Council proposed a comprehensive reform plan for the financial and securities markets based on the following recognition:

1. It is necessary to conduct wide-ranging reforms for the securities market from a mid- to long-term viewpoint towards the 21st century;
2. In Japan's financial and securities markets, the emphasis until now had been placed on procuring and allocating funds mainly for the core industries. However, as the population ages, its role as a place to effectively invest the 1200 trillion yen in individual financial assets will gain in importance. Also, in terms of fund procurement, the provision of financing to various new industries that require risk-taking will become an important issue.
3. The traditional system of indirect financing centered on banks is unable to sufficiently fulfil these roles. It is necessary to strengthen the functions of the securities market, which is better fitted for carrying and distributing risk.
4. The past framework of preventive regulation may have hindered development of innovation and self-responsibility among market participants. It is also necessary to reform market infrastructure such as accounting, taxation and legal systems into a framework that encourages product development and transactions.

Based on this recognition, the council divided the subjects into investment instruments, markets, and market intermediaries, and proposed wide-ranging reform plans for each (Table 2.1). And on December 1, 1998, an omnibus 'Financial System Reform Bill' comprising 22 revisions in related regulations took effect, thus raising the curtain on the 'Big Bang'.

In the post-war era, the Japanese securities market had long remained a limited source for fund procurement under a market intermediary structure where banks enjoyed overwhelming dominance.[4] Due to the low interest rate policy, the bond market had been kept in a condition where a free secondary market was totally underdeveloped, and because of the collateral requirement, companies that were able to issue bonds were limited to the best companies in the heavy, large-scale industries. The situation began to change as a secondary market for bonds rapidly developed following the start of mass issuance of government bonds in 1975, when financial institutions were allowed under limited conditions to sell government bonds they owned, and as newly emerged blue chip companies which were shut out of the domestic market due to the collateral requirement took the move and began issuing bonds in the Euromarket and the Swiss market, which led to the revision of the collateral requirement to allow issuance of non-collateral bonds in an effort to prevent the hollowing out of the domestic corporate bond market. Subsequently, the accord reached by the Yen-Dollar Commission prompted further liberalization in the corporate bond market, to the point that it has now become a more or less free market.

The stock market was similarly limited by the low level of capital accumulation, where most of the issues were conducted at face value until the early 1970s, and was not a market where pricing mechanism functioned. Because of the higher costs of dividend payment involved in raising capital at face value, corporations increased their capital only when they were faced with a shortage of funds as banks tightened lending. Conditions allowing pricing mechanism to function in the stock market were finally met in the latter half of the 1970s, as stock prices began to rise on monetary easing, encouraging a move to stock issuance at market value. However, the post-war breakup of the zaibatsu and the ban against holding companies led to widespread cross-shareholding among former zaibatsu companies, which was followed shortly by commercial banks, and influenced price setting in terms of supply and demand. In other words, since stocks tied up in cross holdings did not circulate in the market unless there was a special reason, they had the effect of providing permanent support for stock prices, thus making stock issuance at market value an advantageous method of fund procurement. However, the functioning of this beneficial cycle depended on the continuous rise in stock prices. If stock prices declined, companies with weak finances were forced to sell the shares, posing a major obstacle to recovery in the stock price. This is the reason behind the latest debate concerning the need for a freeze on the dissolution of such corporate cross-shareholdings.

Putting that aside, until now the securities market had not been designated the role of a market for asset management in official documents. In that sense, this report had an epoch-making significance.

Along with the progress in comprehensive financial reform, the focus on the core business of the financial services industry has gradually been narrowed down. Namely, the change from financial intermediaries centered on the banks to increasing the role for the securities market, and a functional shift in the securities market from that of fund procurement to asset management. These are essential functions to be fulfilled by financial markets for providing financial support to new industries, upgrading industrial structures as well as for future economic development. But in an intermediary system centered on banks, there is a limit to the amount of risk that can be handled. Also, even if venture capital should taken on that role, it would be difficult for investors to take risk without at least developing an IPO and M&A markets to provide an exit. In that sense, it is extremely important to expand the boundaries and to strengthen the functions of the securities market.

There is another aspect concerning the securities market's role as a place to manage assets. Despite the fact that individual financial assets exceed 1200 trillion yen, and despite the prolonged low interest rate conditions, most of the money has remained dormant in savings and deposits. Due to the string of failures of financial institutions and the financial crisis since 1997, this trend has actually strengthened, along with a shift in the direction of safer Postal Savings. At issue is the effective investment of such an enormous amount of assets. Furthermore, along with a rapidly aging population, the collapse of the defined benefit plan of the current pension system is seen to be imminent, making a shift to a defined contribution plan inevitable.

The most important aspect of this system is that management responsibility is left to each policy holder. In other words, self-responsibility will be required of individuals. However, individuals are limited in their effort to acquire investment know-how, making support from an overall asset management service essential. Such operations require considerable investment in systems development, and will not be profitable without a certain degree of concentration in entrusted assets. And such merit of scale is fueling active moves to forge business alliances across traditional keiretsu groups.

From these we can expect that asset management will become an extremely important issue for the Japanese people in the near future. Stated from the viewpoint of the financial services industry, the asset management business is where the biggest business opportunity lies. Furthermore, if such is the case, collective investment schemes such as investment trusts offers the most promise.

In an investment trust, investment capital is collected in small lots and management entrusted to experts. This makes asset dispersion and expert management possible, which would otherwise be difficult for the individual investor. Furthermore, it allows for flexibility in creating products with varied risk profiles through a combination of investment products with varied risk profiles through a combination of investment products. For example, it enables the creation of a low risk product similar to deposits by selecting short-term investment instruments such as short-term government bonds, certificates of deposit and commercial paper. Likewise, if the goal is to achieve returns in line with the market, one can create an index fund that mimics the market portfolio. On the other hand, derivatives can be incorporated to create high-risk Bull-Bear type funds where returns increase with the rise or decline in the market. It is also possible to create sector-specific funds focused on stocks in a specific sector such as venture businesses. As shown above, the greatest attraction of investment funds lies in the ability to offer products in response to the various needs of the investor.

Considering this aspect of investment funds, it is easy to understand why banks and insurance companies have shown extraordinary interest in entering the investment trust business. Above all, adding investment trusts to the product line enables them to offer a full line of financial services. It is not an exaggeration to say that the rapid re-alignment among financial institutions in recent years have been focused on asset management services, and especially those businesses related to investment trusts.

Expected Effects

Aside from these moves towards re-alignment brought about by the reforms, it is true that the banks, placed under strict market scrutiny as an industry following the series of failures, and exhausted by the bad loans problem, have lacked the elbowroom needed to work on a full-scale reform for the future. Rather, a survival race involving re-alignment among banks, securities companies and insurance companies, as well as those outside the industry and foreign financial institutions, is underway at a tremendous speed. And the focus is on the asset management business, which has come to enjoy the spotlight. In addition, the securities industry, which has traditionally been highly dependent on revenue from stock trading commissions under administrative guidance from the Ministry of Finance, has found itself in an extremely serious condition under full liberalization in trading commissions in October 1, 1999. Here again, where a break from commissions-dependent profit structure is the urgent task, most of the large and second-tier brokerages are putting in extra efforts into the asset management business, and especially into operations related to investment trusts. At the moment, these efforts have not entirely been successful, and with few exceptions, the securities industry is suffering from a prolonged downturn. For this reason, there are active moves among securities companies to form joint ventures and business alliances with banks and foreign financial institutions with which they have had close relationships in the past (see Figure 2.1).

Some of the smaller securities companies have increasingly turned to becoming online brokers that aim to compete by offering discounts on commissions. As of May 2000,there are 48 brokerages that take orders via the Internet, and the number of accounts amounted to 77.5 hundred thousand (Bloomberg). In America, price destruction by Internet brokers progressed at a stunning pace over the past few years, but once commissions are fully liberalized, there is a possibility that the same phenomenon will occur in Japan. To survive, it will require systems investment for continuous system upgrades, addition of varied contents as well as capital to pull through the slug match. With brokers like Charles Schwab and E*Trade, survivors of such competition in America, entering the Japanese market or having announced intentions to do so, competition in this area is also expected to increase.

In addition, following the lifting of regulations against trading of unlisted stocks and off-exchange trading, and an easing of restrictions on managing investments, specialized companies are also entering these niche markets. And the change to registration-based entry for securities companies is expected to accelerate this trend.

As we have seen, there is a rush to enter the securities business among companies outside the industry and new entries by foreign financial institutions, aiming to capture the enormous individual financial assets that have remained for the most part in savings and deposits throughout the long period of super low interest rates (see Table 2.2). At least for these newcomers, the securities business is seen as an attractive, underdeveloped business, in contrast to existing companies that are suffering under the prolonged slump.

Remaining Issues

Incomplete Disclosure and Systemic Risk

The series of bank failures have revealed what is lacking or weak in the latest financial system reform (see Table 2.3). Above all, its failure to incorporate the strengthening of disclosure has disabled effective action against growing mistrust within the markets. Published figures on the amount of bad loans changed each time they were disclosed, damaging credibility, and by the time the Ministry of Finance and the Bank of Japan announced that the worst was over with the bad loans problem, the markets met them with complete mistrust.[5] Once bad news surfaced at a specific financial institution, other financial institutions in the same industry were often forced into the corner as their stocks were also sold on 'imagined connections'. For example, Industrial Bank of Japan stocks were sold in the aftermath of the collapse of the Long-Term Credit Bank and the Nippon Credit Bank, simply on the fact that it was also a long-term credit bank stock. This is a classic example of the manifestation of systemic risk, but if we are to part from the traditional 'Convoy administration' and aim to achieve financial administration governed by market principles, accurate and timely disclosure of information remains the only effective strategy.

The disclosure of bad loans at banks began in March 1993, but at the time the definition only covered 'bankrupt loans' and 'past due loans'. Broader figures that take 'restructured loans' into account were not disclosed until March 1996. These figures showed that the amount of bad loans had decreased at an even pace, making it difficult to understand why banks continued to face a serious crisis since autumn 1997. This led to criticism that the definition under which bad loans had been disclosed in the past were too narrow, and national banks began disclosing their more broadly-defined risk-controlled loans from March 1998. These risk-controlled loans included past due loans for which repayment was delayed by six months or more as well as those delayed by three months or more, and not only restructured loans but loans extended by the banks to support companies under operating stress. This definition more or less matches the definition of bad loans adopted in America.[6] These figures showed that bad loans (risk-controlled loans) at 19 major banks and nationwide banks totaled about 22 trillion yen and 30 trillion yen, respectively, in March 1998, a considerably larger figure compared with those defined by the former criteria.

However, even after bad loans figures based on the stricter definitions were disclosed, confidence once lost proved difficult to restore. So the Ministry of Finance, faced with criticism that self-assessment conducted by the banks were too lenient, compiled and disclosed figures on categorized loans based on the banks' self-assessment submitted in response to the ministry's inspections. These consisted of four categories.[7] The first category comprised assets with sound value; the second category, assets which require a certain level of risk control; the third category, assets for which loan recovery was extremely questionable; and the fourth category, assets deemed irrecoverable or valueless. Of these, assets that fell into the second through fourth categories covered all loans for which recovery was questionable to a certain extent, and the total amount reached about 50 trillion yen for the major banks and about 72 trillion yen for nationwide banks as of March 1998. These included assets such as lending to companies that are paying interest but are nevertheless reporting losses, which came under the second category, leading some to point out that the definition was too broad to signify bad loans. However, others pointed out even forcefully that the actual size of bad loans could be even larger because the figures were based on the banks' own assessment. In fact, an examination of cases such as the Long-Term Credit Bank and Nippon Credit Bank, which have been handed over to state-control, reveals that their bad loans far exceeded the total amount reported under the second to fourth categories.

As we have seen, while there has been a significant improvement in the disclosure of bad loans compared to the past, it has come about through a passive gesture on the part of the Ministry of Finance, which was forced to do so in response to the heightened mistrust against its stance, and so far has not been sufficient to restore credibility. Especially because in March 1998, public funds were extended to the major banks as the worsening bad loans problem led to the problem of inadequate capital. This was done on the premise that none of the banks had liabilities exceeding assets, but eight months' later, when the Nippon Credit Bank was placed under state control, it was revealed that the bank's liabilities had already been in excess of its assets at the time public funds were extended, heightening mistrust in the regulatory authorities. Furthermore, in 1999 there was to be a second infusion of public funds, based on the recognition that the economic slump was being made worse by the banks' loan recovery activities and tighter lending policies, which were caused by their inadequate capital levels. However, there has not been a sufficient effort on the part of the banks towards drastically improving their operations, which should be the premise of any extension of funds.

It is certain that the bad loans problem in the banking sector has posed a major obstacle in pursuing financial reform. Its basic principle is to place greater importance on the market and to force speedy exit of banks with unsound operations, and to that end, prompt corrective action has already been adopted. Here, the basic idea is that a bailout of a financial institution and protection of depositors should be treated as separate issues. In other words, the financial system and the depositor are what needs to be protected, and that a shakeup of unhealthy financial institutions should rather be welcomed. Based on this idea, deposits are to be fully protected for the time being. However, as seen from the serious impact left on the regional economy by the collapse of the Hokkaido Takushoku Bank, in reality an extremely critical situation could arise in the real economy, depending on the process of debt takeover. It is also true that prompt corrective action accelerated the tightening of lending by banks, leaving no way out but a further extension of public funds. For this reason, a view has recently emerged in some quarters suggesting the postponement of the pay-off system originally scheduled to take effect from April 2000, for the reason that the withdrawal of large deposits would significantly affect the banks. At last, this measure was postponed until April 2001. There is certainly concern that proceeding with the original reform schedule could further worsen the economic slump. However, the confusion and mishandling of the bad loans issue in the past several years, beginning with the problem of the housing loan companies, were not caused by the reform itself, but may be attributed to the way they were handled and in the moral decline at the regulatory authorities. Therefore, although one cannot rule out the possibility that some need may arise for slowing down the pace of reform, it is necessary to proceed with financial reform while pursuing policies for recovering the economy, which is at the root of the bad loans problem.

Strengthening Depositor and Investor Protection

Another important weakness in Japan's financial reform is the lack of sufficient consideration for the infrastructure of financial transactions. For example, in order to ask the investor to exercise self-responsibility, it is necessary for trustworthy information to be disclosed in a timely manner in order to enable the investor to make the decisions. But we have already seen the situation concerning disclosure of information on the banks' bad loans, and in general, corporate disclosure in Japan has not been sufficient. This is what led to the situation where stocks of targeted companies were sold en masse in the market on speculation borne of uncertainty. To repeat, as long as we are to proceed with financial reform in the direction of respecting market principles, thorough disclosure of information is the only method for avoiding such situations.

With regard to securities trading, the past rule of concentrating orders for listed stocks to existing stock exchanges has been abolished to allow for off-exchange trades. However, as several exchanges come into existence, without a system for distributing pricing information and orders integrating those exchanges, it could lead to a situation where these exchanges remain mutually separated. This issue of 'market fragmentation' has been a recurrent issue in America ever since order concentration rules were abolished in 1975. In America, through reforms in the securities industry undertaken since 1975, the National Market System was created, which consists of integrated bid and offer information and transaction information, and an order distribution system between markets. Unless these conditions are met, any 'competition among markets' will only cause confusion and reduce the fairness and transparency of trading. However, Japan has opted for setting certain pricing limits on off-exchange trades, for the reason that the creation of such a system would be costly. As a result, there arises the possibility that a price of a stock listed on an exchange could differ between the price set at the exchange and the price at which it is traded among brokers. Was it necessary to lift regulations against off-exchange trades at the cost of inviting such a situation?

In the issue of setting up infrastructure, ensuring depositor protection and investor protection is probably the most important. That is because as the abolishment or easing of financial regulations increase competition among financial institutions and lead to more closures, one cannot hope for stability in the financial system without a sure-proof safety net. The revised deposit insurance law of 1996 stipulated that deposits will be protected to the full amount until March 2000, that a Resolution and Collection Bank will be established as a receptacle for the failed credit cooperatives, to which the Deposit Insurance Corporation will extend financial support. Furthermore, following the collapse in November 1997 of Hokkaido Takushoku Bank, one of the commercial banks, the law was revised again in February 1998, making it possible for the Deposit Insurance Corporation to take out a maximum loan of 10 trillion yen from the Bank of Japan with government guarantee. With the revision of the deposit insurance system, the framework for depositor protection in the case of a bank failure has more or less been completed.

In contrast, the issue of securities investor protection has had its twists and turns. In Japan a fund for protecting investors had existed since the establishment of the Compensation Fund for Safekeeping Securities in 1969. However, the upper limit for compensation was 2 billion yen per securities company, which meant that if a securities company with 10,000 customer accounts collapsed, the amount that could be compensated was a mere 200,000 yen for each account. But under the 'Convoy administration', there were no cases of failure among securities companies until 1996, so the weakness of this system was not especially a problem. However, in 1997 Ogawa Securities, Echigo Securities, Sanyo Securities and Yamaichi Securities collapsed one after the other (see Table 2.4), turning under-funding of the Compensation Fund into a serious issue. Furthermore, since more securities companies were expected to close as financial reform progressed, it became necessary to strengthen and expand the securities version of the safety net.

Thus in December 1998 the Investor Protection Fund was established, and securities companies were obligated to join. The upper limit for compensation was raised to 10 million yen per investor. However, here separate management of client assets surfaced as a major problem. Under the Securities and Exchange Act, separate management was limited to securities entrusted by customers such as stocks, leaving cash from a customer's sale of securities, margin accounts, or substitute securities to be used as operating funds by securities companies. Due to this practice, in the case of the collapse of Maruso Securities in Dec. 1997, it was unable to return customers' assets, and required the Compensation Fund for Safekeeping Securities to provide funding instead. Seeing this situation, foreign securities companies demanded complete separation of customer assets as a prerequisite for the establishment of a new investor protection fund, and discussions between domestic and foreign securities companies yielded no compromise. In the end it led to an extraordinary situation where two separate investor protection funds were created. Meanwhile, separate management of client assets was set to start from April 1999.

It is necessary to note here that depositor protection and investor protection differ in substance. While in the former case the subject of insurance is the deposited principal at the time of a bank failure, in the latter case the subject of insurance is in substance the trading of price fluctuating products, and therefore compensation for losses incurred in the course of the transaction is excluded. In other words, the subject of investor protection is limited to any losses caused by accident. In which case the complete separation of clients' assets is the essential issue in investor protection, and the maximum limit of insurance can be said to constitute a secondary issue. Because even if a securities company collapses, investors will be protected as long as customers' assets are managed under a separate account and not used for other purposes. To understand this, it would be helpful to consider the system for investment trusts. Customers who purchase investment trusts from a securities company will not incur losses other than those due to price fluctuation in case that securities company fails, because their assets are managed under separate accounts by trust banks. This is the reason why there is no need to set up investor protection funds for investment trusts.

Strengthening of the System of Supervision

Finally, there is the issue concerning the system of supervision. The Japanese financial system differs from that in America, so we must exercise caution in offering simple comparisons between the two. For example, while both countries adopt a licensing system, the number of commercial banks in America, despite having greatly been reduced in recent years due to mergers, still amount to about 10,000. And in the case of the registration system adopted for securities companies, there are more than 5,000 registered members of the National Association of Securities Dealers.

There is therefore an enormous cost involved in supervising such a great number of companies. While the American supervisory system for commercial banks overlap in a complicated manner, there was a total of about 6,000 inspectors at the OCC, FRB and FDIC as of 1992. The SEC and CFTC supervise securities trading, with a combined total of about 4,500 employees.

In contrast, Japan abolished the Securities Bureau and the Banking Bureau at the Ministry of Finance in 1998, and their supervisory authority was transferred to the Financial Supervisory Agency, which was newly created as an external organ of the Prime Minister's Office. The Financial Supervisory Agency took on the responsibility of inspecting and supervising financial institutions. Seeing only this aspect gives the impression that there has been an improvement in the transparency and independence of financial supervision. However, when we turn to personnel, we find that the Financial Supervisory Agency has 165 officials in its inspection division and 68 in the supervisory division. There were also 98 officials at the Securities and Exchange Surveillance Commission, whose organization moved to the Agency intact, and adding inspectors at the regional finance bureaus would only amount to about 300 officials in all. In general, it is hard to deny that it compares unfavorably with the American financial supervision system.[8]

Certainly, regulatory costs can be kept low through prior regulation under a licensing system, which enables the exclusion of inappropriate companies from the start. The Ministry of Finance has pointed to the effectiveness of Japanese financial administration whenever the number of personnel was mentioned. However, that view is no longer persuasive with regard to the securities industry, which has moved to a registration-based system. Having declared its shift towards retrospective regulation in financial administration, the Finance Ministry needs to set up a supervisory system in line with that stance.

Why then, has Japan's financial reform proceeded in general without making preparations for infrastructure? The reason seems to be related to the ministry's motive in promoting deregulation. In fact, in an environment where fiscal restructuring became the priority following the burst of the 'Bubble', it was unable to depend on fiscal spending to bolster the economy, and further reduction in interest rates did not offer much hope in terms of effectiveness either, in the long period of low interest rates. With no other way out, it gave deregulatory policies the status of the only economic policy that was available.

Since financial reform was placed in the context of deregulation based on such a motive, an increase in regulatory costs was not to be tolerated. It is nothing but ironic that as a result, public funds had to be extended in an even more limitless manner in response to the consecutive collapse of financial institutions.

Summary and Conclusion

The Japanese financial system is experiencing a major turning point amid an unprecedented financial crisis. Though one of the causes for the worsening financial crisis may have been the way the shift in financial administration was handled. At least, the strengthening of the depositor protection system and investor protection fund were never given high priority in discussions concerning financial reform. It is difficult to deny that this amplified concern among depositors and investors, and thus led to the manifestation of systemic risk.

Japan is currently experiencing a brief respite due to the government's frantic use of fiscal spending in its plans to resolve the bad loans problem and to bolster the economy. However, unless banks push ahead with drastic restructuring, no end will be in sight for the bad loans problem. Also, as separate management of assets begins in April, there is growing concern that a large number of securities companies will face financial difficulty and be forced to close. Therefore, moves towards re-alignment in the financial services sector is set to become even more pronounced, and to proceed by involving companies across a wide array of business sectors.

At this point, it is next to impossible to foresee the new financial system that will emerge in the aftermath. Financial reform became inevitable as the system became incompatible with the real economy against the backdrop of globalization, and we can only proceed by experimenting with new financial systems along the way. What should be clear is that there is no return to the old ways, and that such a course would only worsen the crisis.

Notes

[1] On Characteristics of Japan's Post-war Financial System, See Hall (1999), pp.3-15.
[2] Saga (1999), pp.8-14.
[3] MOF (1997).
[4] Saga (1999), pp.17-18.
[5] Horiuchi (1999), p.88.
[6] Ibid., pp.84-85.
[7] Ibid., pp.86-87.
[8] The Financial Services Agency (FSA) was established in July 1, 2000, with integration of the Financial Supervisory Agency and the Financial System Planning Bureau of MOF.

References

Craig, V.V. (1998), 'Japanese Banking: A Time of Crisis', *FDIC Banking Review.*

Fuji Research Institute Corporation (1998), *The Effects of Japan's Big Bang on the Financial System.*

Hall, M.J.B. (1998), *Financial Reform in Japan*, Edward Elgar.

Harner, S. M. (2000), *Japan's Financial Revolution*, M. E. Sharpe.

Horiuchi, A. (1999), *Japanese Economy and Financial Crisis (Nihon Keizai to Kinyu Kiki)*, Iwanami Shoten.

Japan Securities Research Institute (1998), *Securities Market in Japan.*

Minister of Finance (1997), *Financial System Reform*, June 13.

Nakaso, H. (1999), 'Recent Banking Sector Reforms in Japan', *FRBNY Economic Policy Review*, July.

Peek, J. and Rosengren, S. (1998), 'Japanese Banking Problems: Implications for Southern Asia', *FRB of Boston, Working Paper* No.98-7, October.

Saga, T (1999), 'Financial System Reform and Securities Business Management', in Capital Market Research Institute (Shihon Shijou Kenkyukai) (ed.), *Frontier of Securities Business Management (Shouken Keiei no Frontier).*

Securities and Exchange Council (1997), Comprehensive Reform of the Securities Market – For a Rich and Diverse 21st Century.

Table 2.1 Schedule for Reforming the Securities Market

	FY 1997	FY 1998	FY 1999	FY 2000	FY 2001
I. Investment Vehicles (Attractive investment instruments)	▨	▨			
(1) Diversity of the types of bonds	▨	▨			
(2) Diversity of derivatives products	▨	▨			
(3) Developing Investment Trust Products					
1. Introduction of the Cash Management Account	▨				
2. OTC sales of investment trusts products by banks	▨				
3. Private investment trust					
4. Investment company type funds					
(4) Review of the Definition of Securities	▨		▨	▨	
(5) Enhancement of corporate vitality and efficient use of capital	▨				
II. Markets (An efficient and trusted framework for transactions)	▨	▨			
(1) Improvement of transaction system in Stock Exchange	▨	▨			
(2) Improvement of the OTC (JASDAQ) market system	▨				
(3) Deregulation of the solicitation by the securities firms of the unlisted, unregistered stocks	▨				
(4) Improvement of the share lending market	▨	▨			
(5) Improvement of the clearing and settlement system for securities	▨	▨	▨	▨	

Table 2.1 (continued)

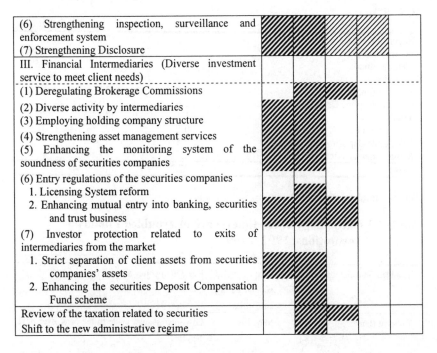

(6) Strengthening inspection, surveillance and enforcement system (7) Strengthening Disclosure				
III. Financial Intermediaries (Diverse investment service to meet client needs)				
(1) Deregulating Brokerage Commissions				
(2) Diverse activity by intermediaries (3) Employing holding company structure				
(4) Strengthening asset management services (5) Enhancing the monitoring system of the soundness of securities companies				

(6) Entry regulations of the securities companies
  1. Licensing System reform
  2. Enhancing mutual entry into banking, securities and trust business				

(7) Investor protection related to exits of intermediaries from the market
  1. Strict separation of client assets from securities companies' assets
  2. Enhancing the securities Deposit Compensation Fund scheme				

Review of the taxation related to securities Shift to the new administrative regime				

Source: Securities and Exchange Council (1997).

Table 2.2 Composition of Individual Financial Assets, Japan VS. USA, Sep., 1998

A. Japan

(Unit: Yen trillions)

Time and saving deposits	620	(50.5%)	
Postal saving		247	(20.1%)
Insurance	353	(28.8%)	
Life insurance		211	(17.2%)
Pension funds		117	(9.6%)
Nonlife insurance		25	(2.0%)
Checkable deposits and currency	145	(11.8%)	
Securities	110	(8.9%)	
Corporate equities		52	(4.3%)
Investment trusts		30	(2.4%)
Bonds		28	(2..2%)
Total	1,228	(100.0%)	

Table 2.2 (continued)

B. U.S.A.

(Unit: $ trillions)

Securities	9.9	(36.6%)
Corporate equities	5.3	(19.7%)
Mutual funds	2.9	(10.5%)
Bonds	1.7	(6.4%)
Pension funds	7.5	(27.7%)
Time and saving deposits	2.9	(10.5%)
Trusts	1.1	(4.1%)
Life insurance	0.7	(2.5%)
Checkable deposits and currency	0.4	(1.5%)
Miscellaneous assets	4.7	(17.1%)
Total	27.2	(100.0%)

Sources: Bank of Japan, FRB.

Table 2.3 Chronology of the Emergence of Troubled Financial Institutions: 1992-1999

Troubled financial institution	Date troubles announced by authorities	Resolution policy adopted
Taiheiyo Bank	May. 1992	Low-interest loan made to the bank over next 10 years
Kamaishi Shinkin Bank	Oct. 1993	
Osaka Fumin Credit Co-operative	Nov. 1993	
Kizu Credit Co-operative	Aug. 1994	Business suspended in Aug. 1995. Performing assets eventually transferred to the Resolution and Collection Bank
Nippon Trust Bank	Oct. 1994	MOF approved merger by Mitsubishi Bank Nov. 1994
Tokyo Kyowa Credit Co-operative	Dec. 1994	Liquidated and performing assets transferred to the newly established Tokyo Kyodo Bank in Mar. 1995 (This Bank was reorganized into the Resolution and Collection Bank in Sep. 1996)
Yuai Credit Co-operative	July. 1995	
Cosmo Credit Co-operative	July. 1995	
Hyogo Bank	Aug. 1995	Business suspended in Aug. 1995. Subsequently liquidated and performing assets transferred to the newly established Midori Bank Jan. 1996.
Fukuiken Daiichi Credit Co-operative	Dec. 1995	
Ibaraki Chuo Credit Co-operative	Dec. 1995	

Table 2.3 (continued)

Osaka Credit Co-operative	Dec. 1995	
Taiheiyo Bank	Mar. 1996	Liquidated and performing assets transferred to the newly established Wakashio Bank
Musashino Shinkin Bank	Sep. 1996	
Hanwa Bank	Nov. 1996	Business suspended in Nov. 1996. Bank liquidated. A New 'bridge bank' was established for the purpose of paying out depositors, recovering performing loans and disposing of collateral. Irrecoverable nonperforming loans transferred to the Resolution and Collection Bank.
Nippon Credit Bank	Apr. 1997	MOF reassured the markets by announcing a restructuring plan
Hokkaido Takushoku Bank	Apr. 1997	Planned to merge with Hokkaido Bank for April 1998.
Naniwa Bank; Fukutoku Bank	Apr. 1997	MOF approved to merger at the end of Oct. 1997
Kyoto Kyoei Bank	Oct. 1997	Assisted takeover by Koufuku Bank
Hokkaido Takushoku Bank	Nov. 1997	Business in Hokkaido region to be transferred to Hokuyo Bank. Business in the Honshu area to be transferred to other financial institutions.
Tokuyo City Bank	Nov. 1997	Closed. Bank of Japan to provide assistance as necessary until the final resolution of the bank.
Long-term Credit Bank	Oct. 1998	Temporarily nationalized.
Nippon Credit Bank	Dec. 1998	Temporarily nationalized.
Kokumin Bank	Apr. 1999	Closed.
Koufuku Bank	May. 1999	Closed.
Tokyo Sowa Bank	Jun. 1999	Closed.
Namihaya Bank	Aug. 1999	Closed.

Sources: Hall (1998), pp.160-165 and various press reports.

Table 2.4 A List of Insolvent and Newly Licensed Securities Companies: 1997-2000

A. Insolvent Securities Companies	
July 1997	Ogawa Securities Co.
Nov.	Sanyo Securities Co.
	Yamaichi Securities Co.
Dec.	Maruso Securities Co.
Jan. 1998	Echigo Securities Co.
April	Matsuhico Securities Co.
June	Nakamura Securities Co.
July	Nisshin Securities Co.
Aug.	Toho Securities Co.
Sep.	Ishizuka Securities Co.
Oct.	Showa Securities Co.
	Yamakichi Securities Co.
Nov.	Tokyo Flower Securities Co.
	Kyosai Securities Co.
Jan. 1999	Nakai Securities Co.
	Wakayama Securities Co.
B. Newly Licenced (Registered since Dec. 1998) Securities Companies	
July 1997	Tokyo Folex Securities Co.
	Nittan Brokers Serucirites Co.
Aug.	D-brain Securities Co.
Oct.	Ueda Tanshi Securities Co.
Feb. 1998	Angel Securities Co.
	Akushies Japan Securities Co.
	Yagi International Securities Co. (closed in Oct. 1999)
July	Nisshoiwai Securities Co.
	Sparks Securities Co.
Aug.	Nippon Investors Securities Co.
	ITM Securities Co.
Nov.	Mirai Securities Co.
	Yamane Prebon Securities Co.
	Nakaizumi Securities Co.
Dec.	Twenty Twenty Securities Co.
	Privier Zurich Securities Co.
	Nippon Denshi Kesisan Securities Co.
	Rabo Asia Securities Co.
	Itochu Capital Securities Co.
Jan. 1999	Hitachi Credit Securities Co.
Feb.	Mitsubishi Shouji Securities Co.
	Nomura Fund Net Securities Co.
April	Jet Securities Co.
	DLJ Direct SFG Securities Co.
	Nippon TPP Securities Co.
July	IBJ Nomura Financial Products Securities Co.
	Star Futures Securities Co.
	Manex Securities Co.
Aug.	Nikko Beans Securities Co.
Sep.	Nippon Online Securities Co.
	Sazare Securities Co.
Nov.	Softbank Frontier Securities Co.
Mar. 2000	Global Net Trade Securities Co.
July	FP Link Securities Co.

Source: JASD.

Figure 2.1 Relationships between Major Banks and Securities Firms

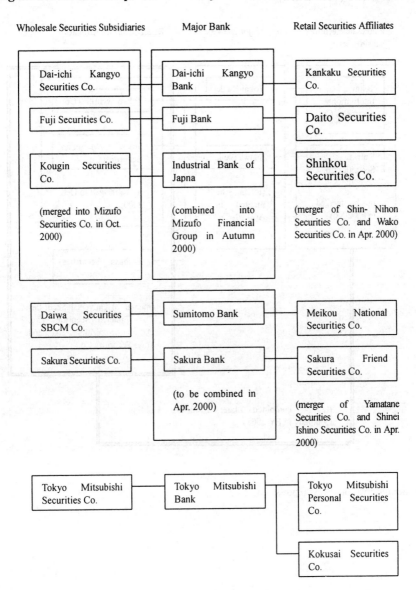

Figure 2.1 (continued)

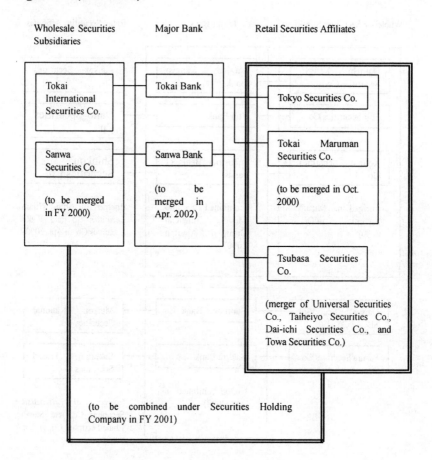

Sources: various press reports.

3 Financial Reform in the Republic of Korea: Past and Present

DONG WON KIM
INN WON PARK

Introduction

The Republic of Korea's (ROK) economy has been taking revolutionary financial reform measures to rebuild a sound financial system after the 1997 financial crisis. These measures could be classified as the third stage of Korea's financial reform history. The first stage, which appeared during the 1960s and 1970s, focused on the supply side role of the financial system for the development of money and capital markets. The second stage in the early 1980s moved toward a more *laissez faire* system through the privatization of banks and gradual opening of financial markets to international society.

This second stage was designed to resolve negative side effects of government-led development plans and shift the economy toward a more market-oriented structure for achieving further growth of the economy. If this second stage of financial reform had been successful, the economy would not have suffered the 1997 financial crisis. This is why structural problems in the financial sector have been blamed for the crisis.[1]

In this paper, we will evaluate the ROK's financial reform policies over time and attempt to characterize current reforms following the 1997 crisis. In Section II, we will briefly summarize patterns of the first and the second stages of reform from the 1960s up to 1997. Section III discusses the process of the third stage aiming to overcome the crisis. In Section IV, we will evaluate the various features of the current stage. Section V will summarize our findings and offer suggestions.

Steady Reform: Before the Financial Crisis

Looking Back on Financial Reform in Korean

Due to the gradual progress in financial reform made since the 1980s, the ROK economy has enjoyed significant gains from openness and deregulation. Interest rates have been fully liberalized, and most of the financial industry has been opened. The ROK's membership in OECD in 1996 was an endorsement by the international community of the successful progress of financial reform. Unfortunately, that endorsement was only valid for a very short period of time. In December 1997, the ROK economy became another victim of the Asian financial crisis. This would not have occurred if the ROK had been successful in building a sound and efficient financial system as OECD endorsed. In this section, we will analyze factors behind the failure of financial reform measures in the ROK, despite the fact that they made significant progress towards deregulation and openness.

The objectives of the reforms were very different from what have become the commonly accepted ones. Financial reform generally aims at achieving financial soundness and efficiency, but in the case of the ROK, they aimed at much more. Reform was accompanied by an overall economic development plan proposed by ROK government. This plan was designed to bring about a systematic transition in the economic management system from a government-led development planning system to a market-oriented economic structure; and as an integral part of the economy, the financial sector should have been restructured to support the overall change to a market-oriented economic structure. Another important difference was passiveness. Financial deregulation in the ROK was not carried out voluntarily to enhance competitiveness in the financial sector, but was pursued under international pressures to globalize into the world economy. These passive, supportive financial reforms had weaknesses from the very beginning.

In order to change an economic management system, the linkage between the real and financial sectors has to be rearranged. In particular, the linkage between financial indices and macroeconomic key indicators, like the economic growth and unemployment rates, will be affected, and relationships among business enterprises, the government, and financial institutions will also change. The main reason behind the failure of financial reform in the ROK is that attempts were made to change the operating system of the real sector through microeconomic reform policies in the financial sector without considering changing the financial linkage to the real sector.

The democratization of ROK politics was taking place at the same time as financial deregulation. The government was forced to pursue growth-oriented expansionary economic policies to satisfy increasing needs created by democratization.[2] It is necessary for a fast growing economy to maintain a high investment ratio and obtain a sufficient supply of capital funds through financial institutions. Therefore, there was no behavioral change in the relationships among business enterprises, the government, and financial institutions. It was, however, very difficult for the government to intervene in the distribution of bank funds, because it had already declared its financial deregulation plan as the core of its economic policy.

None of the three sectors prepared for the problem of massive bankruptcy and resulting unemployment that could be caused by market-determined allocation of funds. As an alternative, the government concluded a special "Agreement on Protection against Bankruptcy" in 1997. The agreement allowed banks to postpone bankruptcy proceedings, subject to certain conditions. It was officially a voluntary arrangement among financial institutions, but was in practice led by the government. Under the agreement, financial institutions could not apply strict rules to corporate loans. In addition, there was a very high possibility of an adverse selection problem caused by the increasing competition resulting from the deregulation of interest rates.

Why Did the ROK Encounter Financial Crisis?

One of the most important reasons why financial reform in the ROK failed and resulted in financial crisis lies in the interrelationship between over-investment by business enterprises and the distorted financial structure. In contrast to the booming period of 1986-88 when business enterprises improved their financial structure by using extra profits, they over-invested through debt financing during the 1990s. Debt financing was made possible by the extra profits during the boom period of 1994-95 and by strong support from the financial system. Enterprises did not focus on structural change for financial soundness, but on expansion of their size by abusing the opportunity to earn short-term profits. The government made it possible by relaxing regulations without taking sound supervisory action during the process toward a perfectly open market economy.

There is a higher possibility of encountering financial crisis when the financial market size is expanded without taking steps to secure the structural soundness of information production and ensure monitoring of the relationships between financial institutions and borrowers. A more severe asymmetric information problem will be created and finally result in financial crisis.[3] If the main source of capital funds for business enterprises is changed from bank loans to direct financing, it is necessary for direct financial markets to establish a system for evaluating and monitoring the financial credibility of those enterprises. The size of a financial system can quickly adjust to changes in regulations and market structure, but it will take time to build enough experience to ensure sound and efficient financial markets by developing a supply system and information production technology for investors.

Instability in the ROK financial system was induced by (1) the unbalanced relationship between financial deregulation and supervisory action, (2) inability on the part of financial institutions to produce sufficient information to support the expanding volume of financial transactions, (3) a mismatched term structure of balance sheets (long-term assets financed by short-term liabilities in the case of financial institutions and long-term investment financed by short-term debts in the case of business enterprises), and (4) over-borrowing of foreign funds. The financial collapse that occurred at the end of 1997 was begun by terms of trade that had been deteriorating since 1996 and the Hanbo and Kia problems that had occurred during 1997.

The failure of financial reforms prior to the crisis may be summarized as follows.

At the beginning, the unstable relationship between the real and financial sectors was first noticed during the restructuring process of the real sector. An asymmetric information problem was deepened because the financial system was quickly moving toward a market-oriented one without preparation for production of appropriate information and a system for supervising borrowing companies. The financial crisis was self-ignited because market participants did not recognize the importance of such a supervisory system, especially in the international financial markets, where borrowing by financial institutions and business enterprises was dramatically increasing.

Secondly, internal instability between real sector and the financial structure was also worsened when the latter's term structure became biased to short-term liabilities, while the former tended to focused structurally on the heavy and chemical industries, which needed long-term investment. Following restructuring, the real sector lost some flexibility regarding the business cycle, while the financial sector's ability to cope with recession was weakened.

Next, both financial institutions and business enterprises failed to make any adjustments because there was no improvement in fund management by large enterprises and financial institutions. While the world economic environment was moving toward a more open market system with tougher competition, business enterprises in the ROK chose as before to borrow their way to expanding their scale, and financial institutions did not improve the ability to produce necessary information.

Finally, the government failed to make the economic system more secure by providing sufficient infrastructure and supervisory functions, despite the fact that t0he financial structure was quickly changing. Such policy mistakes worsened the internal instability of the financial system.

The Big Bang during the Financial Crisis

The Korean government accepted an IMF stand-by arrangement on December 3, 1997. The economy could not meet the demand for foreign exchange resulting from the massive outflows at the hands of individual investors and international financial institutions. The IMF arrangement accelerated the pace of financial reform in the ROK.

Outline of New Financial Legislation

Lawmakers passed a 13-article financial reform package on December 29, 1997, just after the crisis struck, and the bill has been in effect since April 1, 1998.[4] Since the passage of the bill, the so-called "the Bank of Korea (BOK) Act" has been revised to enhance the independence and freedom of the ROK's central bank, together with strengthening its responsibility for achieving price stability. In order to enhance the independence of the BOK, the revised Act stipulates that the Monetary Board, whose chairman is the Governor of the BOK, is the final decision-making committee of the BOK and that the Minister of Finance and Economy is discharged from both the chairmanship and membership of the Board. The board membership is to be converted from part-time to full-time and disclosure of its proceedings is mandatory.

In addition, the financial supervisory role of the BOK has been limited, with most of that role being transferred to the newly established Financial Supervisory Service (FSS). However, the BOK still has the right to request information on financial institutions and the FSS necessary for the implementation of monetary policy and request the FSS to inspect commercial banks and implement corrective measures.

Under the new "Act for Establishing Financial Supervisory Institutions", existing decentralized financial supervisory organization - the Financial Inspector of Ministry of Finance and Economy, the Officer of Bank Supervision, the Securities Supervisory Board, the Insurance Supervisory Board, and the Credit Management Fund - were consolidated into a single body, the FSS, which is under the jurisdiction of the Financial

Supervisory Board (FSB). The FSS, established on 1 January 1999, is a special juridical entity responsible for inspection, audit, and sanction of financial institutions. The FSB, established on 1 April 1998, is in charge of promulgation and amendment of supervisory rules, and licensing of business activities and operations of financial institutions. The Securities and Futures Trade Commission is responsible for overseeing the securities and futures markets under the guidance of the FSB.

Restructuring of Financial Institutions

The IMF stand-by arrangement made the Korean government:

1. close troubled financial institutions if they are not viable;
2. restructure and/or recapitalize troubled financial institutions if they are deemed viable;
3. order financial institutions to accelerate the disposal of non-performing loans;
4. replace the present government blanket guarantees which will end in three years to a limited deposit insurance scheme; and
5. order all banks to establish a timetable to meet or exceed the Basle standards.

Following acceptance of the IMF arrangement, the Korean government decided to close troubled banks and merchant banks, close insolvent non-bank financial institutions during restructuring, and request other financial institutions to implement self-corrective measures, such as increasing capital under the responsibility of major shareholders.

Table 3.1 summarizes the government's restructuring of troubled financial institutions following the outbreak of the crisis.[5] As at the end of April 2000, the total number of banks, including special banks in the ROK,

Table 3.1 Restructuring of Insolvent Financial Institutions

(Unit: Number of Institutions)

	Number of Institutions at the end of 1997(A)	At the End of April, 2000				
		License Revoked	Closure Through Merger	Closure and Others	Total (B)	B/A(%)
Banks	33	5	5	-	10	30.3
Non-banking Financial Institutions	2,069	73	110	247	430	20.8
Total	2,102	78	115	247	440	20.9

Source: Financial Supervisory Service.

was reduced from 33 to 23. The restructuring of non-bank financial institutions was seriously launched in 1999 and resulted in the closure of 430 institutions. The number of non-banking financial institutions at the end of April 2000 was reduced to 79% of the 1997 amount.

Specifically, regarding commercial banks, On January 1998, the government ordered the Korea First Bank (KFB) and Seoul Bank (SB), two of the most troubled banks at that time, to cut their paid capital to 100 billion won, which is the minimum level of capital by stipulated by the Banking Act. After reductions of their paid capital, the government asked the Deposit Insurance Corporation to make an investment of 1.5 trillion won to the two banks (750 billion won for each bank). The action raised the paid capital of each bank to 1.6 trillion won. However, the financial conditions of KFB and SB were deteriorated by the further accumulation of□non-performing loans. The two banks were unable to carry out normal operations without additional recapitalization. Consequently, the Financial Supervisory Committee (FSC) decided to inject 4.2 trillion won as additional public fund to KFB. FSC finally decided to sell the two banks to foreign concerns, having negotiated with the New Bridge Capital Consortium to sell 51% of KFB's total issued shares and Hong Kong Shanghai Banking of China (HSBC) to sell 70% of SB's total issued shares. The New Bridge Capital Consortium took over the ownership of KFB in 1999, but the sale of SB is still not been completed.

Of the other 24 commercial banks, the government ordered six banks with BIS capital adequacy ratios less than 6% (as of the end of fiscal year 1997) to launch business reform measures, and recommended 6 other banks with BIS ratios between 6% and 8% to improve their business management. These 12 banks were requested to submit recapitalization/rehabilitation plans to the government by the end of April 1998.

FSC organized the Appraisal Committee, which included foreign specialists and reviewed the recapitalization plans of the banks until June 30, 1998. Following the review, FSC ordered five banks (Daedong, Dongnam, Donghwa, Kyunggi, and Choongcheong Bank) to transfer their healthy assets and liabilities to five selected banks with BIS ratios over 8% by the P&A method.

Among the above-mentioned six banks with BIS ratios between 6% and 8%,
1. the Korea Foreign Exchange Bank attracted German Com merz Bank's investment,
2. the Commercial Bank of Korea and Hanil Bank were merged and renamed Hanvit Bank in January 1999,
3. a merger between Choheung Bank and Gangwon Bank is in progress as of February 1999, and

4. Choongbuk bank was ordered to find a merging partner.
5. Korea Long-term Credit Bank was merged with Kookmin Bank.

As a result of the bank reform, the number of branches and employees fell by 23.2% and 34.7%, respectively, between the end of 1997 and the end of 1999 (see Table 3.2).

As of the end of 1999, the FSC introduced "forward look criteria" (FLC), which are international standards reflecting borrowers' capability for future redemption. To make sure that all banks practice the FLC, their potential factors of insolvency are to be disclosed in the clearest possible way by the end of June 2000.

For banks to take care of burdens on their own, which is caused by non-performing loans, the Corporate Restructuring Vehicle (CRV) was newly introduced.

The government is trying to provide institutional backup, such as streamlining the financial holding company system and offering incentives to M&A among banks.

Table 3.2 Employees and Branches of Commercial Banks

(Unit: Numbers)

	End of 1997 (I)	End of 1999 (II)	III=(II)−(I)	III/I(%)
Branches	6,225	4,780	1,445	23.2
Employees	114,619	74,744	39,875	34.7

Source: Financial Supervisory Service.

Merchant Banks　Concerning merchant banks, the government ordered them to submit their rehabilitation plans by the end of December 1997, in order to decide whether each merchant bank could raise its BIS capital adequacy ratio to 4%, 6%, and 8% by the end of March 1998, June 1998, and June 1999, respectively. As its first action based on the inspection of these plans, the government ordered the closure of ten merchant banks on February 1998 and forced them to transfer their assets and liabilities to the newly established Hanahrum Merchant Bank, a temporary bridge bank. After a second inspection, the government closed six additional merchant banks. Among them, two were closed because their rehabilitation plans were rejected; three failed to increase their paid capital because their major shareholders gave up; another two went bankrupt due to the bank panic. In the end, 18 of 30 merchant banks were closed, two merged, and only twelve are presently operating.

Insurance Companies With respect to insurance companies, at the end of 1997, the government ordered 18 insolvent life insurance companies (out of a total of 33), two undercapitalized loss insurance companies (out of 17), and two more undercapitalized guarantee insurance companies to submit their rehabilitation plans by the end of June 1998. After the inspection of their rehabilitation plans, the government suspended the operations of four life insurance companies in August 1998 and ordered the above two guarantee insurance companies to be merged. The total number of insurance companies in operation was 39 as of the end of June 2000.

Leasing Companies Turning to leasing companies, reforms are closely related to bank restructuring, because most leasing companies are subsidiaries of commercial banks. In May 1998, the government inspected the financial statements of 25 companies and found that 21 showed more liabilities than assets. Among them, ten were cleared through the transfer of their assets to a bridge leasing company, another eleven were rescued according to their rehabilitation plans, and the remaining four are operating normally. As of May 2000, 17 companies have been either restructured or liquidated, and six are in the midst of restructuring.

Recapitalization / Rehabilitation

The government initially estimated the volume of bad assets owned by all financial institutions at 100 trillion won. Based on this estimate, the government planned to buy 25% with public funds, encourage the financial institutions to sell 25% on the market, and clear the remaining 50% as losses on the books of the financial institutions. However, the actual amount of bad assets according to international standard totaled 112 trillion won at the end of March 1998.

In November 1997, the government ordered the Korean Asset Management Cooperation to establish a special fund for taking over the non-performing bonds of financial institutions. The size of the fund was 20.5 trillion won; and the government, Korean Development Bank, and 32 banks financed 40 billion won each for the fund (see Table 3.3). Most of the bad assets were traded with special bonds.[6] In particular, KAMCO purchased 43.5 trillion won by issuing government-insured bonds. The total public funds came to 64 trillion won, which the Non-Performing Assets Management Fund and the Deposit Insurance Fund have raised by issuing government-insured bonds. All pubic funds have been used. Among them, 18 trillion was recovered, of which 12.1 trillion won was reused. Therefore, a total 76.1 trillion won in public funds has actually been used.

Table 3.3 Breakdown of Public Fund used for Financial Restructuring
(1997.11 ~ End of April 2000)

(Unit: Won trillions)

	Deposit Insurance Fund	NPLs Purchase Fund	Total
Total Amount	43.5	20.5	64.0
Used Amount			
Total	43.5	20.5	64.0
Banks	27.9	17.3	45.2
Non-banks	15.6	3.2	18.8
Recouped Amount at the end of April, 2000	3.7	14.4	18.0
Reused Amount	3.3	8.8	12.1
Remainder in Recouped Amount	0.3	5.6	5.9
Currently Usable Amount	0.3	6.3	6.6

Source: Financial Supervisory Service.

Table 3.4 Extra Fund for Financial Restructuring in addition to 64 Trillion Won (1997.11 ~ End of April 2000)

(Unit: Won trillions)

	End of 1997 - 1st half of 1998	Since 2nd half of 1998	Dawoo related	Total
Special accounting for state-owned asset management	1.5	-	0.9	2.4
Public fund management fund	4.4	2.0	-	6.4
Investment from state-run banks	2.1	8.0	0.9	11.0
Loans from international financial institutions	-	1.4	-	1.4
Borrowings from banking institutions	4.6	-	-	4.6
Total	12.6	11.4	1.8	25.8

Source: Financial Supervisory Service.

Apart from the public funds, another 25.8 trillion won has been used since November 1997 on approval by the National Assembly or the State Council (see Table 3.4). Therefore, the total funds employed to restructure the financial industry come to 101.7 trillion won. Some 48% of these legislature-approved funds, or 25.8 trillion won, was used at the initial stage to cope with the financial crisis itself before the 64 trillion won of public funds was made available.

The 92 trillion won of the total 112 trillion won was recorded as bad assets at the end of March 1998 and was cleared off by the end of December 1999. However, 47 trillion won was added to the total bad assets mainly by the Daewoo Group's work-out (15.6 trillion won) and other work-out corporations (9.3 trillion won). As a result, total bad assets of all financial institutions came to 66.7 trillion won at the end of December 1999. Table 3.5 shows the cost of financial restructuring in the ROK in comparison to other international cases.

Table 3.5 International Comparison of Cost of Financial Restructuring

(Unit: As % of GDP)

Kuwait(1992)	Chile(1984)	Korea(1997-99)	Venezuela(1994)	Mexico(1995-96)	Spain(1980)
45	33	11	17	12-15	15
Hungary(1993-94)	Finland(1991)	Japan(1995-97)	U.S.A.(1986-96)	Poland(1993-94)	Sweden(1991)
12.2	9.9	7	6.6	5.7	4.3

Note: The Korean case (11%) is the ratio of total public fund (102 trillion won) to the sum of GDP (1998-99).
Source: Dzibeck and Pazarbasioglu (1997).

Table 3.6 Changes of Korean Commercial Banks' BIS Capital Ratio

(Unit: %)

	December 1997	June 1998	December 1999
Commercial Banks	7.04	9.19	10.83
Nationwide			
Commercial Banks	6.66	9.14	10.79
Local Banks	9.60	9.72	11.36
Number of Banks	26	20	20
Under BIS 8%	14	7	1

Source: Financial Supervisory Service.

As a result of the government providing fiscal resources to commercial banks, their average BIS ratio rose from 7.04% at the end of 1997 to 9.19% at the end of June 1998 (see Table 3.6). However, bank loans were dramatically cut backs, resulting in a credit crunch throughout the economy during the bank restructuring process. The BIS ratio fell again to 8.23% at the end of 1998, because banks bad assets were being quickly accumulated due to the financial crunch.

Was the restructuring the ROK's financial sector successful in renewing industrial soundness? The government providing fiscal resources for the task contributed to the rapid recovery of the Korean economy by bringing back international confidence and thus relaxing the internal fiscal crunch. The share of non-performing loans of total credits held by the ROK financial institutions was reduced to 8.7% by December 1999, down from

Table 3.7 Non-Performing Credit Ratio

(Unit: Won trillions, %)

	Total		Depository Banks		Other Financial Institutions	
	Mar-98	Dec-99	Mar-98	Dec-99	Mar-98	Dec-99
Total Credit (ç)	773.4	590.2	516.6	474.0	256.9	116.2
Non-performing Loans (ç)/a) b)	112.0	51.3	87.2	24.3	24.8	27.0
Iü ç (%)	14.5	8.7	16.9	5.1	9.6	23.2

Notes:
a) Non-performing credit extended to customers who have been in arrears for no less than three months.
b) Non-performing credit ratio of non-bank financial institutions at the end of March 1999: Security Companies (31.2%), Insurance Companies (12.5%), Merchant Banks (11.9%), Mutual Savings and Finance Companies (40.0%), Credit Unions (26.9%)
Source: Financial Supervisory Service.

14.5% in March 1998 (see Table 3.7). The share of non-performing loans of depository banks was reduced from 16.9% in March 1998 to 5.1% in December 1999. In particular, FSC introduced the "forward look criteria (FLC)", in December 1999 to evaluate the soundness of assets. By then, the number of commercial banks with the BIS ratios less than 8% had fallen from 14 (of 26) at the end of 1997 to 1 (of 20) at the end of 1999.

The government started restructuring non-bank financial institutions at the beginning of 1999. The share of non-performing loans of non-depository institutions increased to 23.2% in December 1999, up from 9.6% in March 1998. This sharp increase was caused by the debt problem of the Daewoo Group, which issued a lot of corporate bonds and commercial paper in 1998, then dishonored it in July 1999. The soundness of investment and trust companies (ITC) was particularly damaged by the Daewoo accident. The government ordered ITC to postpone redemption of funds invested in Daewoo's non-guaranteed bonds. The government arranged for loss sharing to be taken by each financial institution, and the Daewoo work-out followed. To rescue the ITC, public funds were injected to both the Korea and Daehan Investment Trust Companies in June 2000.

Enhancing Prudential Regulation and Supervision

The Financial Supervisory Commission (FSC) revised its "prompt corrective action" system under the Financial Industry Structural Improvement Act and the General Banking Act, in an attempt to provide systematic safety measures by prohibiting enormous amounts of non-performing loans (see Table 3.8). We expect that the toughened

Table 3.8 Revision of Credit Ceiling

	Before	After
Identical Borrower [a]	45% of stockholders' equity of financial institution	25% (with effect from January 1, 2000)
Same Borrower	Loan: 15% of stockholders' equity of financial institution Acceptances and guarantees: 30% of stockholders' equity of financial institution	Less than 20% of stockholders' equity of financial institution (with effect from January 1, 2000)
Large Loan	Sum of the loan amount exceeding 15% of stockholders' equity of financial institution should be less than five times of stockholders' equity of financial institution	Sum of the loan amount exceeding 10% of stockholders' equity of financial institution should be less than five times of stockholders' equity of financial institution (with effect from May 24, 1999)
Large Share Holder [b]	Sum of loan and acceptances and guarantees should be less than smaller value of the 25% of stockholders' equity of financial institution and the large share holder's equity capital ratio to the corresponding financial institution	Credit ceiling within the smaller value of the 25% of stockholders' equity of financial institution and the large share holder's equity capital ratio to the corresponding financial institution (with effect from January 1, 2000)
Sub-sidiary [c]	Individual Subsidiary Loan: 15% of stockholders' equity of financial institution	Individual Subsidiary Credit Ceiling: 10% of stockholders' equity of financial institution
	Acceptances and guarantees: 30% of stockholders' equity of financial institution	Subsidiary as a whole Credit Ceiling: 20% of stockholders' equity of financial institution (with effect from May 24, 1999)
	Subsidiary as a whole Loan + Acceptances and guarantees: 40% of stockholders' equity of financial institution	

Notes:
a) Identical borrower includes same individual, same corporation, and individuals sharing credit risk with them. It indicates the group of firms in the same line of business.
b) Stockholders who own shares more than 10% of issued shares of corresponding nation-wide financial institution (15% in the case of local financial institution).
c) Firms that own stocks more than 15% of financial institution's issued stock based on the General Banking Act.
Source: Financial Supervisory Service.

restriction on individual limits for borrower and the amount of loans will enhance the soundness of banks, since financial fragility has been mainly caused by the enormous amount of loans to Chabols.

Through the introduction of the FLC standard to classify the assets of financial institutions, the market realized and came to distrust the level of soundness of financial institutions. Therefore, the FSC ordered banks to declare their non-performing loans and disposal plans by the end of June 2000, and the disclosure was extended to Daewoo units and other firms under work-out programs.

Corporate Restructuring

Corporate Governance   Following the ROK's acceptance of the IMF stand-by arrangement, the government agreed with the IMF to reform the ownership structure of business enterprises. A detailed plan for a structural adjustment program was prepared to get a World Bank structural adjustment loan (SAL-II).

To begin with, the government ordered listed companies to follow international principles of accounting and auditing. The important reform measures were:

1. Compulsory reporting of quarterly financial statements from the year 2000;
2. Responsibility for reporting combined financial statements of associated companies; and
3. Further restrictions on affiliate payment guarantees.

Secondly, to improve corporate governance structure, the government took the following action:

1. From accounting year 1999, listed companies were compelled to appoint outside directors numbering over 25% of the total directorship;
2. Listed companies were to remove voting restrictions on such institutional investors as investment trust companies and bank trust accounts;
3. Minority shareholders' rights were to be strengthened, such as the right to bring derivative actions; and
4. Class action suits against a director and an auditor were to be permitted.

Other action plans for accelerating corporate structural included:

1. Structural adjustment would be voluntary and implemented by the market mechanism. The use of public funds should not be used for bail;
2. The mandatory tender offer rule on M&As was abolished;
3. Government admission restrictions on foreign ownership of domestic non-strategic enterprises was abolished;
4. Ceilings were abolished on the foreign purchase of domestic non-strategic corporate stocks without permission from the board of directors;
5. Public announcement of corporate management was encouraged;

6. Improvement of the legal structure for the resolution of insolvent business enterprises was urged to speed up procedures; and
7. Implementation of action plans were called for to reduce corporate asset liability ratios.

Work-out   The ROK government and the World Bank agreed to implement structural adjustment plans led by financial institutions subject to the program for the World 'Bank's structural adjustment loan (SAL-II). The plan was applied to all enterprises from the top five Chabols to small- and medium-sized businesses. The work-out involved a voluntary cooperative measure between financial institutions and business enterprises following the "London Rules" The FSC provided a criterion for selecting enterprises to be adjusted and guiding rules for agreements between borrowers and lenders concerning structural adjustment. Creditor financial institutions were to support work-out companies by converting their loans to paid capital or transferring their short-term loans to long-term loans; but the companies were required ask shareholders to dispose of some of their capital shares. The different rates of disposal of shareholders' capital was to be applied to general shareholders and major shareholders.

The top five Chabols were exempted from the work-out and asked to launch their own reform measures. The 15 largest businesses groups ranking from 6th to 64th, which used bank credit exceeding 250 billion won, were selected to be dismantled by the work-out. Among the other 248 companies participating in the work-out, only 14 companies have successfully survived, another 39 companies are still involved in the work-out, and the remaining 195 companies have taken various closing procedures.[7] Another 34 large firms, which used bank credit of no more than 250 billion won, are also under work-out. Creditor financial institutions of 76 firms, including 12 Daewoo companies, whose rehabilitation plans were confirmed, restructured their loans totaling 86.4 trillion won by providing preferential interest rates and debt-equity swaps, and applying normal interest rates to them. These loans accounted for 12% of total domestic private credit at the end of March 2000. New loans to finance these firms' operating costs and L/C opening were also being supported (see Table 3.9).

The work-out program has also induced negative side effects. Moral hazardous behavior of corporations under work-out programs is a continuous problem. Banks also evade accepting equity swap and supply new loans. For these reasons, the government decided to revise the work-out program. To begin with, the FSC investigated the status of work-out corporations and decided to graduate 32 corporations earlier than scheduled. Twenty-nine of them have become financially sound enough to graduate from work-out and the other three were excluded from the program because their creditor banks did not want to supply credit to them. Although 44 established corporations under work-out program were to be kept in their present status, the government reexamined the policy in order to avoid appointing problematic corporations.

Table 3.9 Status of Work-out

						(Units: 100 Million Won, %, the end of March 2000)
	Debt Restructuring					Fresh
	Debt Redemption Extension		Debt-	Others	Total	Loan
	Interest Reduction	Normal Interest Rate	EquitySwap			
Non-Daewoo(64)	194,954	43,876	26,255	22,428	287,513	10,404
Daewoo(12)	531,530	11,888	1,599	32,043	577,060	34,724
Total(76)	726,484	55,764	27,854	54,471	864,753	45,128

Source: Financial Supervisory Service.

Chabol Reform   At the end of June 1998, total outstanding loans the top five Chabols amounted to 207 trillion won, accounting for 27% of the domestic credit in M3. Without structural reform of these enterprise groups, it would be impossible to achieve financial soundness and successful structural adjustment of corporate ROK. The World Bank has especially asked for very strict structural adjustment of these Chabols. As a response, in March 1998 they agreed to improve their financial soundness with major creditor banks by clearing payment guarantees among affiliates in different industries by the end of 1998 and reducing their asset-liability ratios to 200% by the end of 1999. Consequently, 22 subsidiaries were either closed or merged to other group subsidiaries by June 1998. These enterprise groups were able to survive the severe financial repression during the first half of 1998 by issuing corporate bonds.[8] However, on 28 October 1998, the government put restrictions on financial institutions purchasing those bonds.[9]

Structural reform of the top five Chabols and the so-called "big deals" have not been very active, though the government has been pressing them to implement voluntary "big deals" in seven selected industrial sectors since early 1998.[10] Finally, the President of the ROK called in the owners of the top five Chabols and urged them to sign a structural reform agreement, which they did on December 7, 1998.[11] The detailed contents of the agreement are as follow:

1. To enhance transparency of their business operations and management, they agreed to (1) record combined financial statements from fiscal year 1999; (2) abolish illegal internal transactions among group; affiliates; and (3) completely abolish affiliate payment guarantees by the end of 2000 and guarantees among different sectors by the end of 1998.
2. To improve financial soundness, they agreed to (1) reduce asset-liability ratios to 200% by the end of 1999; and (2) increase paid capital.
3. To reform their business structures, they agreed to (1) focus reform on the leading companies of each group; (2) separate non-leading companies from each group; (3) close or sell bad companies (the number of companies under the top five Chabols to be reduced from 264 to 130 by the end of 1999)

Following the presidential meeting, major creditor banks of the top five Chabols revised their arrangement for improving financial disclosure by related business.[12] If the reform succeeds, the top five Chabols will be dismantled into small groups with only a few leading companies, meaning that the "Convoy type" business structure will cease to exist in the ROK business sector.[13] The Daewoo Group collapsed in July 1999, symbolizing the end of Korean crony capitalism.

Table 3.10 Top 30 Chabols' Financial Situation

(Units: Won trillions, %)

	Total 1997	Total 1998	Top 5 1997	Top 5 1998	6th - 30th 1997	6th - 30th 1998
Growth Rateof Total Assets	24.9	8.6	35.2	13.8	10.8	-0.2
Stockholders'Equity Ratio a)	16.2	20.8	17.5	23	14	16.7
(Total Amount of Stockholders' Equity)	68.9	96.6	46.8	70.0 b)	22.1	26.6
Debt Ratio c)	518.9	379.8	472.9	335	616.8	497.7
(Total Amount of Debt)	357.4	366.9	221.4	234.5	136	132.4
Net Income to Sales	-0.8	-4.5	-0.01	-3.3	-2.6	-7.9
Numbers of Companies	804	686	257	234	547	452

Notes:
a) Excluding finance and insurance companies
b) Increase in the top five Chabols' capital by asset revaluation was 14.7 trillion Won in 1998.
c) Share of the top five Chabols' assets over the top 30 Chabols' total assets was increased from 62.7% at the end of 1997 to 65.8% at the end of 1998. The share of the top five Chabols' sales was also increased from 69.8% to 74.9% during the same period.
Source: Fair Trade Commission.

Table 3.11 Top Four Chabols' Financial Situation

	1998(A)	1999(B)	B - A
Debt Ratio (%)	352.0	173.9	-178.1
Hyun Dai	449.3	181.0	-268.3
Sam Sung	275.9	166.3	-109.6
LG	341.0	184.2	-156.2
SK	354.9	161.0	-193.9
Total Debt (trillion won)	165.1	139.6	-25.5
Paid in Capital (trillion won)	46.9	80.3	33.4

Source: Financial Supervisory Service.

The Chabols' share of total bank loans was dramatically reduced after the implementation of reform in 1998. The share occupied by large loans in total bank loans was reduced from 50% at the end of 1997 to 42.8% at the end of 1998. In particular, the five Chabols' share fell from 28% to 21.7%, and its absolute total amount was decreased by 25%.

The financial statements of the remaining four Chabols was improved by the reform policy (see Tables 3.10 and 3.11). Their debt ratios decreased on average from 473% (five Chabols) in 1997 to 173.9% in 1999 and their equity ratios increased from 17.5% to 23% during the same period. However, the Chabols encountered cash flow problems due to the recession and the resulting profit loss in 1998. Their insufficient and passive efforts at restructuring generated harsh criticism from both domestic and international circles, reminding us that the ROK financial crisis was ignited by the unsound financial management of Chabols like Hanbo and Kia.

Deregulation of Foreign Capital Flow

In order to attract more foreign capital, the government allowed foreigners to trade commercial paper and bills of trade beginning in February 1998 and opened short-term financial markets (e.g., CP and RP) to foreign investors, effective April 25. From May 1998, the government abolished the existing 55% limit on foreign ownership sharing and allowed foreign investors to purchase up to 100% of domestic company shares, with the exception of few public enterprises.

Since the passage of the new Foreign Exchange Management Act on 1 April 1999, most foreign exchange transactions have been deregulated. Under the Act, business enterprises can freely incur short-term foreign debts with maturity of less than one year; nonresidents can open deposit accounts with maturity of more than one year and can open trust accounts;

there is no more actual consumer rules for futures transaction; and approval restrictions have been abolished for financial institutions to conduct foreign exchange transactions and money exchanging business.

Foreign exchange transactions will be fully liberalized after the government implements its second deregulation plan by the end of 2000. Then, inflows of foreign portfolio investment with maturity of less than one year will be allowed without having to request the services of domestic securities companies or make nonresident domestic deposits. In addition, individual domestic investors can freely open overseas deposit accounts, make overseas loans, supply credit abroad, and purchase overseas real estate.

However, short-term foreign borrowings by companies with too much liability will be prohibited, and the maximum amount of nonresidential borrowings in local currency (currently 0.1 billion won) will not be changed, in order to avoid negative side effects of deregulation. The key variables of foreign exchange transactions by business enterprises—for example, balance sheet and derivative transactions—must be announced quarterly. An integrated electronic networking system connecting foreign exchange, securities, and futures market will be established for monitoring short-term capital flow.

Regulation of financial institutions has been toughened since the foreign exchange crisis. Since August 1998, more than 50% of foreign currency denominated loans with maturity of more than one year must be financed by the funds with maturity of more than one year, and from July 1999, the percentage was increased to 100%. A gap regulation under which discrepancies between foreign assets and liabilities must be reported was also implemented in January 1999.

Implications and Prospects of Korean Financial Reform

Financial reform in the ROK, which has been implemented since December 1997 under an agreement with the IMF can be seen as bringing about revolutionary change in the system in terms of both depth and breadth. In particular, the traditional chain of procedures making up the government-led development framework—implicit government guarantees, bank supply of funds, dependence of business management on bank loans, high investment ratios, high economic growth rates, and full employment—has been broken by the closure of bad banks. The government made a rapid and proper injection of public funds. The striking evidence for evaluating the financial reform as a successful case is that the ROK recovered it's sovereign credit rating from international rating in about one year's time (see Table 3.12). This success can be summed up in the following points.

1. The first and foremost consideration was to restore the soundness of financial institutions, because the foreign exchange crisis was ignited by the rejection of international financial institutions to roll over their loans to problematic local banks.
2. There was no room for various interest groups to distort the reform because it was strictly implemented under the IMF supervision.
3. It was also the government's most immediate agenda to remove the uncertainty spreading over the whole economy from the time of the crisis. Because the financial repression caused by the crisis brought about problems of bankruptcy and resulting massive unemployment, it had to be resolved by reform measures as quickly as possible.

Table 3.12 Korea's Sovereign Credit Rating

	1997.12	1999. 12
Moody's	Ba1, Negative (12.21)	Baa2, Positive (12.16)
S&P	B+, Negative (12.23)	BBB, Positive (11.11)
Fitch IBCA	B -, Negative (12.23)	BBB, Positive (6.24)

Note: Figures in parentheses are the reporting dates.

The 1997 financial crisis can be recorded as one of the worst economic disasters in Korean history; but on the other hand, it has brought about a market-oriented economy through the IMF's program designed to reform the financial supervisory system, build soundness into financial institutions, and establish market principles to expel bad financial institutions. For the corporate sector, improvements in market transparency, ownership structure and corporate governance were made by forcing companies to take more responsibility for public disclosure of corporate management behavior and implement a system of compulsory appointment of outside directors. Most of Chabols have been dismantled, or at least their traditional Convoy-type management style disposed of. In that sense, we can say that the IMF program contributed a lot to the ROK economy towards moving its economic operational structure toward the U.S. market-oriented system.

However, we should take time to question here whether the miraculous Korean model of economic development can be successfully and quickly transferred to the Anglo-Saxon market system model by means of a financial big bang. Moreover, is the Anglo-Saxon model capable of bringing stronger dynamics and efficiency to the ROK economy? More efforts are needed for the economy to enhance the efficiency of a market-oriented system.

To begin with, there has been no significant change in the dominance of government in its relationships with banks and business enterprises while the reform process was unfolding. No matter how much the government shares the ownership of banks, the government is still forcing banks to follow orders.[14] For example, the government forced major creditor banks of big companies to sign the "Agreement for the Improvement of Financial Structure of Business Enterprises" and used it as an instrument for restructuring the business sector.[15] Relationships between banks and business enterprises is still controlled by the government, and normal relationships have yet to be established. However, since the share of foreign capital in the commercial banking industry is increasing sharply (see Table 3.13), we expect that government intervention will be increasingly restricted in the future.

Table 3.13 Ratios of Foreign Share-holders on Korean Commercial Banks

(Unit: %)

	Government		Major Foreign	Major other
	Deposit Insurance Co.	Others	Share-holders	Share-holders
Chohung	80.05	-	-	-
Hanvit	74.65	-	-	-
Seoul	97.78	2.22	-	-
Shinhan	-	-	-	-
First	45.90	-	New Bridge Capital (51)	-
Kokmin	6.48	-	Goldman Sachs (11)	-
Hana	-	-	Alliabz AG(12.46)	DongWon Group (5.16)
The Exchange	-	EXIM Bank(18.15) Bank of Korea(17.78)	Commertz(23.62)	-
Korea-America	-	-	BOA (16.44)	SamSung Group (16.44) Daewoo Group (12.6)
The Hosing and Commercial	-	Government(11.09)	Bank of New York (11.09) ING Insurance(9.99)	-

Note: Major Share holder means a share-holder who has more than 5% of issued shares.
Source: Financial Supervisory Service.

We also expect that the vertical relationships between the government and banks will quickly disappear, but fear that the market determined relationship between banks and business enterprises may not bring either dynamics or sufficient investment to the economy. If the conservative ROK banks behave like extreme risk averters and evaluate business enterprises myopically, how can it be possible for business enterprises to operate dynamically? Even if we assume that there is no obstacle against the Anglo-Saxon model of market economy, this question is bound to be a hot and sustainable issue concerning financial development in the ROK. In any case, the success or the failure of the ROK's financial revolution will be a very interesting research topic, since none of the other world economies has taken any faster movement toward the Anglo-Saxon model than the ROK is now doing.

Secondly, the adjustment speed of normalizing relationships among the government, banks, and business enterprises will be determined by the success of restructuring policy geared to the Chabols. There will be no more need for government regulation on the relationships between banks and business enterprises if its succeeds in reforming the Chabols.[16] If the "Agreement for Improvement of Business Enterprise Financial Structure" is properly implemented, the top four Chabols will be dismantled into smaller groups, which will enable us to remove the centralized power structure from the economy and allow the government to be only a neutralized supervisor not controlling the business sector by regulating bank business with private enterprises. Consequently, the government will come to perform only the normal financial supervisory role, while the normal buyer-seller relationship between banks and business enterprises will be established.

Thirdly, the financial system, including both market structure and institutions, is not mature enough for the Anglo-Saxon model of market economy to work efficiently. Systematic change in the Anglo-Saxon model is possible through financial reform. In order to achieve successful transition, there must be an efficient monitoring system, in which all the market participants—banks, securities companies, credit rating companies, and institutional investors—can build a multi-staged network. An efficient monitoring network is necessary for a financial system to allocate funds more efficiently and enhance the efficiency of financial institutions. However, the Korean financial system does not have such a multi-staged monitoring system, and financial institutions could not able one because of the lack of depth in the existing financial markets.

Fourthly, there are still problem in ownership and management structure. A revised article of the Banking Act stipulates that part-time directors form the majority of the boards of directors of most banks. These part-time directors will hold the managerial rights over banks and supervise their business operations. However, the article does not allow the top four Chabols, the government, or institutional investors to participate in bank boards. In this sense, bank boards still have a problem in sufficiently representing shareholders' interests, and may not be considered an appropriate decision-making body. In addition, institutional investors, mainly life insurance companies and securities companies, are the major shareholders of private banks in the ROK, but they are not allowed to join their boards because they are usually subsidiaries of Chabols, the major suppliers of industrial capital. As a result, bank ownership is separated from industrial capital. Banks are only taking an intermediate role in the allocation of funds in a market-oriented economic system. The problem here is that the economy does not have any alternative financial capital to replace the industrial capital of non-bank financial institutions.

Next, the most striking feature of the ROK's banking industry after the crisis has been changes that have occurred in its ownership structure; that is, a rising share enjoyed by foreign capital (see Table 3.13). The ROK case reveals that induced foreign capital is a key element to overcoming financial crisis. This ownership shift will affect not only the governance structure and management culture of ROK banks, but also influence their relationships with the government and their customers. This series of changes will push the Korean economy toward a more market-oriented economy. On the other hand, a banking industry managed by foreign capital could be a double-edged sword by forcing the domestic economy to maintain stable economic growth away from shocks in international financial markets.

Concluding Remarks

The ROK's financial system failed to carry out a voluntary process of development and consequently crashed when the Asian financial crisis hit the economy. The implications stemming from the recent Korean experience can be summarized as follows.

First, for developing economies, financial reform not accompanied by overall changes in the system of development cannot improve the efficiency of the financial sector and has difficulty in revising the role of that sector in the overall management of the economy.

Secondly, financial reform brings the closure or relaxation of regulation, but it does not guarantee the development of information and monitoring systems. In order to link deregulation to improved economic efficiency through an enhanced supervisory function, it is necessary to fulfill some other important conditions, such as strict financial supervision, profit-based financial institution management, and an independent position of financial institutions *vis-à-vis* business enterprises.

Last but not least, it would hurt a nation's economy if the transfer of its financial system from a bank-centered one to a market-centered one could not build a multi-staged networking system of information production and technology monitoring operated by financial institutions.

The financial crisis in ROK accelerated the process of financial reform there under the agenda of an IMF rescue program. It is still debatable if the IMF program was suited to the recovery of the ROK economy, but it is certain that the program brought about a big gang type of financial reform leading the economy towards the Anglo-Saxon model of a market-oriented economic system. How successful such a transition to the new system is will be another historical development for the Korean economy. One important lesson we can learn from the ROK case is that the systematic transition of a developing economy to a developed economy through internal evolutionary reform is a very difficult one to achieve. In particular, we find that while financial reform is the core of the transitional process, achieving a successful transition in this way is very painful.

Notes

[1] See Kim (1998), Park (1998), Tomas, Balino, and Ubide (1999), and The World Bank (1998/99).

[2] During the early 1990s, some economists argued that the optimal potential economic growth rate of the ROK economy would be 5%; and the target growth rate set below 5%. Such an opinion was wrong because of unusually high economic growth performances led by exports of semiconductors in the midst of the highly inflated Japanese yen. It was very difficult for the government to cut its target growth rate.

[3] Davis (1995), p.48.

[4] Before the crisis, the Korean government had laid a financial reform bill before the parliament but legislation of the bill had been delayed owing to dispute among political parties at that time.

[5] The government has already rid the foreign exchange trading business of eight insolvent merchant banks in terms of foreign exchange denominated debt as of November 1997, and also suspended the business of 14 merchant banks, two security companies, and one investment trust company on December 1997.

[6] Until the end of 1998, the government issued 19.9 trillion won worth of bonds to purchase 44 trillion won worth of non-performing assets.

[7] Among the 195 companies, 80 companies were disposed of, 47 companies were closed, 43 companies were merged, and 25 companies are under a legal representative's management.

[8] At the end of September 1998, they held 11.4% of all loans, 55% of all commercial paper, and 58.2% of all corporate bonds (*Mail Business Newspaper*, October 28, 1998).

[9] Trust and credit companies, banks, and insurance companies were compelled to invest a maximum 15%, 10%, and 10%, respectively, of their total purchase of corporate bonds to buy the bonds issued by similar companies in the top five Chabols. In addition, the corporate bonds issued by companies that have asset-liability ratios over 500% cannot be purchased by financial institutions.

[10] They are the semiconductor, train and automobile, petroleum and chemical, aircraft, maritime engine, power plant, and petroleum refinery sectors.

[11] The agreement for the 'big deals' was not legislatively but politically decided based on presidential supreme power. It should have been performed based on the financial transmission route. The process as it stands has a problem of punishment if the participating groups violate the agreement. For example, even though there is no legal basis to launching financial repression of LG Semiconductor Co., which has rejected its agreed big deal with Hyundai, major creditor banks of LG pressed LG by stopping new loans since December 28, 1998.

[12] The major arrangements are: (1) the top five groups must submit action plans for reform to creditors, and creditors must check the plans quarterly; (2) the reform process will be checked at quarterly meetings chaired by the President and attended by representatives of concerned business enterprises, government agencies, and financial institutions; (3) performance will be supervised by the Financial Supervisory Committee; and (4) major creditor banks have are responsible for monitoring the enterprise group performance and will honor their promises to support reform by such measures as converting loans to capital.

[13] A report by the Fair Trade Commission shows that the ratio of affiliates of which CEOs of the top five Chabol own the operating right without holding a share of stock are Hyundai 79% (49 of 62 affiliates), Samsung 85.2% (52 of 61), Daewoo 83.8% (31 of 37), LG 65.4% (34 of 52), and SK 77.8% (35 of 45). The average for the five groups is 78.2% (201 of 257) and the average for the 30 largest groups is 69% (555 of 804). CEO ownership sharing of affiliates within the 30 largest groups in the ROK declined from 4.8% in 1996, to 3.7% in 1997 and 3.1% in 1998. On the other hand, capital contribution among group affiliates rose from 33.3% in 1996 to 33.7% in 1997 and 35.7% in 1998 (*Mail Business Newspaper*, November 2, 1998).

[14] At the end of February 1999, the ownership share of the government in Hanvit Bank (merged bank of the Commercial Bank of Korea and Hanil Bank) was 94.8%, 10.4% in Kookmin Bank, 16.1% in Housing and Commercial Bank, 49% in the Korea First Bank, and 30% in Seoul Bank. The government decided to sell its 51% share in the Korea First Bank to Newbridge Capital Consocium Group and 70% share of Seoul Bank to Hong Kong Shanghai Bank of China.

[15] When LG Semiconductor Co. refused to transfer the company to Hyundai Electronic Co., despite the CEOs agreeing to the big deal, the government had LG's creditor banks stop any new loans. As a result, LG finally agreed to give up the business.

[16] The creditor bank of a company is like a regulatory body because of the legal loan management system for big companies. There has been a very uncomfortable relationship between major creditor banks and business enterprises, which is very different from the Japanese main bank system.

References

Chang, Kwang-su, (1997), 'A Trend and Effects of Asymmetric Regulation between Banks and Non-bank Financial Institutions', *Financial Economy Studies*, No. 90, The Bank of Korea, August.

Davis, E. Philip, (1995), *Debt, Financial Fragility and System Risk*, Clarendon Press.

Dzibeck, Claudia and Ceyla Pazarbasioglu, (1997), *Lessons and Elements of Best Practice, Systemic Bank Restructuring and Macro Economic Policy*, IMF.

Kim, Dong Won, (1998),'The Causes of Economic Crisis and Financial Structure Analysis (in Korean)', *Kyong Je Hak Yon Gu*, Vol. XLVI, No. 4, The Korean Economic Association, December.

Park, Yung Chul, (1998),'Financial Crisis and Macroeconomic Adjustments in Korea, 1997-98', in *Financial Liberalization and Opening in East Asia: Issues and Policy Challenges*, edited by Yung Chul Park, Korea Institute of Finance,.

Park, Yung Chul and Dong Won Kim, (1994),'Korea: Development and Structural Change of the Banking System', in *Financial Development of Japan, Korea, and Taiwan*, edited by Hugh Patrick and Yung Chul Park, Oxford University Press.

Tomas J., T. Balino, and Angel Ubide,(1999),'The Korean Financial Crisis of 1997: A Strategy of financial Sector Reform', *IMF Working Paper*, WP/99/28.

World Bank, (1999), *Global Economic Prospects and the Developing Countries: Beyond Financial Crisis*, 1998/99.

4 Economic Development and Financial System Reform in Taiwan

TSUN-SIOU LEE

Introduction

In the last decade, the promotion of financial liberalization has greatly influenced the rapid development of Taiwan's financial markets. Following the interest rate liberalization that took place in the 1980s, many measures have been taken to open financial markets. Major measures have included the following. In 1988, permission was given for the establishment of securities companies. In 1991, similar permission was given for new private commercial banks. The regulations governing bill-financing companies were relaxed in 1994. Regulations on commercial banks engaging in the bill business were relaxed in both 1992 and 1995. Overseas Chinese and foreigners have been allowed to directly invest in the local stock market since March 1996.

Along with the financial liberalization, developments in Taiwan's financial markets during the last three years have shown the following characteristics:

1. the growth rates of both bank deposits and bank loans have declined;
2. the scale of direct financing has broadened;
3. both the bills market and the stock market have grown rapidly; and
4. the transactions system has matured.

Thailand's decision to float its currency against the U.S. dollar in July 1997 induced a chain reaction among the nations, Korea, and Taiwan. Currency, banking, and foreign debt crises hit the region simultaneously and ushered in the most pervasive regional (if not global) financial crisis since the Great Depression of 1929.

However, for the year 1999, all countries in the region enjoyed a return to positive economic growth. Most observers assert that the worst was over as we entered into the year 2000. Although painful, the healing process represents a good opportunity to restructure financial systems. For example, the recent Big Bang in Japan has emphasized the expansion of investment vehicles, the facilitation of corporate fund-raising, the provision of a wider variety of financial services, improvements in market efficiency, the assurance of fair trading, and the preparation of risk controls and techniques to deal with future crises.

Taiwan suffered from a different type of financial crisis than other Asian countries, due to over-leveraging and heavy cross shareholding in the stock market. Although *The Economist* cited the 'creative destruction effect' to be the main factor behind Taiwan's relative success during the turmoil (January 1998), a recent issue of *Fortune* (February 15, 1999) predicts that Taiwan will be the next to fall.

Following the global trend of liberalization and internationalization, the government has been working on financial system reform for years. A strategic plan promoting Taiwan as a regional financial center was proposed in early 1995. The detailed tasks were formulated in January 1998, after a year-long discussion within a special task force called the 'Financial Reform Committee'. The implementation of these measures, however, was stalled by the Asian financial crisis and the local stock market crisis that started in September 1998. To counteract the weakening confidence in the local stock market, the Executive Yuan organized a 'Symposium on the Current Economic Problems and Resolution Schemes' in mid-February of 1999, and came up with some concrete measures to be carried out on a one-year horizon.

The rest of this paper is organized as follows. In Section II, the current economic and financial market situation in Taiwan is described and compared with those in other Asian countries. Future financial reforms in the areas of banking and capital markets are discussed in Section III and Section IV, respectively. Section V discusses some regulatory issues, followed by a brief conclusion in Section VI.

The Current Status of Taiwan's Economy and Financial Market

Peng (1998), Ko (1998), Kuo and Liu (1998), Lee and Yeh (1998), Johnston, Darbar and Echeverria (1997), and the Monetary Authority of Singapore (1997) have confirmed that poor fundamentals and financial disorders may largely account for the recent Asian financial crisis. They include persistent deficits in current accounts, excessive investment,

Table 4.1 Economic Growth Rate, Stock Market Returns and Exchange Rate Changes Before and After the Asian Financial Crisis, 1997

	Taiwan	Korea	Singapore	HongKong	Japan	Philippines	Indonesia	Thailand	Malaysia
A. GDP growth rate (%) a)									
1994	6.5	8.3	11.4	5.4	0.6	4.4	7.5	9.0	9.2
1995	6.0	8.9	8.0	3.9	1.5	4.7	8.2	8.9	9.8
1996	5.7	6.8	7.5	4.5	5.0	5.8	8.0	5.9	10.0
1997	6.8	5.0	8.4	5.0	1.6	5.2	4.5	-1.8	7.5
1998	4.7	-6.7	0.4	-5.1	-2.5	-3.0	-13.2	-10.4	-7.5
1999	5.5	10.7	5.4	2.9	0.3	3.2	0.2	4.2	5.4
2000F	6.2	7.0	5.9	6.0	0.9	N.A.	N.A.	N.A.	N.A.
B. Cumulative exchange rate changes against U.S. dollar (%) - From 1997.6 to b)									
Dec-97	-14.7	-45.7	-14.7	0.0	-11.9	-34.9	-56.0	-45.1	-35.1
Jun-98	-20.1	-36.5	-18.1	0.0	-20.6	-32.6	-82.5	-40.6	-36.8
Dec-98	-16.3	-39.9	-14.8	0.0	-4.7	-49.2	-206.6	-45.3	-36.8
Jun-99	-17.5	-33.0	-20.5	0.0	-3.5	-44.0	-233.3	-49.5	-36.8
Dec-99	-13.7	-30.0	-17.3	0.0	11.9	-54.9	-199.4	-56.8	-36.8
C. Cumulative changes in major stock market indices (%) - From 1997.6 to c)									
Dec-97	-9.3	-49.5	-23.0	-29.4	-25.9	-33.5	-44.6	-29.3	-44.8
Jun-98	-16.4	-60.0	-46.3	-43.8	-23.2	-37.3	-38.5	-49.3	-57.7
Dec-98	-28.9	-24.5	-29.9	-33.9	-32.8	-29.9	-45.1	-32.5	-45.6
Jun-99	-6.2	18.5	9.0	-11.0	-14.9	-11.5	-8.6	-1.0	-24.7
Dec-99	-6.4	37.9	24.7	11.6	-8.1	-23.7	-6.6	-8.6	-24.6

Sources: a) IMF, *World Economic Outlook*, April 2000.
b) Datastream.
c) *Taiwan Economic Journal*.

weakening of industrial competitiveness, and the accumulation of foreign debt. Together with the rapid pace of financial liberalization since 1989, a currency crisis (in the sense of Eichengreen, 1998), followed by a foreign debt crisis, hit the region. The causal relationship is summarized in Figure 4.1.

Taiwan performed relatively well from July 1997 to June 1998, with the sum of the percentage loss in the currency value and the stock market (the so called the index of pain) the lowest among major East Asian countries (Table 4.1). The commonly cited reasons for this performance are (1) a current account surplus and excessive savings, (2) a substantial foreign exchange reserve, (3) technology upgrading [Collins and Bosworth (1996)], (4) flexibility in industrial structural adjustment [Levy (1998 and 1991), Chang (1997), Aw, Chen and Roberts (1997)], (5) a two-stage exchange rate system, (6) a gradual deregulation of foreign portfolio investment and liberalization of financial institutions, and (7) lower financial risks for business corporations (Table 4.2).

However, things began to change in the second half of 1998. Some major shareholders of certain listed companies were unable to service their personal debts. Cash and cash equivalents were stolen from companies by shareholders who were in trouble, subsequently causing the companies' share prices to fall sharply. The stock market as a whole crashed as the confidence of investors weakened. The government came to the rescue with several measures such as a higher margin for short selling, a trading halt in the stocks of the troubled companies, and a NT $280 billion (approximately U.S.$ 8.5 billion) market stabilization fund to invest in the equity market. However, investors still chose to stay on the sidelines for safety reasons. By the end of December 1998, the TAIEX had lost 28.9% compared with its value at the end of June 1997, a loss comparable to the experience of countries in the same period (Table 4.1).

Table 4.2   Comparison of Financial Statistics from Selected Asian Countries, 1997

	Taiwan	Korea	Philippines	Indonesia	Thailand	Malaysia
Foreign debt / GDP(%) [a]	0.0	27.1	54.3	59.9	37.2	47.2
Short term debt / total debt(%) [b]	--	67.9	--	59.0	65.7	52.0
Foreign reserves / average monthly imports [c]	8.8	2.1	3.4	5.3	4.7	4.3
Nonperforming loans / total loans(%) [d]	4.2	15.3	13.0	17.2	19.0	15.7
Foreign share holdings(%) [e]	3.2	10.5	--	59.1	34.3	19.0

Sources: a) IMF, *International Financial Statistics*, January 1998.
          WEFA, *World Economic Outlook*, January 1998.
   b) BIS, January 1998.
   c) *Asia Pacific Profiles* 1998, APEC, ANU.
   d) *Taiwan Economic Research Monthly*, March 1998.
   e) Defined as the ratio of foreign investment in stock market to total market value in 1996. Source: same as c.

For Taiwan's international trade activities, 1998 was a terrible year. Exports and imports fell 9.4% and 8.5%, respectively from the previous year. Exports to ASEAN countries decreased by 29.7% while imports from the United States decreased by 15.3% (Table 4.3). The recession in the foreign sector represented a -1% contribution to economic growth in 1998. Recently revised statistics show that GNP grew only 4.8% in 1998, significantly lower than expected. Growth in industrial production reached only 1.5% in the fourth quarter of 1998, another historical low. The situation improved greatly in 1999, with both imports and exports recovering the ground that had been lost in 1998.

Table 4.3 Growth Rates of Exports and Imports of Taiwan – by Geographical Areas (%)

(Unit:%)

	Exports to						Imports from					
	U.S.	Japan	Europe	H.K.	Other ASEAN	Total	U.S.	Japan	Europe	H.K.	Other ASEAN	Total
1995	8.5	28.7	21.6	22.8	30.1	20.0	15.1	22.1	17.2	20.2	20.7	21.3
1996	1.7	3.8	7.8	2.6	2.2	3.8	-3.8	-9.2	7.7	-7.5	5.7	-1.1
1997	10.0	-14.4	8.7	7.1	4.7	5.3	16.3	5.6	7.2	17.1	19.7	11.8
1998	-0.6	-20.2	6.7	-13.4	-29.7	-9.4	-15.3	-6.9	-4.5	-2.2	-5.1	-8.5
1Q	2.2	-23.8	3.9	-3.5	-27.2	-6.5	2.5	5.0	-5.4	9.1	1.4	0.1
2Q	-0.7	-22.6	9.7	-9.3	-30.0	-7.9	-17.8	-6.1	6.3	1.2	-7.9	-7.0
3Q	2.4	-23.8	13.7	-15.4	-34.7	-9.8	-26.2	-14.5	-16.0	-3.5	-7.2	-15.4
4Q	-5.6	-9.4	1.1	-22.7	-26.2	-12.9	-18.7	-10.7	-1.7	-12.6´	-6.1	-10.7
1999	4.2	28.6	3.0	3.2	22.4	9.7	2.4	13.4	-16.6	4.8	13.1	5.5
1Q	5.3	14.1	2.8	-2.0	5.7	3.3	-22.7	-3.5	-11.5	3.1	3.5	-6.8
2Q	8.0	23.9	0.8	-2.2	20.0	7.4	-0.9	4.3	-22.1	2.4	11.8	-0.8
3Q	-1.0	28.9	-2.3	6.4	26.3	7.7	22.1	15.0	-8.0	4.4	15.0	12.8
4Q	9.0	43.2	11.8	17.0	33.3	21.0	8.2	38.2	-15.6	18.3	29.4	18.3

Sources: Taiwan Economic Journal
Import-Export Statistics Monthly, March 2000, Bureau of Statistics, Ministry of Finance.

As most companies failed to meet their revenue and profit targets, their share prices began to fall, reflecting the worsening fundamentals. Major shareholders, who had collateralized their shareholdings for credit, suddenly found themselves short of collateral and facing credit squeezes from commercial banks. In order to maintain their share prices, companies were desperately in need of capital to buy back their shares through wholly owned subsidiaries. Funds were raised through increased share collateralizations and underground financing channels. Derivative arrangements with foreign investment bankers, in the forms of warrants and equity swaps, were also set up in exchange for shareholdings by the foreign counterparts. Repeated share purchases and collateralizations created very high leverage effects, which worked against the debtors in the bear markets.

When the key shareholders finally became unable to support the share prices, the commercial banks and securities financing industry had to shoulder the burden.

According to the Central Bank of China, NPLs reached a historical high of 4.47% of total loans made by commercial banks at the end of 1998, up 0.65% from the previous year. This figure probably would have been even worse if the NPLs of credit cooperatives, agricultural credit unions, and fishery credit unions had been included. Although major commercial banks strode to write off bad loans, and the Ministry of Finance lowered the sales tax rate for financial institutions from 5% to 2% to make room for more aggressive write-offs, the average NPL for banks nevertheless climbed to 4.88% by the end of 1999. Due to the 7.3 magnitude earthquake that struck Taiwan on September 21, 1999, the NPL is expected to rise again in the first quarter of 2000.

In sum, worsening fundamentals, heavy cross shareholding among companies and their subsidiaries, and over-leveraging by major shareholders are the three most important factors for the 1998 stock market crisis in Taiwan. When all possible short-term rescue plans proved futile, the government had to search for medium and long-term measures to restore stability in local financial markets.

Financial Reforms in the Banking Sector

In the past, Taiwan's banking industry was heavily protected and restricted. No new banks were allowed to be established prior to 1991. Significant trade surpluses and economic growth throughout the 1980s created new demand, both quantitative and qualitative, for banking services. The government, in the face of the global trend toward liberalization, abolished the ban on the issuance of banking licenses in 1991. Cash-abundant conglomerates were soon attracted into putting up the minimum capital requirement of NT$10 billion (approximately US$400 million at that time) to apply for banking licenses, as profitability was excellent for the banking industry at the time, due to limited competition. Sixteen new commercial banks were set up within two years, and each now operates an average of about 30 branch offices. Between 1991 and 1997, the number of branch offices rose from 1,046 to 2,176 for domestic banks, and from 47 to 68 for foreign banks. Competition has become increasingly fierce and profits have gradually shrunk.

In the past, bank deposits, loans, and investments, apart from a few small exceptions, increased at an exceedingly high rate in Taiwan. An annual growth rate of more than 15% was sustained until 1994. Nevertheless, from 1995 up until the present, the financial system has become increasingly pluralized, liberalized, and sophisticated; fund-raising through bills, bonds, and stock markets has become more important as well. Now, medium and large enterprises frequently issue securities in the primary markets to raise capital at relatively low cost, resulting in decreased reliance upon banks. Meanwhile, there have been changes in the way that private wealth is held. People no longer merely store their wealth in bank deposits, but invest in bills, shares, bonds, mutual funds, and loans. The annual growth rates of bank deposits and loans have gradually declined: during the last two years, the annual growth rate of these items has fallen to less than 10%.

Since the financial statements of most small and medium sized business were unreliable, Taiwanese commercial banks, which accounted for most corporate debt, lent mostly against real estate property as collateral, just like elsewhere in Asia. Competition narrowed the spread between the lending rate and borrowing rate from 4~5% to 2~3%. Credit worthiness has deteriorated over time. Common stocks that had once been unwelcome or even unacceptable as collateral became popular among banks. The number of stocks purchased on margin has tripled over the past two years, with many of the borrowers being companies trying to rescue themselves through stock speculation. Since TAIEX has fallen by one third from its 1998 high, banks are pulling in their horns, bringing further selling pressure onto the stock market [Rohwer (1999)]. Taiwanese banks have high capital adequacy ratios (on average, 11% of assets, well above the international standard of 8%), but their pathetic 1% pretax return on assets makes them vulnerable to even slight increases in NPLs (Philippe Delhaise, president of Thompson Bankwatch, Asia).

Taiwan's asset bubble burst in 1990 and the property market has stagnated since then. All of the ingredients of Japan's past decade of bank misery are appearing in Taiwan today. Not much would have to go wrong to bring these ingredients together into a depressing combination (Rohwer, 1999).

Historically, the government has held considerable powers of persuasion over the banks. The 'Symposium on the Current Economic Problems and Resolution Schemes', held in mid-February 1999, reached several concrete conclusions to be enforced within one year. The proposals aim at improving the operational efficiency of banks and strengthening the bank surveillance system.

Ten measures were proposed to improve operational efficiency:

1. Banks must speed up bad-loan write-offs to cut the NPL ratio.
2. Banks will be asked to increase bad-loan provisions from 1% to 2% (the Tax Law must be revised for this purpose).

3. Commercial banks will be allowed to issue corporate bonds (called financial bonds).
4. Banks will be encouraged to issue preferred stocks to further increase their capital adequacy ratios without diluting earnings on common shares.
5. In order to prevent excessive interfere in the operation of state-owned banks, a new law on the supervision of state-owned financial institutions will be legislated.
6. Credit rating will be made mandatory for banks. A new asset restructuring mechanism will buy poor quality assets from low-rated banks.
7. Certain regulations must be instituted to control the use of common stocks as collateral for bank loans.
8. Tax incentives will be provided to encourage bank mergers.
9. Chairpersons of banks should be full time, and should carry full responsibility for preventing corruption in their affiliates.
10. Bank guarantees or joint guarantees will be strictly regulated or even banned.

The symposium concluded with the following proposals to strengthen the financial surveillance system:

1. The responsibility of financial surveillance will be unified under a new financial surveillance committee, which will be elevated to a higher ranking in the government hierarchy.
2. The Banking Law will be revised to provide heavier punishments for violations.

In addition, the Symposium recommended enacting the Trust Business Law as soon as possible so that more business can be created for banks.

In terms of the long term development of the banking industry, the Financial Reform Committee, set up in January 1997, reached conclusions a year later. Basically, it discussed the operational efficiency of state-owned banks, asset securitization, investment banking, asset management, bank surveillance, and evaluation of the firewalls between the banking and securities industries. Its conclusions affecting future financial reform included the following.

To improve the operational efficiency of state-owned banks   After 1992, when new commercial banks began to enter the market, the market share of deposits in state-owned banks dropped from 55.96% to 46.92% in just four years. Similarly, the share of loans dropped from 58.95% to 53.44% during the same period. The lack of an incentive system and the inflexibility in the budgeting process are the major problems. The Committee has decided to privatize those state-owned banks in order to restore their competitive edge. For those with policy-related duties, a new law has to be legislated to lighten most of the existing restrictions on state-owned banks that are absent in the regulations governing private banks.

Asset securitization To create liquidity for bank loans, a mortgage-backed securities (MBS) market will be launched. Conventional housing mortgage loans usually extend over a long maturity period. Periodically resetting interest rates disposes of interest rate risks for the lenders. Liquidity, however, cannot be restored without providing a secondary market for loans. Securitization is an effective way of providing a secondary market for loans. To allow for a legal MBS market, the Banking Law, Corporate Law, Securities Exchange Law, and Civil Law, among others, will need revision. Mortgage insurance and credit enhancement will also be essential to this end. In addition to housing mortgages, auto loans, commercial loans, and even credit card balances are potential underlying assets for securitization.

Investment banking Investment banking generally consists of business activities related to capital markets. Specifically, security underwriting, brokerage, dealing, private placement, M&A, venture capital, project financing, asset management, derivatives, business consulting, and corporate reorganization, are all regarded as within the core business scope of investment banking [Sullivan (1995)]. In order to enhance bank competitiveness, the Committee suggested that banks be allowed to enter into investment banking areas. Banks, with the exception of those that already have investment banking related businesses in place, will be encouraged, for risk control purposes, to set up independent subsidiaries for securities-related business. In effect, the dichotomy between banking and securities will become blurred. Regulations on transactions and information exchanges among banks and their affiliates will have to be strengthened, however.

Asset management Mutual funds, pension funds, and discretionary account management constitute the core of asset management. Worldwide, the size of mutual funds reached a level of more than seven trillion U.S. dollars in 1998, while global pension funds are expected to surpass the eleven trillion U.S. dollar mark in 1999. In major European countries, assets under professional management account for over 60% of GDP. Since the ratio of the sum of mutual funds and pension funds to GNP is only 15.4% in Taiwan, further development remains necessary. The Central Bank has decided to open the business of money market fund management to banks under the Trust Law and Trust Business Law. Article 18-3 of the Securities Exchange Law, which provides a legal foundation for discretionary accounts, passed through the legislature in June 2000.

Bank surveillance and risk control   A minimum 8% risk-based capital adequacy ratio is strictly required for all banks. However, there is still the need for the enforcement of a separate measure of the market risk involved in bank trading books. With regard to liquidity requirements, banks will be asked to self-regulate their own liquidity risk management according to guidelines set by the Ministry of Finance. Limits on transactions with a single customer and its affiliates, through lending, equity investments, and derivative contracts, should be closely regulated. Moreover, regulators will be given the power to dismiss any key bank employee who is deemed unsuitable. Penalties on illegal actions by banks will be increased and charged on a daily basis until the actions are corrected. Permission from the Ministry of Finance will have to be obtained prior to any substantial transfer of shareholdings. More professionals will be required to sit on the boards of directors of banks, in line with prudent management rules. Also, the position of compliance officer needs to be created at all banks.

Firewalls between banking and securities industries   Most countries in the world are moving towards a 'universal banking' system, in which banks are allowed to stretch their commercial activities into the securities and insurance businesses. Even the U.S. Glass-Steagall Act is continuously being challenged in Congress. Japan's Big Bang of 1997 also points toward a spirit of universal banking. In Taiwan, the Financial Reform Committee suggested that banks be allowed to enter the bond market as underwriters, dealers, and brokers. It recommended that full-fledged operations in the equity market either within banks, or through subsidiaries, be allowed, at the discretion of the banks. However, surveillance and risk control should be consolidated. The overall strength of a group to which a bank belongs should be assessed to evaluate the potential impact of other group companies on the bank. Potential conflicts of interest should be prevented. Full disclosure, based on consolidated financial statements and the overall requirement on capital adequacy, is essential to guard against excessive risk.

Financial Reforms in the Securities Industries

Because of the increasing number of channels for fund raising as well as the growing influence of personal financial management, direct financing has developed very rapidly during the last three years. Direct financing comprises the issuing of securities by both the government and private sectors. Instances of direct financing include issues of government bonds, short-term bills, corporate bonds, and overseas bonds (including global depository receipts (GDRs) and overseas convertible bonds), as well as the issuing of shares in both the stock market and the over-the-counter market. Statistics show that the share of direct financing has increased at a faster rate than that of indirect financing, accounting for 15.9%, 18.2% and 22.5% of the two combined in the years 1995 to 1997, respectively. These figures reveal not only that direct financing is increasing in importance, but also that disintermediation is gradually having a large impact on the financial system [Liang (1998)].

The semi-crash of the stock market in the second half of 1998 revealed that highly risky operations prevail in the market and that re-regulation is necessary to restore orderly trading. The recent symposium sponsored by the Executive Yuan recommended urgent improvement in market mechanisms and market scale, and better internal/external controls over business entities.

Strengthening Market Mechanisms and Enlarging Market Scale

Strengthening market mechanisms (1) The Securities and Futures Exchange Commission (SFC) should be given an independent budget. Its ranking in the government hierarchy should be elevated. To unify administrative functions, the SFC and other financial regulators such as the Banking Bureau, Insurance Administration, and financial surveillance units, should be merged into a new regulating unit. In addition, the SFC should be empowered with the functions of investigation, searching, and even arresting. (2) Insider traders and illegal churners should be charged with heavier criminal penalties. (3) Certain measures should be employed to discourage short-term trading. (4) Funds raised through seasoned offerings should be closely audited and followed. (5) Rumors circulated with the intention of influencing market prices should be investigated and penalized. (6) The Securities Investors Protection Law should be pushed into legislation. Class action suits should be encouraged and arbitration enforced. (7) Cross shareholdings and loans against stocks as collateral should be properly regulated.

In order to enlarge market scale   (1) Listing standards on the exchange and OTC markets should be reviewed and lowered if possible, to encourage more companies to go public. (2) Consolidated financial statements should be prepared to improve the transparency of company information. (3) The transaction tax on bonds (currently 0.1%) should be waived. (4) Rules on the buyback of treasury shares should be established. (5) To increase institutional participation in the securities market, hedging vehicles should be provided and the hedging costs should be made reasonable. (6) The business of asset management should be opened quickly, through discretionary account operations. (7) Collateralized shares should not need to be sold when their prices are falling. Securities-financing institutions should be given the discretion to own such shares.

To strengthen internal and external control over business entities   (1) Public companies should be monitored and inspected in a more detailed fashion. Persons found guilty of misconduct should be criminally charged. (2) Underwriters producing underwriting reports and CPAs producing auditing reports should be further regulated and charged with greater responsibility. (3) Misconduct on the part of a company board should be dealt with through the Criminal Law, and board members should be heavily penalized if found guilty. (4) To avoid the double counting of equity capital, reasonable regulations should be applied to guard against improper equity investments in other companies. (5) Share buybacks through subsidiaries should also be reasonably regulated.

Important Issues on Financial Reform

The following discussion focuses on the future direction of developments in the securities markets in Taiwan.

Policy toward foreign portfolio investments   The Central Bank has formulated several guidelines to deregulate foreign investment in Taiwan. These guidelines helped mitigate the impact of the currency crises in this region. In an attempt to conform to the trend of opening capital markets (while, at the same time, averting the drastic impacts of foreign capital), the Central Bank has adopted a gradual approach to deregulation. The inflow of capital to the securities market was opened up in three phases. In phase one, foreign investment was allowed in mutual funds issued abroad. Phase two allowed direct investment in the market by qualified foreign institutional investors (QFII). Finally, phase three (starting 1996) allowed foreign individuals to directly invest in the markets. The ceiling ratio of foreign investment in a single company has been raised from 15% in 1996 to 30% in 1998. By the end of 1998, foreign capital accounted for less than 4% of the total market value of listed stocks. The Ministry of Finance has recently raised the ceiling of foreign shareholdings from 30% to 50% for a single QFII as well as for all QFIIs as a whole, in the hope of attracting more foreign participation in the market. Foreign shareholding has increased to almost 10% as of the first quarter of 2000.

The development of mutual fund business   The mutual fund business represents yet another booming sector. The number of securities investment trust companies (SITCs) has gradually increased from four in 1985 to 36 in the first quarter of 2000, and together they manage 240 mutual funds of contractual type. The total volume of all funds was about NT$ 1,059 billion (about US$ 34 billion) at the end of 1999, accounting for a mere 4% of stock market value and 14% of bond market value. The SFC has decided to authorize the SITC Association to handle the screening process for mutual fund applications. In the near future, indexed futures contracts will also be open to fund management for hedging purposes.

Policy toward discretionary accounts with limited power of attorney Article 18.3 of the Securities Exchange Law in June 2000. The Article provides the legal foundation for SITCs and consulting companies to manage portfolios for individual clients under a limited power of attorney. The new law will be very significant for Taiwan, since increasing institutional participation in the market and the desire to build up asset management business are among the top priorities of market development.

Futures and options market   The Taiwan International Mercantile Exchange (TAIMEX) launched its first futures contract, i.e. Taiwan Stock Exchange Index (TAIEX) futures (tick symbol 'TX') on July 21, 1998. Trading so far has been sparse, with a daily average trading volume of around 4,000 contracts, representing just under 10% of the trading value of the Taiwan Stock Exchange. The SFC has set up a special team called the 'Futures Business Promotion Committee' to promote futures trading, since it is new to local investors. The Committee has decided to recommend the reduction of the futures transaction tax (currently 0.1%) and the relaxation of restrictions on institutional participation. The Ministry of Finance has responded favorably and announced the reduction of futures transaction tax by half, effective May 1, 2000. In addition, two sector index futures (electronic sector and financial sector) were launched in July 1999. Within two to three years, we expect to see bond futures, short-term interest rate futures, foreign exchange futures, and accompanying options trading in the market.

Warrants, warrant bonds and treasury stock   An amendment to Article 28.2 of the Securities Exchange Law will allow listed companies to buy treasury shares (currently banned by the Corporation Law) under three circumstances: (1) for employee stock option plans; (2) for the issuance of convertible bonds, convertible preferred shares, company warrants, warrant bonds, and warrant preferred shares; and (3) for the stabilization of share prices when they are deemed unreasonably low. The amendment has been passed through the legislature in June of 2000. The markets for company warrants (as opposed to sponsored warrants, which were legalized in 1997) and warrant related products will soon be established to enlarge the scope of corporate fund raising and to enrich investment vehicles for investors.

City renovation investment trust (CRIT) funds   The City Innovation Law, which was passed by the legislature in November 1998, encourages the renovation of old communities in the city. The funds needed for renovation can be raised through CRIT funds. Each beneficiary certificate represents ownership in the renovated community, and can be traded in the securities market. In essence, the CRIT fund is a first step toward real estate securitization, which can provide liquidity to real estate properties. Hopefully, the introduction of CRIT funds will inject new blood into the sluggish real estate market.

Regulatory Issues

In view of the issues raised by Tsurumi (1999) concerning the efficiency and robustness of financial systems, Taiwan's policy toward financial liberalization and internationalization clearly reveals the following characteristics:

The sequencing of financial liberalization   Because it long had a closed financial system with respect to portfolio capital mobility, the sudden opening up of financial markets world hurt local financial institutions. A more proper way to deal with the dilemma would be to first liberalize financial service businesses to local capitalists. There are two reasons for this. (1) The new establishments of commercial banks and other types of financial institutions would enhance market competition, and the efficiency of the financial service industry as whole would be improved. (2) Regulators would be provided with the opportunity to upgrade their techniques of financial supervision, so that they would be well-prepared to supervise the incoming foreign counterparts upon internationalization.

Since the early 1990s, license applications have begun to be accepted for several types of financial services businesses. Up until today, foreign financial institutions must still apply for regulatory permission. But because of WTO regulations, Taiwan will have to open up its financial market sooner or later. Its strategy of liberalization first and internationalization later seems like a good way to keep competition and efficiency in good balance.

The prevention of future bubble economies　A bubble economy may be defined as a situation where financial assets prices (as well as real estate prices) exceed their fundamental values. Taiwan has its own experience of an asset price bubble back in the late 1980s. The accumulation of foreign reserves through consecutive current account surpluses in the early 1980s resulted in an abnormal growth of the money supply. Strong sterilization operations were adopted by the central bank, but failed to control inflation as well as rising financial asset prices. The TAIEX index reached a historical high in February 1990, at the level of 12,600. When the bubble burst, the index lost 10,000 points in less than one year.

To prevent any future resurgence of bubbles, two things must be done: (1) The central bank should adopt a more flexible policy toward exchange rates. The pressure of exchange rate appreciation will not affect money supply excessively if the foreign exchange market successfully adjusts itself to a new equilibrium level quickly enough. Speculative funds (or hot money) would not have enough time to take advantage of the pressure. (2) Money supply growth should be kept within an acceptable range. The Central Bank of Taiwan has clearly done a good job with respect to monetary policy, but the 'managed float' exchange rate policy still dominates rate determination.

The structure of corporate governance　The manipulation (or stabilization) of share prices of listed companies through wholly-owned subsidiaries has been quite common in Taiwan. Corporate governance up until now has been largely family-oriented. There have been no requirements on disclosing the names of the ultimate shareholders. In the face of economic downturn and unsatisfactory corporate financial performance, however, even the controlling families are experiencing difficulty maintaining share prices. In particular, if they pledge their shares for credits to support share prices, tragic results are inevitable. This explains the stock market crisis that occurred in the fourth quarter of 1998.

To strengthen the mechanism of corporate governance, we need to make the disclosure of ultimate beneficiaries mandatory. Secondly, treasury share buybacks should be permitted to prevent the manipulation of share prices through wholly owned subsidiaries. Finally, a certain percentage of board directorships should be assigned to independent professionals, for the wellbeing of the general public, as well as to small shareholders.

The role of the banking system and capital markets   In terms of the development of financial systems, there is a worldwide trend toward domination by direct financing. Taiwan is no exception. The banking system, which plays the role of indirect financing, cannot just sit there and watch its share of the pie shrink inch by inch. It should be allowed to step into capital markets to build up possible synergies. The concept of European-type universal banking has been gradually leading to a government policy in which direct and indirect financing are no longer strictly separated. Japan and Korea are also taking similar policies at even faster paces. Risk control and management, as well as the prevention of possible conflicts of interests, are important challenges lying ahead, however.

In total, Taiwan's regulators are strictly adhering to the above mentioned policy guidelines. Yet the execution of strategic plans has been far from perfect and the speed of policy adjustment has been slow. Under the leadership of a new cabinet formed in May 20, 2000, we hope that the traditional conservatism will be changed, and that the pace of related legislation process sped up.

Concluding Remarks

In this paper, we have discussed recent developments in Taiwan's economy and financial markets. Following the turmoil in the local stock market that occurred in the fourth quarter of 1998, a 'Symposium on the Current Economic Problems and Resolution Schemes' was held in February 1999, with the aim of curing the symptoms at their origins. For the long-term development of the financial markets, the trend toward internationalization, liberalization, information transparency, and the cautious integration of banking and securities businesses, will go on. Taiwan has an ample supply of funds and well-educated people; the government's determined efforts to turn the country into a regional financial center and to realize its potential in financial market developments, merit attention.

References

Aw, B.Y., Xiaomin Chen, and M. J. Robert, (1997), 'Firm-level Evidence on Productivity Differentials, Turnover and Exports in Taiwanese Manufacturing', *NBER Working Paper* No.6235.

Chang, M. T., (1997), 'Privatization, Liberalization, Antitrust, International Competition and Vertical Specialization', *International Economics* 1186, 6-22 (in Chinese).

Collins, S. M. and B. P. Bosworth, (1996), 'Economic Growth in East Asia: Accumulation versus Assimilation', *Brookings Papers on Economic Activity* 2, 135-203.

Economist (The), (1998), 'The Flexible Tiger', January 3, 73.

Eichengreen, B., A. K. Rose and C. Wyplosz, (1996), 'Contagious Currency Crises', *NBER Working Paper* No. 5681.

Hu, M. W., (1996), 'The Relationship between SMEs and Taiwan Economic Development', Paper Presented at 2nd Conference on Small and Medium Enterprises, Taipei, Taiwan, R.O.C., May (in Chinese).

Kaminsky. G, S. Lizondo and C. M. Reinhart, (1997), 'Leading Indicators of Currency Crises', Western Hemisphere Department, *IMF Working Paper* 79.

Ko, C. E., (1998), 'Asia-Pacific Financial Crisis and Its Impact on Taiwan', Paper Presented at Kumamoto Gaugen University, Kumamoto, Japan, March 56-27.

Kuo, Shirley W. Y. and Christina Y. Liu, (1998), 'Characteristics of the Taiwan Economy in the Context of the Asian Financial Crisis', *Industry of Free China*, July 57-81.

Lee, T.S. and Y. H. Yeh, (1998), 'Industrial Adjustment Flexibility of Taiwan SMEs in Surviving the Asian Financial Crisis', *Asian Small Business Review*, Vol. 1 No. 1, 1-37.

Levy, Brian, (1988), 'Korea and Taiwan as International Competitors: The Challenges Ahead', *The Columbia Journal of World Business*, 23.

Levy, Brian, (1991), 'Transactions Costs, the Size of Firms and Industrial Policy: Lessons from a Comparative Case Study of the Footwear industry in Korea and Taiwan', *Journal of Development Economics*, 34, 151-178.

Liang, Patrick C. J., (1998), 'Financial Markets in Taiwan: Current Development and Future Prospects', 1998 International Conference on Finance, National Taiwan University.

Monetary Authority of Singapore, (1997), 'Is there cause for concern?' *Current Account Deficits in the ASEAN-3*.

Peng, H. N., (1998), 'Asian Financial Crisis', *The International Commercial Bank of China Monthly*, February.

Rohwer, J., (1999), 'Why Taiwan May Be Next to Fall', *Fortune*, February 15, 53.

Tsurumi, Masayoshi, (1999), 'Financial Big Bang in Asia', presented at the Symposium on Financial Big Bang in Asia, Institute of Comparative Economic Studies, Hosei University, Japan, March.

Sullivan, Edward D., (1995), 'The Structure of the Financial Services Industry', *The Banking Law Journal*, Vol. 122 No. 10, 977-996.

Figure 4.1 Diagrammatic Causal Relationships in the Asian Financial Crisis

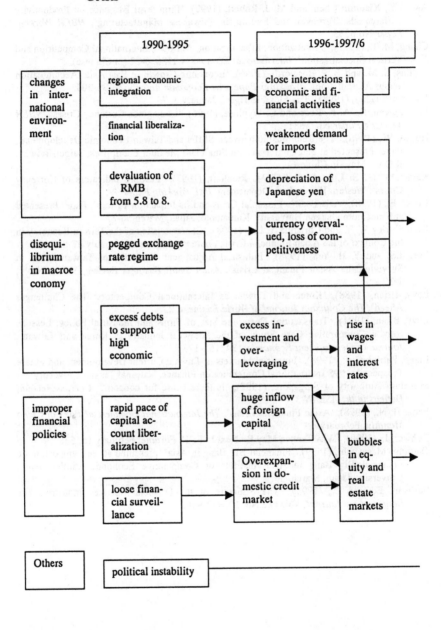

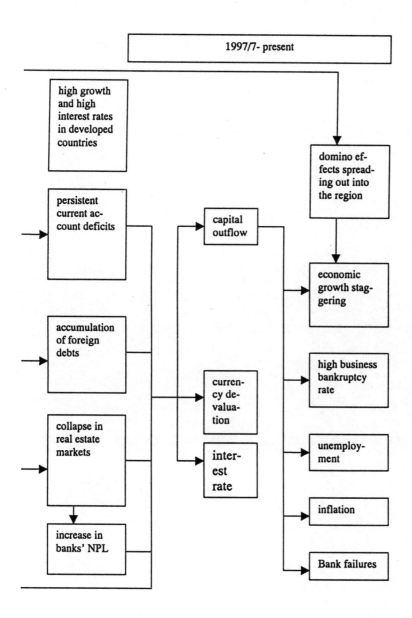

5 Banking Development and the Asian Financial Crisis in Hong Kong

YIM FAI LUK

Introduction

The Asian financial crisis, which started in mid-1997, took the whole world by surprise. It was phenomenal in terms of its severity of infliction, scope of influence, as well as speed of occurrence. It took more than two years or so before the worst situation was over, and economies that were hardly struck by the crisis have finally begun to recover. Given the tremendous impact of the crisis on the region, there are certainly lots of lessons that could be learned from this disastrous experience.

The crisis took place in a period when most of the Asian economies had been undertaking financial liberalization to various extents. It is natural to ask what the relationship between the crisis and liberalization is. Did liberalization expose and aggravate the underlying fragility of the financial system without at the same time introducing suitable measures of control? And would the crisis pose so much pain on the economies that further liberalization has to be postponed?

Among the major economies that were badly affected by the crisis, Hong Kong is different from the others in that there had not been any obvious measures of financial repression. As such, there have also not been any obvious and deliberate policies of financial liberalization. As a matter of fact, the financial system in Hong Kong has been very liberal for a long time, at least in comparison to most of its neighbors. It is true that there were and still are various kinds of government intervention and non-competitive elements in the financial system, but these are not so pervasive and important as to say that the system was once repressed and had to go through an obvious phase of liberalization.

Nevertheless, Hong Kong did suffer terribly in the two or three years after the onset of the Asian financial crisis. The year 1998 was particularly difficult as the economy shrank by over 5% in real terms, the worst in Hong Kong's recent history. Since there was no deliberate policy of liberalization in Hong Kong, while financial liberalization may have something to do with the crisis elsewhere in the region, in Hong Kong, it is not so obvious that the crisis is a result of liberalization.

This paper looks at the banking system of Hong Kong and its experience during the Asian financial crisis. It begins with a brief history of the recent development of the banking sector. It then moves on to highlight some salient aspects of the current situation of banking. This is followed by the experience of banks in the crisis years. The next section discusses other issues of banking reform not directly related to the Asian crisis. The final section looks at some future challenges and concludes.

Some Historical Background

After some bank failures in the early 1960s, the Hong Kong government invited officials from the Bank of England to investigate the banking system of Hong Kong. The findings were that there were too many licensed banks and that their loans were too concentrated in the property market. It was recommended that a Commissioner of Banking be established to undertake prudential regulation of the banks. The idea was adopted and incorporated in the Banking Ordinance of 1964, which, together with later amendments, have since become the legal framework for the operation of banking business. The Ordinance did not stop further bank runs and failures in 1965. As a result, a moratorium on bank licenses was imposed and this was not lifted until 1978. During this period, only one license was granted and after that the number of licensed banks stayed at 74. Another fallout of problem banks in those years was the introduction of the Interest Rate Rule (IRR), which were basically deposit interest ceilings on bank deposits of various denominations and maturities. As in most other economies, deposit interest ceilings in Hong Kong were imposed with the intention to curb excessive competition among banks, and it was believed that bidding for deposits through high deposit rates would lead to undue risk for banks and endanger the banking system.

In the early 1970s, Hong Kong began to emerge as an international financial center. Many foreign banks wanted to start business in the territory, but were not able to get a bank license as a result of the moratorium. However, they were still able to participate in banking business in Hong Kong, either by acquiring shares in existing banks or by setting up finance companies that could not carry out the full range of activities like a licensed bank. These foreign financial institutions were not particularly interested in the local retail banking market. Even if they were, they would find it difficult to compete for shares of the local deposit market, as there were already quite a large number of licensed banks with a long history of local business. The newcomers were actually internationally reputable investment banks with an interest in wholesale banking business in the region.

On the other hand, licensed banks also set up finance companies to bypass the IRR. Given these ceilings, banks found it increasingly hard to compete for deposits as inflation mounted. They therefore set up other financial institutions that were not subject to the IRR. These subsidiaries could offer above-ceiling interest rates to absorb more deposits and lend the funds to their parent banks. In addition, there were numerous local finance companies that received time deposits and lent money to finance stock and property market transactions. As a result, although no new bank license was granted, there were still various kinds of new financial companies in Hong Kong. In 1976, they were all grouped as deposit-taking companies (DTCs) and were required to register as such, which meant they had to fulfil some regulatory requirements, including capital adequacy.

With increasing demand for bank licenses, the moratorium was finally relaxed in March 1978. There was, however, the one-building condition attached to new licenses for foreign banks. By this condition, a foreign bank could have offices in only one building and is therefore restricted in branching. Despite this limitation, the number of applications was so great that a temporary suspension again took place, only to be lifted again in May 1981. In 1981, a three-tier system of financial institutions was introduced that lasted until today. Under this system, depository institutions in Hong Kong are classified into licensed banks, restricted licensed banks (RLBs), and DTCs. They are together taken as "authorized institutions" (AIs) by the Hong Kong Monetary Authority (HKMA). In terms of functions, licensed banks can carry out all kinds of retail banking business and accept deposits of all maturities and denominations. The other two kinds of financial institutions cannot issue demand deposits or savings deposits. In addition, RLBs are barred from taking time deposits of less than HK$500,000 but there is no restriction on maturity, while DTCs cannot take time deposits of less than HK$100,000 or three months maturity. The RLBs are basically involved in investment banking and capital market business, while DTCs are mainly associated with the licensed banks and engage in activities such as consumer finance, trade finance or securities.

One reason for the three-tier structure of depository institutions was to strengthen the IRR. As there were restrictions on RLBs and DTCs in their taking of deposits, there would cease to be effective roundabout ways for the licensed banks to bypass the IRR. This was considered to be very important because the control of interest rates was more or less the only means of money control at that time. In connection with this, the Hong Kong Association of Banks (HKAB) was established as a statutory body to replace the Exchange Banks' Association in January 1981. Since then, all licensed banks are required to be members of the HKAB, and are thus bound by deposit interests set by the HKAB.

There have been fluctuations in the number of the three kinds of AIs over the years. On the whole, the banking industry in Hong Kong, just like most other sectors, has been operating in a very liberal environment, with minimal day-to-day government intervention. Yet, since the economy and the financial landscape has been developing fast, and given the very open nature of Hong Kong, the banking system has experienced sporadic difficulties. The government has been adopting new regulatory measures mostly only in response to problems after they have arisen, rather than imposing regulations to suppress new developments and initiatives.

Some Salient Aspects of the Banking System

By the 1990s, Hong Kong has become a major regional financial center. Of the various financial activities including the foreign exchange market, the stock and derivatives markets, insurance, mutual funds, etc., it is the banking industry that contributes most to Hong Kong's status as financial center. Hong Kong has a high concentration of international banks, with 62 of the 100 largest banks in the world having representation in the city. At the end of June 2000, there were a total of 153 licensed banks, 50 restricted license banks and 65 deposit-taking companies. In comparison, the same numbers for end-1997 were 180, 66, and 115 respectively. The sharp reduction in the number of AIs was the result of the retreat of foreign institutions, mostly those from Japan. Of the total of 268 institutions remaining, 235 are owned by interests from over 30 countries.[1]

The most prominent feature of the Hong Kong banking sector is its openness and international orientation. Aside from the large number of international banks, the media of bank transaction are also easily notable. Foreign exchange transactions account for a large share of total transactions in both bank deposits and loans. Foreign exchange deposits have been a high percentage of total deposits in Hong Kong, reaching levels of over 60% for some months in the early 1990s. This was mainly due to high domestic inflation on one hand, and low nominal interest rates on the other.

Domestic inflation in Hong Kong had been near double digits since the mid-1980s. Although the unit price of export increased by an annual

Table 5.1 Hong Kong Recent Economic Statistics

		Gross Domestic Product	Composite Price Index	Retail Sales (real)	Trade in Goods (real)			Private Residential Price Index	Unem-ploy ment Rate
					Domestic Exports	Re-exports	Imports		
		year-on-year growth rate, %						% change in period	%
1991		5.1	11.6	10.4	0.5	26.5	19.0	37.8	1.8
1992		6.3	9.6	12.0	0.2	28.3	22.2	40.5	2.0
1993		6.1	8.8	6.9	-4.5	19.6	12.7	10.2	2.0
1994		5.4	8.8	5.8	-2.3	13.8	14.0	23.6	1.9
1995		3.9	9.1	-1.4	2.0	14.3	13.8	-7.2	3.2
1996		4.5	6.3	1.6	-8.4	7.5	4.3	9.6	2.8
1997		5.0	5.8	1.1	2.1	6.8	7.2	40.9	2.2
1998		-5.3	2.8	-16.7	-7.9	-3.7	-7.2	-28.8	4.7
1999		3.1	-4.0	-1.5	-7.2	5.4	0.1	-14.4	6.3
1997	Q1	5.4	6.1	2.0	-3.9	5.5	6.4	20.1	3.0
	Q2	6.4	5.7	5.1	-0.1	7.3	6.9	8.6	2.4
	Q3	5.8	6.1	2.5	6.0	4.2	7.1	0.9	2.2
	Q4	2.5	5.5	-4.9	5.6	10.3	8.2	-2.5	2.5
1998	Q1	-2.8	5.0	-14.5	-4.7	2.5	-1.7	-16.1	3.5
	Q2	-5.3	4.4	-16.2	-0.6	-0.5	-1.8	-9.3	4.4
	Q3	-7.0	2.8	-19.6	-9.4	-6.6	-10.5	-17.4	5.0
	Q4	-5.7	-0.8	-16.3	-15.5	-8.6	-13.5	-2.6	5.7
1999	Q1	-2.9	-1.8	-10.2	-9.1	-4.1	-10.3	2.3	6.2
	Q2	1.2	-4.0	-1.6	-12.6	-0.3	-7.9	0.0	6.1
	Q3	4.4	-5.9	1.7	-7.9	10.8	6.8	-3.0	6.1
	Q4	9.2	-4.1	4.7	0.7	14.1	11.9	-4.3	6.0
2000	Q1	14.3	-5.1	14.2	16.2	21.4	22.9	1.2	5.6
	Q2	10.8	-4.5	10.6	8.3	19.1	18.8	-7.7	5.0

Sources: Census and Statistics Department, Rating and Valuation Department, Hong Kong Special Administrative Region.

rate of only 2.2%, mainly a result of low inflation rate in the world market in general and in the U.S. in particular, domestic consumer price index inflation averaged 7.5% per year during the period 1983 to 1997. Figures on consumer price index inflation and other economic variables for the 1990s are given in Table 5.1. Inflation was high despite the fact that U.S. inflation has been low during these years, and that the Hong Kong dollar was pegged to the U.S. dollar with no change in the official exchange rate since October 1983. The main reason for the departure of Hong Kong inflation from U.S. inflation was the rapid structural change in the Hong Kong economy. As a result of economic reform and the opening up of the Chinese mainland, entrepreneurs in Hong Kong took advantage of the cheaper labor and land costs in the mainland and relocated their manufacturing production there. In addition, in order to facilitate such production north of the border, the service sector in Hong Kong greatly expanded. The share of GDP accounted for by services rose from 67.5% in 1980 to 84.7% in 1998. As the law of one price is less applicable to services than goods, Hong Kong inflation could depart from U.S. inflation despite the link between the two currencies. However, on the other hand, because of this link, nominal interest rates in Hong Kong have to follow those in the U.S. This paved the way for very negative real interest rates in Hong Kong, and was instrumental in encouraging speculation, asset price bubbles and sharp wealth effects in Hong Kong over the decade before the Asian financial crisis.

Nevertheless, since the early 1990s, the share of foreign exchange deposits in total deposits has lowered steadily, although it remains at over 40%. This decreasing significance of foreign deposits in the portfolio of Hong Kong people was partly the result of a gradual reduction in the inflation rate since 1991. Moreover, since the early 1990s, there had been several episodes of property market booms with associated speculations. This led to portfolio adjustments towards holding properties and siphoned a great amount of purchasing power from foreign exchange deposits.

Yet, a more important reason for the shift away from foreign exchange deposits was the partial liberalization of the IRR in late 1994. Beginning October 1994, banks were no longer bound by the IRR and were free to set rates on time deposits with maturities more than one month. In January 1995, such liberalization was extended to deposits with maturities longer than seven days, and in November 1995, all rates on deposits of seven days and above were free. Competition in the deposit market raised Hong Kong dollar deposit rates and lowered the share of foreign exchange deposits. The downward trend of foreign exchange deposits continued into the late 1990s, only to rebound in October 1997 following series of speculative attacks on the Hong Kong dollar as the Asian financial crisis befell. Nevertheless, its share in total deposits did not return to the high of 60% as in the early 1990s. At end-June 2000, foreign exchange deposits accounted for 46% of total deposits.

The prominence of foreign exchange transactions in Hong Kong banking is also obvious on the loan side. The share of foreign exchange loans in total loans of AIs had been over 65% before 1995. It came down gradually since then, but still maintains a value of about 40% or so. Among these foreign exchange loans, a large percentage are actually for use outside Hong Kong (about two-third at end-June 2000).

Given the relatively small size of Hong Kong's domestic economy, as well as the presence of a large number of international financial institutions, it is quite natural that a major part of bank activities in Hong

Kong consists of external transactions with both banks and non-banks outside Hong Kong. This is true for both Hong Kong dollar and foreign exchange transactions. In comparison, external transactions in foreign exchange exceeded those in Hong Kong dollars until recently. Moreover, while AIs have net liabilities with the outside world in Hong Kong dollars, they have net claims when it comes to foreign exchange transactions.

It might be surprising to note that AIs in Hong Kong as a whole have to borrow Hong Kong dollars from banks and non-banks outside Hong Kong. Actually, these Hong Kong dollar net liabilities are mostly within the Chinese mainland. Given the close economic ties between Hong Kong and the mainland, especially since the opening of China in the late 1970s, a good amount of Hong Kong dollars now circulate in the mainland, in particular the Guangdong province which is just north of Hong Kong. China is much more important with regard to Hong Kong dollar transactions than foreign exchange transactions, especially for external liabilities of Hong Kong AIs. The net borrowing of Hong Kong dollars from the mainland has been the major element filling the gap between Hong Kong dollar loans and deposits. The Hong Kong dollar loan-to-deposit ratio has been above 100% for many years (Table 5.2), the relatively lower deposits amount being the result of the negative real interest rate mentioned above. Banks had to turn to the mainland for additional Hong Kong dollars.

With regard to external liabilities and claims in foreign exchange, the major country that Hong Kong AIs deal with is Japan. Japan accounts for over 50% in both categories. Transactions in Hong Kong dollars with banks and non-banks in Japan are much less important. The large amounts of foreign exchange transactions between banks in Hong Kong and banks and non-banks in Japan actually reflect the presence of a large number of Japanese banks in Hong Kong. Of the 180 licensed banks in Hong Kong at end-1997, 44 of them have beneficial ownership belonging to Japan. The majority of these Japanese banks in Hong Kong do not have their primary business in the Hong Kong dollar retail banking market. They are mostly in the investment banking business, and the large foreign exchange transactions of Hong Kong AIs with Japan are basically those of Japanese banks in Hong Kong with their headquarters in Japan. However, the presence of Japanese banks had diminished over the years of the crisis: the number falling to 25 at end-1999.

Given that most of the licensed banks now operating in Hong Kong got their licenses after 1978, and that most of them engage mainly in investment banking business, they do not have much Hong Kong dollar deposit base. Moreover, there is one anti-competition regulation that put some banks in particular disadvantage even if they want to pursue retail

Table 5.2   HKD Deposits, HKD Loans and Advances and HKD Loan-to-Deposit Ratio

		HKD Deposits		HKD Loans and Advances		HKD Loan-to-Deposit Ratio
		HK$bn	Year-on-year Growth Rate %	HK$bn	Year-on-year Growth Rate %	%
1991		563.9	24.7	723.8	19.2	128.4
1992		625.4	10.9	812.1	12.2	129.9
1993		786.4	25.8	957.3	17.9	121.7
1994		912.4	16.0	1,119.4	16.9	122.7
1995		1,121.8	23.0	1,237.3	10.5	110.3
1996		1,361.6	21.4	1,447.8	17.0	106.3
1997		1,495.3	9.8	1,742.5	20.4	116.5
1998		1,655.8	10.7	1,695.0	-2.7	102.4
1999		1,732.3	4.6	1,607.1	-5.2	92.8
1997	Q1	1,414.9	20.8	1,582.9	22.9	111.9
	Q2	1,529.0	26.5	1,685.8	24.5	110.3
	Q3	1,563.5	23.6	1,793.4	29.5	114.7
	Q4	1,495.3	9.8	1,742.5	20.4	116.5
1998	Q1	1,516.9	7.2	1,732.6	9.5	114.2
	Q2	1,521.7	-0.5	1,735.6	3.0	114.1
	Q3	1,607.4	2.8	1,707.7	-4.8	106.2
	Q4	1,655.8	10.7	1,695.0	-2.7	102.4
1999	Q1	1,653.3	9.0	1,670.7	-3.6	101.1
	Q2	1,678.0	10.3	1,628.7	-6.2	97.1
	Q3	1,683.7	4.7	1,612.2	-5.6	95.8
	Q4	1,732.3	4.6	1,607.1	-5.2	92.8
2000	Q1	1,716.3	3.8	1,624.4	-2.8	94.6
	Q2	1,749.8	4.3	1,629.0	0.0	93.1

Source: Hong Kong Monetary Authority.

banking. This is the one-building condition mentioned above. As a result of this restriction, Hong Kong dollar deposits are very unevenly distributed among the licensed banks, with a few banking groups receiving the majority of bank deposits. For example, the number of banks with beneficial ownership belonging to the U.S., Europe, and Japan was 108 as at end-1997, which was 60% of the total 180 licensed banks at that time. However, they accounted for only 18.3% of total Hong Kong dollar deposits. The Bank of China group, with a total of only 18 banks, got 28.0% of Hong Kong dollar deposits instead. Another banking group, the HSBC and the Hang Seng Bank, has at least a comparable share of the deposits. One implication of the uneven distribution of deposit base is that those banks with little Hong Kong dollars have to rely on the interbank market for Hong Kong dollar liquidity.

Regarding prudential supervision of the AIs, the HKMA has been following international practices such as those recommended by the Basle Committee for Banking Supervision. The usual standards of paid-up capital and capital adequacy, liquidity, financial disclosure, and on-site and off-site supervision etc. have been closely followed. In fact, banks in Hong Kong have been quite sound and well managed. As indicators, for banks incorporated in Hong Kong, "classified loans", which included "substandard", "doubtful" and "losses", were only 2.08% of total loans gross, and only 0.07% net of all provisions in 1997 when the Asian financial crisis broke out. In September of that year, right before the crisis hit Hong Kong, the ratio of loans overdue by more than 90 days to total loans outstanding was only 0.1%. The equity-to-assets ratio stood at 9.9 while the capital adequacy ratio was 17.5, more than twice the Basle standard.

Despite sound bank management on the whole, there have been episodes of bank failures and panics in Hong Kong. Bank failures in the early 1960s have been mentioned above. There were further failures in the early 1980s following property and stock market booms and then unfavorable expectations about the future of Hong Kong after 1997. A more recent case was the incident of the Bank for Commercial Credit International in 1991. The government has been relying on the market to handle problem banks. If a bank is basically sound but runs into liquidity problems, then it is believed that either the bank could raise money in the market, or there would be potential buyers. The exception was in the early 1980s when the Hong Kong government took over two problem banks. Those were years of Sino-British talks over the future of Hong Kong, and bank failures were considered to trigger broader confidence issues. The two banks have subsequently been sold to the public.

It might be believed that since Hong Kong follows some variant of the currency board system in monetary arrangement, and that the HKMA is not a typical central bank, there is no player of lender of last resort in Hong Kong. However, as the government has been enjoying fiscal surpluses for most years in the past few decades, the amount of accumulated budget reserves is by now quite admirable. These have served the sources of last resort lending should the situation proves necessary, such as after the global stock market crash in October 1987.

Experience in the Asian Financial Crisis

The financial crisis took place in various Asian economies in different forms. The Hong Kong experience differs from that of its neighbors in at least three regards. The first is that while other currencies have depreciated vis-à-vis the U.S. dollar, the Hong Kong dollar has been able to maintain its exchange value, although at great economic costs. The second difference is that while others were plagued by the problem of external debt, this has not been an issue at all in Hong Kong. Foreign exchange reserves in Hong Kong have been close to U.S.$100 billion in recent years, about the fourth largest in the world and the highest on a per capita basis. Thirdly, unlike other economies with financial crisis, bank management was not a factor contributing to problems in Hong Kong, and there has been no bank failure since the crisis began. It is true that there was a short episode of bank run when rumors about a bank brought the depositors queuing outside its branches. However, the panic was easily resolved in a couple of days as the bank showed the ability to mobilize sufficient liquidity. Yet, although banks in Hong Kong were not the originator nor direct victims of the crisis, they nevertheless had to suffer as the economy plummeted into the worst recession in recent history. In other words, once again, the banking sector in Hong Kong has to adjust to shocks in the macroeconomic environment.

As the economy of Hong Kong is extremely open but relatively small, it is natural that it is always subject to disturbances originating from international markets. External shocks, mostly in the form of capital flows, can easily translate into economic ups and downs. Traditionally, there is not much that the Hong Kong government can and would do to offset these shocks with macroeconomic tools. Fiscal policies may be one possibility, but the government has adopted conservative budgets that usually leave the government with surpluses. Even if fiscal policies were intentionally carried out for economic stabilisation, the effects would not be large as most of domestic demand is for imported goods and services. The multiplying effect is small.

As for monetary policy, there has been no central bank in Hong Kong, and the HKMA which is in charge of monetary policy aims to maintain a fixed value of the Hong Kong dollar rather than the quantity of money supply. Since October 1983, the Hong Kong dollar has been linked to the U.S. dollar (the system known as the "linked exchange rate system") and monetary policy in Hong Kong has to follow that in the U.S. Thus on the whole the Hong Kong government does not have much flexibility in employing policies for macroeconomic stabilisation.

The Hong Kong dollar has been on the silver standard, sterling standard, and U.S. dollar standard respectively. In October 1983 it was once again linked to the U.S. dollar to halt the downfall of the value of the Hong Kong dollar resulting from uncertainties arising from talks between China and the U.K. over the political future of Hong Kong after 1997. A Joint Declaration between the Chinese and British governments was reached in 1984 by which Hong Kong was to keep its economic system after 1997. In the run up to the change of sovereignty since then, the economy performed quite robustly, attaining an average real growth rate of 6.1% per year, while unemployment was kept low at an average of less than 2%. Although there were major disturbances including constant bickering between the China and the U.K. over political development and democratisation in Hong Kong, the global stock market crash in 1987, the Tiananmen Square incident in 1989, the bankruptcy of the Bank of Credit and Commerce International in 1991, the Mexican peso crisis in 1995, and the change of sovereignty in 1997, the market value of the Hong Kong dollar has been within less than 1% of the official exchange rate.

One unfavourable macroeconomic outcome under the linked exchange rate system in this period was inflation and its resulting negative real interest rates, as mentioned above. Negative real interest rates over a long period of time fuelled asset price inflation and speculation sentiments. In Hong Kong, the major assets besides bank deposits are securities and properties. The stock market is volatile given the relatively small market capitalisation and free international capital mobility. The property market, on the other hand, is less liquid and more affected by local factors, but can be equally speculative given the uncertainties introduced by government policies in the name of promoting public interests. These policies tended to fine-tune property prices, imposing restrictions on transactions during booms and encouraging, even subsidising, purchases during busts. For the years before 1997, land sales, or more accurately, the auctioning of land use rights, were limited to 50 hectares every year, according to an agreement between China and the British. Land is scarce in Hong Kong relative to the volume of its economic activities, so that land sale has been generating a large share government revenue, allowing relatively low levels of profit tax and salaries tax rates. The limitation on land sale failed to accommodate the large demand for properties during a period of robust economic growth before 1997. Property prices in Hong Kong skyrocketed in the 1990s. Residential property prices increased drastically by 40.5, 23.6, and 40.9% in the years 1992, 1994, and 1997 respectively (Table 5.1). In 1994, the government used several measures to hold down property prices. The HKMA issued guidelines to banks, advising them not to extend more than 40% of total loans to property-related items, including both mortgage loans and loans to property developers. There was also a cap on the loan-to-value ratio of 70% for mortgages. These measures brought down property prices by 7.2% the next year.

The above were the economic situations of Hong Kong when it officially returned to China as a Special Administration Region in July 1997. Three months later, Hong Kong became a victim of the Asian financial crisis. The economy was on the whole quite robust, except possibly for one factor. There was the perception, not necessarily very widespread, that Hong Kong had lost its competitiveness after many years of moderate inflation while the exchange rate was kept stable, that is, a continual real appreciation of the Hong Kong dollar. Whether Hong Kong's competitiveness had actually been eroding vis-à-vis its competitors was not immediately clear, as the real exchange rate could also be affected by changes in real factors such as demand and productivity. However, a change in perception, justifiable or not, is good enough to trigger portfolio adjustments and short-term financial flows. As Asian currencies devalued one after another in the third quarter of 1997, this perception became sufficient excuse for speculators to run on the Hong Kong dollar. The core experience of Hong Kong in the Asian crisis was the attack and defence of the Hong Kong dollar. In the process, the attack was translated into high interest rates and sharp plunges in asset prices, resulting in negative wealth effects, lower aggregate demand, and difficulties for banking business. The way that the Hong Kong dollar is linked to the U.S. dollar is different from the usual fixed exchange rate regime. It is in effect a variation of the traditional currency board system. In a conventional currency board, bank notes are issued only with the availability of foreign exchange at pre-determined exchange rates. As a result, the money supply varies with the balance of payments and adjusts through the price-specie flow mechanism in ways similar to the gold standard. The system represents a monetary system by rule, and the authorities cannot vary the money supply in a discretionary manner. It is completely passive, exchanging domestic currency for foreign exchange and vice versa at a given price on demand. As such, it does not act as a lender of last resort and this is considered to be one of its weaknesses. However, after years of development, the system in Hong Kong is not exactly a conventional currency board. Under the linked exchange rate system in 1997, the HKMA could change the amount of short-term liquidity to licensed banks through what is called the Liquidity Adjustment Facility (LAF). The LAF was a mechanism similar to a discount window whereby banks could borrow Hong Kong dollars overnight from the HKMA using prescribed assets as collateral.

There had been previous episodes of speculation against the Hong Kong dollar, notably during the Mexican peso crisis from late 1994 to early 1995. In that event, the HKMA succeeded in averting speculation by raising Hong Kong dollar market interest rates. Since the attack came mostly from outside, the speculators had to borrow Hong Kong dollar before selling it. They had to face heavy costs due to high interest rates, but did not gain through exchange rate changes if the HKMA succeeded in defending the Hong Kong dollar. This was what happened in early 1995. Speculation subsided in a matter of days and the Hong Kong dollar maintained its value in U.S. dollar. Thus, high interest rates had been considered by the HKMA as a powerful and effective weapon against speculation. However, the same measure failed to forestall speculation during the Asian crisis. In addition, the resulting high interest rates that lingered for months brought immensely disruptive effects to the economy.

Speculators had probably learned their lessons in previous failures to run on the Hong Kong dollar. During the Asian crisis, they perfectly anticipated the reaction of the HKMA and positioned their portfolios to earn lucrative returns rather than being penalised by high interest rates. They sold Hong Kong dollar in the spot market and appeared to have the intention to force a devaluation of the Hong Kong dollar. However, they actually had the stock futures market and the forward exchange market in mind. Before the attack, they might have already held short positions in the stock index futures market and the forward Hong Kong dollar market. When the HKMA raised interest rates as before to defend the spot value of the Hong Kong dollar, stock prices as well as stock futures fell and those with short positions stood to gain. Also, in the forward exchange market, covered interest parity could be considered to be valid on the whole, given the openness and free capital mobility of Hong Kong. Under covered interest parity, as long as U.S. interest rate levels are relatively constant, and if the spot market value of the Hong Kong dollar is successfully defended and so does not change, a higher Hong Kong interest rate necessarily implies depreciation of the forward Hong Kong dollar. Those with short positions in forward Hong Kong dollar would benefit. In fact, the data show co-movements of the interbank rate and the Hong Kong dollar value in the forward market (Figures 5.1 and 5.2). Thus, speculators may seem to lose the battle of the spot Hong Kong dollar market and suffer high interest costs; they actually won handsomely on other fronts and would be happy to repeat the game.

The scale of speculation in October 1997 was much larger than expected and the HKMA had made the situation worse. When there were signs of speculative attacks on the Hong Kong dollar, the HKMA issued a guideline to the licensed banks against repeated uses of the LAF. Banks that did would be subjected to unprescribed penalties. The guideline was intended to limit the amount of Hong Kong dollar available to speculators. The LAF could be a loophole for banks to borrow Hong Kong dollar from

Figure 5.1 Hong Kong Dollar Interbank Offered Rates (daily figures)

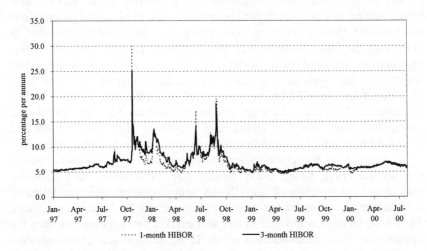

Source: Hong Kong Monetary Authority.

Figure 5.2 HKD Spot Rates and 3-month Forward Rates (daily figures)

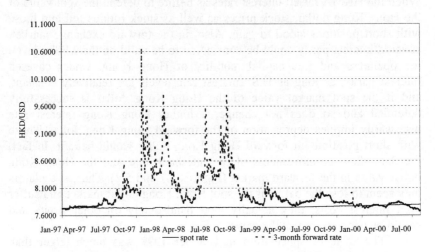

Source: Hong Kong Monetary Authority.

the HKMA on behalf of their speculator customers, and the HKMA would want to restrict this channel and strengthen its high interest rate measure. However, it did not specify what was meant by "repeated uses" of the LAF and what the associated penalties would be. More unfortunately, this guideline came on a day in October when the banks needed lots of Hong Kong dollar for clearing. Their customers had sold large volumes of Hong Kong dollar the days before and it was time for bank clearing of these transactions. These banks were greatly discouraged by the HKMA to get liquidity through the LAF. They were forced to resort to the interbank market for funds. Given the large volume of clearing needs, the interbank rate soared drastically and reached 280% per annum for a couple of hours on October 23, 1997. Interbank rates have remained high and volatile since then. As the U.S. dollar LIBOR have been stable at about 4% or so, Hong Kong dollar rates have been higher by several hundred basis points (Figure 5.1). The interest differentials represent the risk premium on the Hong Kong dollar during the crisis, and were the reason that the Hong Kong economy was dragged into the worst recession in decades.

Speculators had correctly realised that high interest rates was the only weapon the HKMA had to defend the Hong Kong dollar. They seized every occasion to attack spot Hong Kong dollar and reaped profits in the stock index futures and forward exchange markets. Whenever there were uneasy sentiments in the market during the crisis, banks in Hong Kong would increase their hoarding of reserves, liquidity would dry up, interest rates soared, stock prices fell, and the currency weakened in the forward market. These happened when there was fear that the Renminbi might devalue or that the yen might weaken further, or with the official announcement of economic data signifying poor economic performance. The economy was badly pushed into a recession as a result. In the various quarters of 1998, real GDP recorded drops of 2.8, 5.3, 7.0 and 5.7% on a year-on-year basis respectively. These compared bleakly with gains of 5.8% in 1997Q3 when Hong Kong was returned to China, and 2.5% in 1997Q4 right after the Asian crisis started. Along with the fall in real GOP, the unemployment rate climbed from 2.2% in 1997Q3 to a high of 6.1% in 1999Q1 (Table 5.1).

Although speculators repeatedly ran on the Hong Kong dollar and made profits in the way mentioned above, the Hong Kong government was reluctant to admit that speculators were taking advantage of the relationship between the spot exchange market, the stock futures market, and the forward exchange market. Thus controlling liquidity and raising interest rates continued to be the way of defence against speculative attacks. However, when the same kind of attack came again in August 1998, the authorities changed their view and policy reactions completely. They now acknowledge the link between the various markets and confronted the speculators directly in the stock market. The HKMA surprised the whole world by directly intervening in the stock market, buying practically whatever amount of blue chip shares sold to the market to support share prices and the stock price index. The aim was to "penalise" speculators with short positions in the stock price index futures and forward Hong Kong dollar markets.

The drastic move by the HKMA was undoubtedly controversial, especially in an economy that had been acclaimed as the epitome of the free market. The intervention might be considered by some as necessary to safeguard Hong Kong against attacks, but the harmful effects were actually greater and more lasting. Not only was the image of Hong Kong as a free market badly tarnished, the holding of shares by the government has introduced an additional element of uncertainty in the market. Whether and how the government disposed of its holdings of shares remain intriguing problems to investors, and the total holding was enormous. The HKMA spent U.S.$15.2 billion altogether in the operation, making the government the second or third largest shareholders in the economy's 33 largest companies. There was also the problem of conflict of interests, as the government has become both a regulator and shareholder of these companies.

Ironically, one positive turnout of the stock market intervention was that the government changed its attitude to defend the Hong Kong dollar exchange rate. Instead of maintaining the peg to the U.S. dollar through artificially manipulated high interest rates, the HKMA resorted to enlarging the liquidity base and thus relieving the economy through lower interest rates. On September 5 the HKMA introduced the so-called "seven technical measures" to strengthen Hong Kong's currency board system. Among others, these measures include the government's commitment to convert bank clearing accounts (in addition to bank notes as in a traditional currency board) to U.S. dollar at the official rate, as well as a smoother mechanism for banks to get liquidity from the HKMA. The change in HKMA policy orientation was due to the fact that U.S.$15.2 billion spent on domestic stocks amounted to about 15% of Hong Kong's foreign exchange reserves. Although the intention was to safeguard the link of the Hong Kong dollar to the U.S. dollar, the operation actually endangered the link through large depletion of foreign exchange reserves. The authorities might finally realise there was not much room for further manoeuvre if they stuck to previous policy responses. Also, even without the depletion of foreign exchange reserves due to stock market intervention, high interest rate policy might still have to be abandoned as the economy continued to contract. If it is believed that people in Hong Kong might not be willing to go on paying a high price in terms of high interest rates to defend the exchange rate link, there would be further run on the Hong Kong dollar. In this case, even higher interest rates would not be effective, as this would add further pain to the economy and speed up the run. The situation was in line with the so-called second-generation models of currency crisis in the literature. The equilibrium was unstable. In this regard, it was quite fortunate for Hong Kong that interest rates began to fall in October 1998, partly the result of the "seven technical measures" that added liquidity to the market, and partly because the U.S. cut interest rates twice. In addition, the demise of some famous hedged funds and the strengthening of the yen vis-à-vis the U.S. dollar were also helpful in relieving Hong Kong. Thus it is not quite clear if speculation began to subside in late 1998 as a result of HKMA intervention in the stock market, as the Hong Kong government claims. The intervention has made a lot of profit for the government since share prices have gone up, but it is highly doubtful that it was the correct measure *ex ante*.

It has to be added that high interest rates resulting from defending the Hong Kong dollar was not the only major factor that pushed the Hong Kong economy into recession for the first time in a long time. Another factor, which is more institutional and therefore could be more lasting, is the perceived possible change of economic policy regime under the new government of the Hong Kong Special Administrative Region. The government might be very eager to establish credibility and gain popular support. When it came into being in July 1997, Hong Kong was once again experiencing rampant asset price inflation, especially in the property market. There were public calls for the government to curb rising property prices, for both right and wrong reasons. The new government responded by taking housing policy as one of its main policy focuses, and made a sharp turn around by announcing to provide much more land and housing units in the future. The Chief Executive made explicit targets in his first policy address October 1997 to build at least 85,000 units of housing every year, and to achieve a home-ownership rate of 70% in 10 years. However, both figures represented sharp increases from their trend levels. Unfortunately, right after these new targets had been set, the economy ran into high interest rates, credit crunch, rising unemployment and a recession that seem to be protracted. Needless to say, property prices fell sharply. Residential property prices dropped by 2.5% within 1997Q4 and 16.1, 9.3, and 17.4% in the first three quarters of 1998 respectively, a total sharp fall of 40 to 50% in a single year (Table 5.1). As people in Hong Kong have taken property as a major item of investment, this easily translated into very large but negative wealth effects. At the same time, stock values as summarised by the Hang Seng index were also more than halved. The index reached a historic high of 16,600 in August 1997; it came down to 7,300 in August 1998 when the government intervened. Retail sales naturally suffered.

Increasing the supply of land might not be that much a problem, although it would necessarily drive down property prices. What is more disturbing is that, in view of the difficulty in the property market and the importance of this market for the Hong Kong economy, the government wavered in their housing and land policies. It has put forward some policies, such as the suspension of land auction for nine months and the provision of interest-free loans to first-time property buyers, to help increase demand for residential property. At the same time, it makes no further reference to the targets of 85,000 housing units per year and 70% home-ownership rate, and also without explicitly mentioning whether these targets would be maintained or not. The public did not have any clear idea of the direction of housing policy, and perceived this as a very important uncertainty element in the market. In Hong Kong, housing is more an investment asset than consumption asset. There is practically nobody in Hong Kong who does not have any sheltering. About 34% of the population live in public rental housing, and the private rental market is also active. Property has been considered to be a good means of investment because of the limited supply of land relative to the robust economy in the past decades. As an investment, the demand for housing should be forward looking. Given uncertainties in the economy in recession, as well as uncertain government housing policies, potential home purchasers naturally would diminish in number and not be eager to enter the market. This was true even for those who called on the government to curb property prices before. The government perceived that too high or too low property prices would not make it popular, and tried to fine-tune property prices with discretion. It has forgotten that one cannot manipulate both the price and the quantity of a commodity at the same time. It is such intervention in such manner that has tainted the policy-making framework and introduced gaps in understanding between market participants and the government. Economic policies could become economic shocks and introduced unnecessary uncertainties to the market, much to the misfortune of the economy.

Effects on the banking system

Amid all the disasters in economic performance and policy-making, it is inevitable that the banking sector in Hong Kong has been negatively affected in the crisis. A long period of high interest rates and scarce liquidity have alarmed the banks to hoard Hong Kong dollars instead of relying on the interbank market for liquidity. On the other hand, the recession in Hong Kong and uncertain economic future in the region have reduced the willingness of banks to extend loans. Table 5.2 shows a clear downward trend in the amount of Hong Kong dollar bank loans since the inception of the Asian crisis. At the same time, Table 5.2 also shows much slower growth of Hong Kong dollar deposits compared to the period before the crisis. However, deposit growth still dominates loan growth so that the loan-deposit ratio has been falling. Also, banks had to increase substantially their loan loss provisions, and as a result, bank profits were greatly squeezed.

Several indicators show the deterioration of the banking situation in Hong Kong in the one or two years after the crisis. Figure 5.3 illustrates several possible measures of the Hong Kong dollar interest differential. For banks that could absorb deposits at the savings rate and make loans at the best-lending rate (BLR) and above, the differential would be BLR minus the savings deposit rate. There was no change in this differential since when the HKAB changes the savings rate under the IRR, usually after corresponding changes in the U.S., banks would also change the BLR in the same direction and by the same margin. However, this differential does not tell the whole story, as the funds received through issuing deposits are not all transformed to loans: the loan-deposit ratio has been falling and has been less than 100% since early 1999. Those banks with surplus funds might lend the Hong Kong dollar in the interbank market. In this case, the relevant rate differential would be HIBOR minus the savings deposit rate. On the other hand, for those banks that rely mostly on the interbank market for Hong Kong dollar funds, the measure would be BLR minus HIBOR. It is clear that the latter two measures fluctuated widely, especially the year after the crisis began. Banks with surplus funds actually fared better than normal times, and they did so at the expense of those that had to borrow in the interbank market.

The above assumes that the cost of deposits was the savings deposit rate. This is extremely crude, as savings deposits are only one kind of deposits. At end-1998, Hong Kong dollar savings deposits were only 25.2% of total Hong Kong dollar deposits in licensed banks. Item 1 in Table 5.3 gives an appropriate but more aggregate measure of interest differential. This item is the average net interest margin for all locally incorporated banks, calculated as the share of total net interest income in total assets. This value experienced a large drop in 1998 but rebounded moderately the next year.

Net interest margin does not tell the whole picture of financial health of banks. Table 5.3 shows other relevant variables. 1998 was obviously the most difficult year for banks incorporated in Hong Kong. Both operating profits before tax and post-tax return on assets fell sharply in that year compared to the previous year. The main reason for such difficulty was the sharp rise in bad debt charge, from 0.15% in 1997 to

Figure 5.3 HK Dollar Interest Differentials

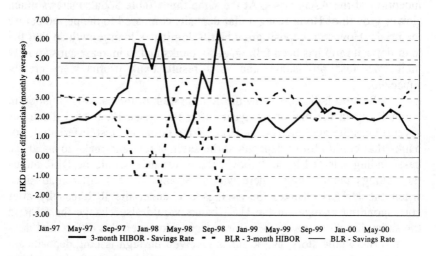

Source: Hong Kong Monetary Authority.

Table 5.3 Return on Assets for the Locally Incorporated Banks

		Contribution to ROA as % of average total assets					
		1994	1995	1996	1997	1998	1999
1.	Net interest margin	2.18	2.33	2.41	2.26	2.07	2.13
2.	Other operating income	1.04	1.08	1.07	1.03	0.95	0.92
3.	Total operating income (1+2)	3.22	3.41	3.48	3.29	3.02	3.05
4.	Operating expenses	1.30	1.31	1.30	1.25	1.20	1.15
5.	Bad debt charge	0.05	0.08	0.18	0.15	0.63	0.60
6.	Other provisions	0.01	0.01	0.00	0.01	0.01	0.02
7.	Operating profit before tax (3-4-5-6)	1.86	2.01	2.00	1.88	1.18	1.28
8.	Profit on disposals and exceptional items	0.24	0.10	0.09	0.04	-0.01	0.06
9.	Profit before tax (7+8)	2.10	2.11	2.09	1.92	1.17	1.34
10.	Taxation	0.28	0.29	0.30	0.27	0.15	0.16
11.	Extraordinary items	0.03	0.03	0.00	0.00	0.00	0.00
12.	Post-tax profit (ROA) (9-10+11)	1.85	1.85	1.79	1.65	1.02	1.18

Source: Hong Kong Monetary Authority.

0.63% for locally incorporated banks. Bad debt charge rose from 0.13% to 0.43% for the banking sector as a whole. The lower percentage for the whole sector was partly the result of a much larger asset size, as well as the possibility that some branches of foreign banks in Hong Kong might have booked their bad debt provisions in their head offices. Fortunately, the situation began to improve in 1999, with larger net interest margin and operating profit and a slightly lower bad debt charge. The improvement continued in the first half of 2000.

While income and profit may recover fast once provisions have been made for possible problem loans, the asset quality may take longer to improve. As a matter of fact, Table 5.4 shows noticeable increases in loans overdue for three months and above in 1998, but the figures worsened further in 1999 for the percentage of classified loans and the share of loans overdue for three months and longer. The latter was the result of rising percentages in loans overdue for over six months, indicating that borrowers with repayment problem in 1998 continued to face difficulty in 1999. Fortunately, the percentage of loans overdue for three to six months had decreased in 1999, hopefully a sign of slow down in new cases of problem loans. Despite all the unfavorable figures after the crisis, the asset quality of banks in Hong Kong is still high by international standards. In addition, the problem loans did not pose serious threats to the stability of the banking system. As a whole, companies in Hong Kong are not as highly leveraged as their counterparts in neighboring economies with serious banking problems, and they do not use funds indiscriminately in fixed investments. Moreover, the high capital adequacy ratio maintained by banks in Hong Kong helped absorb the negative shocks. Although profitability had to suffer after making provisions to bad loans, bank solvency was not threatened at all throughout the crisis.

In addition to high and volatile interest rates, the competition for liquidity and the economic recession, the deterioration in asset quality was also the result of the fall in the value of collateral, most of which were in the form of properties. It was also the result of the fall of the Guangdong International Trust and Investment Corporation in October 1998 which triggered fear of loan exposure to similar Mainland entities.

As the property market has been a major engine of growth in Hong Kong, mortgage loans and loans to other property-related activities such as property development have accounted for a high percentage of total loans and advances of banks. Although the collapse of the property market contributed to increasing bad loans and decreasing profit margins in the banking sector, it should be mentioned that the loan delinquency ratio of mortgage loans has been low relative to that of other loans (Table 5.5). However, the effect of the property market on the banking sector does not

Table 5.4 Asset Quality of All Authorized Institutions

% of total loans and advances	All AIs				Local Banks			
	1996	1997	1998	1999	1996	1997	1998	1999
Pass Loans	96.95	92.29	85.55	84.64	93.31	94.91	84.61	82.14
Special mention loans	1.95	6.46	9.18	8.13	4.01	3.01	8.06	8.05
Classified loans	1.10	1.25	5.27	7.24	2.24	2.08	7.33	9.81
o/w Substandard	0.45	0.59	2.56	2.71	0.87	0.71	3.18	3.72
Doubtful	0.55	0.56	2.29	3.70	1.30	1.30	3.93	5.43
Loss	0.10	0.10	0.41	0.83	0.07	0.07	0.22	0.66
Overdue>3 months and rescheduled loans	2.40	1.81	4.18	5.70	2.40	1.81	5.12	6.96
o/w Overdue > 3 months	2.04	1.58	3.39	4.82	2.04	1.58	4.03	5.85
3 - 6 months	0.37	0.32	1.09	0.71	0.37	0.33	1.45	0.93
over 6 months	1.67	1.26	2.20	4.12	1.67	1.25	2.58	4.92
Rescheduled loans	0.36	0.23	0.79	0.88	0.36	0.23	1.08	1.10
Non-accrual loans	-	-	-	5.32	-	-	-	-

Source: Hong Kong Monetary Authority.

include only mortgage loans. A large percentage of collateralised loans have properties as the collateral. The HKMA conducted two surveys in 1999 and 2000 on the financial situation of small and medium enterprises (SME). As expected, one of the findings was that the majority of bank loans to the SMEs were secured by collateral, mostly by real estate. In general, banks would make provisions for overdue loans equal to the loan size minus the value of collateral. As collateral value falls following the collapse of the property market, banks have to make more provisions and so less profits.

Despite the collapse of the property market, the share of property-related loans in total loans has in fact been rising, exceeding the 40% guideline (imposed by the HKMA in the early 1990s but revoked in July 1998) and approaching 50%. This reflects the fact that other kinds of loans have been sluggish, and that mortgage loans remain a good source of interest income for banks even in times of recession. As the property market has been a dominating market in the economy and for decades it has been booming on the average, banks have found it lucrative and safe to grant mortgage loans and loans with properties as collateral. The information cost of such loans is relatively low. On the other hand, banks in

Table 5.5 Delinquency Ratios of Private Mortgage Loans and Overdue/Rescheduled Loans of All Local Banks

(Unit: % of total loans and advances)

	Private Mortgage Loans		Overdue and Rescheduled Loans		
	Overdue > 3 months	Overdue > 6 months	Overdue > 3 months and Rescheduled Loans	Overdue Loans> 3 months	Rescheduled Loans
1998 Q2	0.29	0.08	-	-	-
Q3	0.53	0.16	3.81	3.18	0.63
Q4	0.84	0.34	5.12	4.04	1.08
1999 Q1	0.84	0.34	6.39	5.41	0.98
Q2	1.13	0.56	7.01	5.92	1.09
Q3	1.14	0.71	7.54	6.32	1.22
Q4	1.12	0.77	6.96	5.85	1.11
2000 Q1	1.13	0.79	6.86	5.90	0.96
Q2	1.23	0.86	6.38	5.53	0.85

Source: Hong Kong Monetary Authority.

Hong Kong are less equipped to make other types of loans, especially in a recessionary environment when uncertainly is high.

Not only have mortgage loans not reduced over the crisis years, banks have actually competed fiercely for such loans. Mortgage loans remained attractive to banks with a much lower delinquency ratio than loans as a whole, even in times of high unemployment. Mortgage loan rates have been sharply reduced from about 1.25% above the BLR before the crisis to over 2% below the BLR. This partly contributes to the narrowed profit margin compared to before the crisis. Also, as a result of the much improved terms for mortgage borrowers, loans to refinance existing mortgages as a percentage of new loans rose from 4.5% in January 1999 to over 51% in December of the same year.

In October 1998, the Chinese government closed the Guangdong International Trust and Investment Corporation (GITIC) due to severe financial problems. GITIC was an investment arm of Guangdong provincial government which had the privilege to deal with external transactions and investments. Its closure led to the liquidation of two of its subsidiaries in Hong Kong, GITIC Hong Kong and Guang Xin Enterprises. It was believed that as GITIC was part of the Guangdong provincial government, the latter would stand behind the former in times of financial difficulty. It was also thought that the Mainland government would not allow government-owned enterprises to fail, especially when they dealt with external business. As such, the closure of GITIC triggered a reconsideration of loans based on official names and implicit guarantees. Banks began to worry about their loans to other International Trust and Investment Corporations and make provisions accordingly. Table 5.6 shows the exposure of Hong Kong financial institutions to non-bank Mainland entities, which was up to 4.5% of total assets in September 1998. This share fell steadily beginning the end of 1998, following the GITIC episode. Since then, banks in Hong Kong have become much more cautious when dealing with Mainland enterprises.

Table 5.6 Hong Kong Banking Sector's Exposure to Non-bank Chinese Entities[a]

(Unit: HK$ billions)

	All AIs					Local Banks				
	GITIC and its subsidiaries	Other ITICs and their subsidiaries	All others[b]	Total	As % of Total assets	GITIC and its subsidiaries	Other ITICs and their subsidiaries	All others	Total	As % of Total assets
1998										
Sep	7.0	40.4	278.0	325.4	4.5	1.9	11.7	75.9	89.5	4.4
Dec	6.2	39.6	251.7	297.5	4.1	1.5	10.2	73.4	85.1	4.1
1999										
Mar	5.8	37.2	237.4	280.4	4.1	1.5	9.6	70.4	81.5	3.9
Jun	5.2	35.3	214.3	254.8	3.8	1.2	9.8	67.3	78.3	3.7
Sep	4.9	34.6	205.1	244.6	3.6	1.2	9.7	63.6	74.5	3.5
Dec	4.2	32.1	197.3	233.6	3.4	1.0	10.1	61.8	72.9	3.3
2000										
Mar	4.1	31.9	188.9	224.9	3.4	1.0	10.0	61.3	72.3	3.3

Notes: a) Total Exposure was spread among 167 institutions, including both local and foreign institutions.
   b) Included red-chips, H-shares, other state, provincial or municipal government owned entities and other entities known to be owned or controlled by Chinese interests.
Source: Hong Kong Monetary Authority.

Other Banking Developments

Despite the crisis and its negative effects on banks, it is fair to say that the banking sector in Hong Kong has been sound and strong, well managed and supervised. All banks except one have declared profits for the year 1998, and no government assistance was needed. Banks also managed to maintain a capital adequacy ratio higher than before the crisis. This, of course, does not mean that there is no room for further improvement. At present there are the following pertinent issues to be handled, and these are not directly related to the financial crisis.

The most obvious issues are that there are still anti-competitive regulations in the Hong Kong banking system, namely, the IRR on bank deposits, and the one-building stipulation for new bank license. As for the IRR, the argument of maintaining control over interest rates as a monetary policy instrument is no longer relevant. Hong Kong has learned expensively that interest rates are not at all a good instrument to defend the exchange rate. Also, the IRR has not been effective in containing excessive risk in banking. After all, banks in Hong Kong have been relatively prudent and well supervised. And in the presence of deposit interest ceilings, they would simply resort to non-price competition for deposits. There was increasing outcry that deposit interest ceilings were anti-competition and were not in the interests of depositors. As such, by the mid-1990s, a series of steps in phasing out the interest rate cartel began to take place. Beginning October 1994, time deposits of less than HK$500,000 and over one-month maturity were no longer subject to restrictions on interest rates by the HKAB. Deposits with a denomination of over HK$500,000 were not subject to the IRR. In January and April of 1995, deposits with maturities over one week and one week exactly were also eliminated from the IRR and could earn different rates at different banks. However, deregulation stopped at this point as large shifts of deposits were observed in early 1995. The share of time deposits in total Hong Kong dollar deposits increased from 46.7% in September 1994 to 53.2% in January1995, while that of current and savings deposits together fell from 41.9% to 37.2%. This shift was partly the result of interest rate deregulation and partly the fact that the HKMA raised interest rates to defend the Hong Kong dollar after the attack on the Mexican peso. Time deposit rates that were no longer constrained by the IRR were free to rise according to market conditions whereas savings deposit rates were changed only at the discretion of the HKAB. As a result of sharp deposit shifts and uncertain market conditions, plans to further deregulate deposit rates were put on hold for a few years.

In 2000, the remaining part of the IRR would be eliminated in two stages. The first phase of deregulation took place in July 2000 and applied to time deposits with maturity of less than seven days. Since then, there has been no restriction on rates of any kind of time deposit. The deregulation has not triggered any appreciable shifts in deposits from saving to time deposits. However, the more important change would be in July 2001 when the cap on interests paid on saving deposits will be removed, and current accounts could become interest-bearing. By then, all restrictions on deposit rates would disappear. As a result, there would be increasing price competition for deposits among banks. At the same time, there will be less cross-subsidization between different kinds of banking services and charges on services that have hitherto been free.

The one-building restriction on foreign banks licensed after 1978 was obviously unfair as all licensed banks had to fulfil the same supervisory and prudential requirements while some had an advantage over others in being able to have multiple branches. This requirement was lifted in September 1999. Instead of one branch, these banks could carry out business at a maximum of three buildings. In addition, there was no further restriction on the number of regional offices and back offices that foreign banks can maintain in Hong Kong. The effects of the three-building condition are supposed to be reviewed in 2001. However, no foreign bank has taken advantage of the liberalization to set up new branches. The restriction itself may be superfluous.

Another issue related to competition is the three-tier system. The RLBs and DTCs cannot compete on equal grounds with the licensed banks and between themselves because of the restrictions on their activities. As these two categories of depository institutions are much less important than the licensed banks in terms of their asset sizes and loan portfolios, it has been proposed that the two be merged to make the system two-tiered.

As for deposit protection, Hong Kong has had no deposit insurance, but there have been consistent calls on the government to set up a deposit insurance scheme, especially in times of financial panics. Due to the uneven distribution of Hong Kong dollar deposits, banks with large shares of Hong Kong dollar deposits are reluctant to endorse deposit insurance if the insurance premium is based on deposit size. Even if the premium is risk-based, there is still the general issue of moral hazard to be reckoned with.

After the failure of the Bank of Credit and Commerce Hong Kong in the early 1990s, an explicit protection scheme was introduced in 1995 whereby depositors of failed local banks and foreign branch banks have the priority to receive their deposits up to a maximum of HK$100,000. This is not an insurance scheme and depositors are not guaranteed, as the failed bank may not have sufficient funds to fulfil all such demand. In addition, depositors may have to wait for a long period of time before the pay-out since bank liquidation is usually a lengthy legal process.

As part of deposit protection, a proposal to introduce a consumer credit insurance agency is being reviewed. This would gather and centralize information of corporate borrowers for participating institutions, making more transparent the credit record and financial conditions of bank customers. Banks would then be in a better position to make credit assessments.

By December 1, 2000, the Mandatory Provident Fund (MPF) will begin to operate in Hong Kong. Except for some exemptions and other stipulations, both the employer and the employee will have to contribute 5% of salaries to the MPF account of the employee. It is not yet clear how much the MPF scheme will affect the savings rate of the economy and deposit growth in the banking sector. Nevertheless, it would represent some degree of disintermediation as funds move from deposit accounts to MPF accounts. This may not be significant at the beginning, but the effect is cumulative. It is estimated that the flow of MPF contributions in the first year of operation would amount to HK$10 billion. As a point of reference, the stock of Hong Kong dollar deposits in all AIs stood at HK$1,750 billion at the end of June 2000. It can be seen that some years after the inception of the MPF scheme, the size of cumulated MPF would be an appreciable percentage of total bank deposits. How much of the MPF growth will be at the expense of bank deposits depends on how the general public reshuffle their portfolios and how savings behavior would be affected by the MPF. As many of the service providers of MPF are banks, the introduction of the MPF basically broadens and diversifies bank portfolios.

Another factor that would affect banks in Hong Kong is China's membership in the World Trade Organization (WTO). It is widely speculated that China is about to be a member of the WTO in the immediate future. Although the terms for China to open up its markets have not yet been fully finalized, the current understanding is that, among other aspects of liberalization, foreign banks can carry out renminbi (RMB) business with Chinese enterprises two years upon China's entry to the WTO. Moreover, five years after China joins the WTO, foreign banks can also carry out RMB business with Chinese residents and will not face geographical restrictions. This represents opportunities for banks from outside, especially those from Hong Kong which have already had a noticeable presence in the Mainland.

Conclusion

The banking sector in Hong Kong has been basically strong and sound, despite some episodes of banking problems. Unlike other Asian economies where banking problems were part of the financial crisis, the banking system in Hong Kong has remained basically intact. It did go through a short period of lean years, but that is the result of poor domestic macroeconomic mismanagement rather than poor bank performance or supervision. It would have been disastrous for the Hong Kong economy during the crisis had the banking system been less strong.

Most economists would suggest that in financial liberalization, capital decontrol should be left to the final stage, so that other reforms would not be easily disrupted or even undermined by unnecessary capital flows. Hong Kong does not have this option, as there is no capital control of any kind to begin with. Given its openness and small size, as well as free capital mobility, any liberalization and financial reform has to be carried out in a gradual and prudent manner. This is additionally true under the linked exchange rate system where external shocks would not be absorbed by exchange rate changes.

Note

[1] Unless otherwise stated, all data in this chapter come from the Hong Kong Monetary Authority, either its publications such as the *Monthly Statistical Bulletin* or information from its website at http://www.info.gov.hk/hkma/.

References

Beecham, B. Julian (1998), *Monetary and Financial System in Hong Kong*, 2nd ed., Hong Kong: Hong Kong Institute of Bankers.

Hong Kong Monetary Authority, *Annual Report*, various issues.

Hong Kong Monetary Authority, *Monthly Statistical Bulletin*, various issues.

Hong Kong Monetary Authority, *Quarterly Bulletin*, various issues.

6 China's Capital Market in the Course of Economic Restructuring

SHI JIN LIU
CHEN GHUI ZHANG

Financial Structure and Capital Markets in China

The Evolution of China's Financial Structure

Financial structure under the traditional mechanism   In order to meet the demands of a planned economy after 1949, China established a financial mechanism that was highly centralized and mostly regulated by administrative means. Hence, an extremely monotonous financial structure was established. Its characteristics can be summarized in two points. First, the People's Bank of China was the country's only bank, and no other banking or non-banking financial institution existed. Secondly, financial assets such as stocks, bonds and commercial paper were not prohibited. All financial activities had to be executed in accordance with predetermined plans, and capital exchanges could not take place either between branches of the People's Bank of China or between enterprises. Commercially-oriented financial activities between individuals were also forbidden.

This financial structure effectively met the requirements for rapid expansion of the economy under the traditional mechanism, but on the other hand, it also led to serious recessive inflation and inefficient capital utilization, among other problems. In light of these problems, the government made several adjustments in the financial system between 1950 and 1975. For example, the Agriculture Bank of China, the Construction Bank of China and the People's Insurance Company of China were founded, but such limited kinds of adjustment could only have a limited influence on China's financial structure. What is more, the small progressive steps that were made were always forced backward due to constant changes in the political climate. For example, both of the Agriculture Bank of China and the Construction Bank of China were established then cancelled three times, and the People's Insurance Company of China was handled roughly the same. Not until economic reform began did the high degree of planning characteristic of China's financial structure begin to change.

A brief review of financial restructuring As China's economic reform proceeded and a socialist market economy was established, some market-oriented reforms were implemented in China's financial mechanism beginning in 1979. First, renovation in financial organization. In the early stages of reform, the government restored the Agriculture Bank of China and the Construction Bank of China and set up a new Bank of China. China International Trust Investment Company and some other regional non-banking financial institutions were also established. These specialized banks and non-banks not only made a breakthrough in the situation of People's Bank of China having to carry many different functions on its shoulders as the only bank in China, but also organizationally proved the need to develop a commodity economy.

After 1984, the People's Bank of China began to function solely as the central bank of China, as the tasks of issuing industrial and commercial credit and receiving deposits were transferred to the newly established Industrial and Commercial Bank of China. Meanwhile, financial institutions of various kinds experienced rapid development and several national or regional commercial banks were set up successively. The pace of development in the non-banking financial sector was even faster, with the emergence of security companies, trust investment companies, financial companies, urban and rural credit cooperatives, leasing companies and various types of funds. At the same time, foreign financial companies began to enter China. In 1994, China established three banks to take over policy-oriented businesses from state-owned banks, and thus created favorable conditions for the commercialization of stated-owned banks.

Therefore, a financial structure had been initially established with the central bank as the main vehicle of guidance, the state-owned bank as the main form, and a number of other forms coexisting and coordinating with each other.

Secondly, reform took place in the credit system in order to change the conventional planned mechanism, in which "deposits were entered into the higher level, while the loans were applied from the higher level". Part of the administrative power regarding credit planning was transferred to banks at lower levels and actual deposits and loans were connected in order to increase bank initiative and capital returns. Meanwhile, the regulation mechanism of current capital was reformed. From July 1983, a state-owned enterprise's working capital was no longer provided fiscally, but through bank loans. More regulatory measures were adopted beginning in 1984. While the government would not provide banks with capital in an across the board manner, capital was allowed to be balanced and financed horizontally among banks, which meant the beginning of competition among the specialized banks. In January 1998, the central bank removed quotas on the size of state-owned bank credit, which had been practiced for

Table 6.1 Securities Issuance in China 1981-1997

(Unit: RMB billions)

Type		1981-85	1986-90	1991-95	1996	1997
National Debt	Issurance	23.7	78.9	377.2	184.8	241.2
	Total Value At Term End	23.7	89.0	330.0	436.1	550.9
Policy-Oriented Bonds	Issurance			161.3	104.1	140.0
	Total Value At Term End			161.3	240.0	348.7
Other Bonds	Issurance		28.0	12.2	1.5	3.2
	Total Value At Term End		8.5	9.5	11.0	14.2
Debentures	Issurance		40.7	163.2	26.9	25.5
	Total Value At Term End		19.5	64.7	59.8	52.1
National Investment Bonds	Issurance			15.5		
	Total Value At Term End			13.9	13.9	
National Investment Corporate Bonds	Issurance		14.9	1.0		
	Total Value At Term End		14.9	11.9	11.9	
Total Bonds	Issurance	23.7	162.5	238.8	317.2	406.7
	Total Value At Term End	23.7	131.9	430.1	611.4	977.2
Stocks (A Share)	Issurance		4.6	7.4	3.8	10.6
	Total Value At Term End		4.6	32.2	22.4	65.5

Source: China's Securities and Futures Statistics Yearbook 1998, p.8.

nearly half a century, and thus the central bank's regulation of overall credit volume was transformed from direct control to indirect regulation.

Thirdly, a financial market was established. China's financial market has been developing since the mid-1980s. It incorporates inter-bank, foreign exchange, insurance and securities markets, among which the stock market has experienced the most rapid development. The Shanghai Stock Exchange and the Shenzhen Stock Exchange were established in November 1990 and April 1991 respectively. As of the end of 1997, the number of listed firms on these exchanges were 383 and 362 and the number of listings 422 and 399 respectively.

China's current financial structure   After 20 years of reform, China has finally set up an indirect financing mechanism where banks play the major role. Although security markets have evolved dramatically since the beginning of the 1990s, financing through stocks and bonds still accounts for only a tiny part of capital financing (See Table 6.1).

Table 6.2 Structure of China's Financial System

Institution Name	Number	Market Share	
		Deposits	Loans
Solely State-Owned Banks	4	63.0	62.5
Other Commercial Banks	13	7.0	5.2
Policy-Oriented Banks	3	0.3	13.8
City Cooperative Banks	60	2.1	1.2
Rural Credit Cooperatives	49530	12.9	10.2
City Credit Cooperative	35000	4.3	3.1
Insurance Companies	13		
Trust and Investment Companies	244	2.9	2.8
Financial Companies	63	1.2	0.9
Security Companies	93		
Leasing Companies	16	0.1	0.1

Note: Statistics are numbers in late October, 1997.

To begin with, the banking sector far exceeds the non-banking sector in terms of the number of institutions and market share (See Table 6.2). The assets held by banks compose over 90% of the total assets held by all financial institutions. Moreover, the trust business has not been properly developed in China, with trust and investment companies mainly involved in the banking business and city/rural credit cooperatives. Therefore China's financial structure is characterized by the predominant role being played by banks.

Secondly, security markets play a small part in the national economy (See Table 6.3).

Table 6.3 The Role of Securities Market in China's National Economy

(Unit: RMB 100 millions)

Year	GDP	Total Market Value (a)	a/GDP	Trading Volume (b)	b/GDP	Fixed Capitalization (c)	Domestic Raised Funds (d)	d/c
1992	26638	1048	3.9	N.A.	N.A.	8317	50	0.6
1993	34634	3531	10.2	N.A.	N.A.	12980	276	2.1
1994	46759	3691	7.9	965	2.1	16856	100	0.6
1995	58478	3474	5.9	938	1.6	20301	86	0.4
1996	67885	9842	14.5	2867	4.2	23336	294	1.3
1997	74772	17529	23.4	5204	7.0	25698	856	3.3

Source: *China's Securities and Futures Statistics Yearbook 1998.*

As demonstrated by Table 6.3, until 1997 the total market value of China's security markets still comprises less than one-fourth of the country's GDP (Gross Domestic Product), while funds raised on capital markets accounted for only 3.3% of the fixed capitalization. It is therefore reasonable to argue that the exemplary and political functions of security markets are far more important than their intrinsic economic function in the Chinese economy.

Thirdly, with respect to the business management system, there are evidently interactive ties between the banking and non-banking sectors. Ever since the beginning of reform, China's central bank, the People's Bank of China, had been until 1998 responsible for supervising the operation of all financial institutions in China. It supervised both commercial banks and other financial institutions. In 1998, its supervision over securities and insurance business were transferred to the Securities Supervision and Regulation Commission and the Insurance Supervision and Regulation Commission, respectively. It was not until then that the situation gradually began to take on a new look. In addition, many trust and investment companies were established by commercial banks, so the non-banking sector relies heavily on commercial banks for both financial sources and clients.

The Crisis of Indirect Financing Mechanism and the Development of Capital Market

Causes for the crisis of indirect financing mechanism   As China's traditional systems have transformed during the country's economic restructuring and reform of the past few decades, significant changes have taken place in allocation patterns as well. This is mostly evidenced by the rapid growth in household income and its increasing share of total government, business and household income. Similarly, a household-oriented trend can also be observed through the allocation of financial assets. As Table 6.4 shows, during the most recent three years, household deposits accounted for an average of 37.8% of all financial assets. Moreover, the household sector would take up over 50% of total financial assets if stocks, bonds and cash items were counted. In addition, from 1990 to 1997, net assets of financial institutions and savings of business and government all declined in their respective shares of total financial assets: financial institutions from 8.1% to 2.8%, business savings from 25.2% to 22.5% and government savings from 2.1% to 1.2%.

These significant changes in the structure of financial assets have made a great impact not only on China's financial system, but also on the country's entire economic structure. In particular, it has led to a crisis in the traditional indirect financing mechanism. As to the reasons behind this, first, the basic pattern of the indirect financing mechanism is that households deposit their savings in banks, and banks make loans to businesses. While a bank's debt against households is a "hard" bond, the bank's credit against businesses is a "soft" one, because banks and businesses are all owned by the state. Given the increasing operational insolvency of state-owned enterprises, the non-performing assets of banks have been on an increase year by year. As bank operations worsen, the ability for self-development diminishes and solvency erodes. This has resulted in low bank efficiency performance and tremendous financial risks.

Secondly, the funneling of capital through banks makes risk diversification difficult, and at the same time cannot meet the household needs for capital growth and diversified use of funds. Furthermore, under strict state restrictions on the scope of banking operations, banks have little room for such activities as interest rate adjustment, financial product innovation. Therefore, household demand on fund management cannot be satisfied within the banking system, so other outlets are sought, including such illegal financial institutions as money houses and various funds. It is for this very reason that bans on illegal financing practices since the beginning of reform have failed over and over again.

Thirdly, indirect financing cannot solve the problem of the high debt ratio of state-owned enterprises. Ever since the government replaced funds allocation with loans for state-owned enterprises in 1993, the state has injected practically no capital into state-owned enterprises, which has resulted in increasingly high debt ratios of these enterprises and the emergence of numerous enterprises which was funded by no capital except loans. Moreover, since these enterprises have very small portions of self-owned operational funds, their business operation is over-dependent on bank loans. The heavy burden of debt in return generates tremendous amounts of bad debts. Therefore, the extreme deficiency of capital and operation with high debt ratios has caused serious negative effects on the survival and development of state-owned enterprises.

Fourthly, one single indirect financing mechanism cannot meet the demands for reform of state-owned enterprises. The ultimate goal of China's state-owned enterprise reform is to establish a modern enterprise system; and one of the most essential ways to achieve this goal is to transform of state-owned enterprises into joint stock companies. As a significant result of these reforms, many state-owned enterprises have successfully changed over from solely state-owned entities to multi-owner entities, a development that has brought about a sharp increase in equity transactions. Moreover, other new large demands for funds in the process of reforming also arose; for example, for mergers and acquisitions. What the indirect financing system can provide is usually far from enough (See Table 6.4).

China's Securities Markets and the Debate over the Financing System

Since the indirect financing system has been far from efficient in supporting economic reform and development, China's capital markets have begun to thrive and become both well-organized and regulated. However, within various limits, development was slow at the initial stage. Although China began to issue treasury certificates in 1981 and debentures in 1986, these movers were basically administrative in nature, and there were no legal secondary markets for the securities that were issued. The first security transaction in a real sense took place in 1986. That year, Shenzhen set up a bond trading counter, which was launched as a pilot project. The bonds were limited to only two kinds with prices set up by the government. Without benefits arising from such transactions, the market became undoubtedly inactive. Later some enterprises started to issue stocks, and two over-the-counter markets emerged. In 1988, the State Council officially approved national bond transactions, and they consequently increased.

Table 6.4 Total Portfolio

(Unit: RMB yuan billions, (%))

	1980	1985	1990	1995	1996	1997
net assets of financial institutions	49.7 (22.7)	84.8 (12.9)	148.1 (8.1)	334.2 (4.6)	366.5 (3.5)	367.8 (2.8)
savings deposits of households	34.0 (15.5)	162.3 (24.6)	712.0 (38.8)	2966.2 (40.9)	3878.1 (37.4)	4628 (35.3)
deposit of institutions	80.3 (36.7)	239.7 (36.4)	461.3 (35.2)	1542.0 (21.3)	2499.6 (24.1)	2951.5 (22.5)
government fiscal deposits	16.4 (7.5)	36.8 (5.6)	38.0 (2.1)	100.3 (1.4)	139 (1.3)	157.2 (1.2)
securities						
1. stock market value			1.2 (0.7)	347.5 (4.8)	984.2 (9.5)	1752.9 (13.4)
2. bonds		23.7 (3.6)	131.9 (7.2)	430.0 (5.9)	611.4 (5.9)	977.2 (7.5)
3. insurance premiums		2.6	15.6 (0.9)	60.1 (0.8)	76.8 (0.7)	108.7 (0.8)
foreign exchange	3.8 (1.7)	10.5 (1.6)	61.2 (3.3)	678.7 (9.4)	934.2 (0.9)	1147.2 (8.8)
cash	34.6 (15.8)	98.8 (15.0)	264.4 (14.4)	788.5 (10.8)	880.2 (8.5)	1017.8 (7.8)
total	218.8	659.2	1833.7	7247.5	10370.0	13108.3

Source: Calculating from *China Year Book*, *China Financial Year Book*, *Statistics Quarterly Report of China Peoples Bank*.

The Shanghai and Shenzhen Stock Exchanges opened in late 1990 and early 1991, respectively, symbolizing the establishment of China's stock market. Thereafter a number of exchanges were established in other places, and trading variety has evolved to incorporate such financial commodities as bonds, investment funds, convertibles and equity certificates, with stock being the most actively traded commodity. China's security markets have developed quickly over the past few years.

Infrastructure preparation in the exchanges has achieved international standards, and some defining indexes have improved greatly. In 1997, the number of companies listed, total market value, trading volumes and accounts opened have increased 14, 16.7, 67.5 and 15.4 fold respectively since 1992 on the Shanghai and Shenzhen Exchanges.

China's state-owned enterprise reform and financial system renovation are at present both going through their roughest phases. Therefore, once latent financial risks have risen to the surface and can no longer be ignored. A debate over the financing pattern that China should or should not adopt has broken out, and many experts argue that in the past China mainly modeled its financing system after Japan's, developing a monolithic banking system, while restraining the capital markets. When the bubble burst in Japan, this approach was severely questioned. The evident problems here are bad-debt ridden banks, dangerously geared companies, and ineffective enterprise regulation and supervision. In facing these problems, China needs to readjust its financing framework for the future; namely, speed up the growth of its capital markets, as well as reform the banking system. The development of capital markets not only opens new channels of finance for businesses, but also will facilitate the establishment of a modern enterprise system. On the one hand, state-owned enterprise facilitated by security markets can be changed to joint stock companies that perform according to the rules of market economy. On the other hand, security markets can act as funnels for state-owned capital to flow in and out of, thus facilitating the relocation of capital and production factors aiming at optimizing the capital structure. It is in this way that developed capital markets can facilitate efficient allocation of national resources. On the whole, China's capital markets will probably go on developing rapidly and play an increasingly important role in the Chinese economy.

The Current Situation and Problems of China's Capital Market

The Development of China's Capital Markets

Securities exchange As milestones of the development of China's security markets, the security exchanges located in Shanghai and Shenzhen have along with China's securities markets undergone a process of growth from small to large and weak to strong. The Shanghai Exchange was the first to be set up in China. Upon approval by the People's Bank of China, it was founded on November 26, 1990. It is a non-profit-oriented legal entity, organized on a membership basis, following the international practice. It has aimed at creating an open, fair and just market environment to ensure the regular exchange of securities. Its functions include providing facilities for the security exchange, laying down operating rules, accepting applications for issuance, arranging the placement of stocks, overseeing transactions, supervising its members and the listed companies, setting up registration and clearance houses, and administrating and disclosing market information. The Shenzhen Exchange began its pilot run on December 1, 1990. It was authorized by the People's Bank of China on April 11, 1991 and opened for business in July of that year. Some basic information about the two exchanges is contained in Table 6.5.

Securities companies and other intermediary institutions   By 1997, there were 97 securities companies in China (merged or eliminated to 15 in 1998), 224 trust investment corporations entitled to conduct securities transactions, 69 financial companies, and 16 leasing companies. There are altogether 450 companies and institutions running 2600 operational branches with total assets of RMB 160 million. Of them, there are eight large companies occupying 80% of the first and second market business. Recently, besides security underwriting, brokerage and business done on their own account, these security companies have become engaged in such business activities as mergers and acquisitions, project restructuring, and other such modern investment banking business.

Besides security companies, there are also 110 accounting firms entitled to conduct securities business, 26 entitled to provide consulting services, 71 professional security consulting agencies, and 288 law firms.

Listed companies   At the beginning of the 1990s, when the security exchanges were first established, there were only 13 listed companies; but by 1997 the number had grown to 745. These companies have raised funds of over RMB 250 billion in the stock market. In 1997 alone, the capital raised came to RMB 132.5 billion. These companies are from the manufacturing (61.2%), commercial (11.5%), real estate (3.6%), public utility (7.5%), financial (0.5%) industries.

Investors   At present, the main portion of investors involved in China's securities markets are individuals, while institutional investors account for only 1%. However, 80% of the capital invested is controlled by institutional investors.

Regulating authorities   The Security Supervision and Administration Commission of China, founded in October 1992, is the state supervisor and

Table 6.5 Exchanges Record in 1997

Subject	Shenzhen Security Exchange	Shanghai Security Exchange	Total
Number of members	373	467	840
Number of listed companies	362	383	745
Number of shares/bonds	399	422	821
A shares	348	372	720
B shares	51	50	101
Capital equity (billions of shares)	79.59	97.54	177.12
A shares	78.34	90.78	164.61
B shares	57.48	67.61	125.09
Circulating Capital (billions of shares)	27.51	28.56	56.96
A shares	22.53	21.80	44.33
B shares	4.98	6.76	11.74
Total market value (yuan billions)	831.12	921.81	1752.92
A shares	812.17	903.25	1715.42
B shares	18.94	18.56	37.50
Circulating market value	69.10	251.35	520.44
A shares	252.82	232.79	485.61
B shares	1.27	18.56	34.83
Turn-over value	1695.87	1376.32	3072.18
A shares	16744.97	13550.24	30295.21
B shares	213.69	212.94	426.63
Number of Accounts (tens of thousands)			3333.33

Source: *China's Securities and Futures Statistics Yearbook 1998.*

administrator of the security market. Its main responsibilities are to set policy for securities and futures markets, control those markets, supervise the issuance, trade, trust and settlement of stock, bonds, and security investment funds, approve company listings and issuance of stocks and bonds, supervise the listed companies in performing their duties of disclosure to their stockholders, to administrate the stock exchanges and other associations in the industry, and supervise securities and future intermediaries. China's securities trading administration reform has gone through three stages: (1) the time before the founding of the Securities Committee of the State Council (SCSC) and the Securities Supervision and Administration Commission (SSAC) of China, when securities exchange was basically regulated by the People's Bank of China or local governments and when the exchanges bore more local characteristics; (2) after the foundation of the SCSC and SSAC, when the exchanges were administrated jointly by local governments and the SSAC; and (3) from August 1997, when the SCSC put the Shanghai and Shenzhen Exchanges under the complete supervision of SSAC and later set up 44 branches to administrate the local supervision committees directly.

Current Problems in China's Capital Markets

Imperfect Market Conditions

Unbalanced market structure   For a variety of reasons, a lot of problems have cropped up during the process of market restructuring in China: more stress has been laid on the securitized than on the unsecuritized market; more emphasis has been put on the development of stock than on the development of bond markets, especially debentures markets; and too much importance has been attached to the growth of on-the-spot trading while over-the-counter trading has been limited or even on occasion prohibited.

China's debenture markets were initiated during the mid-1980s; however, their development has continued to be restrained during the recent decade, and its circulation scale is very small and weak. Registered debentures reached their peak at twenty on the Shanghai and Shenzhen Exchanges in 1995; but as some of them reaching maturity, only six remained as of March 1998. Compared with national treasury bonds and stocks, both the Exchanges are very limited in assortment and volume of debentures. Although there is some private trading besides listed trading, diverted exchange and its small volume can hardly be called a market. Furthermore, since the credit level for China as a whole is not very high, the long-term notes market has never been well developed.

The structure making up securities investors is not very sound either. Institutional investors are very limited in number and the prevailing funds are small in scale and lacking in long term investment. Moreover, insurance funds and pension funds have not been permitted to enter the security market, so the security market is volatile and drastic fluctuations in prices are commonplace, presenting ever-present opportunities for speculation.

In addition, there is a serious problem concerning the division of the security markets in China. They have been divided security market into A share markets and B share markets. A shares of stock are defined as state-owned, legal entity and circulated shares. The capital stock circulating in the market, however, only accounts for 31.6% of the total stock that has been issued. Thus, the whole transaction process in the market can be easily rigged, causing great difficulties for enterprises in merger and acquisition activities.

Insufficient scope of coverage For a long period of time China has held to a kind of discriminatory policy regarding stocks and bonds issuance, which favors large and state-owned enterprises. Non-state-owned and small and middle-sized enterprises encounter great difficulty in obtaining listing permission. Moreover, non-state-owned enterprises do not enjoy the preferential policy of merger and acquisition. For example, in order to encourage mergers and acquisitions of enterprises, the government exempts the parties involved from the interest payments for a certain period of time. However, this exemption can be enjoyed by the acquiring and acquired enterprises only if both parties are state-owned.

Disorder in the Market as a Whole and Fairly High Latent Risk

Big bubbles and stocks not worthy of long term investment In order to insure that stock can be sold at a large premium in the primary market for a long period of time, the market expansion speed was controlled under administrative supervision, and other measures were taken to prevent the stock market from declining. As a result, the supply and demand in the stock market were kept in disequilibrium for a long time, and stock prices in the secondary market were divorced from their enterprises' actual performance, making it not worthwhile to invest in stocks in the long run. From 1993 to 1997, the average market profit earning ratio reached 30.6 and 27.8 on the Shanghai and Shenzhen Exchanges respectively, higher than the average level of the world's major exchanges. In addition, during dramatic stock price rises, the market profit-earning ratio of some stocks has even reached 300. Regarding selling frequency, China's stock market is characterized by too much speculation. The average selling frequencies during this time on the Shanghai and Shenzhen Exchanges were 488% and 477% respectively, much higher than the 299% average in Taiwan, 57% in New York, 28% in Tokyo, and 68% on the London Stock Exchange.

Listed companies are of poor quality, lacking in momentum and not up to standard   Some local governments and enterprises treat stock issuing only as a means of raising funds and solving financial problems. A lot of enterprises and intermediary institutions collaborate in order to force issue prices up for the purpose of accumulating capital, make false financial statements and overestimate profits. There are some extreme cases in which enterprises have even presented false documents and hid unfavorable facts. As an inevitable result, the quality of the listed companies differ and the problem that some are not up to standard is very serious. The performance of a lot of enterprises has turned for the worse and their profitability has declined over the years. Many enterprises make false statements, which seriously affects shareholders' interests.

Driven by the opportunity to earn great profits and use management loopholes, security companies disseminate false information and resort to backstage manipulation, as insiders are very common. Investors are frequently cheated and their interests harmed. All these practices not only violate the "three open principles" of security markets but also bring great risk to the market. In 1995, over-speculation by a few big security companies caused huge losses and a payment crisis. The fact that large shareholders always take advantage of small shareholders represents another serious problem. It is a said that usually "large shareholders put up their hands to vote, while small shareholders take money from their pockets to pay". To be specific, large shareholders vote for proposals to ration their stock made by the board of directors, who is acting in their interest, but when the time comes to pay for the funds to ration the stock, they give up their rights to rationing. What is more, at shareholders' meetings, which are controlled by large shareholders, resolutions are passed to purchase non-performing assets and thus waste the funds raised directly or indirectly from small shareholders, enabling big shareholders to liquidate their holdings. The listed company thus suffers an insurmountable setback.

Weak supervision of market   At present, one conspicuous problem facing China's capital markets is that government supervision and the market mechanism are seriously dislocated. Open and truthful disclosure and open and fair transactions, both of which should be strictly guaranteed by the government are not well controlled. That is why fraud and backstage trading are so common. On the other hand, the government often interferes in aspects that should be left the forces of the market, such as determining criteria for issuing securities and the type, amount and timing of issuance. Consequently, the final result is sure to be that administrative orders distort the market mechanism, create market risk and incur corruption.

Take the stock market for example. At present, the three characteristics of China's stock market supervision may said to be that (1) the overall volume of stock issuance is controlled on a quota basis; (2) both the choices of issuing companies and the type of issuance are determined by administrative authorities; and (3) the issuance of shares is automatically linked to public offering (that is, the approved companies can submit an application to get listed as soon as permission is granted). Such a supervisory model, with its strong color of planned economy and administrative control has completely twisted the inherent mechanism in which supply and demand are balanced and resources are allocated for the purpose of maximum returns. By choosing companies to be listed, the administrative authorities take into consideration such elements as the balance between different regions, industries and departments, the stability of society and so on, rather than the principle of efficiency. Therefore, it is no surprise that equal distribution and relief from financial difficulty through the stock market are common. Enterprises with excellent profitability and bright futures are not eligible to issue stocks and get listed, while those with low economic returns are supported for membership by the government.

At present, the self-regulation of China's security industry is rather weak. Founded as a self-disciplinary organization, China's Security Association mainly functions to train professionals and has little binding authority over security companies, security investment and consulting institutions, certified accountants or law firms engaged in the security business. The lack of a self-disciplinary mechanism is the main reason why China's security markets are in disorder, and their latent risk very high.

The Capital Market Development and State-Owned Enterprises

China is at present in a transitional stage from a planned to a market economy, in which the reorganization of state-owned enterprises has become an extremely important task. During this transition period, the development of capital markets will play an important and indispensable role.

There are at least three functions to be performed by capital markets in the strategic reorganization of state-owned enterprises: (1) to collect money (i.e., the "fund-raising function"); (2) to promote a transformation of the property rights and inner management structures of such enterprises (i.e. the "reform function"); and (3) to promote the re-allocation of resources, (i.e., the "re-allocation function"). Capital markets in China were initiated to a high degree under the pressure of fund-raising. For enterprises that are in great debt and urgently need capital, it is surely a good thing to raise funds without cost through the new channels provided by capital markets. However, problems may also rise at this point. If the above mentioned three functions are compared with each other, the importance of "reform" and "re-allocation" surpasses to some extent that of "fund-raising". This is one of the characteristics of the development of China's capital markets under present conditions. The fundamental difficulty faced by state-owned enterprises is not "a lack of money", but the lack of a system under which money can be efficiently utilized. Therefore, the "reform" and "re-allocation" functions of capital markets should be analyzed and understood in depth.

Looking first at the "reform function", the capital market has several positive functions. First, it helps to promote the transformation of enterprises into a corporate system. The present situation in China is that companies do not adopt standard corporate systems until they have to enter the stock market. Therefore, these enterprises must transform their management systems into the corporate type under "the Corporation Act", before they can enter the stock market, where the number of enterprises is limited. Although such a transformation is rudimentary and hardly satisfactory, it is an indispensable beginning.

Secondly, capital markets promote positive changes in the property rights structure of state-owned enterprises. When a state-owned enterprise enters a capital market, their property rights structure becomes open and mobile, since new investors can "come in" to become new shareholders and the original ones can "leave", a flow that results in the change of the company's property rights structure. This change will thus fundamentally alter a situation in which the property rights structure cannot be changed by choosing to enter a competitive market. Experience shows that a multiple property rights structure thus formed is beneficial to the improvement in an enterprises' efficiency. Even with the precondition of entire state ownership, a property rights structure including several state shareholders is, with a few special exceptions, still more advantageous than a structure with exclusive investment.

Lastly, capital markets are helpful in the transformation of the inner management structure of enterprises. Within a management structure possessing a general meeting of shareholders, board of directors and senior managers, changes in shareholders composition will affect decisions made by the board of directors and senior managers, and in turn affect the behavior of the enterprise. This is only a possibility, though. In order to turn it into a reality, there should be large institutional investors among the shareholder in order to avoid a situation in which new shareholders are scattered about.

Turning to the "re-allocation function", capital markets play an even more important role. First, capital markets offer a mechanism in which assets can be transformed and flow. With the transformation from assets in kind to their market value form, and then from money form to stock form, their mobility is increased accordingly, and the efficiency of initial allocation and re-allocation of assets is greatly enhanced in terms of time and space. Although it appears almost impossible to allocate some resources in kind, allocation can be realized conveniently in an advanced capital market. The significance of developing capital markets for the strategic reorganization of state-owned enterprises lies not only in the flow of state-owned assets between industries and enterprises, but also in cutting down the cost of circulation by great margin, making it possible to allocate resources that can not be done so in kind.

Secondly, capital markets offer various low cost mechanisms for asset re-allocation. The organizational structure of the enterprise is optimized, and its allocation efficiency is enhanced by means of acquisition, merger, etc.

If the introduction of capital markets is more closely observed, unprecedented solutions may be found to those problems that have remained unsolved for a long time in the reform of state-owned enterprises. To begin with there is the problem of separating the functions of the government and the enterprise. It is no secret that separating these functions is significant for the transformation of state-owned enterprises, but it is also extremely difficult. If the personnel in an enterprise and the governmental department responsible for its behavior have hardly changed for several dozens of years or so, it is very difficult to apply the general theoretical description to the complicated historical background of the relations between the government and the enterprise. As a result, measures to separate functions are usually distorted and dissolved in this closed and historically developed environment. Therefore, changes should be made in the relationship through, for example, the introduction of new owners. The original owners should be replaced partially or even totally, so that the old system can be broken apart by openness in the enterprise's property rights structure. The new owners can be non-state, but this is not always necessary. Even under entire state ownership, the relationship between an enterprise and its owners can be quite different from before, so long as there is the participation of state-owned assets from other localities, departments and enterprises. This has been partly proved by the recent practice of setting up "neo-state-owned enterprises" with multiple shareholders. The openness and mobility of the property rights structure that appears along with the development of capital markets are very likely to bring about a breakthrough in separating the functions of the government and enterprises, a problem that has been under discussion for many years.

Secondly, there is the problem of determining the qualifications of state capital administrators, which has been a controversial problem for years. Many plans have been put forward by the researchers and many departments, institutions and enterprises have put forth all sorts of arguments to prove that they are the best administrators. However, only the market can make such a determination, not subjective arguments. In a capital market, there are at least two preconditions for a qualified administrator of state capital: can the administrator bear management risks, and is the capital competitive in the market? Presently some institutions enjoy competing for the position of state capital administrator, because in this position they can become very powerful without taking any responsibilities for management failures. In political economic terms, this is due to the low price of the state assets in question. Even for several institutions that are willing to or forced to bear risks, they still cannot be judged as the most qualified to manage state capital until market competition proves it. This is not to say, however, that there is no need to lay down in advance some standards and regulations for "accession" to the position of state capital administrator. The most essential thing is not the initial accession, but competitive power after entering a capital market. Those who are competitive will expand their operation scale, while those less competitive will have to reduce their operation scale and may even lose their qualifications.

Thirdly, there is the problem of allocating state capital in competitive fields. Under the new system, there some state capital that still exists in competitive fields and occupies a greater share at the primary and intermediate stages of the strategic reorganization of state assets. The allocation of this part of state capital should be decided basically by market competition, in addition to the enlightened government policy. Doing so will result economically in a more rational distribution of state capital than if the decision were made according to subjective judgement.

Next, there is the problem of inspecting and supervising the management of the state capital. Supervision is critical to the management of the state capital, and actually the of property rights problem can be summed up to a high degree as a problem of supervision. Supervision involves two basic aspects: who is to supervised and in what way? What should be emphasized here is improving the system of supervision after the introduction of capital markets. The degree of openness and transparency of enterprises involved in capital markets, especially those that are listed, should be increased, there should be an auditing system within the company and the company should be subject to audit by outside auditing institutions, and the company should publish in detail its operational and financial data according to set regulations. These procedures not only help national shareholders to understand and supervise the management of state capital, but also offer opportunities for the general public as the final owner of the property to understand what is going on. The public can thereby play a role of "supervising the supervisors". Although at present there still exist plenty of problems concerning self-auditing and the publication of information about listed companies, it is after all great progress that such a system has been established, enabling the situation to be gradually improved. Openness and transparency are valuable to state capital because nominal public supervision is realizable to a certain degree.

One more issue is "right of credit" as a solution to the problem of "stock right". Right of credit and stock right seem to be two independent subjects, because there will only be a structural change in capital when the minimum capital requirement is increased and debt is decreased by means of fund-raising through stock right. However, the shareholders are the main actors exercising their rights behind such a structural change. It is the shareholders and the administrators they have elected who use funds raised through borrowing. The problem of financing practices in state-owned enterprises does not lie in the debt rate itself, but in the lack of risk and the consequent trend toward a high debt rate when the present shareholders and their agents are managing funds raised through borrowing. Therefore, in solving the debt problem of state-owned enterprises, the most essential task besides increasing capital and reducing debt is to alter the behavior of shareholders and their agents; otherwise the debt already reduced will again rise, and much of the debt can never be repaid. In this regard, the development of capital markets can bring more capital to the enterprises on the one hand, and provide conditions for fundamentally solving the debt problem, on the other, by altering the structure of property rights and internal management of the enterprises.

Finally, there is the problem of reducing repetitive production. This problem may be viewed from two perspectives. On the one hand, given a "shortage economy" and a great contrast between demand and supply, it is usually inevitable that over a period of time supplying capacity will be strengthened rapidly and include some kind of repetitive production. There is almost no difficulty in entering the market, since super-profits exist due to high demand. Since large monopolistic enterprises have not yet emerged in China, the rationality of investor behavior cannot be denied, so long as they are able to retrieve their investment plus a profit after a certain period of time. To explain this point further, there will be neither full competition nor the emergence of large enterprises on the basis of competition if repetitive and excessive production forces to some extent do not exist. On the other hand, under the absence of a risk binding mechanism for state capital, there is the problem of "strips" formed by different industries and "squares" divided up according to regions both rushing headlong into mass action towards repetitive production, without counting the cost or minding the consequences. However, the immediate cause of the problem is not the managerial method of "strips" and "squares", but the failure to separate the functions of government and the enterprise. This means that the leading units in the "strips" and "squares" are all busy developing new industries and starting new projects to meet the need for more "administrative achievements" regardless of the consequences, since they directly operate the enterprises and decide on production and investment. Furthermore, lacking a system for exchanging, transforming and transferring the assets of enterprises (i.e., the market), the "strips" and "squares" are all striving to set up their own enterprises in popular industries so that they can get a share of the profits being brought about by economic growth. During recent years, nearly every province has had its own television set factory, refrigerator factory and automobile factory, applying policies of administrative blocking and monopoly in order to occupy a corner of the market. When products and enterprises become so divided, the existence of "strips" and "squares" can hinder the annexation of disadvantageous enterprises by the advantageous ones. As the latter expand, they waste more resources when they develop new industries. The solution to these problems lies in the development of capital markets. If capital markets mature, the "strips" and "squares" will be able to exchange investment. Thus it will become unprofitable to invest in similar projects, and investors will be encouraged to select and develop projects according to their own economic interests. Regarding the point at hand, re-allocation of state assets, the opportunities offered by capital markets will make it more profitable to reform old industries than to start new ones, so that existing assets can be re-allocated through internal motivation.

The above problems comprise some of the most "difficult and complicated" in the task of reforming state-owned enterprises and the management of state capital. Through nurturing and developing capital markets, completely new solutions will be found that can be applied over the long term. We thus come to understand what is meant by the statement "capital markets are indispensable", and further understand the role of market in solving the problems related to uncertainty that exist beyond the rationale of any individual or organization. For many years now planners and policy makers have at times believed that they knew the "proper" lay-out of resources, and hoped to make things easier through advance examination, approval and "assignment" of them, in order to avoid repetitive production, excessive competition and their consequent disadvantages. With regard to the management of state capital, these authorities also decided in advance the allocation of state assets and who were to manage them. However, such good intentions have never failed to be dashed by reality. Technically speaking, if government planners were not unable to answer these questions about resource allocation, we would not be justified in asserting that planned economy is inefficient. However, in correctly answering such questions, the market is neither unnecessary nor unimportant, but rather indispensable. Without market competition, people will never know what is the "proper" way to allocate state capital, or who is best qualified to manage it. Actually market competition is not only a "discovery" process, but also a "calculation" process (i.e., allocating assets) and a "development" process (i.e., determining asset managers). Market competition may bring trouble, and even cause some loss and/or incur costs, but it just may be the most economical means in the long term.

Future Reform and Development of China's Capital Markets

The East Asian financial crisis of July 1997 was a warning to China. In order to protect against and avoid financial risk, China must accelerate reform of its banking system to realize the steady and safe operation of its commercial banks. On the other hand, China should also protect against and diversify risk in its security markets more effectively, and ensure their sound and stable development. The Securities Act of the PRC, which was promulgated in December 1998, is the first piece of legislation that regulates China's security markets and a significant event in the development of China's market economy. It will play an important role in administering security markets, regulating the issuance and the exchange of securities, and protecting the legitimate rights and interests of investors. Under the guidelines set by the Act, China's securities markets will enter a new stage of development centering around the following agenda of reform.

Reform of Direct Interference by the Government

To some extent, government interference in securities markets has been one of the reasons for high risk. In light of the fact that the Security Supervision and Administration Commission exercises both the authority to approve the issuance of securities and supervise securities markets, to require that the supervisory institutions disclose and correct problems caused by listed companies amounts to asking that they admit their own errors, since all the companies were judged by the SSAC to be free of problems before their listing. Due to institutional reasons, this should not be one of the tasks of a supervisory institution, since they may be tempted to neglect and even conceal problems. Japan and Korea also have too much government interference in their markets, which has caused negative impacts on market efficiency and normal operation, leading to financial crisis, and thus show that only when the government keeps a proper distance from the market can its power be properly exercised.

China's Securities Act revises the security issuance system, changing government approval of the public issuance of securities into a provision that states,

> "Public issuance of securities must be in accord with the requirements stipulated in the relevant laws and regulations, and go through legal assessment and review by the security supervisory and administrative institution of the State Council or institutions that have been authorized by the State Council."

The process is now also conducted in a different manner. In the past, the process was conducted by special departments set up by the SSAC. Now, the Security Issuance Examination Committee, made up of professionals in the SSAC and experts invited from outside, will be responsible for examination and approval through voting and open hearings. Meanwhile, the Securities Act increases the legal liability of such service organizations to the level of asset evaluation and accounting firms. Hence, the status and function of these intermediary institutions as "economic police" have been strengthened. In addition, the Act stipulates that SSAC can no longer set the standard issuance price when stocks are issued at premium. The Act allows the issuer and the underwriter to negotiate at the issuance price.

Reinforcement of the Supervision and Control by the Market

First, higher standards for listed companies will begin to solve the existing problems of currently listed companies. The quality of listed companies is the cornerstone of sound securities market development. Therefore, the quality of listed companies must be improved. In order to achieve this goal, we must begin by improving the pattern used to approve applications, setting higher standards for listed companies and selecting truly profitable and promising companies in accordance with industrial policy.

1. Asset restructuring of the listed companies and improve the quality of their stock assets must be carried out. The Securities Act targets this problem by providing special stipulations to lift restrictions on mergers and acquisitions. The Act has also made definite provisions to avoid mergers by means of backstage information to manipulate secondary markets and protect the interests of mid- and small-scale investors.
2. The Act appropriately prolongs the interval between successive issuance by listed companies. Recovery of the funds raised should be the principal criterion in deciding whether a company can ration its shares.
3. The Act implements an information disclosure system and strengthens the supervision over the information disclosed by listed companies. Companies that do not disclose information in accordance with Act's regulations will be punished strictly according to the law.

Secondly, securities companies are to be separated according to their main business, and different types of companies are to be administered accordingly. Stringent restrictions have been placed on security company qualifications and strengthen the supervision of their market behavior has been strengthened.

1. According to the stipulations in the Security Act, China's financial industry is to be divided into several sub-industries: securities, banking, trust, and insurance. At present, over 200 trust and investment companies will be involved in the changes taking place in the securities business pattern. Eventually, the securities industry will be separated from the trust industry.
2. Securities companies will be divided into comprehensive securities companies and brokerage firms according to the size of their equity

capital. The former can carry on brokerage, underwriting and business on its own account, while the latter can be engaged only in brokerage. This reform aims at changing the current situation in which the quality of securities companies vary and competition is blind by regulating the order of competition in the market, increasing corporate strength, and reducing supervision difficulties. Moreover, the Act contains a clear stipulation on the qualifications of professionals and chief directors of securities companies. It requires that comprehensive securities companies do brokerage and business on their own account separately and that the funds of client for transaction and settlements be deposited into designated banks. The companies must not appropriate these funds. According to the Act, the issuance price of stocks will no be longer set by the SSAC, resulting in competition in the smaller spread between the primary and secondary market. Securities companies must change the prevailing practice that generated huge profits from this spread.

The above policies demand better management on the part of securities companies and make their operations more difficult. One can foresee China's securities companies entering an era of radical adjustment and restructuring in the midst of the enactment of the Securities Act.

Thirdly, the management requirements of stock exchange service agencies will be strengthened and legal responsibility will be increased and violations punished. For historical reasons, accounting firms in China have hardly been fair or just. Many of them have even helped companies to meet qualifications for listing through fraud and have deceived shareholders with false information. There are main two causes of such behavior. First, most accounting firms that are subordinated to administrative departments lack any consciousness of risk or reputation, and have been often interfered with by administrative agencies. Secondly, the former system of responsibility was disadvantaged by lax supervision and light punishment.

To alleviate this situation, on the one hand, the separation between accounting firms and administrative departments should be accelerated and standards for qualified accounting firms and CPA should be raised. On the other hand, the institutional establishment and supervision should be strengthened, their activities standardized, and legal responsibility increased, punishment for violations made stricter.

Compared with the previous laws and regulations, the Securities Act has greatly raised the related responsibilities of major underwriters, accounting firms and law firms, and clearly specified and tightened punishment criteria. Other necessary laws and detailed regulations will come out in time.

Promoting Debenture Markets

What should be done firstly is to develop a debenture market with moderate speed. From a general view of China's present situation, financing through issuing debentures will probably become one major occupation for the country's capital markets in the future. To meet the demands of a developing debenture market, the present regulation style should be reformed, administrative control over debenture issuance gradually weakened, the focus of supervision turned away from setting and allocating quotas, directly selecting bond issuers, and controlling the pricing in bond issuance and the "three public" principles of the market upheld. Also, a credit rating system should be established and perfected, tighten the standard for entering the market, the independence, neutrality and justice of the credit rating institutions maintained, and the rating criterion system standardized.

At present, administrative control over bond issuance has been weakened somewhat, while the overhaul and standardization of existing intermediary credit institutions is also underway. With the establishment of a modern enterprise system and the strengthening of the corporate risk-binding system, the debenture market should develop even faster.

Secondly, diversifying capital markets is important. Presently, China's capital markets are facing the practical problem of "regular" capital markets being too small to meet the requirements of security issuance and transactions. In particular, high-tech companies that represent the developing direction of industry find it very difficult to obtain financial support in the market. Meanwhile, under reform of operational mechanism of state-owned companies, a large number of small shareholding companies will be formed that will require equity trading. If that need cannot be met, those enterprises will face more difficulty in further improving their asset allocation. Therefore, already been a hotly debated theoretical issue has risen as to whether a "secondary" capital market needs to be established with reference to foreign countries.

Clearing Up Illegal Over-The-Counter Trading and the Stock Exchanges

Due to a lack of supervision and regulations, over-the-counter trading in China is a high-risk business. In contrast to normal stock trading with strict listing qualifications, advanced electronic exchange facilities and the corresponding management method, over-the-counter trading is small-scale and diffused, with backward facilities, management styles, and institutions, leading to such problems as over-speculation, loose supervision, transaction disorder, and threats to the legal rights of investors. To guarantee the healthy development of securities markets, the government has decided to clear up and correct illegal over-the-counter trading and adjust the focus of various stock exchanges by shutting down those exchanges that fail to meet its criteria. This project is supposed to be completed by the end of 1999.

Advantageous Enterprises

Advantageous enterprises that have performed outstandingly during many years of market competition and possess dependable institutional bases and great potential should be granted priority and given great importance when they are listed. Objectivity and transparency in selecting listed companies should be emphasized, which means comparison and selection should be done out in the open according to objective standards that reflect the true operational situation of applicants. The national position of a company should be made one of the basic standards, so that in not too long a period the "pacemakers" of every industry will be able to enter the stock market, for it is the largest enterprises and enterprise groups with the most potential in China's future that will not doubt appear from them. Since the quota distribution system is still under operation, these pacemakers should be given priority by the localities and departments setting those quotas. The term "pacemaker" here refers not to partial regions, but to the whole country, for some enterprises do not rate very high nationally despite indeed excellent performance in several localities. The principle of equality among the various kinds of ownership form should also be adopted in selecting listed companies to replace the present system of "ownership discrimination". Any truly advantageous enterprise, be it entirely state-owned, state-share-held, state-share-purchased, or non-state-owned, should all be eligible for listing. It should be made clear that to list a company is to "add flowers to its brocade", rather than "sending coal in snowy weather". Any enterprise having operation problems ought not to be listed before it has satisfactorily solved its financial. Besides direct listing, unsuitable restrictions barring advantageous enterprises which enter the stock market by means of "shell-borrowing" and "shell-purchasing" should be lifted, and incentives should be enacted to promote leaving the good and weeding out the bad apples from the existing batch of listed companies.

The Fate of "Public Shares"

State-owned and the legal person shares of stock in listed companies — i.e. "public shares" — should be allowed to enter market circulation. Since the market and the technical conditions for the circulation of "public shares" have now come to maturity, circulation of the latter should not be delayed any longer. However, as market accession to "public shares", which account for three-quarters of the total capital of listed companies, may have some impact on the market, so access should be enacted step by step over a certain period according to the principle of positiveness and reliability. The first step may be to give the market access to the part of the state-owned and legal person shares that have already been transferred.

Reorganization of Assets by Advantageous Firms

Advantageous enterprises should be encouraged to reorganize their assets into various forms. In addition to acquisitions, mergers and "shell-purchasing" in the stock market, those advantageous enterprises among listed companies should be encouraged to re-organize into various forms other enterprises with advantages in capital, technology, brand, management and marketing networks. In some regions, listed companies have formed enterprise groups orchestrated on the basis of reorganization of other enterprises. This experience can be useful to other regions as well. Importance should be attached to eliminating the barriers posed by "strips" and "squares", as well as ownership bias, and encouraging reorganization beyond regional boundaries, business lines, and ownership system. Especially for those advantageous enterprises whose products will enter national and international markets, the reorganizational activity of eliminating such barriers will become their most important task. The government should implement necessary support policies in the fields of taxation, debt management, rearrangement of personnel, bank credit, and registration. A lack of capital is the major barrier in merging the enterprises at present. Financial channels supporting mergers are few and far between. For example, there is no such category for securing a bank loan anywhere in China. In the western countries, a financial system geared to mergers has developed to a complex degree. The "leverage purchase", which has become popular since the 1980s, includes more than ten kinds of financing methods. Among the available financial resources, first-class bank loans account for 60%, "double-layer bonds", also referred to as "trash bonds", 30%, while the internal capital of the purchasers accounts for only 10%. Therefore, there is a great deal of international experience in financial channels supporting mergers to help China on its way to corporate reorganization.

The Development of Investment Banks

Investment banks that can support the reorganization of enterprises should be actively developed by means of transformation, building and international cooperation. The reorganization of enterprises is a highly specialized activity that requires high intellectual input and support from all resources. In the developed countries investment banks usually provide this kind of service. Along with the daily increase in reorganizational activities, the need for investment banks emerges as the times demand, because the efforts of the enterprises by themselves is insufficient and far from effective. There are institutions in China that conduct securities and investment trust activities, but they have been involved in over-speculation to a certain degree in recent years, because many of them have paid too much attention to activity in the secondary market and "relation-building" in the primary market. Thus they lack knowledge of such modern investment banking operations as enterprise merger and the inner financial management of enterprises.

Under such circumstances, there is more than one measure that should be taken simultaneously to develop the business of investment banks. The first would to "transform", which means that the existing securities- and trust-related institutions will partly direct their profit-making activities towards the investment business. What should be pointed out here is that since most of these institutions are state-owned at present, they are very likely to turn to over-speculation under the current system. In the meantime, unlawful financing activities are encouraged due to a lack of financial resources. To solve these problems effectively, these institutions could be transformed into multiple share-holding companies. A second measure would be to "build new institutions". Generally speaking, there is still some room for developing such institutions in China, but any new ones must have a good start and high standards in their operating system and quality of business. Thirdly, there is the aspect of "international cooperation". This measure can be combined with the former two, but the foreign partners should be first-class institutions able to incorporate their experience into China's present reality.

The Development of Institutional Investors

During recent years a large number of individual investors have swarmed into the stock market; and since it is only possible to conduct stock transactions in large or intermediate sized cities, we may say that most families who reside there have had some relations with the stock exchanges. Although it is not surprising that "everybody plays the stock market", it is equally obvious that such a phenomenon has brought along with it risk and loss of efficiency. This is why it is an urgent task to develop institutional investors. Furthermore, the original management structure of enterprises cannot be influenced positively if there are too many individual investors in the stock market. By "institutional investor" we meant all types of investment fund, such as mutual funds, trust investment funds, and pension/insurance funds. They are all long-term and stable forces in the stock market, since specialists operate these funds with security, profit, flexibility and farsightedness.

Relationships between Enterprises and Banks

Relationships between enterprises and banks should be reconstructed during the development of capital markets. When we stress the importance of capital markets, we do not mean that bank financing is no longer important as a capital source for business enterprises. Actually, indirect financing by banks will continue to play the main role in the foreseeable future of supplying capital to enterprises. Consequently, the acceleration of restructuring and developing the banking system should become a mutually stimulating force to the development of capital markets. Along with continuing to accelerate the commercialization of state-owned specialized banks, new types of commercial banks should also be set up gradually under the principle of the modern corporate system. One of the experiences of China's economic reform has been to develop enterprises "outside the system" first, then promote the reform of enterprises "inside the system" when the latter cannot reform on their own. The reform of China's financial system may also not be able to avoid this process. Presently, in addition to solving similar problems faced by enterprises in other industries, the national banks also have their particular problems that they are finding hard to tackle. However, some newly founded commercial banks have shown business vigor and advantages. It is necessary to institute more and new types of commercial banks, for China's commercial banking system is insufficient in the light of the development of its economy and financial needs. Such a scarcity problem will be beneficial to promoting moderate competition among the country's financial institutions, and thus increasing the number of financial channels. At the same time, in instituting new types of commercial banks, advantageous enterprises will be encouraged to participate in each other's shares, so as to create more opportunities for the combination of industrial and financial capital.

References

China Statistics Yearbook, 1993-1998, China Statistics Press.

China Financial Yearbook, 1995-1998, China Financial Press.

China Stock and Futures Yearbook, China Financial and Economics Press, 1998.

Ma Hong and Lu Baifu (eds) (1998), *Macroeconomic Policy Report of China*, China Financial and Economics Press.

Ma Hong and Wang Mengkun (eds) (1998), *China Development Research*, China Development Press.

Statistics Quarterly Report of China Peoples Bank.

Wu Jingliam and Liu Shijin (1998), *Strategy Reorganization of the State-owned Economy*, China Development Press.

7 Financial Liberalization and Financial Crisis: The Case of Thailand

PRAKARN ARPHASIL

Introduction

Prior to the 1990s, the Thai financial system was highly regulated and well protected from both domestic and foreign competitions. Then Thailand launched the first stage of a series of financial reforms aiming at enhancing competition and efficiency in the system, relaxing restrictions on international capital flows, and developing Thailand as a restricted financial center. Success in sustaining high economic growth in the past and establishing strong economic fundamentals (see Table 7.1), maintenance of stability in the financial system, and international pressure on the financial opening of the country are the reasons attributed to the adoption of financial deregulation and liberalization. Despite a steady process in financial liberalization, huge foreign capital inflows via non-resident baht accounts and a rapid increase in international banking facilities to take an advantage of high rates of return exposed the Thai financial sector to rapid changes in the world financial market. Hence, Thai authorities expressed concern over the implementation of economic stabilization policies, particularly the impact of the foreign capital movement on the economy. Controlling inflation, stabilizing exchange rates, domestic liquidity management, prolonged current account deficit, and rising short-term debt would become critical problems in economic stabilization.[1] In addition, the integration of the Thai financial sector into the world financial market to some extent nullified the effectiveness of traditional monetary management policies.

The financial crisis broke out on July 2, 1997, seven years after the beginning of financial deregulation and liberalization. The crisis has been much deeper than anticipated and has affected not only individual countries, but also the whole East and Southeast Asian regions, contiguously spilling

Table 7.1 Macroeconomic Indicators, 1985-1997

	1985	1990	1995	1996	1997p	1998e
GDP Growth Rate	4.6	11.2	8.8	5.5	-0.4	-8.0
Inflation Rate	2.4	6.0	5.8	5.9	5.6	8.0
Current Account (as % of GDP)	-4.0	-8.3	-7.8	-7.9	-2.0	11.0
Investment (as % of GDP)	28.2	41.4	41.6	41.7	N.A.	N.A.
Savings (as % of GDP)	24.4	33.0	34.9	33.2	N.A.	N.A.
Exports (% change)	10.5	15.1	24.8	-1.9	3.8	-3.1
Imports (% change)	4.6	29.8	31.9	0.6	-13.4	-32.4
Balance of Payments a)	0.5	3.8	7.2	2.2	-10.6	1.7
Foreign Exchange Reserves a)	3.0	14.3	37.0	38.7	27.0	28.5
Fiscal Balance b)	-38,978	107,046	134,965	34,118	-26,707	N.A.
Exchange Rate (Baht/$)	27.16	25.59	24.92	25.34	31.37	41.37

Notes:
a) US$ billions
b) Baht millions
Sources: Bank of Thailand, NESDB, Stock Exchange of Thailand.

over into some Eastern Europe and Latin American countries. This diffusion makes remedial measures even more difficult, since its contagion has plagued the Thai economy through trade and capital movements. Some critics blame the crisis on financial deregulation and liberalization that the government initiated prior to liberalization that began in 1990. They were bereft of adequate and proper safeguards, adequate supervisory and financial infrastructure and efficient management of resource allocation. As is typically the case, such problems are rarely attributable to any single factor, but must be explain by a permutation or combination of numerous factors. The objective of this paper is to examine Thailand's financial deregulation and liberalization policy and the outbreak of financial crisis.

A brief review of the process of financial liberalization will be presented in Section 2. Section 3 investigates whether financial liberalization and financial crisis are related. Policy responses and measures implemented are assessed and discussed in Section 4. The final section provides some concluding remarks.

Financial Deregulation and Liberalization

Financial deregulation basically means relaxing supervisory constraints and less intervention by political authorities in financial markets, thereby allowing the market mechanism to work more freely. Deregulation began with the abolishment of interest rate ceilings in 1989. The acceptance of the obligations listed under Article VIII of the International Monetary Fund and the implementation of the first phase of exchange rate control relaxation in

1990 marked the first steps in financial liberalization. A chronology of the major reforms during 1989-1995 is presented in Appendix 7.1.

Removal of Interest Rate Ceilings

Under the first three-year financial reform plan, the Bank of Thailand fully liberalized the interest rate structure, thereby enabling the domestic financial system to adjust interest rate movements on the basis of supply and demand conditions. All types of interest rate ceilings for financial institutions were completely lifted in June 1992. Interest rate liberalization produces higher flexibility for commercial banks and financial institutions to manage their interest rate policies in accordance with their strategies and economic environments.

Foreign Exchange Control Relaxation

The official acceptance of the obligations listed under IMF Article VIII and implementation of the first phase of exchange control relaxation were important steps in the process of exchange control deregulation. Under favorable economic conditions in the late 1980s (*i.e.*, a strong position in foreign exchange reserves, a low debt-service ratio, manageable inflation rates, and a surplus in government balances), Thai authorities deemed that it was an appropriate time to liberalize the country's foreign exchange system.

Several foreign exchange controls were relaxed, rendering greater flexibility to private business and the general public in the purchase and sale of foreign currency, while retaining minimal controls to monitor and safeguard the system. The remaining controls are in the area of capital outflows. For example, residents and legal persons can open foreign currency accounts in Thailand. The requirement for government approval in capital outflows has been steadily minimized, except for the transfer of foreign exchange above a certain limit and the acquisition of real estate or investment in the stock market abroad.

Establishment of Bangkok International Banking Facilities

As part of the liberalization process and the regional financial center plan, the Bank of Thailand proposed the establishment of Bangkok International Banking Facilities (BIBF) in 1993 to (a) serve the increasingly sophisticated needs of international trade and investment, (b) promote the role of Bangkok as a center for raising capital and meet the needs of the Indochina countries in reconstructing their countries, (c) enhance the capacity of the financial and commercial banking business, ensure efficient services, prepare the system for intensified competition and open the Thai financial system in accordance with the WTO, and (d) finance government and private projects with cheap sources of funds.

The BIBF operations included taking deposits or borrowing in foreign currency from abroad, lending in foreign currency within Thailand (out-in) and abroad (out-out), non-baht cross currency foreign exchange transactions, giving to bills guaranteeing any debts denominated in foreign currencies to non-residents, undertaking financial transactions that involve international trade among currencies to non-residents, search-financing from foreign sources, and acting as a party in loan syndication. In addition, BIBF could also engage in other investment banking services, such as undertaking financial transactions which involve investment feasibility studies, financial advisory services for business acquisitions, takeovers or mergers, and arranging or underwriting debt instruments for selling abroad.

To promote financial services in provincial areas, the government also granted licenses for Provincial International Banking Facilities (PIBF). The funding of PIBFs had to originate from overseas, and its offices were to be located outside of Bangkok and its periphery. In addition to extending credit in foreign currency, PIBFs were allowed to extend out-in credit in baht to provincial customers and do foreign exchange business (against baht) with customers.

Relaxation of Constraints on Portfolio Management of Financial Institutions

In the past, a mandatory measure had stipulated that commercial banks hold a specified minimum amount of government and other eligible bonds as a branch-opening requirement. However, the requirement was completely abolished in 1993 to allow commercial banks to manage their tapped financial resources better. Moreover, the Bank of Thailand encouraged commercial banks and financial institutions to open branches in rural areas. This policy attempted to promote savings mobilization and financial redistribution by making credit availability and providing financial services in rural areas. It implicitly gave financial advantage to local financial institutions to widen and network their customer bases in preparation for foreign competition.

Expansion of the Scope of Activities of Financial Institutions

To improve the quantity and quality of financial services and encourage competition among local financial institutions before a full-scale liberalization, the Bank of Thailand broadened the scope of financial operations in gradual steps to maintain stability in the system. The concept of a universal banking system was basically applied, so that financial institutions such as commercial banks, finance companies, and capital companies would be able with certain reservations for particular lines of financial business, to compete more freely and fairly in the same activities.

To maintain stability and solvency of the financial system in a more competitive environment, the quality of supervision and regulation of financial institutions and their activities was modernized and made more advanced and efficient in step with financial liberalization. To this end, policy transparency, prudential requirements, and efficiency of supervision in terms of regulatory guidelines and supervisory techniques were introduced. Important measures included the adoption of the risk-asset ratio, the establishment of a Securities and Exchange Commission (SEC), and the separation of finance and security companies.

Capital Adequacy

The adoption of the Bank for International Settlements (BIS) guideline on capital adequacy for financial institutions beginning in 1993 to replace the capital risk asset ratio was a consistent move to comply with international standards in the process of financial liberalization.

The Bank of Thailand practically modified capital adequacy into first-tier and second-tier capital. First-tier capital comprises paid-up capital, retained earnings, reserves appropriated from net profits and statutory reserves. Second-tier capital includes revaluation of land and buildings and certain types of instruments issued by banks, such as hybrid debt capital instruments and subordinated term debts. Risk assets are then weighted by degree of risk according to the BIS guideline.

Establishment of a Securities and Exchange Commission

In synchronization with the liberalization of the money and financial markers, the Securities and Exchange Commission Act was enacted in March 1992. The Act established the Securities and Exchange Commission to supervise, lay down a framework for, and facilitates the development of securities businesses. Qualified companies are now able to mobilize funds through debt instruments in domestic and foreign markets, lowering the costs of debt in comparison to borrowing from financial institutions. The Act allows other financial institutions, in addition to capital companies, take part in the securities business, thus fully expanding the scope of the securities industry under licenses and resulting in more competition in capital markets.

The SEC Act also provided for the Over-the-Counter Center (OTC) to be set up in 1995 to handle unlisted securities trading. The Bangkok Stock Dealing Center (BSDC) was established as an alternative fund-raising source for small and medium enterprises. Unfortunately, it has failed to attract many of these firms to its listing. Only three companies were registered at the end of 1998. The capital gains tax represents the most serious impediment to the development of the BSDC. Currently, BSDC-listed stocks are not exempt from capital gains taxes while stocks listed on the Stock Exchange of Thailand (SET) enjoy the benefits of tax exemption. To facilitate and promote the development of debt instruments for long-term finance, a credit rating agency, the Thai Rating Information Service (TRIS) was established in July 1993. TRIS's credit ratings provide important information for investors in the form of fair and objective assessment of the quality of its bonds.

The Onset of the Financial Crisis

Various studies (for example, Radelet and Sachs, 1998 and Corsetti, Pesenti, and Roubini, 1998) have extensively outlined the outbreak of the Asian financial crisis. Most of them point out that growing imbalances and financial weaknesses in the Asian economies are responsible for the crisis, even though their economies achieved rapid growth during the early 1990s. A rapid buildup of short-term external debts into a weak financial system is cited also as an important factor. Their successful track records of high economic growth with stability and steady financial market liberalization, which opened new channels for foreign capital flow into domestic markets, led to overconfidence concerning policy management and underestimation of the risks caused by the financial liberalization. Capital inflows led to appreciating real exchange rates, rapidly expanding bank lending, sharply rising external debt, and especially increasing vulnerability to reversal in capital flows.

In this section, rather than analyze the various causes of the financial crisis in Thailand, the discussion will focus on role played by financial liberalization; that is, how the process of financial liberalization and deregulation initiated in 1990 led to the financial crisis of 1997.

Surges in Capital Flows

From 1990, international capital flows to emerging countries, particularly to Asia increased remarkably. A rapid internationalization of savings in most developed countries led to the international diversification of investment portfolios. Surges in capital flows to emerging markets were therefore in response to slowdowns in the industrialized countries and concurrent rapid growth in the emerging economies.

In addition, these markets, particularly in Asia and Latin America, were in the process of financial liberalization and financial deregulation as a means to attract and capture the vast amount of available financial resources from the developed countries at relatively low costs, resulting in a sharp rise in external debt.

Two characteristics distinguish foreign capital flows in Asian market from those in Latin America. First, during the early 1990s, foreign capital in Asian markets was much more aimed towards short-term flows than was the case in Latin America. Secondly, unlike Latin America, capital flows into Asia were preceded rather than followed by surges in investment (Pedro Alba, *et al.*, 1998).

After financial reform towards deregulation and liberalization in 1990, a surge of international capital inflows into Thailand became evident, averaging about 10% of GDP during 1990-1995. At the macroeconomic level, foreign capital inflows bridged a rising investment-savings gap, leading to high investment and robust growth and paid for the ballooning current account deficit of the early 1990s. Moreover, these inflows generated positive microeconomic effects, such as lowering firms' costs of capital.

The composition of capital inflows evolved over the period and appeared responsive to regulatory reforms and incentives for capital inflows. The major composition of capital inflows during 1992-1998 were BIBF borrowing, portfolio investment, non-resident baht accounts, and foreign direct investment (see Table 7.2). Net direct investment inflows (FDI) had contributed to the initial strengthening of capital accounts in the late 1980s; however, net portfolio inflows became important with the establishment of BIBFs and the occurrence of large interest rate differentials. A growing proportion of the net inflows—BIBF borrowing, portfolio investment, and non-resident baht accounts—was short-term in nature. The sharp increase in non-FDI caused a buildup in the banking system's short-term foreign liabilities and Thailand's short-term private debt. As a result, Thai financial markets became more vulnerable to a risk of the sudden reversal of short-term capital, which eventually led to balance of payments and banking crises.[2]

Table 7.2 Private Capital Flows

(Unit : US$ millions)

	1992	1993	1994	1995	1996	1997
Bank	1,931.14	3,595.30	13,910.74	11,222.83	5,002.80	-8,104.18
Commercial bank	1,931.14	-4,034.83	3,833.64	3,099.64	427.90	-5,630.16
BIBFs	-	7,630.13	10,077.10	8,123.19	4,574.90	-2,474.02
Non-bank	7,407.44	6,710.35	-1,908.39	9,549.32	13,172.22	-1,544.95
Direct investment	1,977.56	1,437.44	900.95	1,166.29	1,453.16	3,355.63
Foreign direct investment	2,113.82	1,730.33	1,321.71	2,001.89	2,268.03	3,751.64
Thai direct investment abroad	-136.26	-292.89	-420.76	-835.59	-814.88	-396.02
Others loans	2,722.76	-2,417.97	-5,832.60	1,528.61	5,446.80	-4,246.89
Portfolio investment	555.28	4,843.13	1,093.56	3,279.33	3,482.32	4,430.35
Equity securities	453.23	2,679.70	-408.87	2,117.13	1,122.22	3,899.30
Debt securities	102.05	2,163.43	1,502.43	1,162.20	2,360.10	531.05
Non-resident baht accounts	1,752.64	2,679.03	2,033.52	3,377.33	2,910.97	-4,981.67
Trade credits	306.89	538.47	455.15	255.34	-146.09	-404.18
Others	997.83	-369.75	-558.97	-57.58	25.06	301.82
Total	9,338.58	10,305.65	12,002.35	20,772.15	18,175.02	-9,649.12

Source: Bank of Thailand.

The causes of the continuous rise in capital inflows during the early 1990s can be summarized as follows:

1. High domestic investment-savings gap about 6-8% and financing rising current account deficit. The fact that the investment-savings gap and the current account deficit rose steadily during the early 1990s to a high of 8% of GDP in 1996 required financing by foreign savings. Financial liberalization rendered new avenues and opportunities for access to cheap financial sources to finance them, such that the gap was widened through substituting domestic savings the deficit widened through higher domestic spending.
2. The establishment of BIBFs and incentives to engage into aggressive lending, particularly to BIBFs, in order to gain commercial bank licenses due to licensing being asset-based rather than capital-based.
3. A relative fixed exchange rate against the US dollar and implicit public guarantees to financial institutions. These factors encouraged excessive private foreign borrowing, most of which was financed substantially by unhedged and progressively greater short-term borrowing.
4. High interest rate differentials. The 7-8% differentials were the result of weak competition in financial markets and government policy to maintain high domestic interest rates in order to control inflation and rising current account deficits. The relatively high domestic interest rates, together with fixed foreign exchange rates, attracted short-term foreign funds, especially in the form of non-resident baht accounts, to reap a higher rate of return to deposits in Thai financial institutions.

Adverse Impacts of Massive Foreign Capital Flows

The heavy influx of foreign capital into Thailand during the early 1990s generated both positive—increased competition in financial markets and new opportunities for financial development—and negative impacts. The negative impacts that led to the financial crisis were:

High debt-equity ratios Except for the subsidiaries of the multinational corporations, companies in the Thai private sector, including those listed on the Stock Exchange of Thailand (SET) have long been dominated by family businesses. In general, families have displayed little willingness to relinquish control over their firms; and as the economy rapidly grew along with the capital account liberalization of the early 1990s, they borrowed heavily to finance aggressive investment expansion. As a result, their debt dependence continuously rose (see Table 7.3). The highly leveraged firms among them, especially those borrowing from abroad, thus became vulnerable to increased interest rates and baht devaluation.

Table 7.3 Debt-Equity Ratios of Listed Companies

Sector	Debt to Equity ratio (times)					
	1992	1993	1994	1995	1996	1997
Construction materials	1.78	1.99	1.95	2.1	2.73	6.71
Chemicals and plastics	2.07	1.88	1.07	1.32	1.79	2.87
Communications	0.61	0.78	1.03	1.28	1.85	3.11
Electrical products and Computer	2.3	2.04	1.89	2.36	2.38	4.93
Energy	1.15	1.46	1.24	1.4	1.51	2.49
Property development	1.32	1.56	1.76	1.81	1.91	2.79
Paper and pulp	2.26	2.33	1.78	1.9	2.65	8.42

Source: Stock Exchange of Thailand.

Table 7.4 Sources of Corporate Funding in Thailand

				(Unit : US$ billions)
	1995	1996	1997	1998(Jan.-Jun.)
Recapitalization in SET	5.20	4.60	2.00	4.50
Issuance of corporate debentures	3.51	5.60	1.40	0.09
Private capital flow (non-bank)	9.50	13.20	-1.50	-1.90
Change in bank lending (including BIBF credits)	33.60	24.10	12.50	-6.60
Change in finance company lending	11.50	8.20	-6.50	-19.20
Total	63.31	55.70	7.90	-23.11

Source: Bank of Thailand, (1998).

The structure of corporate financing in Thailand indicates that before the crisis, the major source of corporate financing was debt-finance through financial institutions, rather than equity-finance via the (see Table 7.4). Direct financing and the development of long-term debt instruments were new to Thai corporations, from the time the Securities and Exchange Commission Act was enacted in 1992. In addition, fear of relinquishing family control over a firm and strict procedures for public offering explain why Thai companies preferred indirect financing through financial institutions prior to the SEC Act.

Misallocation of resources and asset price bubble According to the Bank of Thailand, most commercial bank loans were made to priority sectors, mainly the manufacturing and export industries. However, it was discovered that a significant proportion of these loans were re-lent by these firms to their subsidiaries to purchase land and invest in real estate (Bank of Thailand Economic Focus, 1998 "Focus on the Thai Crisis"). This caused a rapid increase in land prices and the value of real estate.

Real estate and property loans played a significant role in the Thai credit market during 1990-1997, accounting for about 13-15% of total loans (see Table 7.5). With a real estate price boom in full swing, financial institutions provided loans readily without spending many resources on valuing the underlying collateral, because of the belief that the gains would be substantial. Financial institutions therefore, tended to take on risky investments in expectation of high profits, making them less prudent in monitoring their clients' investment and in taking appropriate action against borrowers who showed signs of financial deterioration. The growing risk inherent in the financial system was unfortunately overshadowed by the real estate and stock market booms.

The establishment of the BIBFs enhanced resource misallocation. For example, this move unexpectedly provided a second boom in the real estate sector. As early as 1994, it became obvious to observers of real estate

Table 7.5 Bill, Loans and Overdrafts of Commercial Banks According to Industry (As of December 1997)

					(Unit: Baht millions)
Type	1990	1991	1995	1996	1997
Construction	59,321.8	72,095.1	185,850.3	236,340.8	273,064.4
Real Estate	177,699.0	207,140.3	400,184.3	426,100.1	490,521.2
Construction and Real Estate	237,020.8	279,235.4	586,034.6	662,440.9	763,585.6
Total	1,494,062.3	1,807,558.1	4,250,824.5	4,855,687.5	6,059,956.0
Share of Construction and					
Real Estate in total (%)	15.86	15.45	13.79	13.64	12.60

Source: Bank of Thailand.

prospects that oversupply had finally arrived. Sales began to falter. Without the BIBFs, many real estate firms would have gone under sooner and caused a credit crunch and instability of the financial system a few years earlier; but their collapse would have not been as critical as what has happened recently (Siamwalla, 1998).

The stock market boom of 1990-1994 (see Table 7.6) helped fuel an upswing in the real estate cycle. During this period, 46 property companies and 35 construction firms were newly listed on the Stock Exchange of Thailand for the purpose of exploiting the boom in mobilizing a cheaper source of funds from the public. Moreover, many of them issued various kinds of debentures, such as convertible debentures and debentures with warrants in the Eurobond market. These property firms as a group were highly leveraged with the debt-equity ratio of about 150%. Therefore, it is not surprising that the liabilities of property and construction companies represented a majority share (53%) of the total liabilities of all distressed listed companies whose operating cash flows could not cover interest expenses by September 1997 (Bertrand Renaud, Ming Zhang, and Stefan Koeberle, 1998).

Table 7.6 SET Index Movement: 1990-1998

	1990	1991	1992	1993	1994	1995	1996	1997
SET index								
Daily Trading	613	711	893	1,683	1,360	1,281	832	373
Value								
(average)	2,539	3,237	7,531	8,984	8,628	6.24	5,341	3,764

Source: Stock Exchange of Thailand.

Table 7.7 External Debt

							(Unit : US$ billions)
	1991	1992	1993	1994	1995	1996	1997
1.Total Debt	37.9	43.6	52.1	64.9	82.6	90.5	86.2
Public Debt	12.8	13.1	14.2	15.7	16.4	16.8	17.2
Private Debt	25.1	30.6	37.9	49.2	66.2	73.7	69.0
Banks	4.5	6.3	13.0	28.0	41.9	41.7	39.6
Commercial banks	4.5	6.3	5.3	9.9	14.4	10.6	9.5
BIBFs	-	-	7.7	18.1	27.5	31.1	30.1
Non-banks	20.6	24.3	24.9	21.2	24.2	21.3	29.5
2.Short Term Debt/							
Total Debt (%)	40.5	43.3	43.4	44.9	48.0	41.5	37.3
3.Debt/Export (%)	103.7	104.2	107.2	112.9	114.2	111.4	119.6
4.Debt/GDP (%)	38.3	39.2	41.7	45.3	49.3	48.9	N.A.
5.Debt Service Ratio (%)	10.6	11.3	11.2	11.7	11.4	16.5	20.5

Source: Bank of Thailand.

Sharp rise in short-term external debts   Corresponding to massive capital flows during the early 1990s, the structure of Thailand's external debt changed remarkably with bank debt (including BIBFs loans) increasing from US$ 4.5 billion at the end of 1991 to US$ 41.7 billion at the end of 1996. However, the figure moderately fell in 1997 as foreign creditors called their money back (see Table 7.7) as a result of the financial crisis. Meanwhile, non-bank private debt continuously rose from US$ 20.6 billion in 1991 to US$ 29.5 billion in 1997. Altogether the share of total external debt occupied by bank and non-bank external debt—i.e., private external debt— rose significantly from 66% in 1991 to 80% in 1997.

BIBF operations led to a shortening of Thailand's external debt maturity. Prior to their establishment, Thai residents tended to borrow directly from abroad mainly through banks in such offshore financial centers as Hong Kong and Singapore. These inflows were recorded as non-bank borrowings in balance of payments accounting. The maturity structure of these inflows was based on the wording of original loan contracts concerning either short-or long-term maturity. BIBF banks are treated as a part of Thailand's banking system. To measure capital inflows, balance of payments accountants record inflows to BIBFs from abroad rather than the amounts lent by BIBFs to Thai residents. While this change did not affect the total size of the inflows, it affected their maturity structure. For example, in the case where Thai residents borrowed long-term from BIBFs, while the BIBFs fund this lending through a revolving facility of short-term credit from abroad, the balance of payments accountants recorded this transaction as short-term capital inflows. This mismatching caused debt and bank crises when the currency crisis struck.

From that time on, with rapid growth in BIBF lending, the reported short-term liabilities of banks in Thailand increased dramatically, reflecting short-term funding by BIBFs, despite a significant amount lending through revolving facilities. As a result, Thailand's reported short-term external debt rose from US$ 15.3 billion in 1991 to US$ 37.6 billion in 1996. By contrast, the continued fiscal surplus during 1988-1996, together with the government's cautious policy regarding external public sector borrowing, helped external debt to rise only marginally and lowered the share of public external debt from 33.8% in 1991 to 18.6% in 1996.

Some ratios may assist in analyzing Thailand's ability to repay its external debt. During 1991-1995, the debt service ratio and the ratio of debt to exports were stabilized to some extent (see Table 7.7). These ratios moderately rose in 1996 and 1997 as Thai exports unexpectedly declined 1.9 % in 1996 and slightly rose in 1997 as a result of the sharp devaluation of the baht, indicating relative inability to service external debt.

Appreciation in the real effective foreign exchange rate One of the consequences caused by the heavy inflow of foreign capital during the early 1990s was a slow rise in the real foreign exchange rate. Even though the baht was relatively fixed against the dollar, rising inflation rates in Thailand after 1994 relative to declining annual rates in the U.S. steadily inched up the real exchange rate.

Based on Thailand's real effective exchange rate (REER) against the composite REER of 25 countries during 1990-1998, we find that real

Table 7.8 Comparison between Thailand's REER and Composite REER of 25 Competing Countries a)

Year	Thai REER b)	REER of 25 competing country b)	Baht/US$
Dec-90	92.8	99.1	25.17
1991	92.3	90.0	25.35
1992	92.4	99.3	25.45
1993	92.9	99.6	25.42
1994	92.2	98.9	25.07
1995	95.1	98.3	25.14
1996	98.1	99.6	25.53
1997	63.5	99.2	47.25
1998	81.2	99.8	36.68

Notes:
a) Competing countries include 9 in Europe, 3 in Asia, 2 in Latin America, Canada and the United States.
b) June 30, 1997 is the base year.
Source: Bank of Thailand.

Table 7.9 Net Private Capital Movements

(Unit: US$ millions)

Period	Banks			Non-banks				Total
	Commercial Banks	BIBFs	Direct Investment	Portfolio	Loans	Non-resident baht Accounts	Others	
1996 Q1	-2325	1,751	486	1,138	922	3,701	121	5,794
Q2	589	1,893	307	910	1,756	209	27	5,691
Q3	1,661	145	341	830	1,681	-1202	-216	3,240
Q4	419	4,579	1,454	3,484	5,447	2,922	-120	18,185
1997 Q1	1,768	662	514	507	-112	-1590	190	1,939
Q2	41	-96	540	1,071	-853	-1786	51	-1032
Q3	-3057	-761	855	2,137	-900	-3800	357	-5169
Q4	-2321	-1575	581	279	-1680	2,199	98	-2419
1998 Q1	491	-2507	1,340	482	-1951	-2116	118	-4143
Q2	-2866	-2322	1,555	140	-1070	-2312	-215	-2466
Q3	-4175	-1927	1,220	-15	-753	780	0	-4852

Source: Bank of Thailand.

appreciation of the baht significantly increased after 1994. This implies thatThailand's competitiveness against those 25 countries slowly eroded as the difference between the two REERs was very small in December 1996 (see Table 7.8). This real appreciation undermined the competitiveness of Thailand's traded goods, leading to a contraction in exports in 1996, and widened the current account deficit. Moreover, real appreciation indirectly encouraged domestic resources to be utilized to produce for domestic demand rather than for export. Thailand's currency competitiveness improved markedly after the sharp baht devaluation in July 1997.

Reversal of capital flows   To date, major reversals of capital flows have occurred in many developing countries, such as Mexico, Turkey, and Venezuela. A common reason for most of these reversals is a lack of confidence in domestic macroeconomic policy. Reversals usually take place in a fixed exchange rate system. If the growth rate of domestic credit permanently exceeds that of the nominal demand for money, the minimum level of reserves will eventually be reached, creating a balance of payments crisis. Authorities have no choice but float or devalue the exchange rate. A speculative attack and reversals of capital flows then take place because economic agents will try to avoid capital loss on their domestic money holdings once the fixed exchange rate collapses (Krugman, 1979).

Recently, several symptoms of currency crisis have been studied in order to provide an early warning system for governments to adopt preemptive measures. For example, Calvo (1996) points out that the 1994 experience in Mexico showed that a balance of payments crisis could result not only from current accounts and fiscal deficits, but also from financial vulnerability. Thailand's net private capital inflows were a sign of heavy reversal of foreign capital flow in the first quarter of 1997, as total net private capital sharply declined compared to previous periods. Capital flows into a non-resident baht account and loans are recorded negative (Table 7.9). From the second half of 1997 to the third quarter of 1998, commercial bank loans, BIBF loans, private loans, and capital in non-resident baht accounts played a vital role in capital reversals after the onset of the currency crisis. Loss of confidence by both foreign creditor and investor was attributed to these reversals.

Policy Responses and Measures Implemented

The massive capital inflows during the early 1990s caused concern on the part of monetary authorities because they created excessive liquidity in the money markets, resulting in higher inflation, rising current account deficits, and mounting external debt. While several measures were being introduced to stem the influx of foreign capital, instability gradually emerged in financial system, requiring the government to take urgent action. The currency crisis broke out in July 2, 1997 after a series of speculative attacks on the exchange rate system. This currency crisis demanded immediate actions to restore foreign investor confidence and restructure the weakening financial system as foreign creditors and investors pulled their money back, causing a credit crunch and a banking crisis. The more important measures implemented shortly before and after the crisis can be summarized as follows.

Measures to Deter Capital Inflows

Successive measures were adopted to slow down short-term capital inflows. In April 1996, finance and securities companies were required to maintain liquidity reserves at the Bank of Thailand equal to 7% of non-resident baht borrowing or deposits with maturity of less than one year, including the issuance of promissory notes, bills of exchange, and non-certificate deposits.

This measure was later extended to short-term borrowing or deposits from abroad (in baht and in foreign currency) of commercial banks, finance companies, and BIBFs. In addition, the minimum requirement for BIBF borrowing was raised from US$ 500,000 to US$ 1,000,000 so that small sized borrowings were excluded from offshore funds. These measures succeeded in slowing capital inflows to some extent, as total private capital inflows were reduced moderately from US$ 20.77 billion in 1995 to US$ 18.18 billion in 1996. However, they could not correct resource misallocation to unproductive sectors.

Foreign Exchange Market Intervention

A series of major speculative attacks on the Thai baht were observed in December 1996, February 1997, and May 1997. These attacks stemmed from deteriorating economic fundamentals, looming problems in the financial sector, and widespread rumors of baht devaluation. Foreign investor confidence was shaken, prompting withdrawal of investment capital out of Thailand. However, various forms of market intervention helped restore confidence as well as expel the baht devaluation rumors.

Sterilization   Typically, the first line of defense in a fixed exchange rate regime involves some form of sterilized intervention in the spot and/or forward exchange market. When intervention takes place in the spot market, reductions in the monetary base resulting from central bank sales of foreign exchange apply upward pressure on the interest rate. To keep the rising interest rate in check so that it will not jeopardize the real sector, the central bank will have to partially or completely sterilize the monetary impact of its intervention by injecting the money supply back into the system, usually through open market operations. While intervention in the forward market does not involve any immediate reduction in the monetary base, it involves an offsetting action at the time the forward contract matures. The ability to sustain a program of sterilized intervention is ultimately constrained by the size of a country's foreign exchange reserves and the resources the country can obtain from other official institutions or by borrowing in the international market.

Because a speculative attack requires the establishment of a net short position in domestic currency, Thailand employed a number of tactics to raise the cost of short positions. When sterilized intervention fails to stem capital outflows, short-term interest rates are allowed to rise making it more costly for speculators to obtain a net short position by borrowing domestic currency.

During the period of heavy capital outflows from late 1996 to the middle of May 1997, foreign exchange market intervention was carried out by the Bank of Thailand to defend the currency peg. The Bank of Thailand heavily manipulated not only the local exchange market but also offshore spot and forward exchanges markets, such as those in Singapore and Hong Kong. In addition, buy/sell swap transactions were occasionally used in order to prevent a sharp rise in interest rates.

Imposition of a two-tiered foreign exchange market Another form of speculative defense was the creation of a two–tiered foreign exchange market consisting of an onshore market, where there was normal supply of baht, and an offshore market, where baht was scarce. This selective capital control aimed specifically at denying foreign speculators access to domestic currency credit.[3]

In response to government pressure, banks refused to provide short-term credit to speculators, effectively segmenting the onshore and offshore markets, and sales of baht for dollars by speculators to nonresidents were limited to the spot foreign-exchange markets, raising speculators' costs. In addition, it was required that proceeds of sales of foreign holdings of Thai stocks for baht on the Stock Exchange of Thailand be converted into dollars at the onshore rate.

In the absence of extensive liquidation of baht positions by domestic residents, Thailand was able to withstand pressures on the baht through these two measures until early July 1997. Attempts to arbitrage the differential between onshore and offshore rates continued. The Bank of Thailand also intervened quietly to supply foreign currency to the market. The foreign reserves depleted continuously as a result of defending the baht against at least three major attacks by speculators from late 1996 to mid-1997.

Reserve depletion was hidden from the public by the forward sale of its dollars to support the baht. The reported foreign exchange reserve came down from US$ 38.7 billion at the beginning of 1997 to US$ 33.8 billion at the end of June 1997. Net foreign reserves after deducting forward sales were about US$ 2.5 billion at the end of June 1997. Finally, on July 2 the Bank of Thailand abandoned the baht's peg to its traditional currency basket and the baht immediately depreciated sharply against the US dollar.

Measures to Avert Financial Fragility

The liberalization of interest rates and capital account transactions set off a credit boom mostly financed by short-term borrowings from abroad. When the real estate market collapsed in 1996, the loan problems of finance companies began to spread, causing them liquidity problems. In March 1997, 10 finance companies were ordered to increase their capital. The property Loan Management Organization (PLMO) was set up to purchase and manage property loans from financial institutions, thereby helping to ease pressure on their balance sheets. This did not prevent a further loss of confidence, and translated into an increase in withdrawal of funds from other finance companies as well as smaller banks and deposit of them into larger domestic and foreign banks. This flight resulted in the build-up of excess liquidity in some institutions. Larger banks were reluctant to lend their liquidity to other financial institutions.

The inter-bank market became segmented between larger banks, on the one hand, and smaller banks and finance companies, on the other. This prompted the Financial Institutions Development Fund (FIDF)[4] to extend liquidity support through revolving-lending of the excess liquidity of the larger banks to weaker institutions, accelerating reserve money growth.

These difficulties forced the authorities to suspend additional 42 finance companies in August 1997. The authorities also extended a comprehensive guarantee to the depositors and creditors of the remaining financial institutions. Financial restructuring plans were announced in October 1997 and early 1998. In December 1997, 56 out of the 58 suspended finance companies were closed.

The IMF Package

A few weeks after baht floatation, Thailand finally sought assistance from the International Monetary Fund (IMF) for stand-by credit in order to restore foreign investors' confidence and build up depleting foreign reserves. A package of US$ 17.2 billion, including bilateral and multilateral assistance from other donors, was granted in August 1997. The package included a policy framework aimed at price and exchange rate stability, restructuring the weakening financial system, and economic recovery. Thailand followed the IMF's guidelines with some adjustments as follows.

Monetary policy   The primary objective of monetary policy during the early crisis period was to stabilize the baht and prices. A high interest rate policy was initially implemented to relieve inflationary pressures from the sharp devaluation and restore the stability of the baht. However, achieving baht and price stability by means of tight monetary later caused a sharp contraction of the economy in 1998 and increased financial instability as non-performing loans were continuously rising to critical levels.[5] As a result, monetary policy was later relaxed in recognition of an unexpected economic depression in 1998 and that the exchange rate and prices had became more stable.

Fiscal policy   The original IMF program required the overall public sector to accumulate a surplus of 1% of GDP for partially funding FIDF in its financial sector restructuring efforts. However, due to a misinterpretation of the impacts of the currency crisis, this fiscal austerity policy was partially responsible for throwing the Thai economy into a deep recession. Acknowledging the problem, the IMF later allowed Thailand to pursue fiscal stimuli for cushioning against rapid contraction, particularly of domestic demand, and for safeguarding against adverse social impacts arising from increased unemployment.

Financial sector restructuring   To strengthen the financial system, the government adopted a more structured approach to deal with suspended financial institutions, strengthen the remaining opened institutions, and restore confidence and stability in the economy. For example, the FIDF was authorized to provide guarantees for deposits and liabilities of the financial institutions to prevent further bank runs and systematic risk as well as quickly restore public confidence. In addition, the Financial Sector Restructuring Authority (FRA) and the Asset Management Corporation (AMC) were established. The FRA was to oversee the liquidation process of the 58 suspended finance companies, whereas the AMC was to bid for the lowest quality assets as a buyer of last resort to prevent "fire sales" of assets of closed finance companies.

Modernization of legal and regulatory framework Upgrading the legal and regulatory framework of the financial sector is necessary to improve and strengthen prudential regulation and supervision, as well as facilitate corporate debt restructuring. Modernization was planned to restore creditor confidence to extend credit to troubled firms without undermining their right of subsequent recovery and to lure foreign investors back to Thailand. For example, revising foreclosure and bankruptcy laws in line with international standard was hoped allow and accelerate the orderly resolution of the rising amount of non-performing loans.

Conclusion

Seven years after financial deregulation and liberalization, Thailand's whole financial system found itself badly damaged by financial crisis, which plunged Thailand into a severe recession. Although the crisis of July 1997 was triggered by an unsustainable macroeconomic policy mix of financial liberalization without effective management of capital flows and the foreign exchange rate, weaknesses in the financial sector and in financial supervision were the major factors behind the depth of the crisis.

Two points regarding the connection between financial liberalization and financial crisis require special attention. First, financial deregulation and liberalization exposed threats to financial stability through capital movements. They allowed financial intermediaries to gain too easy access to risky investments and to misallocate resources. Secondly, it was not financial liberalization per se that lay at the root of the problem, but rather the inadequacy of prudential supervision and regulation. There are important roles for policies that encourage adherence to international standards for accounting, auditing, and information disclosure, that facilitate enforcement of sound rules of corporate governance, and that protect investors and creditors from fraud and other unfair practices.

The crisis has taught Thailand an expensive lesson — expensive because its impact has dragged on and spread across economic and social sectors. Many experts have begun questioning continuing commitment to economic and financial liberalization. Various forms of capital controls have recently been discussed. Nevertheless, in comply with the IMF's guidelines, the crisis has in fact accelerated the need to liberalize across all economic sectors and to welcome in greater foreign participation, since Thailand sorely needs foreign capital to repair the damage that has been done. Such is the case in the financial sector. Foreign capital will soon account for a notable share of banking equity, bringing a structural change to the finance industry. To maximize the economic benefits of increasing foreign participation, financial and supervisory reform is required to introduce more effective mechanisms in monitoring and addressing banking problems, as well as enforcing sound regulation. It should be noted that if the IMF program fails to bring about the concrete rebound that the public anticipates in the near future, political and social forces could lead to modification and political change.

Notes

[1] See, for example, 'Analyzing Thailand's current account deficit' Jan-Mar 1996, and 'Analyzing Thailand's short-term debt', Jul-Sept 1996, Bank of Thailand.
[2] The rise in short-term foreign debt through foreign capital inflows after the introduction of BIBFs concerned the Bank of Thailand. However, the low risk of capital reversal due to strong economic fundamentals and high foreign exchange reserves mitigated that worry (see 'Analyzing Thailand's short-term debt', *Bank of Thailand Economic Focus*, 1996).
[3] Foreign exchange transactions associated with trade flows, foreign direct investment, and equity investment were excluded from this measure.
[4] The role and duties of the FIDF are to provide liquidity assistance to financial institutions, provide guarantees to depositors and creditors, act on behalf of the authorities in exchanging promissory notes for depositors and creditors, and souring liquidity for the note exchange scheme.
[5] At the end of 1998, non-performing loans in the banking sector accounted for about 46% of the total.

References

Alba, Pedro, Amar Bhattacharya, Stijn Claessens, Swati Ghosh, and Leonardo Hermandez, (1998), 'Volatility and Contagion in a Financially-Integrated World: Lessons from East Asia's Recent Experience', *Working Paper*, World Bank.
Arphasil, Prakarn, (1996), 'Financial Liberalization and Its Impacts on Thai Financial Market', Paper presented at the East Asian Economic Association.
Bank of Thailand, (1996), 'Analyzing Thailand's Current Account Deficit', *Bank of Thailand Economic Focus*, Vol. 1, No. 1.
Bank of Thailand, (1996), 'Analyzing Thailand's Short-term Debt', *Bank of Thailand Economic Focus*, Vol., 1, No. 3.
Bank of Thailand, (1998), 'Focus on the Thai Crisis', *Bank of Thailand Economic Focus*, Vol. 2, No. 2.
Calvo, G., (1996), 'Capital Flows and Macroeconomic Management: Tequila Lessons', *International Journal of Finance Economics*, Vol.1.
Jolmson, R. Barry, Salim M. Darbar, and Claudia Eche verria, (1997), 'Sequencing Capital Account Liberalization: Lessons from the Experiences in Chile, Indonesia, Korea, and Thailand', 1997, *IMF Working Paper*, International Monetary Fund.

Kochhar, Kalpana, Prakash Loungani, and Mark R. Stone, (1998), 'The East Asian Crisis: Macroeconomic Developments and Policy Lessons', *IMF Working Paper*, International monetary Fund.

Krugman, Paul, (1979), 'A Model of Balance of Payments Crises', *Journal of Money, Credit, and Banking*, Vol.11.

Min, Hong G, (1998), 'Dynamic Capital Mobility, Capital Market Risk and Exchange Rate Misalignment: Evidence from seven Asian Countries', *Working Paper*, the World Bank.

Radelet, Steven and Jeffrey Sachs, (1998), 'The East Asian Financial Crisis: Diagnosis, Remedies, Prospects', *Working Paper*, Harvard Institute for International Development.

Renaud, Bertrand, Ming Zhang, and Stefan Koeberle, (1998), 'How the Thai Real Estate Boom undid Financial Institutions: What can be done now?' Competitiveness and Sustainable Economic Recovery in Thailand, A Joint Publication of the Office of the National Economic and Social Development Board and the World Bank Thailand Office.

Siamwalla, Ammar, (1997), 'Can a Developing Democracy Manage its macroeconomy? The Case of Thailand', J. Douglas Dillon Lecture, Queen's University, Ontario.

Appendix 7.1 Chronology of Major Financial Reforms in Thailand: 1989 – 1997

1989 June	Abolition of interest rate ceiling on commercial bank time deposits with maturity exceeding one year.
1990 May	Foreign exchange liberalization, commencing with the official acceptance of obligations under article VIII of the Articles of Agreement of the International Monetary Fund and followed by two subsequent relaxations of exchange control regulations in late 1990 and 1991.
1992 Jan.	Abolition of interest rate ceiling on savings deposits at commercial banks.
1992 May	Further relaxation of exchange controls. · Exporters allowed to receive payments in baht from non-resident baht accounts, in addition to those in foreign currencies, and to use such foreign currency receipts either to pay for imports or reduce foreign liabilities to non-residents; receipts either to pay for imports or reduce foreign liabilities to non-residents; · Residents allowed to withdraw from foreign currency accounts to repay debts on behalf of subsidiaries or transfer currency to creditors' foreign currency accounts at commercial banks in Thailand; · Expatriates working temporarily in Thailand allowed to purchase foreign currency for deposit in their foreign currency accounts at commercial banks in Thailand · Government departments, government organizations, state enterprises and legal persons allowed to purchase, exchange, borrow or withdraw freely from their foreign currency - accounts and to deposit an unlimited amount of foreign notes and coins into their foreign currency accounts. (The limit was formerly set at US$ 2,000 per day.)
1992 Mar	Scope of financial institution operations expanded to allow greater competition in the supply of financial services. Commercial banks now allowed to act as selling agents for public debt instruments, arrangers, underwriters and dealers in debt instruments and act as financial advisers in mergers, acquisitions, and takeover cases.
1992 Jun-Oct	Finance companies and finance and securities companies allowed to operate leasing services, act as selling agents for public debt instruments, act as arrangers, underwriters and dealers in debt instruments, and acts as mutual fund supervisors.
1992 Jun	Removal of ceilings on lending and borrowing rates of finance and credit finance companies. Remaining ceiling on bank lending rates removed.
1992 Jul	Commercial banks allowed to issue NCDs with minimum maturity of 3 months, maximum maturity of 3 years, minimum face value of not less than Baht 500,000 and subsequent denomination and multiples of Baht 100,000.
1993 Jan	Adoption of the BIS standard for commercial banks. Commercial banks required to maintain 7% (increased to 8% by Jan. 95) of capital to risk asset ratio. · Foreign bank branches required to maintain 6% of tier 1 capital to risk asset ratio.
1993 Mar	Permission given to 46 commercial banks to operate BIBF international banking businesses.
1993 Jul	Thailand's first credit rating agency TRIS established.
1993 May	Requirement for commercial banks to hold government bonds lifted to fulfill branch opening requirements.
1993 Oct	Commercial banks required to disclose their minimum loan rates (MLR), the minimum retail rates (MRR), and maximum margin to be added to MRR as a reference rate for customers not eligible for MLR.

1994 Feb	Further liberalization of foreign exchange controls.
	· Limit raised from ฿ 250,000 to 500,000 on the amount of baht that can be taken to countries sharing contiguous border with Thailand and Vietnam.
	· Limit on the amount of foreign currency that travelers can be taken out abolished.
	· Limit raised from US$ 5 million to 10 million on the amount of foreign investment by Thairesidents without seeking prior approval;
	· Thai residents allowed to use foreign exchange originating from abroad to service external obligations without surrendering or depositing it into domestic accounts.
1994 May	BIBFs allowed to open branches outside of Bangkok and its vicinity. Regional BIBF branches allowed to take deposits in both baht and foreign currency from in or outside the country; but may grant credit only in baht in areas outside of Bangkok. BIBFs also allowed to operate conduct exchange activities.
1994 Jun	Commercial banks allowed to invest in equity of more than 20% of their total capital.
1994 Aug	Guidelines initiated to separate the finance and securities businesses.
1994 Sep	Commercial banks allowed to open ATMs without seeking prior approval.
1994 Nov	Ceilings on commercial bank net position on foreign assets and liabilities to capital reduced to 20% and 15%, respectively.
	· BIBFs allowed to mobilize funds by the issuance of NCDs.
1995 Jan	Provincial International Banking Facilities (PIBFs) outside Bangkok and its vicinities were granted.
1995 Oct	Minimum disbursement from BIBFs out-in lending increased from US$ 500,000 to 2 million.
	· Finance companies allowed to issue bills of exchange and certificates of deposits denominated in foreign currency, with maturity of over one year, to investors overseas or commercial banks authorized to undertake foreign exchange transactions.
1996 Apr	Second-round of application for BIBF licenses begins.
1996 Jun	Commercial banks, BIBFs, finance companies, and finance and securities companies required to maintain liquidity reserves in the form of deposits at the Bank of Thailand averaging no less than 7% of new short-term foreign liabilities, including non-resident deposits.
1996 Oct	Capital-to-risk asset ratio raised from no less than 8 % to 8.5 % for Thai commercial bank and from no less than 7% to 7.5% for finance companies.
1997 May	Measures preventing currency speculation implemented.
1997 Jun	Guidelines initiated for financial institutions undertaking mergers or acquisitions Property Management Corporation set up to receive transfers of property loans from commercial banks, finance companies, and finance and securities companies.
1997 Jul	Foreign exchange rate system changed from a basket of currencies to a managed float.

Source: Compiled from various documents of the Bank of Thailand.

8 Financial Policy and Financial Sector Development in Indonesia since the 1980s[1]

ANWAR NASUTION

Introduction

The purpose of this paper is to analyze the policy since the early 1980s in Indonesia to develop a modern financial industry. Financial sector development according to Khatkhate and Riechel (1980) refers to the evolution of a financial system, its structural form, its mode of operation, and the types of financial instruments it offers. In the case of the Indonesian economy, the banking industry is the core of the system, and credit is the main source of the external financing of the corporate sector. Deregulation of the banking industry will surely produce long-term benefits for the economy. In the short-run, however, deregulation inevitably exposes financial institutions to new risks; and if it is not properly managed, financial reform can lead to economic crisis like that now facing Indonesia. Moreover, fragility of the system limits the severity of both monetary and fiscal measures required in a short-term macroeconomic stabilization program for solving the crisis.

The remainder of this paper is divided into six sections. The following section is a brief analysis of recent macroeconomic policies and developments. Section 3 describes the structure of the financial sector and it recent reforms. Section 4 investigates the current problems being faced by the financial industry. Section 5 examines foreign exchange systems and exchange rate management. Section 6 describes the policy to restructure the banking industry and the corporate sector. The main conclusions of the paper are in contained in the final section.

Table 8.1 Indonesia: Selected Key Indicators, 1990 - 1998

(Unit: in % of GDP, unless otherwise indicated)

	1990	1991	1992	1993	1994	1995	1996	1997	1998 *
Internal Stability									
Gross Domestic Product									
Real GDP (% of growth rate)	9.0	8.9	7.2	7.3	7.5	8.1	8.0	4.6	-13.6
Consumption	63.7	63.9	62.0	67.5	65.1	69.1	70.3	70.4	78.6
Private	53.9	54.0	52.2	58.5	56.5	61.0	62.7	63.1	71.2
Government	9.8	9.8	9.8	9.0	8.6	8.0	7.6	7.3	7.4
National Saving	27.5	26.9	26.9	27.0	28.4	28.0	29.3	28.0	N.A.
Private	19.1	19.8	20.5	20.4	22.0	22.4	23.0	N.A.	N.A.
Public	8.4	7.1	6.4	6.6	6.4	5.6	6.3	N.A.	N.A.
Investment	30.1	29.9	29.0	28.3	30.3	31.3	32.7	32.0	20.9
Private	23.5	21.7	20.9	20.9	24.0	25.8	27.4	N.A.	N.A.
Public	6.6	7.7	7.8	7.4	6.3	5.5	5.3	N.A.	N.A.
Inflation (CPI)	9.5	9.5	4.9	9.8	9.2	8.6	6.5	11.6	
Fiscal Balance	0.4	0.4	-0.4	-0.6	0.1	0.8	0.2	-0.2	
External Stability									
Current Account Balance	-2.8	-3.7	-2.2	-1.6	-1.7	-3.6	-3.7	-2.7	0.1
Real Effective Exchange Rate (1997 = 100)	95.1	93.2	90.8	85.6	82.5	80.1	78.0	100.0	315.83
Nominal Exchange Rate / CPI (1997 = 100)	111.3	107.7	104.2	97.7	93.2	88.6	85.5	100.0	238.14
Net Capital Inflows	4.9	5.0	3.8	1.7	2.0	4.0	5.4	-1.1	0.1
Of which:									
Net Direct Investment	1.0	1.3	1.4	1.0	0.8	1.9	2.5	2.1	
Net Portfolio Investment	-0.1	0.0	-0.1	1.1	2.2	2.0	2.2	-1.2	
Other Capital	3.3	3.6	3.5	1.4	-0.9	1.2	0.1	-0.2	
Net Error and Omissions	0.7	0.1	-1.0	-1.9	-0.1	-1.1	0.6	-1.8	
Net Resourse Transfer / GDP (1997 = 100)	-100.1	-86.1	-535.6	-749.0	-309.7	396.3	198.5	100.0	N.A.
Reserves (in months of imports)	4.7	4.8	5.0	5.2	5.0	4.4	5.1	4.4	5.2
Ratio M2 to Reserves (%)	596.8	539.0	552.6	602.3	643.4	690.3	638.6	419.9	
Total External Debt	65.9	68.4	69.0	56.7	61.0	61.5	56.7	63.4	N.A.
Total External Debt (in % of Exports of Goods and Services)	222.0	236.9	221.8	211.9	231.8	233.9	219.8	227.0	N.A.
Short term Debt (in % of Total External Debt)	15.9	17.9	20.5	21.0	19.6	22.2	27.1	27.2	N.A.
Short Term Debt (in US$ billion)	11.1	14.3	18.1	18.8	21.1	27.6	35.0	37.0	N.A.
Debt-Service Ratio (in % of Exports of Goods and Services)	30.9	32.0	33.0	33.6	30.7	30.9	29.5	30.0	N.A.
Exports Goods & Services (in % of GDP)	25.1	28.1	30.2	26.8	26.9	27.2	27.1	27.5	40.3
Exports of Goods (% of growth rate)	15.9	13.5	16.6	8.4	8.8	13.4	9.7	7.5	15.4
IM (1997 = 100)	112.0	123.4	131.7	134.6	136.9	165.0	175.4	100.0	N.A.

Note: * Up to September 1998.

Sources: IMF, *International Financial Statistics*, various issues.

World Bank, *World Debt Tables: External Finance for Developing Countries*, 1996.

World Bank, *Indonesia in Crisis; A Macroeconomic Update*, July 1998.

Bank Indonesia, *Indonesia Financial Statitics*, January 1999.

Macroeconomic Setting

Indonesia's economy was indeed in need of adjustment, particularly because of weak economic fundamentals and a fragile banking system. Massive capital influx since the early 1990s has caused bouts of domestic overheating. Domestic economic management has become more difficult with the increasing size of that influx and changes in its composition towards short-term private capital. As a result, the rapid economic growth achieved during this period has been accompanied by rising domestic inflation, interest rates, and current account deficits (see Table 8.1). On the other hand, capital influx has helped strengthen the external value of the rupiah and checked the rise in both inflation and interest rates.

Having been maintained at below 2% of annual GDP in 1993 and 1994, the current account deficit rose to 3.6% in 1995 and then to 3.7% in 1996. This deterioration in the balance of payments does not only reflect higher investment which increased from 28.4% of annual GDP in 1990 to 33.4% in 1996, but also having been channeled through the banking system and relatively narrow and shallow capital markets or direct borrowing, the private sector was the main recipient of those inflows. As indicated by a slight decline in the savings rate in national account data, part of influx has been partly used for financing consumption expenditure, while another part has been used to finance the rapid growth of "off-budget expenditures" and government-sponsored projects. Those projects include "strategic industries" (such as aircraft manufacturing) controlled by J.E. Habibie, the Minister of Research and Technology, and the national car project[2] owned by Mr. Hutomo Mandala Putra, the youngest and favorite son of former President Suharto.

High rates of economic growth during the early 1990s were mostly associated with "bubble" industries, including construction, public utilities, and services in the non-traded sector of the economy (see Table 8.2), indicates that a large portion of the capital influx was invested in this "bubble" part of the economic sector. Moreover, most of the growth of non-oil exports during that period occurred in industries like electronics, sport shoes, and textiles and apparel, which relied least on domestic inputs and were associated with firms from East Asia (mainly Japan, Republic of Korea and Taiwan) with strong currencies during the 1980s. In contrast, domestically owned sectors or those relying heavily on domestic inputs fared poorly. Part of the problem was that the exportation of palm oil and wood products was subject to quotas. Export revenues from natural gas and oil also been declined because of a fall in their prices to the lowest levels in the past ten years.

Table 8.2 Indonesia: Share and Growth Rate of Real Gross Domestic Product by Industrial Origin

(at 1983 constant market prices for 1985-1993, and 1993 constant market prices for 1994-1998)

	Share		Rate of Growth								
	1985	1995	1990	1991	1992	1993	1994	1995	1996	1997*	1998** a)
Gross Domestic Product	100.0	100.0	7.2	7.0	6.5	6.5	7.6	8.1	8.0	4.6	-13.6
Gross Domestic Product non Petroleum	78.7	91.3	7.6	6.5	8.4	7.8	8.1	9.1	8.3	5.3	-14.7
1. Agriculture, Livestock, Forestry and Fishery	22.6	16.1	2.0	1.6	6.7	1.4	0.9	3.8	3.2	0.6	0.3
1.1 Farm Food Crops	14.0	8.6	0.5	-0.5	7.7	-1.2	-2.1	4.6	2.4	-1.8	-1.7
1.2 Non-food Crops	3.6	2.6	4.9	5.4	4.8	5.8	5.1	4.7	4.2	4.3	5.9
1.3 Livestock and Products	2.4	1.8	3.7	6.0	7.9	5.6	4.0	4.2	6.1	4.1	-6.0
1.4 Forestry	1.0	1.6	3.0	0.0	-2.2	1.7	0.5	0.0	1.3	-0.6	3.0
1.5 Fishery	1.6	1.6	5.0	5.2	5.8	5.7	8.8	1.9	4.6	5.0	7.0
2. Mining and Quarrying	18.2	9.3	5.2	10.2	-1.9	2.2	5.6	6.7	5.8	1.6	-4.5
2.1 Crude Petroleum and Natural Gas	17.1	6.2	4.2	9.3	-4.5	-0.3	2.6	0.0	1.4	-1.4	-1.8
2.2 Other Mining and Quarrying	1.1	3.1	18.0	20.1	24.0	20.8	13.9	23.5	14.6	7.0	-9.0
3. Manufacturing Industries	15.8	23.9	12.5	10.1	9.7	9.3	12.5	10.7	11.7	6.2	-16.8
3.1 Non-oil and Gas Manufacturing	11.5	21.3	13.0	10.9	11.0	11.6	13.5	13.0	11.7	7.4	-18.7
3.2 Oil/Gas Industry	4.3	2.5	11.0	7.4	5.3	1.3	5.6	-5.4	11.1	-3.4	0.5
4. Electricity, Gas and Water Supply	0.4	1.1	17.9	16.1	10.1	10.1	12.5	15.5	13.2	11.8	1.8
5. Construction	5.3	7.6	13.5	11.3	10.8	12.1	14.9	12.9	12.8	6.4	-38.2
6. Trade, Hotel and Restaurant	14.6	16.7	7.1	5.4	7.3	8.8	7.6	7.7	8.2	5.5	-19.5
6.1 Wholesale and Retail Trade	12.2	13.4	6.8	5.1	7.4	9.0	6.8	7.7	8.2	5.9	-20.4
6.2 Hotels and Restaurants	2.3	3.3	8.7	7.0	7.2	7.7	11.1	7.9	8.2	3.8	-16.0
7. Transportation and Communication	5.3	7.2	9.6	7.9	10.0	9.9	8.3	9.4	7.8	8.4	-8.7
7.1 Transportation	4.7	6.0	8.6	7.3	10.0	8.9	6.5	7.3	6.4	6.5	-11.7
7.2 Communication	0.5	1.2	16.9	12.3	10.0	16.4	20.4	21.1	14.5	17.3	3.7
8. Financial, Ownership and Business	6.4	9.0	10.1	9.7	9.8	10.3	10.2	11.2	8.8	4.8	-18.3
8.1 Banking and Other Financial Intermediaries	3.5	4.7	14.1	13.1	13.0	13.0	13.8	13.9	9.6	3.5	-20.3
8.2 Building Rental	2.9	2.8	4.2	4.0	4.2	5.0	4.0	5.5	5.8	5.0	-17.7
8.3 Business Services	n.a.	1.4	n.a.	n.a.	n.a.	n.a.	12.0	14.2	12.1	8.5	-13.9
9. Services	11.3	9.2	4.7	3.7	4.3	4.3	2.8	3.3	3.4	3.0	-5.8
9.1 Public Administration and Defense	7.6	6.0	4.6	3.1	3.0	2.0	1.3	1.3	1.3	1.2	-8.3
9.2 Private Services	3.7	3.2	5.0	5.2	7.3	8.9	5.8	7.2	7.4	6.3	-1.7
Traded Sector b)	40.2	38.9	8.5	9.3	4.5	6.2	9.5	8.5	9.1	4.7	-10.9
Non-traded Sector c)	59.8	61.1	6.4	5.3	7.8	6.7	6.5	7.9	7.3	4.6	-15.3

Notes: * Preliminary data, ** Very preliminary data.
a) Growth of the total first three quarter GDP in 1997 to 1998.
b) Comprise of Non-food Crops, Forestry, and Fishery, Mining and Quarrying, and Manufacturing Industries.
c) Comprise of Farm Food Crops, Livestock and Products, Electricity, Gas, and Water Supply, Construction, Trade, Hotel, and Restaurant, Transportation and Communication, Financial, Ownership and Business, and Services.

Source: Central Bureau of Statistics, *Economic Indicators*, various issues.

The low rates of inflation and rapid growth in GDP and non-petroleum exports, all of which were often quoted as indicators of sound economic fundamentals, were largely artificial. The government had to pay large subsidies (whether implicit or explicit) to control the prices of state-vended products and were thereby able to keep inflation rates below 10% per annum between 1990 and 1996. Moreover, these low inflation rates were also due to the appreciated external value of the rupiah.

The Financial Sector: Structure and Recent Reforms

Table 8.3 shows that in terms of total assets and the number of institutions and branch offices, the core of the financial sector in Indonesia is still the banking system. Other financial institutions such as capital markets, leasing companies, insurance companies, etc. (including unit trusts, building societies, and housing bonds) are rapidly growing segments within the financial system, but as a group still form a relatively small portion.

Through networks of ownership, and management overlapping, all of the domestic private banks in Indonesia are closely connected to large business conglomerates. The collapse of a number of large conglomerates since 1990 implies that certain sectors within them could become burdensome, in part because of their high leverage strategies. Such financial strategies involving high debt-to-equity ratios may have been suited to the past era of subsidized interest rates and highly protected domestic markets (Nasution, 1995, pp. 185-86), but no longer.

The Driving Force behind the Reforms

Financial sector reforms were implemented during the early 1980s as an integral part of economy-wide deregulation. The scope and sequencing of the reforms were much wider and faster in Indonesia than the gradual approaches adopted in other countries in ASEAN. The "technocrats" at the Ministry of Finance and the Planning Agency have been the driving force behind economic reform, while the central bank plays a supporting role. Bank Indonesia, the country's central bank, is governed by the Monetary Board. Chaired by the Minister of Finance, the Monetary Board is the country's monetary policy-making authority. The other members of the Board are cabinet ministers appointed by the President. After the economic crisis, which began in August 1997, reform efforts were driven by a combination of domestic needs and external pressures.[3]

Banking reform in Indonesia has been adopted in stages, starting with the end of repressive financial regulation and followed by opening up

Table 8.3 Structure Growth of Financial Structure, 1969-1997

	Number in								Share in Assets (%)								Asset Growth (%)				
	1969	1982	1988	1991	1994	1995	1996	1997	1969	1982	1988	1991	1994	1995	1996	1997	1970-	1983-	1989-	1992-	1995-
Bank Indonesia	1	1	1	1	1	1	1	1	57.7	42.4	36.8	23.8	21.3	16.4	16.4	14.4	31.1	18.8	9.2	6.6	50.11
Deposit Money Banks	179	118	111	195	240	240	237	238	42.3	52.9	56.9	68.5	78.7	83.6	83.6	85.6	37.6	22.4	32.6	37.4	75.27
State Commercial Banks	5	5	5	5	7	7	7	7	30.3	37.9	34.5	30.2	30.4	33.4	30.4	32.1	36.6	19.7	20.7	16.7	64.66
Private Banks	126	70	63	129	166	165	162	160	3.7	5.8	13.1	25.2	34.9	39.3	43.2	39.6	34	41.5	56.9	67.9	72.16
Private Forex Banks	3	10	12	28	53	75	79	N.A.	N.A.	3.6	2.8	5.2	6.9	N.A.	N.A.	N.A.	N.A.	36.1	64.9	75.7	N.A.
Private non-Forex Banks	123	60	51	101	113	90	83	N.A.	N.A.	2.2	4.3	5.5	4.4	N.A.	N.A.	N.A.	N.A.	32.2	37.3	28.7	N.A.
Foreign Banks	11	11	11	29	40	41	41	44	4.3	3.6	2.8	5.2	6.9	8.2	7.7	12	32.6	16.8	55.4	44.6	149.3
Development Banks	25	29	29	29	27	27	27	27	4	4.1	4.4	6.3	6.5	2.7	2.3	2	34.6	22.1	42.2	21.3	25.65
Saving Banks	12	3	3	3	...	...	...	...	0.1	1.4	2.1	1.6	...	...	...	...	60	27.9	14.5		
Non-Bank Financial Institution	N.A.	13	13	13	N.A.	N.A.	N.A.	N.A.	N.A.	2.5	2.7	2.1	N.A.	N.A.	N.A.	N.A.	N.A.	22.3	14.9	N.A.	N.A.
Insurance Companies	N.A.	83	106	145	145	155	163	N.A.	N.A.	1.6	1.6	3.5	N.A.	N.A.	N.A.	N.A.	N.A.	21.2	62.3	N.A.	N.A.
Leasing Companies	N.A.	17	83	88	N.A.	N.A.	N.A.	N.A.	N.A.	0.4	1.5	1.8	N.A.	N.A.	N.A.	N.A.	N.A.	45.4	33.6	N.A.	N.A.
Other Credit Institutions	8568	5808	5783	6243	N.A.	N.A.	N.A.	N.A.	N.A.	0.3	0.6	0.4 a)	N.A.	N.A.	N.A.	N.A.	N.A.	33.4	15.9 b)	N.A.	N.A.
Total	8748	6040	6097	6725	386	396	401		100	100	100	100	100	N.A.	N.A.	N.A.	34.2	21.2	21.3	29	73
Total (Rp Trillions)									0.7	32.3	115.5	218.5	319.6	N.A.	N.A.	N.A.					
Memo items																					
M1/GDP									0.07	0.09	0.1	0.12	0.14	0.12	0.12	0.13					
M2/GDP									0.09	0.14	0.3	0.44	0.55	0.49	0.55	0.57					
Total Assets of Financial Inst. (TAFI)/GDP									0.26	0.52	0.81	0.96	1.01	N.A.	N.A.	N.A.					
M2/TAFI									0.33	0.34	0.36	0.45	0.55	N.A.	N.A.	N.A.					

Notes : a) December
b) Average

Sources : Bank Indonesia, *Indonesian Financial Statistics and Annual Reports* , various issues.
Cole, David C. and Betty F. Slade. (1992), 'Indonesian Financial Development: A Different Sequencing ?' in Dimitri
Vittas (ed.), *Financial Regulation - Changing the Rules of the Game* , EDI Development Studies, Washington D.C.: The
World Bank.

Department of Finance, *Statistics Data of The Finance Companies 1991* .
Department of Finance, *Statistics Data of The Insurance Companies 1991* .

market entry and efforts to strengthen prudential rules and regulations governing the financial industry. Interest rate ceilings were lifted in June 1983. The October 1988 reforms also significantly reduced the role of the central bank and commercial banks as development-oriented institutions.

Protection of domestic banks from foreign competition was reduced, as were special market preferences for state-owned financial institutions. Moreover, before the reforms, the central bank was required to undertake quasi-fiscal operations, which included subsidized credit to favored economic activities and development finance institutions through selective credit policies, subsidized deposit insurance, bailing out insolvent financial institutions, and assuming exchange rate and interest rate risk incurred by offshore borrowing by favored groups of individuals and companies. The third stage of the reform was introduced in 1999 as part of the implementation of an IMF restructuring program.

Scope and Chronology of the Reforms

Table 8.4 summarizes the scope and chronology of banking sector reform in Indonesia since the early 1980s. The reforms have removed the traditional functional specialization among various types of banks and major areas of specialization for state-owned banks in Indonesia. Following the reform, there were no more statutory public development agencies to extend credit to targeted individuals or enterprises for investment in commerce, agriculture and industry. Since then, there have been only two types of banks operating in Indonesia; namely, commercial banks and rural banks. Called *bank perkreditan rakyat (BPR),* a rural bank is an unitary local bank prohibited from accepting demand deposits.

Table 8.4 Reform in the Banking Industry in Indonesia, 1969-1998

Policy Measures	Before Reform	After Reform	Date
I. Competitive Measures			
1. Entry of New Banks			
(a). Private Banks	moratorium since 1970	permitted	October, 1988
(b). Foreign Banks	moratorium since 1970	permitted to enter as joint venture	October, 1988
2. Branching Power			
(a). Private Banks	restricted 1)	permitted to sound banks	October, 1988
(b). Foreign Banks	restricted to Jakarta	permitted to seven cities (later Batam)	October, 1988
3. Forex License	restricted [a]	eligible for sound banks	October, 1988
		eligible for sound banks	September, 1995

Table 8.4 (continued)

4. Type of Loans

(a). State Banks	mainly the extended subsidized credit programs, as set and refinanced by Bank Indonesia	the scope and coverage of the subsidized credit programs reduced	June, 1983 January 27, 1990
(b). Private Banks	free to set	20% of total credit must be extended to small business [b]	October, 1988
		22.5% of total credit must be extended to small business [b]	April, 1997
(c). Foreign Banks	free to set	50% of total credit must be extended to export related activities	October, 1988

5. Types of Saving and Deposit Schemes

(a). State Banks	set by Bank Indonesia	free to set	June 1, 1983
(b). Private Banks	free to set	free to set	
(c). Foreign Banks	free to set	free to set	

6. Deposits of the Public Sector	restricted to state banks	restricted to state banks	October, 1988
7. Deposits of the State Enterprises	restricted to state banks	up to 50% with private banks	October, 1988

8. Deposit Rates

(a). State Banks	set by Bank Indonesia	free to set	June 1, 1983
(b). Private Banks	free to set	free to set	
(c). Foreign Banks	free to set	free to set	

9. Loan Rates

(a). State Banks	controlled by Bank Indonesia	free to set	June 1, 1983
(b). Private Banks	free to set	free to set	
(c). Foreign Banks	free to set	free to set	

10. Credit Ceilings

(a). State Banks	set by Bank Indonesia	eliminated	June 1, 1983
(b). Private Banks	set by Bank Indonesia	eliminated	June 1, 1983
(c). Foreign Banks	set by Bank Indonesia	eliminated	June 1, 1983

11. Loan Restriction	not regulated	Prohibition to land provision and land usage of the real estate developer	July, 1997
12. Forex Power (limited to licensed banks)	subjected to ceilings set by Bank Indonesia	net open position [c]	November, 1989
		30% of bank capital	March, 1997
13. Reserve Requirements	15% of deposits (differentiated between banks)	2% of deposits	October, 1988
		3% of deposits	December, 1995
		5% of deposits	April, 1997

Table 8.4 (continued)

14. Electronic Local Clearing	not regulated	All banks in the local clearing area	August, 1998
15. Entry to New Activities			December, 1988 [d]
(a). Leasing	not regulated	subsidiary	
(b). Venture Capital	not regulated	subsidiary	
(c). Securities Trading	not regulated	not for own account, not as broker/dealer	
(d). Factoring	not regulated	directly	
(e). Consumer Finance	not regulated	directly	
(f). Credit Cards	not regulated	directly	
(g). Underwriting Shares [e]	---	prohibited	
(h). Custodian	not regulated	approval required for capital otherwise can do as market	
(i). Trustee and Guarantor	not regulated	approval required for capital part of usual activities market	
(j). Securities Administrative Agency	not regulated	prohibited	
(k). Investment Manager	not regulated	subsidiary	
(l). Derivative Transaction	not regulated	by permission of Bank Indonesia	February, 1996
(m). Swap and Forward Facilities	not regulated	applicable to banks with foreign exchange license	October, 1997

II. Prudential Measures

1. Capital Requirements			
(a). General banks			
(I). Private Banks	---	Rp. 10 billion	October, 1988
		Rp. 50 billion	October, 1992
(II). Joint Venture Banks	---	Rp. 50 billion	October, 1988
(minimum 15% of Indonesia Ownership)		Rp. 100 billion	October, 1992
(b). Bank Perkreditan Rakyat		Rp. 50 million	October, 1988
2. Legal Lending Limits	none	1. Old credit : (% of bank capital)	May 29, 1993
		Individual Group	
		20%	by May 29, 1993
		50%	
		20%	By Dec, 1995
		50%	
		20%	by March, 1997
		50%	
		2. New Credit	
		Individual Group	
		20%	
		20%	
3. Loan to Deposit Ratio	none	110 %	February, 1991 [f]
4. Capital Adequacy Ratio	none	(% of risk weighted assets)	February, 1991
		5% by March, 1992	
		7% by March, 1993	
		8% by Dec, 1993 [g]	

Table 8.4 (continued)

		4% by December, 1998 [h]	
5. Net Open Position	none	25% of capital	March, 1989
6. Accounting Standard	none	Standardized - *Standar Khusus*	January 1, 1993
		Akuntansi Perbankan Indonesia (SKAPI) - Accounting Standard for Indonesian Banks	
7. Measures of the Soundness of Banks			
a. State Banks	none	weighted average of prudential measure	May,1997
b. Private Banks	none	weighted average of prudential measure	May,1997
c. Bank Perkreditan Rakyat	none	weighted average of prudential measure	May,1997
8. Government's Warranty			
a. Payment obligation of Private Banks	none	Sanction to the unobeyed party	March, 1998
b. Deposits and Interbank call money	none	No more than acquired interest rate	May, 1998
9. Bad Debt restructuring	none	Funding creation and debt elimination	November, 1998

III. Money Market

Reintroduced in February 1984, SBI is the most important money market instrument at present. On June 1, 1993, the auction system of SBI changed from "cut-off rate" (COR) to "stop-out rate" (SOR). The private sector commercial paper (SBPU) introduced in January, 1985. Until now, the government has not floated treasury bonds in domestic market.

IV. Transparency and Accountability of Reporting and Management

1. To improve banking supervision by (i) standardizing accounting and reporting system; (ii) requiring commercial bank to submit detailed business plans to the central bank and banning person involved in fraudulent transactions or defaulted on significant loans from becoming shareholders, executives or member of the board of commissioners of banks.	January, 1995
2. Banks are required to (i) submit detailed credit plan to Bank Indonesia and those with uncollectible amounted to 7.5% of total credit or more are required to submit credit recovery plans; (ii) standardized internal audit system and (iii) adopt standardize information system technology.	March, 1995
(iv) improvement of the financial report; to include the detail on the items with exchange rates value	September, 1995
3. The criteria of person who may not be involved in bank management	January, 1995

Notes:
a) Permitted in principle, but economic and social requirements made it prohibited in practice;
b) Since May 29, 1993 can be channeled through other banks and BPRs;
c) Overseas borrowing for public sector is subject to ceilings set by TKPLLN (Coordinating Team for Management of Commercial Offshore Loans) since October 1991;
d) Item (g) to (j) are subject to Ministry of Finance's Decisions No. 1548 of Dec 4, 1990;
e) Can underwrite bonds and other debt instruments;
f) Since May 29, 1993 own capital; included in the denominator;
g) In May 29, 1993, this schedule was extended to December 1994.
h) In November 12, 1998, this schedule was extended to December 1998.

Table 8.4 (continued)

Sources:
Bank Indonesia, *Annually Report*, various issues.
Bank Indonesia, *Directors' Act*, various numbers.
David Cole and Betty F. Slade, (1991) 'Development of Money Markets in Indonesia', *Development Discussion Paper*, No. 371, Cambridge, MA: Harvard University, HIID, January.
John Chant and Mari Pangestu, (1992) 'An Assesment of Financial Reform in Indonesia: 1983-90' in G. Caprio Jr., *et al.* (eds), *Financial Reform: Theory and Experience*, mimeo.
Nasution, Anwar, 'Financial Institution and Policies in Indonesia' Singapore: ISEAS (1983).
Pakmar (1988), Pakto (1988), Pakjan (1990), Pakfeb (1991), *Banking Law*, No.7, 1992; Banking Regulation, May 29, 1993.

As of March 1994, the banking system in Indonesia consists of Bank Indonesia, serving as the central bank, seven state-owned commercial banks, 163 national private commercial banks, 39 foreign banks, 27 commercial banks owned by provincial governments',[4] one Islamic bank (Bank Muamalat), 8,757 rural banks, 13 merchant banks, and a number of money and foreign exchange brokers. All of these institutions are regulated and supervised by Bank Indonesia. 67 commercial banks are licensed to conduct foreign exchange transactions. A number of private commercial banks are partly or wholly owned by Bank Indonesia, the central bank. Ten of the foreign banks are full branches licensed between 1966 and 1970. There is no regulation concerning new entries of foreign bank branches in Indonesia, but no new licenses have been issued since 1970.

The other 29 foreign banks are joint ventures with local financial institutions. Until recently, the only mechanism by which foreign banks could currently penetrate the Indonesian domestic market was through such an avenue. The foreign partners in the ventures must already have representative offices in Jakarta, be reputable in their countries of origin, and be from countries that have reciprocity agreements with Indonesia. Domestic partners must be recognized as "sound" for at least 20 of the last 24 months. The maximum share held by foreign partners in a joint venture bank is set at 85%.

The 1999 reform abolished both the share limit of foreigners in local banks and the geographical restriction of foreign banks. Foreign investors can now own 100% of the equity share of banks in Indonesia. Foreign banks and joint venture banks can now open branches anywhere in Indonesia, outside the formerly designated seven major cities.

The Credit System

Prior to 1999, Bank Indonesia ran roughshod over the financial system through a very detailed system of ceilings cum selective credit policies with subsidized interest rates. Under such a system, the central bank refinanced credit programs and determined the economic sectors and classes of their recipients. Moreover, credit was given with virtually no risk. During the "oil boom" of 1974-83, the credit program was partly used as an instrument for distributing the resulting economic windfall to the lower income and favored groups. Banking sector reform implemented since 1988 gradually reduced the scope of the credit programs. Their refinancing by the central bank was discontinued beginning in 1999 with the introduction of a new law passed in May 1999 concerning Bank Indonesia, which eliminates the role of the BI as an agent of development. Since then, interest rate subsidies on credit programs have been directly provided through the government's budget.

The six state-owned banks, which controlled over 60% of the market in the 1980s, were the main providers in the credit programs. For decades, the loan decisions of these banks had been subject to explicit or implicit government direction. All to often, creditworthiness of the borrowers was not given sufficient weight in credit decisions, with the result that loans by state banks became vehicles for extending government assistance to particular industries and a handful of politically well-connected business groups. These conglomerates control a large proportion of the GDP and a vast range of mainly rent-seeking activities. Deregulation had not ended government intervention in lending decisions of state-owned banks and other financial institutions. On example is direct government intervention in providing credit to Edi Tansil and to PT Timor Putra Nusantara after the banking reform and allegedly by those who promoted it.

Current Problems in the Financial Industry

Along with implementing reform, since early 1991 Indonesia has adopted prudential rules and regulations suggested by the Committee on Banking Regulation and Supervisory Practices, under the auspices of the BIS in 1988. In line with BIS recommendations, the authorities raised the minimum initial paid-in capital for any new banks, set the capital adequacy ratio at 8% and loan-to-deposit ratio at 110%, linked new loans to the level of deposits, and required banks to provide reserves for all loans. Bank Indonesia has even adopted the more restrictive CAMEL (capital adequacy, asset quality, management, earning, and liquidity) system to regulate and supervise banks. The implementation of the strict prudential rules and regulations has however been very weak. This is partly because of structural weaknesses in legal and accounting systems. Another part of the problem is poor governance. Four bank supervisors of Bank Indonesia were arrested in early August 1997 for allegedly receiving bribes during inspections made during 1993-1996 (*The Jakarta Post*, August 28, 1997).

Table 8.5 Indonesia: Banking Sector Indicators

(Unit: %, unless otherwise indicated)

	1985	1990	1991	1992	1993	1994	1995	1996	1997	1998 *
Loans to Deposits Ratio	102.9	118.2	130.7	129.3	132.4	134.9	137.7	131.0	123.7	
LGR Minus GDPGR	14.7	48.1	-9.9	7.7	6.9	5.7	4.0	4.7	12.1	62.8
LGR Minus IPGR	29.0	61.4	9.0	25.9	22.4	16.0	23.1	22.5	N.A.	N.A.
NFL to TBL	-20.0	0.9	0.7	2.2	4.9	5.8	3.8	2.8	5.2	14.23
M2 Multiplier [a]	3.4	6.7	7.7	7.0	7.8	7.4	8.0	7.5	7.6	7.8
M2/Forex Reserves	414.2	596.8	539.0	552.6	602.3	643.4	690.3	638.6	419.9	
Non-performing loan [b]	N.A.	N.A.	9.2	N.A.	14.2	12.1	10.4	8.8	14.0	N.A.
of which: Bad Debt [b]	N.A.	N.A.	1.7	N.A.	3.3	4.0	3.3	2.9	N.A.	N.A.
Cash Assets to Deposits Ratio	15.9	6.5	13.7	3.2	2.6	2.5	2.6	4.7	5.8	
Loans to Assets Ratio	N.A.	73.4	76.2	73.7	75.4	80.3	79.2	77.0	71.9	60.7

Notes: * Up to September 1998.

            LGR; Loan Growth Rate.   NFL; Net Foreign Liabilities.

            GDPGR; GDP Growth Rate.   TBL; Total bank Liabilities.

            IPGR; Industrial Production Growth Rate.

            a) Ratio of M2 to Reserves Money.

            b) As percentage of total loan outstanding of Commercial Banks. Non-performing loan data tends to be underestimated. The decline of non-performing loan to 8.8% of total credit in 1996 was mainly due to write-off of the bad loans at state commercial banks and private 'non-foreign exchange' banks. As end of March 1998, bank Non-performing loan reach 19.8% of total loan.

Sources: IMF, *International Financial Statistics*, various issues.

            Bank Indonesia, *Annual Report*, various issues.

Lending Sprees

A combination of lifting restrictions on financial institutions (such as banks and security companies), lowering reserve requirements (and gearing ratios) and giving greater access to offshore markets has encouraged rapid rates of credit expansion. On average, bank credit grew by over 20% per annum during the decade prior to the crisis of August 1997, a figure more than double the annual rate of economic growth (see Table 8.5).

The presence of new entrants in a more competitive market environment may well increase pressure on financial institutions to engage in riskier activities. Yet their credit officers, who were reared in the earlier controlled environment, may not have the expertise needed to evaluate new sources of credit and market risk. When the economy is booming, it is difficult to distinguish between good and bad credit risks because most borrowers look profitable and liquid. The lifting of restrictions on bank lending immediately expanded credit to the non-traded sector of their economies. Land, buildings and other physical goods are the main collateral in this region of the credit system. Part of the credit expansion was financed by foreign borrowing. The perception of Indonesia as a stable country and one of the shining lights of the international economy has generated massive capital inflows since the early 1990s.

As indicated earlier, there are three aspects of banking sector reform that have increased the role of banks a intermediaries in short-term capital inflows to Indonesia. First, the reforms removed the traditional functional specialization between various types of banks and major areas of specialization for state-owned banks. Secondly, requirements were relaxed for domestic banks in conducting foreign exchange transactions, opening branch offices overseas, and allowing greater penetration of foreign banks in the domestic economy. Finally, rules and regulations replaced the ceilings on offshore borrowing by commercial banks by a system of net open position (NOP) and abolished the limits for inflows of FDI as of November 1989.

Increasing Bank Liabilities with Large Maturity and Currency Mismatches

A combination of liberal capital accounts, financial sector reform, advances in technology, and information processing have made it easier for money holders to alter the currency composition of their deposits. These factors combined with relatively sound financial policy (including exchange rate management), a relatively stable macro-economy, and high rates of growth have significantly deepened the financial system. The ratio of broad money (M2) to GDP has increased rapidly (Table 8.1 and Table 8.5).

When domestic interest rates are high, there is a strong temptation for the banking system and bank customers to denominate debt in foreign currency. Commercial banks with licenses to conduct foreign exchange transactions turn to short-term, foreign-currency denominated borrowing in the inter-bank market to fund longer-term loans. Consequently, external borrowing by the financial sector rose rapidly in Indonesia between 1993 and 1996.[5] Partly because of historically predictable, low rates of the rupiah depreciation, a large portion of the external debt is not hedged. This not only makes banks and their customers in Indonesia more vulnerable, but also makes it harder to deal with the banking crisis. This and the traditionally high debt to equity ratio of the banking and corporate sectors make it more difficult to impose tight monetary and austere fiscal measures required by a stabilization program.

The risk of maturity mismatches is higher for unlisted banks, which have no access to mobilizing long-term sources of funding by selling bonds, shares and other types of securities in stock markets. Selling equity in stock markets can also help spread or share risk.

Banks with Weak Financial Positions and Highly Concentrated Problem Loans

Despite a relatively high rate of economic growth continuing at 6% plus per annum since 1990, the problem of bad loans of national banks in Indonesia appears to have worsened. The problem is likely to be more severe at state-owned banks and non-"*bank devisas*". The former were the main providers of credit programs with subsidized interest rates during the long era of financial repression. This group of banks is also the main victim of erratic government policies, such as shifting their public deposits to the central bank.

Bad debts in the banking system grew rapidly during the economic crisis, which struck in the third quarter of 1997 due to stagnant economic growth, high interest rates, sharp devaluation and tight internal and external liquidity. This has stimulated a rise in interest rates and tightened the credit crunch even further. Between 1997 and 1999, commercial banks suffered from losses partly because their deposit rates were constantly higher than lending rates. Of the 240 banks that were in operation before the crisis in June 1997, 23 private banks have been shut down by the authorities since November 1997, and four state-owned banks have been merged. The 55 private-banks under IBRA's management are technically insolvent with negative net worth. According to Bank Indonesia estimates, about 40% of all bank loans are classified as problem loans, the amount for some banks being as high as 80%.

The 1995 actual risk-based capital ratio of almost 12% for all commercial banks in Indonesia was higher than the Basle minimum standard of 8%. Nevertheless, according to the World Bank (1996), there were 22 banks (out of a total 240 banks in mid-1995) that did not meet the capital adequacy ratio standard, and 65 banks did not conform to legal lending limits regulations. To give some breathing space to banks and allow them to reduce interest rates and expand credit, in June 1998 the authorities temporarily reduced the CAR ratio to 4%. The ratio is to be raised back to 8% by the end of 2001.

The Foreign Exchange System and Exchange Rate Management

Indonesia has obtained IMF Article 8 status and adopted a relatively liberal exchange rate system. This liberal exchange rate system was introduced in October 1966, long before it deregulated its current accounts and domestic commodity, labor and assets markets during the second half of 1980s. The system was further relaxed with a devaluation and unification of exchange rates in April 1970. Under this system, there is no surrender requirement for export proceeds and taxes or subsidies on the purchase or sale of foreign exchange. Foreign nationals and Indonesian citizens are free to open accounts in either rupiah or foreign currencies with all "*bank devisas*", which are authorized to conduct foreign exchange transactions. These banks are free to extend credit in foreign currency with a 15% withholding tax on interest rates. It turns out that the more liberal system of capital accounts has not been followed by significant improvements in the implementation of prudential rules and regulations. Consequently, banks and the corporate sector in Indonesia borrow heavily from overseas to finance their domestic operations particularly consumer credit and credit for construction and land-based industry.

Foreign Exchange Exposure

In general, the financial sector reforms have replaced the complicated direct controls or ceilings on foreign borrowing by financial institutions with a more rational system of daily net open position (NOP). In Indonesia, NOP amounts to 20% of the capital of the bank and 25% of loans to a single borrower and that borrower's group of companies. In reality, this rule has been barely enforced.

To encourage inward foreign investment, from January 1979 to December 1991, a special effective exchange rate was made available to domestic borrowers by providing explicit subsidies on the exchange rate.

The foreign exchange subsidy was extended through the exchange rate swap facility at Bank Indonesia. Under this facility, the central bank provided forward cover to foreign borrowing contracts or swaps to banks and non-bank financial institutions, as well as for their customers with foreign-currency liabilities. The swap premium was set below the level of the real depreciation of the rupiah. The size of the subsidy depends on the choice of interest rates used to calculate the interest rate differential. In reality, the swap facility was also used for liquidity purposes by financial institutions, either to fund themselves, to hedge, or even speculate against a declining rupiah.

In the beginning, Bank Indonesia determined the amount of the swaps and allocated the premiums through a non-market mechanism. The ceiling was abolished in October 1986, as Bank Indonesia allowed the swap premium to be determined by market forces. In reality, the swap premium remained subsidized until December 1991. The subsidy was caused by a time lag in either an upward adjustment of the swap premium or a nominal depreciation of the rupiah, or a combination of both. Beginning from December 1991, Bank Indonesia on average set the swap premium above the market rate. This further induced speculation on the rupiah.

Control on Short-term External Borrowings

Despite the deregulation in their capital accounts, the authorities in Indonesia have taken a number of measures to limit the size and affect the structure of capital inflows by resorting back to controls on certain types of transactions and classes of customers. In October 1991, they re-imposed special quantitative ceilings on offshore borrowing by the public sector at large, including state-owned enterprises. The ceilings were also applied to offshore borrowing by the private sector, which relies on public entities for their "bankability". The control was included in Bank Indonesia's regulations that set ceilings on commercial foreign borrowing by BI itself, state-owned banks, privately-owned "foreign exchange banks", and state-owned and private companies for five fiscal years ending 1995-96 (see Nasution, 1996). Bank Indonesia established a queuing system to obtain and use the ceilings and abolished the implicit subsidy on the premium of the exchange rate swap facility. The queue system allows the authorities to set the size and timing of capital inflows and check their terms and conditions, as well as what they are to be used for. Banks will be fined for failing to report external borrowings or exceeding their ceilings and NOP requirement. Effective from April 1, 1997, at least 80% of offshore borrowing has to be channeled to export related activities.

Quantitative restrictions or capital controls, however, are perceived as inferior to a tax on foreign borrowing, which is regarded as the first and best policy. In the short run, administrative restrictions and controls are seen as measuring devices to bring about a reduction in capital inflows quickly without having to lower interest rates. They are also effective tools to change the composition of capital inflows in the short-run. In the longer-run, however, quantitative controls on capital movement have several major disadvantages. Since they are inevitably involved with non-price rationing, they result in very different effective rates of tax on different domestic borrowers. They are administratively cumbersome, and there is potential policy rigidity or pressure group activity which ensures that restrictions, once imposed, are not eased or removed even when the original macroeconomic rationale is gone. Because of such macroeconomic crisis-protection ratchet effects, capital controls are subject to abuse and dissipation as inducements to rent seeking, since the application of such quantitative controls is based on a non-price mechanism.

The principal of less-distorting alternative policy, such as the so-called "Tobin tax" (Tobin, 1979; Spahn, 1995; and Eichengreen, *et al.* 1995) could have been temporarily introduced to help lessen the motivation to shift capital around. As a strategy to throw "sand in the wheels" of the relatively efficient currency market, Tobin (1979) has proposed the imposition of "an internationally uniform tax on all spot conversions of one currency into another, proportional to the size of the transaction". The tax includes a non-remunerated reserve requirement deposit at the central bank on deposits associated with direct borrowing in foreign currency.[6] The tax would be an insignificant burden for exchanges in goods and services markets, labor markets and long-term capital investment. It, however, would significantly add to the cost of short-term arbitrage to reduce speculative transactions. The proceeds from such a tax increase government revenue and can be used to reduce speculative transactions and exchange rate volatility.

Since it would hurt currency speculators more than traders or investors, the Tobin tax could control erratic exchange rate volatility and attract attention of direct traders to long-run fundamentals and away from transient contagious market sentiment. The variant of the Tobin tax proposed by Spahn (1995) imposes a tax only on currency conversions that occur when the exchange rate moves beyond some band. The Spahn tax is equivalent to the difference between the band and the market exchange rate. From a microeconomic point of view, the Spahn tax internalizes externalities associated with currency instability into currency prices.

The feasibility of collecting the Tobin-Spahn tax is dependent on the existence of an international cooperation agreement over collection within national borders. As of now, a tax on short-term capital inflows is not covered in double-taxation treaties between nations. However, such a transaction tax (particularly the reserve requirement deposit associated with external borrowing) can be unilaterally imposed in one country. The tax rate should not be too high as to act as a disincentive to borrow overseas, particularly on instruments of short-term maturity. Moreover, a high tax can be avoided or re-routed through other channels. These include the over-invoicing of imports or under-invoicing of exports when export credits are exempted from the tax. Again, because excessive capital influx is a temporary phenomenon, the tax ratio should be immediately readjusted once short-run capital inflows return to a more manageable level.

There are two other tax schemes that can be used to discourage destabilizing short-term capital inflows. The first is to eliminate tax advantages and regulatory and policy distortions that have been normally used to stimulate short-term capital inflows. The second is to limit the extent of tax deductability for interest on debt denominated or linked to foreign currencies.

Exchange Rate Management

The exchange rate is the single most important relative price in the open economy. Monetary transmission in such an economy operates through exchange-rate effects on net exports and interest rate effects on financial portfolios. Exchange rate policy in Indonesia has included devaluation, speed up depreciation, widening the intervention band, and raising transaction costs in foreign exchange markets. This exchange rate policy together with other policies has traditionally been used to remove distortions in the domestic economy and help international competitiveness. Until recently, the related authorities have avoided the use of prolonged nominal and real exchange rate overvaluation as a principal instrument for generating fiscal revenues and curbing domestic inflation and rising interest rates. In fact, such an active exchange rate policy is an integral part of the "outward looking" or "export-oriented" development strategy in this region.

To offset the so-called "Dutch disease" effect of the oil boom, in November 1978, the Indonesian authorities devalued the rupiah by 50% against the US dollar. At the same time, they adopted the US dollar as the external anchor along with an undisclosed basket of major currencies, then moved to a managed floating exchange rate system. The rupiah was further devalued by 40% in June 1983 and by another 31% in September 1986. In normal cases, the authorities would target depreciation of the rupiah against the dollar at between 3 to 5% per annum. Bank Indonesia intervenes in the foreign exchange market by buying and selling the rupiah in an "intervention band" encircling the central rate.

To allow market forces a greater role in setting the exchange rate, Bank Indonesia had widened the intervention band six times since 1992 to 6% effective from September 1996 (see Figure 8.1). In theory, this greater exchange rate flexibility introduces uncertainty that may well discourage part of the purely speculative capital flows and allows a higher degree of freedom for monetary authorities to exercise control over monetary aggregates. As it allows temporary, slight appreciation of the rupiah, the present policy reduces the need for sterilization of surges in capital flows.

Figure 8.1 Indonesia: Rupiah Exchange Rate and its Intervention Bands, November 1995-August 1997

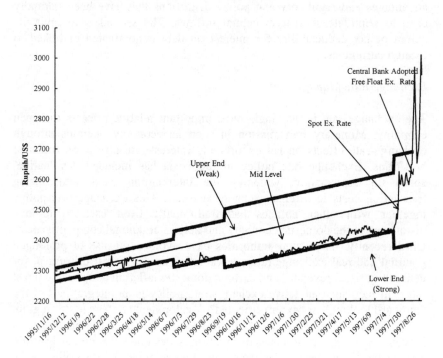

Source: Bank Indonesia, *Indonesian Financial Statistics*, various issues.
University of British Columbia Data Base, Canada.

The adjusting factors in the active management of exchange rate policy have been rising domestic inflation rates and interest rates. Inflationary pressures in Indonesia have been partly suppressed by government policies to narrow the budget deficit and subsidize prices of "state-vended" products,[7] control wages and to adopt a more vigorous trade liberalization program. The trade and financial sector policy reform and productivity gains generated by the economy-wide reform and increasing market competition, help relax the supply constraint and check the inflationary pressures and upward pressures in interest rates.

Partly due to surges in capital inflows, the rupiah was slightly appreciated between 1990 and 1996 (see Figure 8.2) to help reduce inflation rates and interest rates. This currency appreciation, however, erodes external competitiveness of the economy, distorts savings and investment decisions, and squanders scarce savings on unproductive investment projects to impede the efficiency of the economy at the micro level. As has been pointed out earlier, massive capital inflows have also been used for financing expansion in the non-traded sector of the economy and private sector consumption expenditures.

**Figure 8.2 Indonesia: Real Effective Exchange Rate Index
January 1990-June 1998** (1990=100)

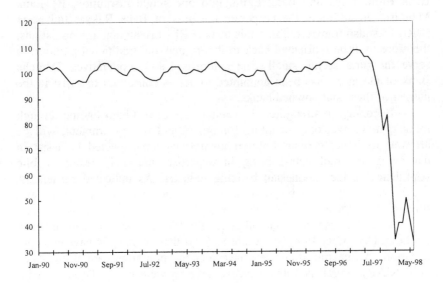

Source: JP Morgan, *Emerging Markets Data Watch*, various issues.

Until June 1997, Indonesia defended the external value of the rupiah against a succession of major speculative attacks by depleting external reserves. However, this strategy had to be abandoned because of limited resources, so Bank Indonesia floated the rupiah on August 14 of that year.

Between June 2, 1997 and March 1, 1999, the nominal value of the rupiah to the US dollar depreciated by over 80%.

Sharp increase in interest rates and the devaluation of a domestic currency deteriorate bank and corporate balance sheets, because of the high leverage strategy based on high debt equity ratios. The substantial fall of the external value of a domestic currency rapidly raises the cost of renewing or rolling over the short-term floating rate of foreign borrowing in real terms. The indebtedness of domestic banks and firms rises and their net worth falls.

Banking Restructuring

The IMF program introduced in November 1997 contains seven measures to restructure the banking system. First, to encourage banks to merge rather than letting distressed one's fail, the authorities announced on October 3, 1998 the merger of four state-owned banks, Bapindo, Bank Dagang Negara, Bank Bumi Daya and Bank Exim, into one single institution, PT Bank Mandiri.[8] In addition, the corporate business of Bank Rakyat Indonesia (BRI) was also transferred into this bank. BRI's orientation and operations, therefore, will be reoriented back to its original and traditional purpose: to serve the rural sector, small-scale enterprises and cooperatives. Deutche Bank of Germany has been appointed to act as consultant to assist in the merger of these state-owned banks.

Secondly, to strengthen the capital base of bad banks going through merger, new investors, including foreigners and the government, will be allowed to inject capital. Foreign institutions are expected to assist in packaging the bad debts, bring in expertise, and help restore public confidence in the Indonesian banking industry. As indicated earlier, the problems are likely to be more severe for state-owned bank group and foreign exchange non-banks.

The audit report of due diligence for 150 domestic banks was made public in December 1998 (see Table 8.6). Of these banks, 54 have been put in Group A, meaning that they have met the minimum capital adequacy ratio (CAR), which is above positive 4%; 56 were put in Group B with CARs between minus 25% and positive 4%); and the remaining 40 banks have been classified under Group C with CARs less than minus 25%. All of the six audited state-owned banks belonging to Group C, indicated their financial problems are more severe than elsewhere. As pointed out earlier, the state-bank group was the main provider of the credit programs with subsidized interest rates during the long era of financial repression. This group of banks has also been the main victim of erratic government policy, such as the shifting of their public deposits to the central bank.

Table 8.6 Classification of Banks by Capital to Asset Ratio and Cost of Bank Restructuring

(As of December 1, 1998)

Ownership	Audit Groups[a]					Cost (Rp trillion)
	A	B	C	Being Audited	Total	
State-owned	-	-	6	1	7	136.4
Domestic private[b]	45	45	30	15	132	119.7
Regional development	12	11	4	-	27	1.3
TOTAL	54	56	40	16	166	257.5

Notes: a) Group C: banks with capital ratio below minus 25%.Group A: banks with capital ratio above 4%; Group B: banks with capital ratio between 4% and minus 25%;
   b) Includes two joint venture banks, namely: PT Bank Uppindo and Bank PDFCI.
Source: Ministry of Finance (1998), 'Program Restrukturalisasi Perbankan', *Press Release*, 9, December, Table 1.

Traditionally, state-owned financial institutions have been undercapitalized based on the presumption that the state will always stand by its banks, and any insolvency will carry through to the fiscal balance. Because state-owned banks are protected from closure on constitutional grounds and have their losses covered by the public budget, these banks tend to have lower incentives to innovate or control costs, and promptly identify problem loans at an early stage. Their loan loss performance is usually inferior to that of their private counterparts.

Banking systems with relatively high state ownership are characterized by a greater intrusion of the political objectives of government in almost all aspects of operation, including personnel and technology policies. At the same time, such banking systems also show greater recourse to the public financing of bank bailouts. Because risk involving state-owned banks is assumed by the state, lending skills (including risk appraisal) of their officers are generally poor. Because of state control, both physical infrastructure (such as computer systems) and human resources are inferior to that of their counterparts in the private sector. Overstaffing and overextended branch networks are also more prevalent for state-owned banks and financial institutions. This is partly because during the long period of financial repression, public financial institutions were operating at arm-length to the bureaucracy.

Thirdly, the process is being assisted by the Indonesian Bank Restructuring Agency (IBRA), an independent "bridge" agency acting under auspices of the Ministry of Finance. Established in January 1998,

IBRA has two main functions: first, to supervise banks in need of restructuring and manage the restructuring process and, secondly, to manage the assets it requires in the course of restructuring. The interdepartmental Financial Sector Action Committee sets the overall policy guidelines for the restructuring program. The members of this committee are the Coordinating Minister of Economy, Finance and Industry, the Governor of Bank Indonesia, the Minister of Finance, the Minister of Trade and Industry, the State Minister of Planning cum Head of the National Planning Agency (*Bappenas*).

The Assets Management Unit (AMU) of IBRA purchases non-performing loans (NPL) from distressed banks. These include the NPLs of the four state banks and non-performing corporate credit issued by BRI. The takeover of NPLs allows banks to focus on the traditional activities of deposit receiving and lending and not use too much of their resources in managing their heavy load of NPLs. The sharp reduction in the amount of NPLs from the peak in the second quarter of 1998 (see Figure 8.3) has been mainly due to IBRA purchases. This has allowed banks to resume credit expansion. Through the purchase of NPLs, the function of lender of last resort has been shifted via IBRA from the central bank to the Treasury.

Figure 8.3 The Development of Non-Performing Loan (NPL), June 1997–May 2000

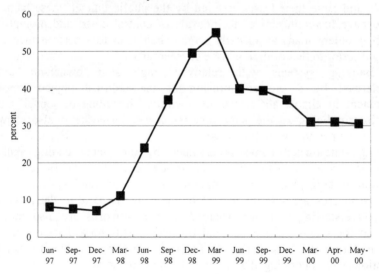

There were 54 banks placed under IBRA supervision in early September 1998. Of these, three were state-owned banks (PT Bapindo, PT BBD and PT BDN). As pointed out earlier, these banks, along with PT Bank Exim, have been merged into PT Bank Mandiri. Eleven of the banks under IBRA were Bank Pembangunan Daerah (BPDs) owned by provincial governments. The 40 privately owned banks under IBRA supervision are divided into two groups: four banks (PT BCA, Bank Danamon, PT Bank PDFCI and PT Bank Tiara) are classified as viable; the other 30 as not. A viable bank has some franchise value and a useful infrastructure, while a non-viable bank has none. Since April 1998, operations of ten of the non-viable banks have been either suspended or frozen.[9] Consequently, 23 banks have been closed or 10% of the 240 banks originally existed in July 1996.

The shareholders of the viable banks are required to focus more on banking by repaying inter-group loans and injecting fresh capital and management methods into their organizations, for the purpose of improving credit evaluation, credit management and risk. The banks were given a deadline of 21 September 1998 to repay their inter-group loans and liquidity supports received from Bank Indonesia. Those unable to meet the deadline were classified as non-viable banks. Their operating licenses were immediately revoked, and their shareholders are liable to repay losses and transfer all of their assets to IBRA's AMU. To give them some breathing space, the CAR standard was temporarily reduced on June 1988 to 4% until the end of 1998. The standard is to be raised to 8% by the end of 1999, then to further 10% by the end of 2000.

Table 8.7 The Cost of Bank Restructuring as of July 31, 2000

(Unit: Rupiah trillions)

	Total bonds	% of total	Fixed rate bonds					Variable rate bonds	Hedge bonds
			Total	5yr	6yr	7yr	10yr		
Bank Indonesia	218	34	0	0	0	0	0	0	0
Program Credit	10	1.6	0	0	0	0	0	0	0
Recapitalized banks:	402	64	150	55	31	31	34	218	35
State banks	265	64	102	40	18	18	28	127	35
Private banks (seven banks)	27	7	13	4	3	3	2	15	0
BTO in 1998	109	26	34	11	10	10	4	75	0
Regional development banks	1	0	0.4	0.1	0	0	0.3	0.8	0
Non-Recapitalized Banks:	9	1.4	7	0	0	0	7	2	
Bonds issued to date	639	100	157	55	31	31	34	219	35

Backed by government guarantee, Bank Indonesia provided the funds for financing the initial operations of IBRA. Additional funds are to be raised by issuing government bonds on domestic markets. The preliminary estimate of the cost of bank refinancing comes to Rp630 trillion (see Table 8.7), which is equivalent to around 55 to 60% of Indonesia's annual GDP. Banks under category B in Table 8.7 (56 banks as of December 1998), with capital to asset ratios between minus 25% and plus 4% are eligible for government support provided through IBRA. The shareholders of the eligible banks are required to mobilize 20% of the capital restructuring, and the government will provide the rest in form of loans to be repaid in five years. Since the government has no resources, IBRA will take over Bank Indonesia's liquidity credit to these banks and pay with Treasury bonds with an interest burden appearing in the national budget.

IBRA has a limited life span and will be disbanded once the bank rehabilitation program is completed. Given its expected longevity, IBRA can hold on to purchased asset until their values rise again. Any financial loss incurred by IBRA will be covered by the public budget. Currently the collateral backing NPLs ranges from prosaic real estate and shares to toll road and logging concessions. IBRA is able to buy a combination of performing or viable loans and NPLs, then restructure them together and inject fresh capital and/or better management methods in the hope of reviving the whole package. On the other hand, the distressed banks themselves have an option on what NPLs they want to retain. To determine the price of an NPL, IBRA has hired international accounting firms to evaluate its value based on international commercial standards.

Fourthly, to restore the confidence of domestic and international communities in Indonesian domestic banks, the authorities will explicitly provide full guarantees on demand, saving and time deposits of all banks in the country. Government guarantees will also be extended to cover credit received and guarantees and letters of credit issued by the banks. The debts incurred by failed banks to depositors and creditors are also covered by the scheme. Credit received by the bank owners and subordinated debts, however, are not covered by the program. In two years time, the scheme will be taken over by the yet to be established Deposit Insurance Scheme, administered by IBRA. Participating banks are required to contribute a half-year fee of 0.05% of guaranteed deposits and debts to the government guarantee scheme. The funds used by Bank Indonesia to bailout depositors and creditors will be credited to the government's annual budget in trances of five years.

In the short-run, the existence of such a scheme will reduce bank runs, which began following the closure of 16 banks in early November 1997. In exchange for guarantees, all locally incorporated banks are subject to enhanced supervision, to be done mainly by international accounting and law firms. Those who fail to meet Bank Indonesia standards are to be reviewed by IBRA. The scheme is expected to restore the confidence of both the domestic and international communities in the financial system. Since the outbreak of the crisis in August 1997, foreign banks have refused to accept letters of credit issued by Indonesian banks. In the long run, however, the credit insurance scheme will certainly create moral hazard problems, particularly with a relatively weak economic infrastructure.

Fifthly, to make operations of state-owned enterprises, including state-owned banks, more transparent and accountable, the performance of managers will be evaluated according to criteria set out in performance contracts. Political corruption can be significantly reduced by making state-owned enterprises more independent and by cutting their links to government bureaucracies.

Next, to strengthen Bank Indonesia by giving full autonomy in formulating and implementing monetary policy, a new central bank act will be introduced in May 1999. There are three main features of the draft: (1) raise the initial capital of the central bank to a minimum Rp two trillion and to link the capital to at least 10% of Bank Indonesia's monetary liability; (2) focus the role of Bank Indonesia in controlling inflation and stabilizing the external value of the rupiah, thus eliminating the development role of the central bank; and (3) move the role of banking supervision to a yet to be established financial sector supervisory agency, FRA.

The seventh and final element of the bank-restructuring program is to upgrade the quality of human resources and market infrastructure. Human resources can be improved through various programs, such as selection through proper testing and twinning programs with reputable foreign institutions. Prudential financial rules and regulations should be upgraded along the Basle core principles. Meanwhile, the capability of Bank Indonesia and FRA to enforce such rules and supervise the banking industry must also be upgraded.

Private Sector Debt Overhang

Rehabilitation of corporate financial strength and resumption of access by the corporate sector to international and domestic financial markets are preconditions for the restoration of production and exports. Exclusion from international capital markets affects the private sector most, since it is the main debtor to foreign creditors. Over 60% of the external debt as of March 1998 ($77.5 billion) were owed by the private sector, and nearly 90% of that was owed by non-bank corporate entities. The average maturity of this external debt is approximately 1.5 years (J.P. Morgan, *Global Data Watch*, January 16, 1998, p. 70). In addition, there is short-term external debt denominated in local currency amounting to $15 billion.

To relax external constraints, the IMF program of April 1988 has addressed problems of the private sector's short-term external debt. Out of $66 billion corporate external debt outstanding, about $30 billion will fall due in March 1998. In a policy statement issued on 27 January 1998, the government proposed a temporary freeze on servicing the private sector's external debts. It also made clear that the corporate debt problem should be solved on a voluntary basis between borrowers and lenders. The government will not provide financial resources, subsidies or guarantees to bail out those companies that cannot survive surging real interest rates, sharp devaluation of domestic currency, and/or falling sales. Private sector default will be permitted in all sectors, including the financial sector, and the government will neither those in financial difficulty nor guarantee their external debts and try to repackage into government bond issues. Since it is creditors that will certainly lose out (as in the case of Peregrine), Indonesia's access to international financial markets will be reduced. Some of the lost can be shifted to taxpayers through tax credits in the source countries.

An agreement between representatives of the government and domestic private sector and the steering committee of foreign lenders was reached in Frankfurt, Germany on June 4, 1998. According to this agreement, the private sector's external debt problem is to be solved based on a combination of Mexico's Ficorca program and the Korean scheme. The Korean idea takes the short-term, non-trade debts of Indonesian banks (amounting to $8.9 billion) and restructures them into loans with one- to four-year maturities. Interest on the new loans will be paid based on LIBOR plus margins, ranging between 2.75% and 3.5%, about 50 basis points wider than the Korean agreement. The non-bank corporate external debt ($58.79 billion) will be rescheduled and restructured along the lines of Ficorca program. A trust institution, called INDRA, is to be established by the government of Indonesia and administered by Bank Indonesia. INDRA "will provide exchange rate risk protection and assurance to the availability of foreign exchange to private debtors that agree with their creditors to restructure their external debt for a period of eight years, with three years of grace during which no principal will be payable".[10]

In September 1998, the Jakarta Initiative was announced to help solve the $65 billion private sector domestic debt by forming a Task Force to facilitate and coordinate the restructuring process. The Task Force is to work closely with the Corporate Restructuring Advisory Committee, consisting of representatives of domestic and foreign financial institutions, IBRA and INDRA, and providing recommendations to solve the workout problems. The legally non-binding principles so proposed to solve the problems at hand will be based on out-of-court commercial negotiations between debtors and creditors. The elements of the framework include the appointment of professional legal and financial advisors by each distressed debtor. Debt restructuring requires accurate and timely financial information from debtors. On the other hand, creditors will agree to a "standstills" (i.e., not charging default interest payment and/or other penalties). The creditors are to be treated the same as equity holders who have suffering their first losses.

As of October 1998, neither INDRA nor the Jakarta Initiative has made significant progress to solve the debt issue. Anticipating a rebound by the rupiah and taking advantage the scheme's weak legal sanctions, many debtors are adopting strategies to slowdown the negotiation process. They include delays in providing required information and blocking auditors, valuers and lawyers from conducting their investigations. Some debtors continue to move funds and shift assets from one distressed subsidiary to the other without consent of their creditors.

Conclusions

Prior to the crisis, all financial indicators (M1/GDP and M2/GDP) were rapidly rising in Indonesia following its financial sector reforms of the 1980s. In terms of assets and number of institutions and branch networks, the banking system remained the core of its financial systems. Other financial institutions are fast growing segments of the system, but their role is not yet as important as that played by banks.

Highly trained economists at the Ministries of Finance and Planning have become Indonesia's financial liberalizers. Bank Indonesia, the central bank, has played a supporting role and retains its direct control over the banking system.

Indonesia has adopted a different sequencing of economic and financial sector reforms since the early 1980s. In general, the coverage and speed of financial reform has been much wider and faster than in the real sector of the economy. Financial reform began in June 1983 with the relaxation of controls on interest rates and the elimination of sectoral loan allocation. However, the short-term money market was only beginning to develop in April 1984. More drastic reforms were introduced in October 1988, but new prudential rules and regulations would not be announced until two years later. The reforms of 1988 removed special purpose development type banks, reduced protection of domestic banks from foreign competition, and reduced special market preferences for state-controlled financial institutions.

Furthermore, since many banks, including state-owned institutions, were having difficulty in meeting the prudential standards, the authorities had to retreat back by relaxing the rules and regulations or by not imposing them as strictly as they could be. Since legal and accounting systems cannot be built overnight, the focus of bank supervision in Indonesia is likely to remain more on its regulatory aspects. Inherited from the colonial past, the base for securing contract and credit transactions is weak, and the laws and procedures for exit and bankruptcy are unclear. Financial disclosure is poor due to the difficulties in implementation of accounting standards and training of public accountants.

The transition to a more competitive environment and stricter rules and regulations is a very difficult task for the banking system. Problems are not limited only to state-owned banks, which are traditionally undercapitalized and have inherited a larger portion of low-yield, non-performing assets from past credit program; the number of bank crises faced by private banks and their clients has also been rising in recent years.

The fragility of the banking system limits strictness in monetary policy and austerity in fiscal policy. Tight liquidity, high interest rates, and a wide spread between deposit and lending interest rates have headed both the banking and corporate sector in the direction of bankruptcy. The extra burden for paying coupons on government bonds to refinance the banking system weakens support for fiscal austerity

Notes

[1] A paper presented at the "Symposium on the Financial Big Bang in Asia" held at Institute of Comparative Economic Studies, Hosei University, Tokyo, Japan, on 27-28 March 1999.

[2] The national car policy was contained in Presidential Instruction No. 2/1996, which gives "pioneer status to PT Timor Putra Nasional". This exclusive status exempts the company from paying a maximum 65% import duties for spare automobile parts, and maximum 35% import duty and luxury goods sale tax, both of which make up over 60% of the cost of automobile production in Indonesia. While completing its own production and assembling capacity in Indonesia, the company is allowed to import the first 45,000 units of diassembled cars from JIA of Korea. To boost car sales, the public sector is required to buy them. In return, the company promises to manufacture in stages an Indonesian-made car with local components comprising 20% in the first year of operation, over 40% in the second year, and over 60% in the third year. Fully backed by the Government and Bank Indonesia, a consortium of four state-owned banks and 12 private domestic banks extended $960 million worth of credit to the company to construct a production and assembly facility. PT Timor Putra is jointly owned by Hotomo Mandala Putra and KIA Motor Company of South Korea.

[3] Between October 1997 and May 1999, Indonesia signed six letters of intents (LoIs) with the IMF and three Supplementary Memoranda. Each LoI contains specific policy target and time schedule.

[4] Each provincial government has one RDB. In reality, the RDBs only operate as fiscal agents for their owners.

[5] J. P. Morgan. 1997. *Emerging Markets Data Watch*. July 1. page 3.

[6] Chile imposes a 30% reserve requirement ratio on gross inflows to be deposited with the Central Bank for one year.

[7] The authorities in Indonesia control prices of staple foods (such as rice, sugar and wheat flour), building materials (such as Portland cement), energy (such as electricity and petroleum products), and services (such as fares of ground, sea and air transportation and school tuition). The government of Singapore controls prices and rents of public housings.

[8] Previously, in January 1988, a number of private banks announced plans to merge. Bank Internasional Indonesia (BII), Bank Dagang Nasional Indonesia (BDNI), two of Indonesia's largest private banks, agreed to merge with three smaller banks (Bank Tiara Asia, Bank Sahid Gajah Perkasa and Bank Dewa Ruci). Four banks owned by President Suharto's four foundations (Bank Duta, Bank Tugu, Bank Umum Nasional, and Bukopin--Bank Umum Koperasi) are also to be merged into one bank. The widely diversified Bakri Group announced its plan to merge its four banks, Tirtamas Group issued a similar statement to merge its three banks, and Ramako Group will merge its two banks. It turns out that many of these large and small banks were forced to close by IBRA in September 1998.

[9] They are Bank Surya, Bank Subentra, Bank Istismarat, Bank Pelita, Bank Hokindo, Bank Deka, Bank Centris, Bank Dagang Nasional Indonesia (BDNI), Bank Umum Nasional, and Bank Modern.

[10] *"Joint Statement of the Indonesian Bank Steering Committee and Representatives from the Republic of Indonesia"*. Press Release. June 4, 1998.

References

Caprio Jr., Gerard and Patrick Honohan (eds) (1991), *Monetary Policy Instruments for Developing Countries,* A World Bank Symposium, Washington, D.C.: The World Bank Group.

Caprio Jr., Gerard, Izak Atiyas and James A. Hanson (1996), *Financial Reform, Theory and Evidence,* New York: Cambridge University Press.

Chandravarkar, Anand (1996), *Central Banking in Developing Countries,* New York: Macmillan Press Ltd.

Claessens, Stijn (1998), *Systemic Bank and Corporate Restructuring, Experiences and Lessons for East Asia,* Washington, D.C.: The World Bank Group.

Cole, David C. and Betty F. Slade (1996), *Building A Modern Financial System, The Indonesian Experience,* Cambridge, England: Cambridge University Press.

Cole, David C., Hal S. Scott and P.A. Wellons, *Asian Money Markets,* New York: Oxford University Press.

Dewatripont, Mathias and Jean Tirole, *The Prudential Regulation of Banks,* The Walas-Pareto Lectures at the Ecole des Hautes Etudes Commerciales, Universite de Lausanne. Cambridge, Ma.: the MIT Press.

Eichengreen, Barry, James Tobin, and Charles Wyplopsz (1995), 'Two cases for sand in the wheels of international finance', *Economic Journal* 105 (January): pp.162-172.

FAIR--Foundation for Advanced Information and Research, The Committee for the Development of Financial and Capital Markets in the Asia-Pacific Region, (1991), *Financial and Capital Markets in Asia,* Tokyo, September.

FAIR--Foundation for Advanced Information and Research, The Committee for the Development of Financial and Capital Markets in the Asia-Pacific Region, (1991), *Financial and Capital Markets in Asia*, Tokyo, September.

Frankel, J.A. (1994), 'Sterilization of Money Inflows: Difficult (Calvo) or Easy (Reisen)?', *IMF Working Paper*, No WP/94/159, December.

Fry, Maxwell J, Charles A.E. Goodhart and A. Almeida (1996), *Central Banking in Developing Countries, Objectives, Activities and Independence*, London and New York: Routledge.

Khatkhate, Deena R. and Klaus-Walter Riechel (1980), 'Multipurpose Banking: Its Nature, Scope, and Relevance for Less Developed Countries', *IMF Staff Papers*, Vol. 27, No.3, September: pp.478-516.

Krugman, Paul R (ed.) (1986), *Strategic Trade Policy and the New International Economics*, Cambridge, M.A.: the MIT Press.

Lindgren, Carl-Johan, Gillian Garcia, and Matthew I. Saal (1996), *Bank Soundness and Macroeconomic Policy*, Washington, D.C.: IMF.

McKinnon, R.I. (1991), *The Order of Economic Liberalization: Financial Control in the Transition to a Market Economy*, Baltimore: The Johns Hopkins University Press.

Nasution, Anwar (1983), *Financial Institutions and Policies in Indonesia*, Singapore: Institute of Southeast Asian Studies.

Nasution. Anwar (1986) 'Instruments of Monetary Policy in Indonesia after the 1983 Banking Deregulation', A paper prepared for *Conference on Financial Research in Indonesia*, sponsored by Ministry of Finance, Directorate of Financial Institutions, and Harvard Institute for International Development, Lembah Bukit Raya, August, mimeo.

Nasution. Anwar (1992) 'The Years of Living Dangerously: The Impacts of Financial Sector Policy Reforms and Increasing Private Sector External Indebtedness in Indonesia, 1983-1992', *Indonesian Quarterly*, August.

Nasution, Anwar (1994), 'Banking Sector Reforms in Indonesia, 1983-93', In Ross McLeod (ed.), *Indonesia Assessment 1994: Finance as a Key Sector in Indonesia's Development*, Singapore and Canberra: Institute of Southeast Asian Studies and Australian National University.

Nasution, Anwar (1996), *The Banking System and Monetary Aggregates Following Financial Sector Reforms, Lessons from Indonesia*, Research for Action 27, Helsinki: The United Nations University, WIDER.

Nasution, Anwar (1996), *Financial Sector Reforms: Indonesia versus Malaysia Since the 1980s*, A research to IDRC, September 1, Processed.

Nasution, Anwar (1997), 'Indonesian Economic Development Since the 1980s', in *East Asian Development Experience, Economic System Approach and Its Applicability*, Toru Yanagihara and S. Sambommatsu (eds), Tokyo: Institute of Developing Economies, Chapter 23, pp. 519-552.

Schumpeter, Joseph A. (1955), *The Theory of Economic Development*, translated from the German by Redvers Opie, Cambridge: Harvard University Press.

Shahid N. Zahid, (ed.) (1995), *Financial Sector Development in Asia*, Country Studies, Manila: Asian Development Bank.

Spahn, Paul Bernd (1995) International Financial Flows and Transaction Taxes: Surveys and Options, *IMF Working Paper*, No. WP/95/60 (June).

Stiglitz, J.E. (1994), 'The Role of the State in Financial Markets', in *Proceedings of the World Bank Conference on Development Economics 1993*, Supplement to the World Bank Economic Review and the World Bank Research Observer, Washington, D.C.: The World Bank Group.

Stiglitz, J.E. and Andrew Weiss (1981), 'Credit Rationing in Markets with Imperfect Information', *American Economic Review*, Vol. 7, No. 13, June.

Tobin, James (1979), 'A proposal for international monetary reform', *Eastern Economic Journal*, Vol. 4, July: 1953-159.

World Bank (1996), *Indonesia: Dimensions of Growth,* Report No. 15383-IND, Country Department III, East Asia and Pacific Region, May 7.

9 Financial Reform and Crisis in Malaysia

KOK FAY CHIN
K.S. JOMO

Introduction

Once considered by the World Bank (1993) as an impressive example of successful development, the Malaysian economy was transformed from an economic 'miracle' into a 'debacle' from mid 1997. With the exception of large current account deficits and worsening savings-investment gaps, Malaysia's macroeconomic fundamentals were generally sound prior to the crisis (see Table 9.1). Over the previous decade, Malaysia had enjoyed rapid growth, stable inflation, falling unemployment and fiscal surpluses. As such, the first generation of currency crisis theories—which focused on public sector debt related to fiscal deficits—were clearly irrelevant for explaining the financial crisis in Malaysia.

Table 9.1 Malaysia: Selected Macroeconomic Indicators, 1991-1997

Year	Real GDP (%)	Inflation (%)	Unemploy- ment (%)	Fiscal Balances (% of GDP)	Current Account (% of GDP)
1991	8.7	4.4	4.03	-2.0	-9.2
1992	7.8	4.7	3.7	-0.8	-3.8
1993	8.3	3.6	3.0	0.2	-4.8
1994	9.2	3.7	2.9	2.3	-6.3
1995	9.5	3.4	2.8	0.9	-8.5
1996	8.6	3.5	2.6	0.7	-4.9
1997	7.7	2.7	2.6	2.4	-5.1

Sources: Bank Negara Malaysia, *Annual Report*, 1996 and 1998.

One popular explanation for the East Asian crisis emphasises corruption, cronyism as well as lack of transparency, resulting in moral hazards, with adverse consequences for the economy. This diagnosis,

225

however, fails to provide a satisfactory explanation of why the crisis—which started in Thailand—spread to the rest of the region so quickly, leading to massive economic disruptions. Crony capitalism—which has existed for some time—fails to explain how Malaysia sustained rapid growth for four decades after independence in 1957 without experiencing any earlier financial crisis of comparable magnitude. More importantly, as pointed out by UNCTAD (1998), this explanation also ignores the similarities between financial crises in developed and developing economies, which have been occurring with increasing frequency since the late 1970s.

In this chapter, we argue that the roots of the currency and financial crises in Malaysia can be traced by examining pre-crisis financial developments in the country, before considering the broader macro-economic situation.[1] Given the dominance of the banking system and the growing importance of stock markets, our discussion will be mainly concerned with evolving banking and stock market developments in order to provide insights into the structure of Malaysia's financial system. Unlike some other East Asian economies that experienced sudden and extensive, if not comprehensive, financial reform packages, or a financial 'big bang', financial reforms in Malaysia have been undertaken gradually over the years. Notwithstanding the gradualist approach,[2] our analysis of the characteristics of financial developments and reforms in the years leading up to the crisis will shed light on how financial interests and liberalisation have undermined effective financial governance, both at the international and national levels, causing greater vulnerability of the system to crisis.

Financial Developments before the Crisis

Although Malaysia's financial system was relatively well developed, compared to other developing economies, during the British colonial era and in the early post-independence period, its intermediation role was limited. During that era, the main function of banking services was to facilitate trade. Banks mainly provided funds for the agency houses that dominated exports of the country's primary commodities (tin and rubber) as well as imports of consumer and capital goods.[3] Thus, financing was essentially short-term and self-liquidating in nature—mainly in the form of bills of exchange, documentary letters of credit, overdrafts and trust receipt facilities, which normally did not exceed 180 days for maturity—and were repaid as soon as the goods concerned were received or exported [Hing (1987)]. While the percentage of loans advanced for general commerce was high during this period, reaching 42% of total loans advanced by the commercial banking system, or about 25% of total loans advanced by the financial system in 1960, the amount of loans to productive sectors (such as agriculture and manufacturing) were low, amounting to less than 20% of total commercial bank loans, or less than 15% of total advances disbursed by the financial system. As Ho (1990) commented: 'Banks concentrated on discounting of trade bills, providing the letters of credit and checking the credit-worthiness of traders and merchants. In this sense, they were nothing more than foreign outfits to process trade papers and to act as insurers for merchants'.

Conscious efforts to develop the financial system only began after the establishment of the Central Bank of Malaya, which was renamed Bank Negara Malaysia (BNM) after the formation of Malaysia in September 1963. Since then, the financial system has been restructured, reorganised and reshaped to meet the increasing investment needs of the growing economy. It has certainly become much deeper, broader and more diverse, with a host of institutional developments taking place over the decades. The banking system, which has always been the core of the financial system, not only consists of monetary institutions (comprising BNM and commercial banks including Bank Islam),[4] but also non-monetary institutions (including finance companies and merchant banks).[5] The turn of the decade also saw the aggressive promotion and rapid growth of the capital market. In order to facilitate the mobilisation of financial resources for technological development in the manufacturing sector, the government has adopted several measures in recent years to promote venture capital industries.[6]

The indicators in Table 9.2 and Figure 9.1 capture the development of monetarisation and financial deepening in Malaysia. It is clear from Table 9.2 that the M2/GNP ratio rose from 0.46 in 1975 to 0.70 in 1985, and subsequently to 1.11 in 1997, reflecting rapid monetarisation in Malaysia. This is also reflected in the sharp increase of the M2/M1 ratio—from 2.3 in 1975 to 3.71 in 1985 and subsequently to 4.61 in 1997. This increasing monetarisation of the economy has been followed by a further deepening of Malaysia's financial system. As shown in Figure 9.1, the M3/GDP ratio in 1997 was more than double its value in 1980, although the transaction demand for money (M1) relative to GDP remained fairly stable over the period.

The Banking System

Generally, differences between different financial systems are the result of interactions of a number of different factors that have exerted influence over a long period of time [Rybczynski (1984)]. In other words, the evolution of different financial systems can be traced back to the political, social and economic histories of the countries concerned. Given that

Table 9.2 Malaysia: Monetarisation and Financial Deepening, 1975-1997

	1975	1980	1985	1990	1994	1995	1996	1997*
M1/GNP	0.20	0.19	0.19	0.22	0.26	0.25	0.25	0.24
M2/GNP	0.46	0.54	0.70	0.76	0.89	0.96	0.98	1.11
M2/M1	2.30	2.87	3.71	3.46	3.45	3.83	3.85	4.61
Currency/M1	0.51	0.49	0.46	0.41	0.34	0.34	0.31	0.34

Note: * Bank Negara Malaysia estimates.
Sources: Bank Negara Malaysia, *Quarterly Bulletin*, various issues.

Figure 9.1 Malaysia: Deepening of Financial System, 1980-1997

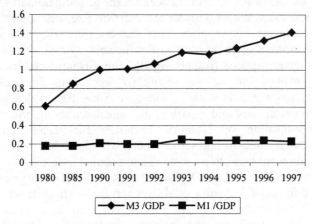

Sources: Bank Negara Malaysia, *Quarterly Bulletin*, various issues.

Malaysia is a former British colony which was greatly influenced by trends in the UK and US since independence, its financial system has exhibited many features of the Anglo-American model, which restricts banking activities to accepting deposits, granting loans and other specified activities. In contrast to the German and Japanese experiences, banks in Malaysia are prevented from becoming involved in corporate governance and management. Under the Banking (Control of Acquisition and Holding of Shares) Regulations, 1968,[7] a bank could only invest up to 10% of its paid-up capital and reserves (or 10% of net working funds in the case of a foreign bank) into trustee shares. Domestic banks were not permitted to hold shares in companies exceeding 25% of their paid-up capital and reserves, while foreign banks were not permitted to invest in such shares exceeding 25% of their net working funds [BNM (1989)].

Beginning from 1 September 1989, however, the scope of permissible investments by commercial banks was broadened to allow them to invest in Malaysia Airline System Berhad (MAS), the Malaysian International Shipping Corporation (MISC), and other approved "blue chip" shares, as well as into shares of manufacturing companies and property trusts, though subject to prescribed limits [for details, see BNM (1989), Lee (1992)]. Investments in manufacturing companies by a commercial bank cannot exceed 10% of the bank's paid-up capital and reserves (or 5% of a foreign bank's net working funds), whichever is lower. The sum of these shares should not exceed 25% of a domestic bank's paid-up capital and reserves, or 25% of a foreign bank's net working funds. As the Japanese and German experiences show, allowing banks to own non-controlling shares in companies, even in limited amounts, is desirable, as it helps to develop and maintain close bank-firm relations and banks gain an incentive to monitor the firms. This does not imply that the Japanese or German model can be easily replicated in Malaysia–as will be seen in the ensuing paragraphs.

Apart from historical accidents, many institutional arrangements and developments in Malaysia's financial system are the result of the regulatory framework that has evolved over the decades. Commercial banks—the oldest established financial intermediaries—have remained the largest institutions within the banking system, with total assets worth RM362 billion, or 57.5% of the total assets of the banking system, in 1996 [BNM (1997a)]. Their significance results from the role they play as retail deposit takers as well as providers of current accounts. They provide financing in the forms of overdrafts, trade bills and term loans. During the early post-independence period, Malaysia's financial structure was relatively simple, with a few commercial banks basically serving trading requirements. This traditional pattern of lending has, however, changed significantly over time, as reflected by the declining share since independence of general commerce in total loans and advances. Another positive development in the evolution of commercial bank lending has been increased term lending, involving a lengthening of the average maturity period for credit. There was a decline in the use of overdrafts for short-term financing—from 37.2% of total loans and advances in 1978 to 29.7% by the end of 1990 [Zainal *et al.* (1994)]. This can partly be attributed to the BNM urging commercial banks to emphasise term lending in view of the rising demand for long-term credit accompanying rapid industrialisation and economic growth.

The 1965 establishment of Bank Bumiputera, Malaysia's first state-owned commercial bank, marked the beginning of active direct government intervention in finance. Following a resolution of the First Bumiputera[8] Economic Congress in 1965, this state-owned bank was set up in 1966 to provide commercial loans to Malay entrepreneurs. The government became a major shareholder of Malayan Banking in 1969 after a run on the bank in 1966. By 1976, when the then United Malayan Banking Corporation (UMBC)[9] came under government control, the government dominated the banking system, owning the three largest commercial banks in the country. These state-owned banks were used to facilitate the implementation of the New Economic Policy (NEP), introduced in 1970, especially in terms of redistribution, as well as the government's heavy industrialisation programme which was launched in 1981. State-controlled joint ventures with foreign capital began to invest in heavy industries such as Perwaja Steel and Proton (Perusahaan Otomobil Nasional). These state-sponsored corporations received loans at subsidised interest rates.

The first half of the 1980s saw many abuses by directors and staff at banks and finance companies in terms of lending operations. Some major Bumiputera-controlled conglomerates emerged, usually under the patronage of powerful politicians, e.g. with soft loans from state-owned banks and awards of major projects and lucrative licenses as well as other business opportunities including privatisation [Gomez (1994)]. The ownership of financial institutions as well as top corporations by the government and state-owned enterprises, and later, the privatisation of some of them, served to encourage such developments. Huge loans could be obtained without proper procedures, and were often extended to highly speculative get-rich-quick schemes rather than for productive investments. Because of this, other national developmental priorities, e.g. industrial policy, have been neglected.

Meanwhile, many major corporate groups controlled by non-Bumiputeras have also grown thanks to political patronage, arising from close ties with powerful, usually Malay politicians [Gomez and Jomo (1997)]. During the height of the implementation of the ethnic redistributive NEP, many Chinese capitalists minimised their vulnerability to long-term risks by moving capital abroad, mainly from the mid-1970s until the mid-1980s [Jomo (1990)]. It was estimated by Morgan Guaranty that total capital flight during the period from 1976 to 1985 amounted to US$12 billion [Khoo (1994) as cited in Gomez and Jomo (1997)]. In addition, many of those who remained within the country preferred short-term investments in construction, commercial property and residential housing at the expense of more productive investments, e.g. in manufacturing.

Following the liberalisation of interest rates in October 1978,[10] coinciding with a property boom, there was another tendency toward short-termism in the banking sector, favouring short-term loans with high rates of return rather than productive long-term investments. As noted by

Zainal *et al.* (1994), the shares of different sectors among total loans and advances extended by commercial banks have generally moved in line with changes in capital productivity and share of gross domestic product (GDP). However, the share of bank credit to the property sector rose from 21% in 1978 to a peak of 36.6% in 1987 [Zainal *et al*, (1994)]. This huge increase stood in stark contrast to an only modest increase in the relative importance of building and construction in GDP, and rather reflected the greater profitability of real estate investments due to rapid price rises. Loans made by the banking system for consumption credit also rose, together with loans for the purchase of stocks and shares. As a result, the share of credit going to the manufacturing sector declined during this period despite a sharp increase in the manufacturing's share of GDP.

Efforts to liberalise the financial system were underway even before the strong institutions needed for effective prudential regulation and supervision became well-established, thus exacerbating the situation. This led to the mushrooming in the eighties of poorly regulated deposit-taking cooperatives (DTCs), with weak capital bases, who engaged in speculative and unproductive investments as well as connected lending to or investments in subsidiaries and related companies. Taking advantage of the more liberal interest rate regime and lax regulations, most of these DTCs, which were already insolvent due to hidden losses from investments in shares and property—began to offer higher deposit rates and attractive commissions for their staff to attract deposits—giving the illusion of high liquidity and disguising the rapid deterioration of their actual assets [BNM (1987)]. By the mid 1980s, 24 ailing DTCs had collapsed, involving over 522,000 depositors and total deposits of RM1.5 billion [Sheng (1989)]. As pointed out by Hino (1998), 'the presence of small institutions came to pose systemic risks, not only because of the large number of such institutions that failed, but also because these weaker institutions had attracted larger shares of banking system deposits'.

The lack of incentives for Malaysian bankers to favour long-term lending for productive investments is one reason behind the limited development of Malaysian manufacturing capabilities, especially in non-resource-based export-oriented industries (which are dominated by foreign investors). Export-oriented manufacturing accounts for only a very small percentage of total outstanding loans extended by commercial banks. With the exception of export credits and some relatively minor financial institutions, there is little evidence of financial policy serving as an important industrial policy tool in Malaysia [Chin and Jomo (2000), Chin (2001)]. Only slightly over a quarter of Malaysian commercial bank lending goes to manufacturing, agriculture and other productive activities;

this percentage is likely even smaller with foreign borrowings, most of which have been collateralised with assets such as real property and stocks.

Malaysian banks also tend to be conservative, extending loans principally on the basis of collateral rather than project viability. 'These policies ... impose on industry a similarly cautious and short-term view of investment, profitability and profit allocation and inhibit long-term or high-risk industrial investment' [Hing (1987)]. In times of bullish property and stock markets, this emphasis on loan security has encouraged loans to the real property sector, for share purchases and for consumption, rather than for production. A BNM Survey of Private Investment in Malaysia found that this reduction in the share of bank credit to the manufacturing sector caused firms to rely increasingly on internally generated funds. On average, the surveyed firms financed 52 to 66% of their capital expenditures from internally generated funds in the 1986-90 period. Bank financing accounted for just 10 to 14% of total financing. Although banks still provided a larger share of external finance than the capital market (ranging from 1 to 8%), this probably reflected the less developed state of the capital market vis-à-vis the banking system at the time. Company size was also found to be an important determinant of access to credit, with larger companies enjoying lower average credit costs. This could be due to the less stringent requirements imposed by financial institutions on bigger companies with better track records and reputations [see Zainal *et al.* (1994)]. This 'discrimination' was more pronounced during the recession of 1985-86, when the average cost of credit for large companies was almost 11% lower than for small and medium-sized enterprises.

Despite restrictions on entry and branching imposed on foreign banks in Malaysia, special incentives have been provided to entice foreign banks to open up in Labuan, which the government designated as an international offshore financial centre (IOFC) on 1 October 1990. Various measures have been taken to make Labuan comparable to some of the 'best' IOFCs around the world, enhancing the attractiveness of Malaysia as an investment centre. To this end, a relatively liberal regulatory environment has been established on the island: exchange rate control regulations pertaining to offshore business activities have been made very liberal; and preferential tax treatment for income, profits, dividends and interest earned from offshore business activities has been offered.[11] As of the end of 1993, 21 banks had been granted licences by the Minister of Finance to conduct offshore banking activities [BNM (1994)].

In 1989, the Banking and Financial Institutions Act (BAFIA) was passed by Parliament, with vast implications for the governance of the financial system. In the mid 1990s, well before the crisis, BNM began trying to consolidate Malaysian banks, in anticipation of further financial liberalisation. A new two-tier regulatory system was introduced in December 1994. The new system sought to provide incentives for smaller banks to recapitalise and merge. Only bigger 'tier one' banks were allowed to handle certain lucrative kinds of transactions denied to other banks, such as opening foreign currency accounts. To qualify for 'tier-one' status, banks must have an equity base of at least RM500 million. Hence, while 'financial restraint'[12] exists in Malaysia, it has primarily sought to ensure bank profitability, especially with the increasing Bumiputera dominance of the Malaysian banking system from the 1970s. Banks in Malaysia have also been heavily used by the state to redistribute and accumulate wealth, ostensibly in line with the NEP. As Bumiputeras advanced their interests in the financial sector, rents were created by limiting competition in some areas, especially from foreign banks. However, this was not complemented by other policies to restrict wasteful competition in the banking sector that might erode these rents. For example, generous banking margins fostered wasteful competition, e.g. too many bank branches competing for limited business in particular areas, resulting in socially wasteful duplication of services, which also has undermined the possibilities of economies of scale in the provision of banking services [Chin and Jomo (2000)].

Stock Market Development[13]

Although share trading in Malaysia began as early as in the 1870s, involving British companies dealing primarily in rubber, tin and international trade, the public trading of stocks and shares was not undertaken until May 1960 when the Malayan Stock Exchange was established [Drake (1969), Zeti (1989)]. It was renamed the Stock Exchange of Malaysia in 1964 after the formation of Malaysia on 14 September, 1963 and then the Stock Exchange of Malaysia and Singapore after the separation of Singapore from Malaysia in 1965. After that, it had continued to operate as a unified stock exchange with separate trading rooms in Kuala Lumpur and Singapore [Zeti (1989)]. In 1990, it broke away from its Siamese twin, paving the way for its subsequent rapid expansion.

As noted by Singh (1995), contemporary stock market development in many developing countries has not been a spontaneous response to market forces; governments have played a major role in the expansion of these markets. This is particularly true of Malaysia. Between September 1961 and June 1964, the embryonic stock market enjoyed a boom [Drake (1975)], before turning bearish in 1965,[14] as a result of the existence of counterfeit shares, in spite of the fact that economic conditions during the year were relatively buoyant. Under the supervision of the Capital Issues

Committee (CIC) and following a government requirement that companies granted pioneer status tax relief go public, there was marked growth in new market issues from 1968 [Zeti (1989)].

With the promulgation of the NEP in 1970, redistribution, especially along inter-ethnic lines, became the government's top public policy priority. Since 1976, firms issuing shares to the public have had to offer 30% of their equity to Bumiputeras. The Foreign Investment Committee (FIC) has became an important government body monitoring and influencing non-Bumiputera and foreign owned corporations, encouraging them to restructure their equity to comply with the NEP's ownership regulations. Together with the FIC, the CIC sets the prices of shares issued by local Chinese and foreign firms in the interest of Malays, including special government-financed trust agencies and investment funds for Bumiputeras. The prices are usually set below market prices[15] to ensure positive returns for these special investment funds, in order to accelerate capital accumulation and speed up the acquisition of corporate assets by Bumiputeras. Mohamed Ariff *et al.* (1993) argue that the excessive underpricing of Malaysia's initial public offerings (IPOs) was mainly due to government intervention in price setting, and not merely the consequence of asymmetric information, winner's curses or *ex ante* uncertainty or seasoning.[16] The excessive underpricing of new issues has created good prospects for capital gains through immediate sale in the market after successful subscription allocations, resulting in the over-subscription of new issues, particularly in the case of KLSE Second Board new listings.[17] The possibility of making quick tax-exempt capital gains, encouraged many to subscribe to new shares [Ng (1989)].

The stock market has grown with considerable support from the government and those who have sought to use the stock market and publicly-listed firms to capture various types of rents and to secure better access to relatively cheap funds through the securities markets or from financial institutions, which increasingly used stock market listing and performance as loan market signals [Chin and Jomo (2000)]. The political influence of many key players encouraged such developments. In August 1985, the Finance Minister gave banks permission to give up to 100% loan support for share purchases, despite persistent warnings from Bank Negara Malaysia against extending loans for share speculation [Khor (1987)]. Thus, increased bank lending for the purchase of shares led to rises in share trading and stock values. He also directed government-controlled investment institutions, such as the Employees Provident Fund, to invest into stocks. The privatisation of state-owned enterprises further contributed to stock market growth in the country. The substantial funds raised by the capital market since 1990 can be partly attributed to the government's privatisation programme, which has undoubtedly considerably deepened Malaysian's stock market.

This period also saw sharply increased equity flows into the Malaysian stock market. This swelling was partly due to the gradual liberalisation of financial markets and regulations. The government announced an eighteen-point financial market liberalisation program to enhance Malaysia's position as a major international financial centre. One strategy was to attract foreign institutional investors by allowing fund managers to buy more equity in Malaysian corporations and to reduce the tax rate on their profits to 10%. Table 9.3 shows the withholding tax rates for dividends and long-term capital gains offered by selected emerging markets to US-based institutional investors, as well as restrictions on foreign ownership of listed stocks, in 1996. Malaysia is clearly the most liberalised market. With greater access to the Malaysian stock market as well as the reduction or removal of withholding taxes on capital gains and dividends, the interest of international investors in the emerging Malaysian stock market grew rapidly. Enormous inflows of foreign portfolio investment accelerated the growth of Malaysia's stock market.

Table 9.3 Barriers to Portfolio Investments in Selected Emerging Stock Markets, 1996

Country	Withholding Taxes		Foreign Investment Ceiling for Listed Stocks
	Dividends (%)	Long-term Capital Gains (%)	
Malaysia	0.0	0.0	100% in general
Indonesia	20.0	0.1	49% in general; 85% for securities companies
Philippines[a]	15.0	0.5	40% in general; 30% for banks
Thailand	10.0	0.0	10%-49% depending on company by-laws
India	20.0	10.0	24% in general
Korea[b]	16.5	0.0	20% in general; 15% for KEPCO and POSCO
Taiwan	35.0	0.0	25% in general

Notes: a) Transactions tax in lieu of a capital gains tax
b) Rates are for funds in which US investments total more than 25%. Tax rate shown include a 10% resident tax applied to base rates
Source: IFC, *Emerging Stock Market Factbook*, 1997.

In 1993, the Malaysian stock market gained a reputation as a kind of casino, with active trading fuelled by heady optimism, sudden interest from foreign institutional investors and a frenzy of speculation over corporate takeovers (*Asian Wall Street Journal*, 26 March 1996). The KLSE Composite Index (KLCI) nearly doubled to 1275 points, before crashing to

971 points in the following year, while market capitalisation as a proportion of GDP rose more than two-fold from the previous year's figure. The volume of shares traded jumped by more than 450%, and rose by more than 650% in value terms to reach RM387 billion.

Successful promotion of the stock market in the 1990s brought about significant financial disintermediation from the banking system to the securities markets, particularly in the bull-run years of the early 1990s (see Table 9.4), though corporate savings continue to account for much of corporate financing. When the stock market was booming, Malaysia's banks lost much of their deposit base to the stock exchange, particularly during the bull periods in 1993 and 1996. Higher returns on equities, with opportunities for making quick tax-free capital gains, resulted in portfolio substitutions. The Malaysian stock exchange's share of the total deposit base increased significantly from 48.8% in 1991 to 53.3% in 1992 before reaching almost 70% in 1993, while the commercial banks' share dropped from 23.1% in 1991 to 13.4% in 1993. This disintermediation was reversed as the stock market turned bearish in 1994.

Table 9.4 Malaysia: Classification of Deposits by Financial Institutions, 1990-1996

(Unit: % Share)[a]

	1990	1991	1992	1993	1994	1995	1996
Commercial Banks[b]	22.8	23.1	20.1	13.4	16.1	17.3	16.1
Finance Companies[b]	10.4	10.6	8.5	5.3	6.2	6.3	5.7
National Savings Bank[c]	1.0	0.9	0.8	0.5	0.6	0.5	0.5
Employees Provident Fund	16.9	16.0	13.4	8.1	10.3	10.5	9.2
Life Insurance Companies	0.6	0.6	0.5	0.3	0.4	0.5	0.4
Unit Trust Funds	N.A.	N.A.	3.4	3.1	4.4	4.7	4.7
K.L. Stock Exchange	48.2	48.8	53.3	69.4	62.1	60.2	63.4

Notes: a) Allow for +/- 3% variation;
   b) Figures do not include Negotiable Certificates of Deposits (NCDs) issued and Repurchase Agreements (Repos)
   c) Figures consist of 'amount standing to credit of depositors' plus 'Premium Savings Certificates depositors'
      N.A. - Not available

Sources: *Asian Banker*, cited by *Banker's Journal Malaysia* (1995), BNM, *Annual Report*, 1997, Ministry of Finance (1996 and 1997) and Kuala Lumpur Stock Exchange (1997).

Recent data suggests that in 1990, the Malaysian stock market emerged as a more important source of funds than commercial banks. The share of equity market financing in total funds raised by the private sector rose significantly from 9% during 1980-85 to 19% during 1990-96. But the stock market boom of recent years has not raised the effectiveness of mobilising funds for productive investment, since more than 50% of the total funds raised in the equity market through initial public offerings (IPOs) during 1990-96 went to privatised projects [BNM (1997)]. Adam and Cavendish (1995) suggest that these privatisation issues may well have crowded out other private investment issues, unless total foreign capital and portfolio inflows were very high. Since 1993, the increased funds raised through rights issues were reflected in an expansion of existing stocks or capitalisation. Table 9.5 shows that much of the funds raised from the equity market in 1996 were from rights issues, which mobilised 43% of all funds raised during 1993-7, while initial public offers only accounted for 31%. With privatisation, 'capital resources—which might otherwise have been invested into expanding productive capacity—have instead been diverted into acquiring or transferring existing public sector assets' [Jomo (1995)].

Table 9.5   Kuala Lumpur Stock Exchange: New Issues of Shares[a], 1992-1997

(Unit: Ringgit millions and % Share)

	1992	1993	1994	1995	1996	1997
Initial Public Offers	5,415.8	912.7	2,972.9	4,175.0	4,099.2	4,781.0
	(59.0%)	(26.6%)	(35.1%)	(36.5%)	(25.7%)	(26.0%)
Rights Issues	3,437.8	1,176.9	3,436.7	5,240.2	5,268.5	8,524.9
	(37.4%)	(34.3%)	(40.6%)	(45.8%)	(33.1%)	(46.4%)
Special Issues[b]	300.4	684.2	1,249.4	875.5	2,002.3	1,818.8
	(3.3%)	(19.9%)	(14.8%)	(7.7%)	(12.6%)	(9.9%)
Private Placements[c]	27.5	658.8	798.9	1,146.9	4,554.4	3,233.6
	(0.3%)	(19.2%)	(9.4%)	(10.0%)	(28.6%)	(17.6%)
Preference Shares	-	-	-	-	-	-
Total	9,181.5	3,432.6	8,457.9	11,437.6	15,924.4	18,358.3
	(100.0%)	(100.0%)	(100.0%)	(100.0%)	(100.0%)	(100.0%)

Notes: a) Excluding funds raised by the exercise of Employee Share Options Schemes, Transferable Subscription Rights, Warrants and Irredeemable Convertible Unsecured Loans Stocks.
   b) Issues to Bumiputera investors and selected investors
   c) Including Restricted-Offer-For-Sale
Sources: Adapted from Bank Negara Malaysia, *Annual Report,* 1997 and 1999.

In addition, banks are no longer assured of easy and stable sources of income from large loans given to well-established corporations as more and more corporate borrowers resort to tapping funds directly from the securities market. Due to the shrinking customer base in the lending business following growing competition from the securities market, banks have had to turn to servicing small and medium enterprises (SMEs) and households, which generally do not have direct access to the capital market. However, the tendency of Malaysian banks to emphasise loan security–rather than project viability–has discouraged loans, even to viable SMEs, due to their lack of collateral.[18] They are more attracted to giving direct loans for consumption, especially with the steady increase in income due to rapid growth and rising household wealth, because of the appreciation of property and stock market prices from the late 1980s.

Financial Fragility and Crisis

In the preceding section, we showed how increased liberalisation of the financial sector reduced the franchise value of the banking sector, which according to Hellmann, Murdock and Stiglitz (1997) is so crucial in inducing banks to effectively monitor and manage the risk of their loan portfolios.[19] Although no more new banking licences were granted to foreign banks from 1974 and various restrictions were imposed on them, the franchise value of large banks in Malaysia declined. The share of deposits of the ten largest banks declined from about 84% of the total in 1975 to 77% in 1990, while their share of total assets fell from 80% in 1975 to 72% [Zainal *et al.* (1994)].[20] Thus, banks underwent disintermediation on both sides of their balance sheets. In the absence of strong institutional arrangements for effective prudential regulation and supervision to realign incentives, the erosion of franchise values led to a distortion of the banks' risk-taking behaviour, thus exacerbating moral hazard problems and hence the fragility of the banking system.[21]

High Exposure to Loans for 'Non-tradeables'

Notwithstanding its efforts to improve the regulatory and supervisory systems, the BNM was rather ineffective in checking the growing fragility of the financial sector, particularly due to the direction of bank lending. Despite several warnings from the BNM, banks continued to lend to the property sector, which in 1986 accounted for 55% of all new loans, compared to 32% in 1980 [Zainal, *et al.* (1994)]. When the property and stock markets collapsed following the recession in the mid-1980s, a string of banks–particularly those with weak and dishonest managements–fell into serious trouble, causing a large percentage of property-based loans to become non-performing. This large overhang of non-performing loans in the banking system required substantial provisions for interest in suspense and bad debts.

The banking crisis in the mid 1980s was short-lived, thanks to improving external conditions and a manufacturing expansion following selective deregulation and other new incentives to attract foreign direct investment which had been implemented in the late 1980s, contributing to revivals of the stock and property markets. It is perhaps due to this speedy recovery that Malaysian policymakers did not learn to become much more prudent in lending despite erecting the Banking and Financial Institutions Act (BAFIA) in 1989. Moreover, in the face of greater lending competition from a more liberalised market, banks sought alternative lending opportunities such as funding real estate and share purchases, and competed fiercely to lend as long as the loans were collateralised. Thus, their exposure to property and share purchases grew quickly in the first half of the 1990s, as it had in the 1980s. This heavy lending encouraged over-investment in non-tradeables, aggravating current account trade deficits and fuelling asset price bubbles in the economy. As noted by Rasiah (1998), 'over-expansion in construction before achieving industrial maturity has created a big dent in Malaysia's capacity to finance growth'.

Thus, the economic boom from the late eighties was built on shaky and unsustainable foundations. Rapid growth in Malaysia became increasingly heavily reliant on foreign resources, both in terms of capital and labour. Foreign direct investment significantly supplemented domestic investment, accounting for, on average, 19%[22] of gross fixed capital formation during the 1990-6 period.[23] As a result of intense competition from lower-cost exporters, especially China,[24] and rising production costs, Malaysia's future economic progress could no longer be secured by reliance on its previous economic strategy of utilising cheap labour and keeping other production costs low. Inappropriate investments in human resources continued to limit the development of greater industrial and technological capabilities in the country, as elsewhere in the region [Jomo and Felker (1999), Jomo, Felker and Rasiah, (1999)]. Inappropriate financial policy also continued to limit the commitment[25] of financial institutions to provide long-term resources for manufacturing, let alone more innovative and higher technology-based activities requiring long gestation periods [Chin (2000)].

The Build-Up of External Private Debt

Stock exchange listing has been an important means to gain access to bank borrowing on better terms. The establishment of the Labuan International Offshore Financial Centre (IOFC) facilitated greater access for Malaysia, on better terms, to international funds. According to the BNM's Cash Balance of Payments Reporting System, net international funds sourced from the Labuan IOFC increased from RM69 million in 1991 to RM7,441 million in 1996. On the supply side, intense competition among 'debt-pushing' Japanese and continental European banks (who appreciated the higher interest rates available for dollarised short-term loans to the region) further eased access to foreign funds. These and other financial reforms as well as the growth of 'private banking' and 'relationship banking' in the region, weakened the scope and efficacy of national-level prudential regulations. On the demand side, more Malaysian corporations seeking lower financing costs began to tap funds from abroad.

As a result, there was a surge of private sector debt in the mid-90s, especially from abroad (see Table 9.6). As in Thailand and Indonesia, the non-bank private sector was the major recipient of international bank loans, accounting for more than 50% of total foreign borrowings by the end of June 1997 (see Table 9.7). The foreign borrowings of almost 90 of Malaysia's largest listed and KLCI-indexed companies have been estimated at around RM35 billion, with the three largest borrowers–Malaysian Airline Berhad, Tenaga Nasional Berhad and Telekom Malaysia Berhad–alone accounting for three-quarters of this foreign corporate debt.

Tables 9.6 and 9.7 show that the banking sector has also been borrowing extensively from abroad. According to BNM, commercial banks' net foreign liabilities increased from RM10.3 billion at the end of 1995 to RM25.2 billion in June 1997, while their net external reserves position deteriorated from –RM5.3 billion to –RM17.7 billion over the same 18-month period.

Table 9.6   Malaysia: External Short-term Debt of the Banking and Non-Bank Private Sector Outstanding, 1988-1997

(Unit: Ringgit millions)

	Banking Sector	Non-bank Private Sector
1988	2,464	N.A.
1989	3,343	N.A.
1990	4,415	N.A.
1991	7,171	N.A.
1992	13,157	N.A.
1993	17,320	N.A.
1994	9,840	4,404
1995	11,293	4,911
1996	17,648	8,098
1997	32,665	11,322

Note: Short-term debt refers to debt with tenure of one year and below.
Source: BNM *Quarterly Economic Bulletin*, various issues.

Table 9.7   Lending by BIS Reporting Banks to Selected Asian Economies by Sector (as of end-June, 1997)

(Unit: US $ billions)

	South Korea	Thailand	Indonesia	Malaysia
Total Borrowings	103.4	69.4	58.7	28.8
Banks	67.3	26.1	12.4	10.5
(%)	(65.1)	(37.6)	(21.1)	(36.5)
Private Non-bank	31.7	41.3	39.7	16.5
(%)	(30.6)	(59.5)	(67.6)	(57.3)
Government	4.4	12.0	6.5	1.9
(%)	(4.3)	(17.3)	(11.1)	(6.6)

Source: Bank for International Settlements (BIS) as cited by Jomo (1998a).

From the beginning of the decade, Malaysia sustained current account deficits. The over-investment of investible funds into 'non-tradeables' only made things worse. In so far as such investments–e.g. into power generations and telecommunications–did not contribute to export earnings, they aggravated the problem of currency mismatch, with foreign borrowings being invested in activities which did not generate foreign exchange. An additional problem of 'term mismatch' also arose as a high proportion of these foreign borrowings were short-term in nature (see Table 9.8) but were deployed to finance medium- to long-term projects.

Table 9.8   Maturity Distribution of Lending by BIS Reporting Banks to Selected Asian Economies

(Unit: US $ billions)

	All Loans			Under 1 Year			1-2 Years		
	June 1996	Dec 1996	June 1997	June 1996	Dec 1996	June 1997	June 1996	Dec 1996	June 1997
South Korea	88.0	100.0	103.4	62.3	67.5	70.2	3.4	4.1	4.1
Thailand	69.4	70.1	69.4	47.8	45.7	45.6	4.1	4.9	4.6
Indonesia	49.3	55.5	58.7	30.0	34.2	34.7	3.5	3.6	3.5
Malaysia	20.1	22.2	28.8	10.0	11.2	16.3	0.8	0.7	0.6

Source: Bank for International Settlements (BIS) as cited by Jomo (1998a).

The Surge of Portfolio Investment

Like other emerging markets in the region, Malaysia experienced an unprecedented surge of portfolio investment inflows in the early 1990s. This surge was attributable to the interaction of various push and pull factors.[26] The gradual liberalisation of the financial market provided the impetus for the massive portfolio inflows that sought to maximise capital gains in the bullish Malaysian stock market (Table 9.9). During the 1991-1995 period, portfolio investment funds accounted for 88% of identified gross capital inflows, while net foreign portfolio investment averaged 5.1 percent of GDP [Ong (1998)]. In 1993 and 1994, portfolio inflows alone surpassed GDP in current market prices, reaching US$67 billion and US$87 billion, respectively. Inevitably, the encouragement of the entry of foreign financial institutions into the stock market made the national economy much more vulnerable to international macro-economic fluctuations as well as capital flight, and rendered the tasks of exchange rate management and controlling inflation much more difficult. The huge short-term capital inflows proved to be destabilising as they involved closer links between two inherently unstable markets, i.e. the stock and currency markets. The central bank was reported to be incurring high costs as it managed a tight monetary policy to neutralise the potentially destabilising inflows of speculative foreign funds.[27] After a sudden exodus of such funds in early 1994, temporary controls aimed at limiting portfolio inflows were put into place, but were removed once speculative pressures on the ringgit declined by the end of the year.

Table 9.9   Malaysia: Annual Capital Inflows by Major Category, 1989-1995

(Unit: % of GDP)

	1989	1990	1991	1992	1993	1994	1995
Net Capital Inflows	3.5	4.2	11.9	15.2	16.8	1.6	8.5
Official Development Finance	-2.4	-2.4	-0.5	-1.4	0.6	0.3	2.7
Foreign Direct Investment	4.4	5.4	8.5	9.0	7.8	6.0	4.7
Commercial Bank Funds	1.1	2.0	2.8	6.3	6.6	-7.0	0.1
Portfolio Equity	N.A.	N.A.	-1.5	5.6	14.5	5.7	1.2

Source: BNM's Cash BOP Reporting System, as cited by Ong (1998).

It has been estimated by stock market analysts that by mid-1997, about a quarter of the stocks in the Kuala Lumpur Stock Exchange were in foreign hands, with another quarter held by Malaysian institutions, and the remaining half by 'retail investors'. While most small Malaysian shareholders only operate within the Malaysian stock market, foreign institutional investors see the Malaysian market as only one of many different types of capital markets in a global financial system that includes many national markets. In other words, the global financial system is hardly a market of equals. Foreign investment institutions could shift their assets among securities markets as well as among different types of financial investment options all over the world. Because of poor information, exacerbated by limited transparency, the nature of fund managers' incentives and remuneration, the short-termism of their investment horizons and their global reach, if not global presence, foreign financial institutions were more prone to herd behaviour and contributed greatly to the regional spread of panic, the so-called "Asian contagion". Although foreign funds never owned a majority of shares in the market, their influence grew disproportionately as they tended to become market leaders, with greater turnover than domestic institutions and far greater clout than local 'retail players'.

Speculation and Contagion

The increased fragility of the financial system brought about by increased financial liberalisation–that reduced effective prudential regulation and supervision–ultimately caused vulnerability to crisis as it inflicted additional burdens on a shaky real economy already bleeding from the consequences of overheating. It did not take very long for the contagion from the Asian financial crisis–that began with the floating of the Thai baht on July 2 1997–to spread to the rest of the region, including Malaysia. With the baht down, currency speculators turned their sights on the other economies in the region that had similar unsustainable quasi-pegs to the US dollar. Speculators, anticipating a glut in the property market due to an over-expansion in recent years, and noting Malaysia's high exposure to short-term foreign borrowings (albeit generally smaller than many of its neighbours in the region), began to mount attacks on the Malaysian ringgit. The BNM–that initially put up a spirited defence of the ringgit–finally gave up currency support operations after suffering hefty losses of several billion US dollars. The ringgit began to collapse beginning in mid-July 1997, eventually reaching RM4.88 to the US dollar in early January 1998–i.e. a fall of almost one half in six months from a high of RM2.47 in July 1997. The stock market fell more severely, with the main Kuala Lumpur Stock Exchange (KLSE) Composite Index dropping to 262 on 1 September 1998, from almost 1,300 in the first quarter of 1997.

Nevertheless, Malaysia was relatively better off than its neighbours who were also affected by the crisis. Although prudential regulation had been weakened in recent years by various changes, especially some relating to financial liberalisation, it remained better than in most other countries in the region with the exception of Singapore. This saved Malaysia from some of the worst problems witnessed elsewhere in the region. Lower domestic interest rates also limited the extent of foreign borrowings, most of which were hedged, owing to the relatively lower costs of hedging in Malaysia.

Conclusion and Policy Implications

In short, high investments in non-tradeables, along with private external debt and an unrestricted surge of portfolio investment inflows arising from financial liberalisation, increased the risk of a systemic financial crisis. Thus, one of the lessons of the financial crisis was the importance of prudentially managing risk in the financial system; failing to do so enhanced the vulnerability of the financial system. While financial restraint can promote a commitment by banks to act as long-run agents and can enhance their capability to cope with risks, it has failed to do so in Malaysia. In so far as financial restraint has been practised in Malaysia, it has sought primarily to ensure bank profitability, especially with increasing ethnic Bumiputera dominance of the Malaysian banking system from the 1970s. Banks in Malaysia have been heavily used by the state for the wealth redistribution policies of the NEP. Though financial restraint was utilised to support inter-ethnic economic redistribution and other public policies, it has not been used much in order to favour long-term productive investments, especially in non-resource-based export-oriented manufacturing, which continues to be dominated by foreign direct investment. Increasing financial liberalisation has exacerbated most of these trends, and has served to further reduce the financial sector's support of productive long-term investments.

Our analysis of financial reforms and developments prior to the present crisis suggests that the roots of the Malaysian financial crisis since mid-1997 can be traced to financial liberalisation and its consequent undermining of effective financial governance both at the international and national levels. Domestic liberalisation of the financial system–meaning the elimination of controls on interest rates and credit allocation, and hence the granting of a freer rein to market forces –before the establishment of the strong institutions needed for effective prudential regulation and supervision, led to moral hazards. The promotion of securities markets before an effective and mature banking system was well-established diminished the franchise value of the banking system. This resulted in increased risk-taking, aggravating the fragility of the banking sector. This was evident as excessive bank lending to property and stock markets was observed in the years leading up to the banking crisis in 1985-88 as well as the present financial crisis since mid-1997.

Meanwhile, external liberalisation in the early 1990s e.g. encouraging investment by foreign financial institutions into the stock market, and allowing the free international movement of capital, made the national economy much more vulnerable to both external shocks as well as capital flight, and rendered the tasks of exchange rate management and controlling inflation much more difficult. Unlike the previous banking crisis, which was triggered by a prolonged world recession that began in the advanced economies in the early 1980s, the present crisis stemmed rather from the turbulence of the financial market, involving massive withdrawals of funds. Notwithstanding the imposition of some temporary controls aimed at limiting portfolio inflows in 1994, Malaysia–in its enthusiasm to enhance its position as a key financial centre in Southeast Asia by attracting foreign institutional investors–did not have any well-conceived prudential regulatory instruments in place to deal with the surge of destabilising portfolio investment inflows. What started off as a currency and financial crisis in Malaysia soon became a crisis of the real economy because of the injudicious government policy and response to the crisis [Jomo (1998b)].

An important lesson of the East Asian crisis is that Malaysia should have been more prudent in reforming its financial sector. Prudential regulation by the government is necessary to help maintain a balance between the competitive efficiency of markets and the security of the banking system [Park (1994), Chowdhury and Islam (1993)]. Prudent and effective regulation of the capital account, with the aim of constraining exit, might have helped mitigate some of the worst excesses that contributed to the recent financial crises in Malaysia and Southeast Asia. Rather than encouraging developing countries to engage in excessively rapid financial market liberalisation, Stiglitz (1999) argues that they should focus on finding the right regulatory structure to manage the incentives and constraints which affect financial institutions' exposure to and ability to cope with risk.[28] This is due to the fact that financial institutions are both a source of risk to, and are also affected by risks from, the rest of the economy. According to Stiglitz (1999), 'the best way to manage risk management in developing countries may differ markedly from that in developed countries, simply because they face larger risks, with poor information and typically have weaker risk management capacities'.

Notes

[1] For a critical review of how the currency and financial crises in Malaysia became a crisis of the real economy, see Jomo (1998b).

[2] To defend the McKinnon-Shaw thesis in the face of disappointing empirical evidence, proponents of financial liberalisation have sought refuge by focussing on what has come to be known as 'sequencing of financial liberalisation', providing several justifications for the importance of sequencing in financial reforms. For some details, see Fry (1997).

[3] For a brief historical review of the development of commercial banks in Malaya and later Malaysia, see [Lee (1990),Chapter 4].

[4] Those institutions whose principal liabilities are generally accepted as money.

[5] Those institutions which are closely linked to monetary institutions and whose liabilities are generally accepted as near money.

[6] For details, see Chin (2000).

[7] Initially, these regulations were imposed on commercial banks but from 1979 were extended to merchant banks.

[8] Bumiputera refers to the 'indigenous' population of Malaysia, mainly comprising the Malays of Peninsular Malaysia.

[9] It became known as the Sime Bank after its takeover by Sime Darby Group and subsequently was acquired by the RHB Bank.

[10] except for interest rates on loans to priority sectors.

[11] For details, see [BNM (1994), pp.46-47].

[12] As advocated by Hellmann, Murdock and Stiglitz (1997), financial restraint attempts to create and channel rents in the financial and productive sectors in order to induce agents in the financial sector to engage in desirable or beneficial activities to economic agents. Unlike financial repression, where the government extracts rents from the private sector, financial restraint involves the government creating rent opportunities for the private sector. With financial restraint, the government can create rent opportunities, but allows profit maximising firms to pursue and capture these rents, thus enabling private information to be utilised in making allocation decisions.

[13] Part of this section is drawn from Chin (1999).

[14] There was only one public issue in 1965 [Drake (1975)].

[15] Some examples are provided by [Jesudason (1989), p.126, endnote 31].

[16] One may disagree by arguing that shares issued at their intrinsic values can be bid up by an overly optimistic market, leading us to wrongly interpret demand pressures as underpricing. However, demand pressure at or after listing may push up prices above their intrinsic values in the short-run, as prices of new issues decline in the longer run after demand pressure subsides.

[17] See Securities Commission (1996).

[18] In a televised interview with a local TV station, Looi Teong Chye, the President of the Small and Medium Industries Association of Malaysia, said that some bankers had requested collaterals double the value of loans applied for by small-scale entrepreneurs.

[19] As discussed in Hellmann, Murdock and Stiglitz (1997), an important aspect of the franchise value is that it creates long run equity that cannot be appropriated in the short run since banks have an ongoing interest to stay in business. Thus, franchise value creates an incentive and commitment for the banks to act as long-run agents, to effectively monitor the firms they finance and to manage the risk of their loan portfolios.

[20] A similar declining trend over the same period was observed for the three and five largest banks [Zainal *et al.*(1994), p.305].

[21] In examining the empirical relationship between banking crisis and financial liberalisation, Demirgüç-Kunt and Detragiache (1998) show that the adverse impact of financial liberalisation on banking sector fragility is stronger where the institutions needed for the correct functioning of financial markets are not well-established.

[22] Computed from Table 2 in UNCTAD and ICC (1998).

[23] The share of foreign direct investment in gross capital formation in Malaysia was exceptionally high. Not only did it rise from 10.7% during the period 1980-90 [Rasiah (1998)], but it was also much higher than in other Asian countries affected by the crisis (i.e. South Korea, Thailand, Indonesia and the Philippines), in which the ratio never surpassed 10% [see Table 2 in UNCTAD and ICC (1998)]. Foreign direct investment also accounts for very significant shares of exports, particularly in electrical and

electronic industries, making up more than half of manufacturing exports and more than 40% of total exports [UNCTAD and ICC (1998)].
[24] Bhattacharya, Ghosh and Jansen present evidence that recent growth of China's market share for its top 10 manufactured exports was associated with a small decline in the market shares of these products for Malaysia as well as Thailand [see World Bank (1998)].
[25] Commitment here refers to financial institutions' willingness to assume a major role in industrial finance, promoting longer time horizons, rather than mainly lending short-term working capital.
[26] See Akyuz (1995) and Griffith-Jones (1997).
[27] For further details, see BNM (1993). For instance the BNM had to absorb large interest payments issuing bonds to mop up the extra liquidity in the financial system.
[28] Stiglitz calls this approach to effective financial regulation, from the perspective of risk management, the Dynamic Portfolio Approach.

References

Akyuz, Y. (1995), 'Taming International Finance' in J. Michie and J. G. Smith (eds) *Managing the Global Economy*, Oxford University Press, New York.
Bank Negara Malaysia (1987), *Quarterly Bulletin*, Vol. 2, No. 3: Kuala Lumpur.
Bank Negara Malaysia (1989), *Annual Report, 1988*, Kuala Lumpur.
Bank Negara Malaysia (1994), *Money and Banking in Malaysia*, 35th Anniversary Edition 1959-94, Kuala Lumpur.
Bank Negara Malaysia (1997), *Annual Report, 1996*, Kuala Lumpur.
Banker's Journal Malaysia, October/November, 1995, Kuala Lumpur.
Chin Kok Fay (1999), *The Stock Market and Economic Development in Malaysia*, IKMAS Working Papers No. 16, March, Universiti Kebangsaan Malaysia, Bangi.
Chin Kok Fay (2001), 'Financing Manufacturing in Malaysia: Experience, Issues and Challenges' in Jomo K. S. (ed.) *Southeast Asia's Ersatz Industrialisation*, Macmillan, Basingstoke.
Chin Kok Fay and Jomo K. S. (2000), 'Financial Sector Rents in Malaysia', in Mushtaq Khan and Jomo K.S. (eds) *Rents, Rent-seeking and Development*, Cambridge University.
Chowdhury, A. and Iyanatul Islam (1993), *The Newly Industrialising Economies of East Asia*, Routledge, London.
Demirgüç-Kunt, A. and Detragiache, E. (1998), 'Financial Liberalization and Financial Fragility', paper prepared for the 1998 World Bank Annual Conference on Development Economics.
Drake, P. J. (1969), *Financial Development in Malaya and Singapore*, Australian National University Press, Canberra.
Drake, P. J. (1975), 'The New-Issue Boom in Malaya and Singapore, 1961-64', reprinted in D. Lim (ed.) *Readings on Malaysian Economic Development*, Oxford University Press, Kuala Lumpur.
Fry, M. J. (1997), 'In Favor of Financial Liberalisation', *Economic Journal*, Vol. 107, pp.754-770.
Gomez, E. T. (1994), *Political Business: Corporate Involvement of Malaysian Political Parties*, James Cook University of North Queensland, Townsville.
Gomez, E. T. and Jomo K. S. (1997), *Malaysia's Political Economy: Politics, Patronage and Profits*, Cambridge University Press, Cambridge.

Griffith-Jones, S. (1997), 'Regulatory Challenges for Source Countries of Surges in Capital Flows', paper prepared for FONDAD Conference, 18-19 November, Available from: URL: http://www.ids.ac.uk/ids/research/easia.html

Hellmann, T., Murdock, K. and Stiglitz, J. (1997), 'Financial Restraint: Towards a New Paradigm', in M. Aoki, Kim Hyung-Ki and Okuno-Fujiwara (eds), *The Role of Government in East Asian Economic Development: Comparative Institutional Analysis*, Clarendon Press, Oxford.

Hing Ai Yun (1987), 'The Financial System and Industrial Investment in West Malaysia', *Journal of Contemporary Asia*, Vol. 17, No. 4, pp. 409-435.

Hino, Hiroyuki (1998), 'Maintaining a Sound Banking System: New Lessons of the Asian Miracle', mimeo, Kobe University.

Ho Ting Sing (1990), *The Financial Industry of Malaysia: Toward a New Era of Technological Change*, Malaysian Institute of Economic Research Discussion Papers, No. 33, September, Kuala Lumpur.

International Finance Corporation (1997), *Emerging Stock Market Factbook*, 1997, Washington, D.C.

Investor Digest, February 1997, Kuala Lumpur.

Jomo, K. S. (ed.) (1990), *Growth and Structural Change in the Malaysian Economy*, Macmillan, London.

Jomo, K. S. (ed.) (1995), *Privatizing Malaysia: Rents, Rhetoric, Realities*, Westview, Boulder.

Jomo, K. S. (ed.) (1998a), *Tigers in Trouble: Financial Governance, Liberalisation and Crises in East Asia*, Zed Books, London.

Jomo, K. S. (1998b), 'Malaysia's Debacle: Whose Fault?' *Cambridge Journal of Economics*, Vol. 22, No. 6, pp. 707-722.

Jomo, K. S. and Felker, G. (1999), *Malaysian Industrial Technology Policies*, Routledge, London.

Jomo, K. S., Felker, G and Rasiah, R.. (1999), *Technology, Competitiveness and the State: Technology Development in Malaysia*, Routledge, London.

Khor Kok Peng (1987), *Malaysia's Economy in Decline*, Consumers' Association of Penang, Penang.

Kuala Lumpur Stock Exchange (1997), *KLSE Statistics*, 1997, Kuala Lumpur.

Lee Hock Lock (1987), *Central Banking in Malaysia: a Study of the Development of the Financial System and Monetary Management*, Butterworths, Singapore.

Lee Hock Lock (1992), *Regulation of Banks and Other Depository Institutions in Malaysia: A Study in Monetary, Prudential and Other Controls*, Butterworths, Singapore.

Lee, Sheng Yi (1990), *The Monetary and Banking Development of Malaysia and Singapore*, Singapore University Press, Singapore.

Ministry of Finance, Malaysia (1996), *Economic Report*, 1996/1997, Kuala Lumpur.

Ministry of Finance, Malaysia (1997), *Economic Report*, 1997/1998, Kuala Lumpur.

Mohamed Ariff *et al.* (1993), 'A Market Micro-Structure Explanation for the Excessive Underpricing in Malaysian IPOs', paper presented at a seminar on 'Underpricing on New Issues International Comparison', KLSE Research Division, 20 September.

Ng Beoy Kui (ed.) (1989), *The Development of Capital Markets in the SEACEN Countries*, South East Asian Central Banks (SEACEN) Research and Training Centre, Kuala Lumpur.

Ong Hong Cheong (1998), 'Coping with Capital Flows and the Role of Monetary Policy: The Malaysian Experience, 1990-95', in Kwan C. H., Donna Vandenbrink and Chia Siow Yue (eds) *Coping with Capital Flows in East Asia*, Institute of Southeast Asian Studies, Singapore and Nomura Research Institute, Tokyo.

Park, Y. C. (1994), 'Concepts and Issues' in H. T. Patrick and Y. C. Park (eds.), *The Financial Development of Japan, Korea and Taiwan: Growth, Repression and Liberalisation*, Oxford University Press, New York.

Rasiah, R. (1998), 'The Malaysian Financial Crisis: Capital Expansion, Cronyism and Contraction', *Journal of Asia Pacific Economy*, Vol. 3, No. 3, pp. 358-378.

Rybczynski, T. (1984), 'Industrial Finance Systems in Europe, U.S. and Japan', *Journal of Economic Behaviour and Organisation*, Vol. 5, pp. 275-86.

Securities Commission, Malaysia (1996), *Annual Report*, 1996, Kuala Lumpur.

Sheng, A. (1989), *Bank Restructuring in Malaysia 1985-88*, Policy, Planning and Research Working Papers, WPS54, September, The World Bank.

Singh, A. (1995), *Corporate Financial Patterns in Industrialising Economies: A Comparative International Study*, IFC Technical Paper, No. 2, Washington, D.C.

Stiglitz, J. (1999), 'What Have We Learned from the Recent Crises: Implications For Banking Regulation' Remarks at the Conference on Global Financial Crises: Implications for Banking and Regulation, Federal Reserve Bank of Chicago, Chicago, IL, May 6, 1999.

UNCTAD and International Chamber of Commerce (ICC) (1998), 'Financial Crisis in Asia and Foreign Direct Investment', Available from: URL: http://www.unctad.org/en/press/bg9802en.htm

United Nations Conference on Trade and Development (UNCTAD) (1998), *Trade and Development Report*, Geneva: United Nations.

World Bank (1993), *The East Asian Miracle*, Oxford University Press, New York.

World Bank (1998), *East Asia: The Road to Recovery*, World Bank, Washington D.C.

Zainal Aznam Yusof, *et al.* (1994), 'Financial Reform in Malaysia', in Gerard Caprio Jr. *et al.*, *Financial Reform: Theory and Experience*, Cambridge University Press, New York.

Zeti Akhtar Aziz (1989), 'Development of Capital Market in Malaysia', in Ng Beoy Kui (ed.) *The Development of Capital Markets in the SEACEN Countries*, South East Asian Central Banks (SEACEN) Research and Training Centre, Kuala Lumpur.

10 The East Asian Economic and Financial Crisis: The Case of the Philippines
JOSEPH Y. LIM

Introduction and Historical Background

The East Asian crisis has revealed the interconnections between the frailties of the real sector of the Philippine economy and the rapid financial and capital account liberalization undertaken in the nineties by the Philippines. More than any other crisis in the past, the current East Asian crisis has shown the vulnerability of the Philippine economy to regional 'contagion' and to an international financial architecture that is not sensitive to sudden financial panics and the ensuing liquidity crisis.

Before the financial and currency turmoil hit the East Asian region in mid-1997, the Philippines had been lagging behind its "tiger" neighbors in terms of economic growth, penetration of export markets, technological advancement and social and human development. This inability to replicate the earlier successes of the so-called East Asian "tigers" is crucial to the analysis of the impact of the East Asian crisis on the Philippines. Aspects of this inability include a low domestic savings rate compared with that of its East Asian neighbors and high trade and current account deficits during periods of growth and boom. In the other East Asian countries, growth before the eruption of the financial crisis was more or less accompanied by high export growth. High foreign exchange earnings matched their import needs. This meant that their high growth could be sustained.

Table 10.1 shows some key macroeconomic indicators of the Philippines. It is clear that the Philippines has been left stagnant in the long run by a bust-boom cycle of recession and growth. In the mid-1980s, there was a sharp economic decline comparable to the decline of Indonesia today. It included political instability, massive foreign debt problems and overhang, sharp devaluation, high inflation and high interest rates. The years 1984 and

251

1985 alone brought the Philippines back more than ten years in terms of GNP per capita. There was an economic recovery from 1986 to 1990 but it was short-lived as the foreign debt overhang wiped out foreign exchange reserves and military coups against the Aquino government killed the 'animal spirit' of both domestic and foreign investors. The Philippines also missed out during this period on the East Asian 'takeoff' of its Southeast Asian neighbors which received massive foreign direct investments from Japan as a result of the Plaza Accord and the yen's appreciation. Another stagnation occurred in 1991 and 1992, a period marked again by some initial devaluation, high inflation and high interest rates. This stagnation, together with the economic collapse, threw the Philippines back even further in terms of GNP per capita, by 15 years. In 1997, the year when the crisis hit, the Philippines' GNP per capita was just at the level of the early 1980s (see Table 10.1). Just when growth regained respectability in the 1994-1997 period, the currency turmoil rocked the region in July 1997 and dragged the economy down in 1998.

It can also be seen from Table 10.1 that every growth period saw increases in trade and current account deficits that made economic growth unsustainable without sufficient foreign capital inflows. In a way, the present crisis can be seen as a continuation of the boom-bust cycle in Philippine economic history. What gave the present crisis its specificity was that foreign capital inflows stopped (aggravated most likely by significant capital flight as evidence seems to indicate) mainly because of "contagion" from the Thai, Indonesian, South Korean, and Japanese economic crises.

Another special feature of the crisis was that foreign capital flows became exceedingly volatile after foreign exchange and capital accounts were liberalized in 1992. While net foreign direct investments increased, external inflows and outflows were dominated by short-run portfolio flows which went initially to domestic treasury bills but starting in 1993 streamed heavily into the domestic stock market. Unhedged short-run foreign borrowings also increased significantly from 1995 up to early 1997. Together with the significant external deficits, the nature of the capital flows in the latest growth period of the Philippines made it vulnerable to the financial turmoil that was to erupt in mid-1997.

Economic and Financial Conditions Before the Crisis

The 1980s

In the mid-1980s under the Marcos regime, the Philippines was a victim of the foreign debt crisis, extremely high interest rates and a tight monetary policy (imposed by the IMF and an over-zealous Central Bank) as well as an "Indonesia-size" political and economic decline. The economy recovered from 1987 to 1990 with the assumption of power of the Aquino government in 1986, but this recovery could not be sustained because of the high net capital outflows due to foreign debt and interest payments as well as political instability and coups against the Aquino government. Still, the Aquino government was able to implement important structural reforms, which included:

(1) Import liberalisation, which lifted almost all quota restrictions. Many quota restrictions were converted into tariffs at the same time that tariff reduction schemes were also drawn up.

(2) Financial liberalisation, which was started in the early eighties but was implemented in earnest during this period, effectively lifted all interest rate ceilings, substantially reduced credit subsidies and allowed banks and financial markets to operate using market processes.

(3) Tax reforms, which included a shift towards more global taxation and value-added taxation.

(4) Rehabilitation of many state enterprises and the privatisation of a considerable number of them; and the sale of non-performing and sequestered assets inherited from the crisis of the mid-1980s.

These reforms—trade and financial liberalization and the emphasis on the privatized sector and market forces—would provide the basic thrust of the economic strategy of the succeeding Ramos and Estrada governments.

The 1990s

As the foreign debt overhang and political instability intensified and as a crippling power shortage gripped the entire country, the economy entered another recession from 1991 to 1992, which was aggravated by high interest rates and tight monetary policy. But the implementation of the Brady Plan significantly reduced the debt burden of the country. The remittances of Filipino overseas contract workers (OCWs) —already a growing item in the eighties—intensified in the nineties. And the energy crisis ended with the fast-tracking under the Ramos administration (1992-93) of the construction of hydroelectric plants. The Ramos government was finally able to inject political and economic stability and confidence into the system. This was further heightened with the dissolution of the debt-strapped Central Bank and its recreation into the Bangko Sentral ng Pilipinas (BSP), as well as the liberalization of bank entry to domestic and foreign banks, and most especially the liberalization of the foreign exchange and capital accounts.

The Ramos administration deepened the market liberalization and privatization processes started by the Aquino government. On the domestic front, deregulation of key industries (telecommunication, oil, banking) was undertaken in earnest with the telecommunications industry exhibiting significant improvements in productivity and growth.[1] On the external front, the government locked in the country on trade liberalization by joining the World Trade Organization (WTO), the ASEAN Free Trade Area (AFTA) and the Asia Pacific Economic Cooperation (APEC) and reducing its tariffs unilaterally ahead of the schedule it was bound to by international agreements and way ahead of its neighbors. The economy exhibited extreme confidence, impressed foreign investors and appeared as if it was ready for a strong economic take-off.

The strong confidence in the Philippines manifested itself initially in the sharp rise of the local stock exchange as foreign and domestic investors scrambled to enter the "emerging market" marked for high take-off. The stock index jumped several-fold in 1993. From then on, volatility and large volumes of short-term portfolio inflows and outflows dominated the external capital accounts although net direct foreign investments and net medium and long-term borrowings also increased significantly (see Tables 10.2a and 10.2b).

The Fundamentals of the Real Sector

The macroeconomic fundamentals looked like they were leading to an economic take-off:

(1) The inflation rate, which was very volatile and had gone to very high levels during the stagflation and bust periods, started to be tamed and fell into the single digits in 1993, continuing until 1998 when the country was well into the financial crisis—see Table 10.1.

(2) GDP growth rates started to pick up, with the economy growing by more than 4% in 1994 and 1996 and more than 5% in 1996 and 1997–see Table 10.1.

(3) Remittances by Filipino overseas workers also increased rapidly and made GNP growth around 1% (or more) higher than GDP growth–see Table 10.3.

(4) The national government posted surpluses from 1994 to 1997 and the consolidated public sector deficit turned positive in 1996 and 1997.[2]

(5) Interest rates, which had been raised as part of the stabilization measures to stave off external deficits and which had made recessions quite severe in the mid-1980s and early 1990s, started to go down towards the low tens (11% to 13%). Meanwhile liquidity increased tremendously but did not cause inflationary pressures as income velocity decreased and the money multiplier expanded. At first this seemed to indicate financial deepening but proved later to be a symptom of the "overborrowing" syndrome of the McKinnon-Pill type.

The trade sector—both exports and imports—expanded with annual growth rates for most years surpassing 15%. The high growth rate of exports during this period was unprecedented in the economic history of the Philippines, although import growth still surpassed export growth.

The picture above, however, hid some important figures. The trade deficit in merchandise goods as a percentage of GNP shot up to more than 11% from 1993 to 1995 and increased to around 13% from 1996 and 1997. Lower foreign debt and interest payments and, more importantly, large remittances of overseas workers kept the current account deficit lower but still significant at substantially more than 4% of GNP in the period from 1994 to 1997—see Tables 10.2a and 10.2b. This happened when the currency was appreciating in nominal terms between 1992 and 1995 and was kept very stable until the financial crisis hit East Asia.

The stable and appreciating currency was the result partly of the net external inflows brought about by the exuberance during that period and partly of a conscious policy by the Bangko Sentral ng Pilipinas (BSP) to have a stable currency as part of macroeconomic stability.

The appreciating currency accompanied by growing trade deficits and high current account deficits was the single most damaging evidence to show that economic fundamentals were not as nice as the government and private investors had painted them to be. Furthermore the twin effects of currency appreciating in real terms and substantial tariff reductions in the mid-1990s made imports exceedingly cheap and increased import intensity. This can be seen in Table 10.4 which shows the ratio of imports to GDP increasing from 40% of GDP in 1992 to 64% of GDP in 1997 (Exports grew from 33.6% of GDP in 1992 to 52% of GDP in 1997). This contributed to making the trade deficits grow.

Furthermore, a look at the composition of exports (Table 10.5) reveals that much of the export growth was due to only one commodity—electronics and electrical equipment/parts and telecommunications—which comprised more than 50% of merchandise exports in 1997 from less than a third of dollar-dominated exports of merchandise goods in 1992. Perhaps this lack of diversification of export growth could be attributed partly to an appreciating currency and partly to little growth in labor productivity.

This raises an important point. Labor productivity has been on a long-run downward trend in the Philippines partly because of the booms and busts and the stagnant growth (see Table 10.1). Moreover, the latest growth period from 1994 to 1997 was not accompanied by any significant improvement in labor productivity except for a small increase in 1997.

If one looks at the growth rate of the economy by sectors—Table 10.3—one can see that although manufacturing grew respectably (more or less near the GDP growth rate) in the period from 1994 to 1997, the biggest growth rates came from construction and finance (followed by transportation/communication/storage and electricity/gas/water) which translated into a higher output share for non-tradeables. It is clear in hindsight that the lead sectors in the growth were the non-tradeable sectors rather than the tradeables in agriculture and manufacturing. This again might be an indication that the currency appreciation and tariff reduction in the nineties had made relative prices of non-tradeables more attractive than those of tradeables.

The Financial Conditions Before the Crisis

As mentioned earlier, the high "animal spirit" that pervaded 1994-1997 was accompanied by looser monetary policy. Money supply grew annually by more than 15% in real terms for most years from 1993 to 1997 (see Table 10.1). The high monetary expansion was accompanied by a "boom" lending spree marked by a growing money multiplier and sharp declines in the reserve requirement ratio (as prescribed by the monetary authorities) and currency deposit ratio (a sign of increasing volume of lending). The liquidity to income ratio (M3/GDP) increased significantly (Table 10.1).

Interest rates of various instruments fell significantly in pace with inflation. T-bill rates for 91 days (the most circulated) fell from 16% in 1992 to between 11% and 12% in 1995 and 1996. Average bank lending rates fell from 19.4% in 1992 to less than 15% in 1995 and 1996 (see Table 10.6). The real interest rates for T-bills (91 days) and average bank lending rates fell substantially from 7.1% and 10.4%, respectively, in 1992, to less than 4% and 6%, respectively, in 1995 and 1996. Easy money and easy credit became the name of the game.

The annual growth rate of outstanding loans for banks (in nominal terms) from 1993 to 1996 was more than 30% (see Table 10.7). The biggest increase was in the years from 1995 to 1996. Table 10.7 shows that while outstanding loans for manufacturing grew tremendously from 1994 to 1996, they were increasingly outpaced by loans to finance/real estate/business service; construction and transportation/storage/communi-cation and electricity/gas/water, especially from 1995 to early 1997. Again the increasing attractiveness of non-tradeables began to manifest itself in 1995 and intensified in 1996 and early 1997.

Even if the domestic interest rate was going down from its 1992 level, it was still significantly higher than the dollar interest rates. The significant interest rate differential could have been due to the following:

(1) the higher inflation rates in the Philippines compared with those in the US and other developed countries;

(2) a risk premium that had to be added due to an overvalued currency that was not consistent with the levels of trade and current account deficits; and,

(3) the Central Bank policy of sterilizing external monetary inflows to keep the peso stable or appreciating.

The potential cause for the interest rate differential (particularly the third one mentioned above) was quite controversial, and instigated intense debates between the Bangko Sentral ng Pilipinas (BSP) and mainstream economists, particularly from the University of the Philippines (UP).

Whatever the reasons for the interest rate differential, the semblance of a very stable currency over the medium term encouraged unhedged dollar borrowings vis-à-vis domestic peso borrowings. As long as the currency remained stable (or appreciated) and was backed up by a credible Central Bank, borrowing in dollars at a lower interest rate and then converting them to peso to invest in higher-yielding domestic assets or investments brought windfall gains. The expectation that foreign inflows would continue to flow in and the general belief that the BSP would defend the peso and keep it from depreciating made much of the dollar borrowings unhedged. Table 10.8 gives us the foreign currency deposit unit (FCDU) loans by borrower. It must be noted that the sharp borrowings from FCDUs occurred in the second half of 1995 and accelerated in the first half of 1996. The growth rate declined but remained at high levels in the second half of 1996. In terms of composition, we can see that starting in 1996, the share of loans of commodity exporters (the naturally hedged borrowers) started. Their share was increasingly taken over by "others" which turned out were mostly unhedged borrowers investing in real estate and speculators out to make a quick killing. It must be pointed out that the borrowings of "others" continued at a high pace up to the first half of 1997 even if borrowings from FCDUs started to slow down in the first half of 1997.

Table 10.9 gives us the foreign exchange liabilities broken down in various ways. It must be pointed out that the share of the commercial banks' foreign exchange liabilities to total foreign exchange liabilities increased from 5.66% in 1993 to 18% in 1997. Private firms' liabilities increased from 15% in 1993 to 27.5% in 1997. The banking and private firms' combined share of foreign exchange liabilities increased from less than 21% in 1992 to more than 45% in 1997.

In terms of institutional creditors, the share of foreign exchange lending held by foreign banks and other financial institutions increased from 14.6% in 1993 to 22.4% in 1997. "Other" institutional creditors (mostly private) increased their share from around 13% in 1993 to 24.1% in 1997. All these facts point to a drastic shift to private borrowings by financial institutions and private firms. The growth of public foreign debt was outpaced by that of private foreign debt. Table 10.9 also shows the shift towards short-term foreign debt with the increase coming mainly from non-trade short-term debt. This means that private financial institutions and private firms were increasingly incurring short-term debt that was not given as trade credits.

Table 10.10 shows us that based on the BSP's data on non-performing loans, the Philippine banking system was not exhibiting very worrisome trends in non-performing loans before the crisis. The only worrisome factor was a rise in the ratio of non-performing loans to total loans for commercial banks in the first half of 1997 right before the crisis (from 2.8% in December 1996 to 3.4% in June 1997). Another trend was the decline in the ratio of loan loss provision to total loans from 1993 to 1996 when domestic credit was expanding at a very rapid rate. Still, overall, the ratio of non-performing loans was low.

Perceptions About Economic Fundamentals

Academics had already warned about the volatility that short-run capital flows and an appreciating currency accompanied by growing trade and current account deficits could bring (see Montes and Lim (1996)). The Mexican crisis had already given warning on what McKinnon and Pill (1996 and 1998) called the "overborrowing syndrome" during a time of overconfidence (on the benefits of structural reforms) made perverse by "moral hazards" brought about by the belief of inevitable bailouts of banks by the monetary authorities and by multilateral agencies during times of financial crises. Yet, despite these warnings, the government and private sector continued to assume that the capital flows would continue indefinitely and that asset inflation (in the stock and real property markets) would not create bubbles leading to a financial crisis. In November 1996, the World Bank (1996) warned that domestic credit in the Philippines was growing too fast. Nobody listened and the stock market zoomed to its peak in February 1997 after the release of the high growth figures for 1996.

What most people—including the strongest doomsayers—did not foresee was the extent of and the grave dangers entailed by unhedged dollar borrowings which ballooned especially in 1996.

In summary, the lower inflation, the much higher growth, the improved fiscal performance and the large capital inflows and growing international reserves were seen as strong economic fundamentals which would bring about the birth of another "baby tiger" (to use the words of President Ramos) in the region. The financial "earthquake" that hit the region in mid-1997 caught most policy makers and businessmen by surprise and it took them several months to accept the gravity of the crisis and the strong negative impact it would have on the economy.

The Philippines, though, was not in as dire shape on the eve of the crisis as, say, Thailand and South Korea were, although there was a common perception that the current account deficits might have been understated due to an overestimation of the foreign currency deposit unit (FCDU) from exports and remittances of overseas workers. The Philippines by itself would not have fallen into crisis in mid-1997. However, it was very vulnerable, in both the real and financial sectors, to strong, negative external shocks, as indeed happened in mid-1997.

The Impact of the East Asian Crisis

Contagion and Responses by the Monetary Authorities

The contagion from Thailand actually began as early as May 1997, when the asset bubble (stock market and real estate market) burst and the baht came under tremendous pressure to depreciate. This affected the external accounts of the Philippines. As can be seen in Tables 10.2a and 10.2b, net portfolio investments turned largely negative in May 1997 and continued to register negative figures for most of the succeeding months. Net unclassified items registered large negative outflows starting as early as March 1997 and lasting throughout the year. These unrecorded accounts may have been actual capital flight, moving from domestic currency to dollars in the spate of speculation on the dollar. Also in May and June 1997, the peso came under speculative attacks just as the baht was under tremendous pressure to depreciate. In May and June 1997 the BSP increased the overnight lending and borrowing rates, as can be seen in Table 10.6. The overnight rate set by the BSP had gone close to 10%—its lowest ever—before it was raised to an average of 15% in May and June of 1997.

The baht finally caved in on 2 July 1997, but still the BSP tried vainly to defend the peso by raising overnight rates to an average of 25% for July 1997 (see Table 10.6). When this did not succeed, the central bank used up somewhere between $1.5 billion to $2 billion in defending the peso. This was equivalent to at least 13.4% of its gross international reserves (around $11.2 billion) as of the end of June 1997 (see Table 10.6). When this measure still failed, the BSP allowed the peso to float on a wider band on 15 July 1997, effecting a more than 10% depreciation (from P26.37 to more than P29 to the dollar). The pressure on the region's currencies increased in the succeeding months as portfolio investments continued their outward flow and as unhedged dollar borrowings aggravated the speculation against the peso. The BSP kept overnight rates above the 20% level until August. The interbank call loan rate replicated the high BSP overnight rates. When high overnight rates still failed to keep the peso from depreciating, the monetary authorities moved on to another tactic.

Before the baht's depreciation, the total reserve requirement ratio was 15%—13% for the statutory reserve requirement and 2% for liquidity reserves (which were allowed to be invested in market-yielding government securities). The liquidity reserve ratio was increased to 4% at the end of July 1997 as part of the attempt to reduce liquidity in the system in order to discourage speculation on the dollar. This tactic was used to the hilt in August as the liquidity reserve ratio was further raised to 8%, raising the total required reserve ratio to 21%. The total reserve ratio was kept high in September. Again, this strategy failed to reduce speculation against the peso, which continued to deteriorate. But at the same time it aggravated the rise in interest rates that had started when overnight rates were raised. Table 10.6 shows that from August onwards, there was an increase in treasury bill rates starting in August 1997. Bank lending rates increased dramatically from August 1997. The squeezing of liquidity brought another risk to the system. There arose new fears of high defaults on loans, especially from the real estate and construction sectors which had borrowed heavily at variable interest rates. The real estate bubble followed the stock market bubble and burst from August 1997 onwards.

The gradual realization of the extent of unhedged dollar borrowings, the high exposure of the financial sector to real estate and financial sector loans (see Table 10.7), the high interest rates and the effect of the peso depreciation on import-dependent firms all increased the perceived risk of defaults in the system. Victoria Millings, the largest sugar firm, had already defaulted on its loans months before the baht depreciated, which caused ripples in the financial sector. Between September and December two large firms also fell into trouble. EYCO—an electrical appliance firm that had diversified into real estate—defaulted on its loans and caused some financial panic. A businessman closely associated with President Ramos—Ramon Jacinto—nearly went bankrupt and caused another wave of bank jitters to hit the financial system. It became obvious that many firms which had previously done well became troubled due to their dollar borrowings and/or their diversification into real estate.

In October the monetary authorities made one last attempt to reduce liquidity in the system in order not to exceed an IMF-imposed liquidity target. This took the form of direct mopping-up operations. This operation jacked up interbank call loan rates to more than 100% for a few days in October with the monthly interbank rate averaging 34% (see Table 10.6). Bank lending rates again increased significantly, which rocked the system further. Bank failure rumors began to circulate and heavy withdrawals started to hit many banks which were seen as small or medium-sized (with shaky loans) and would therefore not be bailed out by the BSP. Bank failure rumors and sporadic withdrawal of funds persisted until February 1998.

The instability brought to the financial system finally convinced the BSP that its very tight monetary policy was counterproductive and would not stem the peso's depreciation. Liquidity reserve requirements were lowered just as overnight BSP rates were also reduced. The continued currency instability, however, kept interest rates high even under the more lax monetary stance of the BSP. When South Korea became embroiled in the crisis and the Indonesian crisis took a turn for the worse, the currencies started to plunge again in December 1997 and January 1998. Interest rates shot up significantly (see Table 10.6). Actually, the official figures underestimated the average bank lending rates shown in Table 10.6 as many loans had been received at close to a 30% annual rate. The figures on interest rates also hid significant credit rationing as many firms (especially small and medium-sized firms) were rationed out due to the high risks of default, the weakness of domestic sales and the high costs of production.

The BSP used another strategy to stave off currency depreciation. It provided non-deliverable forward covers (NDF) to buyers of dollars at a future date to stem speculation on the peso. In effect, the scheme insured dollar purchasers from future fluctuations in the exchange rate. It ensured that the payment at the future date of the differential between market and contracted price would be made in pesos rather than in dollars, thus preventing the further depletion of international reserves. In order to increase the supply of dollars, the BSP offered a similar guarantee scheme to foreign banks that were willing to supply dollars to the foreign exchange market. This strategy was used intermittently in the succeeding months but the movement of the exchange rate still followed the regional fluctuations, which finally stabilized in the final quarter of 1998.

The Currency Market and the External Sector

Between July 1997 and January 1998, transaction volumes in the foreign exchange market shrank as dollar holders (except for the BSP in the beginning), anticipating further peso depreciation, refused to release the money into the system while there was strong demand for dollars from speculators, importers and dollar debtors. This caused the currency to depreciate at a rapid rate. When regional currencies temporarily stabilized between February 1998 to April 1998 (see Table 10.6), volumes went back to normal levels. When currency instability started again in May 1998 (triggered by the release of poor first quarter earnings throughout the region coupled with the Indonesian riots and violence and change of government, and culminating in the rapid deterioration of the Japanese economy and the sharp yen depreciation), volumes failed to shrink back to the earlier low levels which had partially cushioned the impact of this latest round of currency instability. Exchange rate stability finally became more permanent starting in the last quarter of 1998, but by that time the battering of the 'animal spirits' had already taken its toll and the country was in a serious recession.

Tables 10.2a and 10.2b show us that the crisis and recession effected a drastic reduction in imports, so that the high current account deficits swung strongly into surpluses at the end of 1998 and even more so in 1999. The current account surplus was also made higher by continued high inflows of remittances by overseas workers. On the capital account side of the balance of payments, the high net inflows in 1996 and 1997 fell drastically in 1998 as there were high net outflows of short-term capital and changes in the net foreign assets of commercial banks. Overall, though, the balance of payments still registered positive balances in 1998 and 1999, due to the high current account surplus. Table 10.6 also shows the increase in foreign reserves starting in the second quarter of 1998, culminating in the peak international reserves position in late 1999.

The Financial Sector

The interest rate (measured mainly by the treasury bill rate and the bank lending rate) declined starting in February 1998, after the unsuccessful experience of using high interest rates to stave off currency speculation. It finally settled to a historic low of below 9% in mid-1999. Although the average bank lending rate also declined, it was clear that most banks were still rationing loans because of the high risks and bearish outlook of the financial system. A serious credit crunch and 'liquidity trap' had set in. Table 10.7 shows the rapid decline of loan growth from very high levels from 1992 to 1997 into the negative territory in 1998, especially affecting loans to manufacturing, agriculture, and trade. The general trend continued in 1999. Table 10.8 also shows the rapid decline of FCDU loans to all types of borrowers (commodity exporters, service exporters, manufacturers, oil companies and others). Loans denominated in both domestic and foreign currency declined drastically during that year. Table 10.9 shows clearly that in 1998, foreign exchange liabilities in the form of trade credits again contracted significantly, affecting the production of traded goods. Tables 10.7, 10.8 and 10.9 show some slowing down of credit decline in 1999 but it is clear that the credit crunch and the bearishness of the financial markets persisted.

The crisis caused the financial sector to weaken. This was seen in the rise of the share of non-performing loans to total loans for commercial banks, thrift banks and rural banks. Table 10.10 shows that the official non-performing loan ratio (to total loans) of the commercial banks steadily deteriorated from 3.4% in June 1997 (on the eve of the crisis) to 13.4% in January 2000. A similar story can be told for the smaller sectors of thrift banks and rural banks. One can also see from Table 10.10 that although coverage for loan loss provisions (as a percentage of total loans) also increased due to stricter rules by the BSP (from 1.3% for commercial banks in June 1999 to 6.2% in January 2000), it did not increase as fast as the non-performing loans themselves. Thus the unprovisioned non-performing loans for commercial banks also increased from 2% of total loans in June 1997 to 7.2% in January 2000.

Stricter Rules by the Central Bank

The deteriorating financial conditions created a quandary for the BSP. It was clear that in order to allow financial liberalization to effect further financial deepening and improvements in financial intermediation, the financial house would have to be strengthened and confidence in the system restored. The former could be done partly by strengthening prudential and supervisory regulations, such as insisting on tighter loan loss provisioning, higher capitalization requirements and capital adequacy ratios. But imposing these at a time of general financial weakness would only further weaken some banks and discourage further loan expansion, which of course would deepen the credit crunch that was a root cause of the continuing recession. The BSP's quandary was reflected in the changes it made to the rules it had been implementing, as follows:

(1) The schedule for full compliance with the increase in loan loss provisions from 1% to 2% of total loans was moved back to October 1999, to allow banks more time to adjust and to recover lost profits. The rules concerning allowances for probable losses were also made stricter with the schedule of compliance and changes in rules as in Table10.11.

The above provision for loan losses proved a tremendous burden to most banks and discouraged loans from being undertaken during the crisis, so that in April 1999, the BSP relaxed the loan loss provision requirement and applied the above rules only to loans incurred from 31 March 1999. This meant that incremental loans granted over and above the loan portfolio level of banks starting 31 March 1999 were no longer subjected to the above rules.

(2) The definition of past due and non-performing was made stricter right after the outbreak of the crisis but then relaxed later on. Loans which were to 'be repaid in quarterly, semi-annual and annual installments, were considered non-performing if payments had not been made within three months. Before the crisis this period had been six months. For monthly and lump-sum loans, any failure to pay on time would give the loan the label of non-performing. Because of the burdens on the banks caused by the rapid deterioration in non-performing loans and required loan loss provision, the rule was relaxed on 27 May 1999 by Circular No. 202. The BSP now allowed a 30-day grace period before a loan would be considered non-performing. This was applicable to loans payable in lump sum, or in quarterly, semi-annual or annual installments. Loans payable in monthly installments would be considered non-performing if three or more installments were overdue. In addition, restructured loans on which payments had been received would no longer be considered non-performing or past due. This directive effectively reduced the amount of money that banks needed to set aside as provision for bad debts, thereby allowing them to increase available funds for re-lending.

(3) Banks' loan exposure to real estate was limited to 20%. This has actually already been achieved (exposure to real estate declined to 12.3% by June 1999) but there were loans categorized as loans to manufacturing or commercial firms that were being used by firms in real estate projects. These might not have been captured in the figures and the BSP has been correcting these possible loopholes.

(4) The capital requirements of troubled banks were increased. The capital adequacy ratio was maintained at 10% and strictly monitored. On top

of this, a directive issued on 19 March 1998 increased the minimum capitalization of new banks by 20% for universal banks, 40% for regular commercial banks and 60% for rural and thrift banks, from the banks' capitalization requirement for 1998. Existing banks were given two years (until 2000) to comply with this minimum capital build-up. These capital requirements are summarized in Table 10.12.

As of June 1999, the banks' capital adequacy ratio was at 17.6%, above the 10% required by Philippine laws and the 8% standard of the Bank for International Settlements (BIS).

(5) The BSP moved to reduce the foreign exchange mismatch. It issued Circular No. 1389 dated 13 April 1998 which stipulated that dollar lending to borrowers without dollar returns required the BSP's approval, or else that repayment for these loans could not be sourced from foreign exchange purchased from the banking system.

(6) There was a shift in supervision focus from a compliance-based process to a forward-looking and risk-based framework. The BSP started to apply this risk-based consolidated approach to on-site examinations of banking groups. There would also be close monitoring of banks identified as potentially in distress based on a set of both forward- and backward-looking indicators. These indicators include capital deficiency, reserve deficiency, sharp changes in credit and deposits, operating losses and rises in past due loans.

The stricter loan loss provisioning and capital requirements, together with deteriorating non-performing loan ratios of weaker banks, led to a trend of mergers among big banks starting in the second half of 1999. Although the banks became stronger due to higher capitalization, there were concerns that this would reduce competitiveness in the banking sector and possibly lead to cartel-like behavior, which would unduly harm financial intermediation and efficiency. The higher capital requirements, the deadline for which was 2000, were not satisfied by some banks, especially among smaller or medium-sized ones with high ratios of non-performing loans. This caused serious bank runs in April 2000 as some commercial banks faced demotion to the status of thrift banks. Thus moves which supposedly aimed to strengthen the financial system ironically caused more instability and vulnerability to the system.

At the same time the financial sector could not fully recover and credit lines could not be reestablished until "animal spirit" had been brought back into the system. This return of confidence was undermined however by the perception of government mismanagement, cronyism, and the growing budget deficit resulting from weak revenue collection.

Slower Economic Growth and Higher Unemployment

Considering the turmoil in the second half of 1997, the growth rate for that year was rather respectable: 5.1% for GDP and 5.8% for GNP—around 1% short of that achieved in 1996 (see Table 10.1). The unemployment rate was flat, increasing very slightly from 8.6% in 1996 to 8.7% in 1997.

The full brunt of the crisis was felt in 1998. GDP fell by 0.5% and GNP per capita fell by 2.4% (see Table 10.1). Agricultural production fell by 6.64% as the El Niño and La Niña phenomena wreaked havoc on the countryside (see Table 10.3). Industrial production fell by 1.74%, with construction falling by 8.14% and manufacturing, 1.07%. Only services managed to grow in 1998 at a respectable 3.5%. Capital formation fell by a whopping 17.14% while the volume of exports[3] and imports also declined significantly (see Table 10.4). The unemployment rate jumped from 7.4% in 1996 to 9.6% in 1998 with the impact on male unemployment being most severe. Male unemployment in October in urban areas shot up to 13.1% in 1998. Unemployment in October for young males aged 15 to 19 in urban areas went up from 19.4% in 1996, to 30.5% in 1998, and to 31.4% in 1999. Female unemployment in October for the same age group in urban areas went from 16.4% in 1996, to 22.3% in 1998, to 22.6% in 1999.

The year 1999 showed some signs of recovery, with GDP growth averaging 3.6%. But the recovery was mostly the result of a rise in agricultural production after the weather improved significantly. Industry growth was still largely in the doldrums even if manufacturing seemed to have recovered slightly. Construction, however, continued to decline strongly (see Table 10.3).

Higher Inflation The year 1999 saw a recession and a slump in demand, which reduced inflation to 6.6%. However a series of oil price increases rocked major urban and industrial centers in early 2000. Although inflation in April and May 2000 hovered at just 4%, the perception of falling purchasing power continued to hinder a significant rebound in aggregate demand.

The Fiscal Bind Another victim of the crisis was the fiscal sector, which had posted national government surpluses from 1995 to 1997. In 1998, the government (still under Ramos) imposed a 25% mandatory savings (a euphemism for cutbacks) in government expenditures for all departments in order to comply with the IMF program of achieving a fiscal surplus of 1% of GNP.

The decline in revenue collection during a period of serious recession made the government and the IMF relax their fiscal targets and allow a budget deficit for 1998. The year ended with a more than P50 billion national government deficit, amounting to around 3% of GNP.

In 1999, the Estrada government decided to initiate pump-priming activities to spur growth. But the continuing slump reduced revenue collections even further below the targets. The national government deficit by October had exceeded the P85 billion targeted deficit for the year. In 1999 the economy was seen to have accumulated a deficit of around P90 billion or more than 3% of GNP. The overshooting of the fiscal deficit target caused a temporary delay in the release of the $350 million IMF standby facility in 1999 as the IMF advised the government to cut down on pump-priming activities and improve revenue generation.

The growing budget deficit was and continues to be one cause for alarm in the present efforts at economic recovery. Incurring higher deficits would mean incurring the wrath of the IMF, meaning lower credit ratings for the country and continuing lack of confidence.

Loss of Business Confidence Perhaps one of the biggest economic victims of the crisis was the 'animal spirit'. As poor economic performance and financial weaknesses continued, the credit crunch persisted and little private investment took place. The perceived weak performance of the Estrada Administration only added to the bearish feeling of investors and reduced the impact of the pump priming activities. Although there were early signs of positive movements in the manufacturing sector, the climb out of the recession would still be a difficult one. Two things needed to happen before full recovery could take place. One was the resumption of credit lines and the end of the credit crunch. A second was that economic growth needed to incorporate the investment, construction and manufacturing sectors before economic growth could become credible and sustained. Both would require a strong return of business confidence and the 'animal spirits' which the crisis, recession and perceived poor performance of the government, cronyism, and the sudden eruption of war in Southern Philippines had broken.

Evaluation of the Root Causes of the Crisis and the IMF Response

The Origins and Nature of the Economic and Financial Crisis

Following our description of the economic performance of the Philippines on the eve of and during the crisis, it is worthwhile at this point to recapitulate the important trends that had a direct bearing on the currency crisis.

(1) Low domestic savings: The apparent and immediate cause of the bust portion of the boom-bust cycle has usually involved the lack of foreign exchange to finance an economy dependent on imported capital goods, imported fuel and imported intermediate products. The other side of the coin was the low domestic savings rate[4] of the Philippines, which was around half of the usual rates in other East Asian countries (see Table 10.1). This low savings rate forced the Philippines to rely on foreign capital inflows to finance its growth.

(2) Foreign exchange and capital liberalization: Attempts were made in the latest growth period to address low domestic savings and the inability to generate foreign reserves by lifting most restrictions on foreign exchange inflows and outflows. The foreign exchange and capital liberalization in 1992 led to increases in net foreign investments and remittances of overseas workers to the Philippines (see Tables 10.2a and 10.2b). This allowed growth to be sustained for several years even as trade deficits became very large.

(3) The increase in foreign portfolio inflows and outflows: Capital liberalization, however, led to massive portfolio inflows and outflows that increased volatility in the external account as short-run monetary inflows ('hot money') came in and out at very short intervals.

(4) Strength of Globalization: The opening-up of the capital markets was carried out simultaneously in many countries, from Eastern Europe to South Asia to Latin America. The New York Stock Exchange, in the meantime, provided stiff competition for portfolio funds going into the 'emerging markets' in the second half of the 1990s. This opening-up of the capital markets of most countries and the fast development of telecommunications and computer technologies facilitated inward and outward flows of short-term capital, which exited one country and entered another in just a matter of minutes.

Foreign fund managers managing portfolio flows, in the second half of the 1990s, followed a 'herd mentality' that looked at the entire ASEAN region as if it were homogenous even though there were in fact differences in economic fundamentals from country to country. This led to the 'contagion effect' wherein currency depreciation and financial crisis in one country was transmitted to another country in the same region. Although there may have been over-reaction and irrationality toward this 'herd mentality', it is a fact that all the countries in East Asia which were hard-hit by the financial crisis had undertaken, in one form or another and in various degrees, a similar opening up of the capital account (which produced the perverse effects described below) and had financed their growing current account deficits with portfolio inflows and/or unhedged foreign borrowings. When the Thai crisis erupted, these weaknesses of the other East Asian countries were emphasized, further strengthening the 'herd' and 'contagion' effects.

The 'herd' mentality afflicted not only portfolio investors but also foreign private lenders. Once Thailand got hit, foreign commercial banks that had lent to other Southeast Asian countries naturally became jittery and stricter in the rollover and disbursement of additional loans. This contributed to the gravity and depth of the financial crisis.

The intense trade liberalization and tariff reduction undertaken by many countries under the General Agreement on Tariff and Trade (GATT) and the Asia-Pacific Economic Cooperation (APEC) as well as, for the Southeast Asian countries, under the ASEAN Free Trade Agreement (AFTA), and the opening up of China, Vietnam and Eastern Europe to world trade—all these brought intensified competition into the world export market. This contributed to the perception, especially among speculators, foreign fund managers and commercial banks, that if one country devalued, similar currency depreciation would have to be effected by other countries to remain competitive in the world market (especially if the economies of these countries displayed relatively high current account deficits). The specter of China being forced to devalue its currency was a variant of this perception. In the end, the periodic rounds of significant currency depreciation in Thailand, Indonesia, Malaysia, the Philippines, South Korea, and Singapore were most likely events that were unique to this stage of massive opening up of the capital and goods markets to international forces.

(5) Overvaluation of the peso: The net external inflow of capital led to a paradoxical situation wherein the currency was appreciated in real terms (sometimes even in nominal terms) while trade and current account deficits rose partly due to the higher growth.

(6) Rising import intensity and relative price distortions with a bias toward nontradeables vis-à-vis tradeables: The appreciation of the currency in real terms had harmed the export sector (with the exception of semiconductors), and in conjunction with a significant import liberalization (implemented in the late 1980s) and tariff reductions (effected in the 1990s) increased the import intensity of the economy tremendously. This led to

led to what some economists call a 'Dutch disease' —as the perverse effects of positive capital inflows and subsequent currency appreciation led to the deterioration of the trade and current account balances. Furthermore, this bias against tradeables encouraged the fast-growing economy to shift resources into non-tradeables, and particularly into real property, financial, wholesale and retail trade sectors. Together with the overlending syndrome in the financial sector, this created asset bubbles that aggravated the financial crisis.

(7) Weak prudential regulation: The financial liberalization and easing of bank entry allowed the overborrowing and overlending syndrome to unfold in full force without sufficient prudential regulation by the BSP. This regulation should have focused on reducing exposure to risky assets and loans, especially real estate loans, unhedged and mismatched dollar borrowings, and the expansion of consumer lending to high risk groups.

(8) Higher real peso interest rates compared to real dollar rates: The financial liberalization, together with the BSP's sterilization of monetary inflows and the policy of maintaining a stable currency, ensured that domestic interest rates[5] were above foreign rates, particularly those on the dollar. This, together with the stable and appreciating peso, led as a matter of course to high dollar borrowings (which were largely unhedged) by commercial banks and private firms alike.

The Philippines was on an IMF program when the crisis hit in July 1997. Because the BSP spent between $1.5 billion and $2 billion of its reserves defending the peso from speculative attacks, the government borrowed, almost immediately, approximately the same amount from the IMF to beef up its international reserves. The Philippines exited the old IMF program at the end of March of 1998, only to enter into a 'precautionary arrangement' for a standby facility of $1.37 billion. This program pretty much exemplified the IMF ideology. It differed from the packages of the more hard-hit countries only in the extent of the financial rehabilitation and financial prescriptions (inasmuch as the financial sector of the Philippines had not been as severely damaged) and the degree of opening up of the economy to market forces and foreign investments (inasmuch as the Philippines had already opened up much ahead of these countries).

The IMF program contained some disturbing features, and ultimately it failed to tackle the ultimate causes of the crisis which we described above, and even bailed out some of the culprits, particularly foreign portfolio investors and the foreign commercial banks. The following are the program's objectionable features:

(1) The IMF program relied heavily on increasing interest rates to stave off currency speculation and to effect 'current account adjustments' to

offset the capital outflows. This weakened an otherwise healthy financial sector and, together with currency depreciation, increased non-performing loans and brought about a loss of confidence in the financial sector.

(2) The IMF and the BSP also immediately called (without a sufficient grace period and phasing in) for stricter loan loss provisioning and higher capitalization requirements without giving due consideration to short-run instability and weaknesses (which combined with adverse economic and liquidity conditions) of financial institutions.

(3) There was strong emphasis on achieving fiscal surpluses--in the crisis years of 1998 and 1999. This completely ignored the objective conditions wherein currency devaluations cause drastic cuts in imports and thus substantially reduce import tax revenues. The massive currency depreciation was also stagflationary, reducing the government's revenue-generating capacity from direct and indirect taxes. All these should have pointed to the inevitability of fiscal deficits and a policy of allowing a reasonable deficit so as not to drastically reduce basic social services and essential infrastructure spending. Instead the fiscal surplus targets gave the wrong signals. Confidence was shattered when it became clear that significant deficits were for real and the currency depreciated even more so.

(4) The IMF program was also insistent on retaining the policy of complete capital liberalization, even for short-run portfolio inflows and short-run foreign lending. In the previous section, it was shown very clearly that portfolio investments created undue volatility in the system. The money was for mere speculation and, unlike foreign direct investments, did not involve commitments to medium and long-term productive investment in the country. More importantly, it was these unnecessary flows which led to the overvaluation of the peso, which together with tariff reductions,[6] increased the import intensity of the economy, which in turn led to higher current account deficits. It was also the overvaluation of the peso (again together with lower tariffs) that made non-tradeables (real estate, financial instruments, the trade sector) attractive vis-à-vis tradeables and the manufacturing sector. This led to the real estate and financial bubbles which brought the property and financial sectors into trouble. Thus it was not just the lack of prudential regulation (over which there was general agreement and which the IMF concentrated on) that caused the crisis. More importantly, it was the relative price distortions that gave concrete economic incentives to financial capital to flow into the wrong sectors. Many of the mistakes which the IMF blamed on the East Asian countries—high current account deficits, overinvestment in the wrong sectors—could be traced to the capital liberalization policy.

There are many proposals on how to distinguish good foreign inflows (foreign direct investments [FDI]) from bad ones (portfolio investments and short-term foreign lending). There are of course the strict quantitative restrictions on portfolio flows and foreign borrowings as in China. There are the exchange and capital controls being successfully implemented in Malaysia. There is, as in Chile, the use of deposit requirements (30% in Chile, and not to be withdrawn for at least a year) for all financial and portfolio inflows (including foreign lending, financial investments in local financial instruments and stocks, foreign currency deposits[7] and bond issues); there is the Tobin transaction tax imposed on foreign currency exchange transactions (with those earmarked for FDIs possibly exempted). There is also the proposal by Joseph Stiglitz to disallow the treatment of interest payments for foreign loans as expenses for tax purposes.

The problem was that with the IMF program, the Philippines could not implement any of the measures outlined above. Even if the assurance of complete capital liberalization was not included in the IMF program, it would have been difficult for the Philippines to implement capital regulations on its own in this part of the world without becoming the pariah of the region—which would have led to it losing the good direct foreign investments as well. It was precisely the IMF style of presenting a unique package individually to each country that precluded a regional and international solution to the crisis, which would have included regional and international efforts and cooperation to stave off the harmful rounds of currency depreciation and contagion.

(5) It was also clear that in all the IMF packages for the region, foreign banks that were guilty of the 'overlending syndrome' would not be made to share the burden. None of the IMF packages in East Asia had a Brady-like plan for partial debt forgiveness. Especially for the Philippines, much of the recession and credit crunch was caused by liquidity problems as short-term foreign credit lines were cut. Strong workout arrangements and debt rollovers could have kept confidence afloat in a period of intense currency speculation. It is, however, IMF belief and ideology that if a country makes a mistake, it should be the one to undertake the reforms to correct that mistake. Unfortunately, it is the poor, more likely than not, who suffer the most.

(6) The IMF seemed little concerned about the social and human impacts of the financial crisis and the painful reforms required. It was also blind to the more long-lasting effects of the strong recession on human capital (education, health and self-esteem).

The Developed Countries and Other Multilateral Agencies

There was widespread perception that the US was a staunch supporter of the IMF line. Most other developed countries did not venture beyond the space allowed by the IMF. This made the IMF the most powerful player in dealing with the current crisis. But criticism of the high-handed IMF treatment of the hard-hit countries has grown, particularly among UN agencies and the NGOs.

The World Bank, in particular, behind closed doors and via its ex-chief economist, Joseph Stiglitz, was quite critical of the IMF approach to the crisis. The shock treatment that the IMF implemented in Thailand, Indonesia and South Korea—the immediate closure of failing institutions, immediate austerity measures—created greater loss of confidence (both internally and externally) and deepened the regional crisis further than what should have been the case otherwise. (Even Jeffrey Sachs, known as a staunch advocate of market-friendly reform, criticized the role of the IMF in East Asia.) Furthermore Stiglitz's public statements pointed to the need for the regulation of short-run foreign portfolio and credit flows, given the 'moral hazard' and 'market failures' that occur in the financial system.

The UN agencies—ILO, UNDP, UNICEF, and UNCTAD—have all taken the social sector and poverty alleviation seriously, and the World Bank and the Asian Development Bank are setting up funds precisely for this. This makes them less willing in principle to accept very austere measures that will aggravate the conditions of the poor. If we extend this logic even further, then these organizations should have greater inclination to listen to suggestions concerning the creation of social funds to help countries ease the human and social pain of the crisis and provide safety nets to the most vulnerable groups, given that public safety nets are non-existent in most of the affected countries, and that ballooning budget deficits leave little room for improving basic social services and poverty alleviation at a time of extreme need.

One would expect it to be a long-run goal for these United Nations organizations with a more social orientation to espouse sharing the burden of the crisis with foreign investors and creditors, coordinating efforts to fight currency instability and volatility, and creating international solutions to the problem of indiscriminate portfolio flows and short-term foreign borrowings in developing nations. They could spearhead discussion and international forums to address such issues.

The Lack of a Regional and Coordinated Response from Affected Countries

It was disappointing that the countries hit by the crisis failed to coordinate some regional response. Except for some lip service to trading with one another's currencies, there was no attempt to unite in common financial policies and capital regulation, nor most immediately, was there any regional and international effort to stave off the currency attacks on the region. The lesson perhaps is that united and coordinated policies among East Asian countries may not be forthcoming in periods of extreme weakness and crisis. The idea of a common fund, for example, cannot be implemented by countries which have to defend their currencies on an everyday basis. Japan proposed the idea of an Asian Monetary Fund but it was quickly shot down by the US at a time of extreme weakness in the Japanese economy. The idea will be useless without concrete support from countries with very strong currencies and very large reserves--which means some sort of international effort. The IMF's strategy of concentrating on stringent individual programs to hard-hit countries rather than coordinating regional and international efforts contributed to the lack of a genuine solution to the crisis.

Perhaps when their economies are strong again, the East Asian countries will be able to look back to the current crisis and implement, cooperatively and consultatively, common financial and capital regulation policies. The serious consideration in 2000 of reviving the Asian Monetary Fund is a step in the right direction.

Solving the Economic and Financial Crisis

Regionally and Internationally

It is very clear also that a permanent solution to the crisis can no longer be based on the economic fundamentals of each individual country—as the IMF individual country programs would have us believe—but on the soundness of all the countries in the region. This was illustrated in the spate of alternate ups and downs experienced in the financial markets of the countries in East Asia in 1997 and 1998.

It is therefore urgent that international and regional efforts be carried out immediately to prevent a repetition of the spiralling decline in the currency and financial sectors of the region. In this light, it is imperative that, if a crisis like the present one hits the region again, the following policies be implemented:

(1) The multilateral agencies—led by the IMF, the World Bank and the Asian Development Bank, and the strongest economies in the world—led by the US, Europe and Japan—should coordinate efforts to stabilize currencies. Multinational and large commercial banks in developed countries—especially those with large foreign credit exposure in East Asia—should be encouraged and persuaded to assist in this effort. This could take the form of setting up a common fund (the Asian Fund), intervening in the foreign exchange transactions to stabilize affected countries' currencies, and beefing up their international reserves.

(2) The international community should also come up with international rules and regulations to guide short-run capital flows in and out of developing countries. In the long run, this could entail the creation of an international body to monitor and regulate such flows. But at this juncture, there is a need for the multilateral agencies and the powerful countries to draw up common rules to control the entry and (especially) the exit of short-run foreign capital. The Chilean model may be one case to emulate and standardize across all countries. Short-term capital would be forced to put down a 30% deposit on the total value of inflow, which could only be withdrawn after a year. Such regulations in effect impose a tax on short-run capital flows (the shorter the duration, the higher the tax) and reduce financial volatility and speculation emanating from the foreign investors. Economic disincentives (or taxation) of short-run unhedged foreign borrowings should also remove unnecessary exposure to high-risk loans that breed speculation and panic, aggravate currency depreciation and increase financial vulnerability. All these should be allowed by the IMF and other multilateral agencies. In fact, being international coordinating bodies, they should take the initiative in the establishment of common and standard rules for short-term capital flows.

(3) Working out arrangements and debt rollovers during periods of currency speculative attacks and contagion should be part and parcel of an arrangement for a new international financial architecture. This will avoid unnecessary financial panic and liquidity crises that can turn otherwise sound and strong firms and financial institutions into insolvent ones.

(4) The East Asian countries themselves will have to learn to formulate and coordinate common financial, exchange rate and capital flow policies, to cooperate and support one another, and to lobby jointly in international forums for international financial reforms and international support for their battered economies.

(5) While the situation in the region is still quite volatile, the monetary authorities of the East Asian countries should come up with extra efforts to strengthen their financial and banking sectors before things get worse again. This would involve undertaking, during recessions, good prudential regulation that does not bring further weaknesses to the financial sector. Increasing capitalization requirements, encouraging weak banks to increase their capital or merge with bigger and stronger banks, increasing loan loss provision covers—all of these may be eventually required during good times but should be balanced and moderated during a climate of recession and lack of confidence. Grace periods, phasing and forebearance are important during times of extreme financial fragility and liquidity constraints.

(6) Much still has to be done in terms of generating greater transparency and giving early warning data and information in a timely, honest, and accurate fashion. As the financial sector becomes increasingly capable of responding to external and internal shocks, the danger of the crisis deepening further will be lessened. Measures to strengthen the financial system may lead to more concentration in the banking sector and therefore will require even better and more effective prudential regulation, monitoring, and supervision of the financial institutions. Policies should be simultaneously geared towards generating healthy competition in the financial sector, especially as economic recovery becomes sustained. Strengthening the financial system in the individual countries will be greatly enhanced if there are regional and international agreements for mutual surveillance and monitoring of flows, the harmonization of prudential and supervisory regulations over the financial system, and the institution of early warning devices to detect major negative trends and occurrences in the financial systems of the region. No doubt regional cooperation among the countries affected may be greatly beneficial, but more importantly, given that financial capital flows come from developed countries, the involvement of developed countries—the US, Europe and Japan—and their financial institutions would be even more helpful and would ensure a strong and healthy financial system in the region and in the world.

At the National Level

Employment generating programs will have to be undertaken to stimulate job creation and aggregate demand in the economic system, as was done in 1986 and 1987. As a domestic policy, this will be crucial in the recovery stage of the economy. The problem here is that this will require a significant volume of funds, and the terribly tight fiscal bind now—which threatens social services and safety nets as well—will provide a major obstacle to its early implementation. The availability of international funds at concessional rates and with no strings attached will be vital in cushioning the possible negative impact of higher fiscal deficits.

Now that foreign inflows seem to have dried up again, the Philippines should try to avoid returning to the boom-bust cycle. Even if portfolio inflows return, they should not be seen as a stable source of foreign exchange to fund the import needs of the country. What is required is a strong commitment to promote high value-added exports, promote a strong and backward-linking import-substituting sector, and attract foreign direct investments, especially those that help promote and diversify high value-added exports. The other side of the coin should be to improve the domestic savings capacity, but at this stage of development, the domestic savings rate is critically dependent on the boom-bust cycle—rising during booms and falling during busts. The domestic savings rate will go up once the boom-bust cycle is banished and the economy enters onto a permanently upward trend.

Even if foreign inflows cannot go back to the large magnitudes of the mid-1990s, it is alright if GDP rises more slowly than before—say between 4% and slightly less than 5%—as long as we do not be incur large current account deficits and foreign debt. Lower but more manageable and less volatile growth may also be more environment-friendly, especially if it is more equitably dispersed and is not highly concentrated in growth areas, which increases pollution in urban areas and requires increased natural resource extraction in the rural areas. It should also be more gender-friendly, leading to less uprooting of families as laborers, both male and female, are forced less to migrate to urban and high growth areas to search for job opportunities.

Notes

[1] Not all deregulation was successful. The oil deregulation was very controversial and it would take years before its full impact was seen. The attempt at deregulating the shipping industry is known to have been largely unsuccessful.

[2] Actually the old Central Bank liabilities being funded by the national government were put "below the line" which put the national government accounts into surplus (since these did not include the old Central Bank liabilities) but made public sector borrowing requirements (PSBRs) high.

[3] Although export volumes fell in the national income accounts, there was actually a 16.9% increase in the dollar value of exports, which improved the current account and the balance of payment positions (see Tables 10.2a and 10.2b).

[4] Domestic savings and the domestic savings rate are seen by the author as indicators of the capacity of the economy to generate investments without resorting to foreign borrowings and foreign capital inflows. It is the belief of the author that, in the Philippine context, domestic

savings capacity follows a Keynesian trend, that is, domestic savings and its rate grow adequately during periods of reasonably high economic growth and grow slowly or contract during periods of bust and economic decline. Thus the unsustained growth and boom-bust cycles have not allowed Philippine domestic savings capacity to grow over time. Furthermore, the two-gap analysis has emphasized the point that the investment-savings gap in developing countries like the Philippines is maintained due to the incapacity of the economy to generate sufficient foreign exchange earnings via exports and to develop import competing and substituting industries that limit dependence on imports.

[5] The domestic interest rates had actually been falling substantially since 1993, but the levels were still above foreign interest rates

[6] In fact, the overvaluation of the peso subverted the potential beneficial impacts that tariff reductions might have brought about.

[7] A reserve requirement for foreign reserve deposits was originally proposed for the IMF program, but the BSP successfully lobbied against it.

References

Agosin, Manuel R. and Ricardo Ffrench-Davis (1998), 'Managing Capital Inflows in Chile', Presented at the UNU/WIDER seminar on Short-Term Capital Movements and Balance of Payments Crises held at Sussex, on May 1-2, 1997.

Akyüz, Yilmaz (1998), 'The East Asian Financial Crisis: Back to the Future?' UNCTAD, Geneva.

Fischer, Stanley (1998) 'The Asian Crisis: A View from the IMF', speech at the Midwinter Conference of the Bankers' Association for Foreign Trade, Washington D.C., Jan. 22, 1998.

Fischer, Stanley (1998), 'How to Avoid International Financial Crises and the Role of the IMF', International Monetary Fund.

Lim, Joseph (1998), 'The Philippines and the East Asian Economic Turmoil', in Jomo K.S. (ed.), *Tigers in Trouble*, University of Malaysia.

Lim, Joseph (1998), 'The Social Impact of and Responses to the Current East Asian Economic Turmoil: The Philippine Case', United Nations Development Programme.

McKinnon, Ronald and Huw Pill (1997), 'Credible Economic Liberalizations and Overborrowing', *American Economic Review*, Vol 87, No. 2.

McKinnon, Ronald and Huw Pill (1998), 'International Borrowing: A Decomposition of Credit and Currency Risks', *World Development*, Vol.26, No. 7.

Montes, Manuel F. (1998), *The Currency Crisis in Southeast Asia*, Institute of Southeast Asian Studies, Singapore.

Montes, Manuel and Joseph Lim (1996), 'Macroeconomic Volatility, Investment Anemia and Environment Struggles in the Philippines', *World Development*, Vol. 24, No. 2.

Ranis, Gustav and Frances Stewart (1998), 'A Pro-Human Development Adjustment Framework for the Countries of East and Southeast Asia', UNDP.

Stiglitz, Joseph (1998), 'Sound Finance and Sustainable Development in Asia', Keynote address to the Asia Development Forum, Manila, Philippines.

World Bank (1996), 'Strengthening Philippine Resiliency', A Country Paper.

Table 10.1 Some Macro Indicators of the Philippines: 1981-1997

Year	GDP Growth Rate	GNP Growth Rate	GNP per capita (1985 price)	Growth in GNP per cap. (1985 price)	Unempl. Rate (%) (Oct)	Labor Productivity (GDP/Empl)	Exchange Rate	Growth of Exchange Rate	Inflation Rate	T-Bill Rates (91 days)	M3/GDP	Growth of M3/CPI (in %)	Money Multiplier
1981	3.4	3.2	12,643		8.7	38,002	7.90		17.3	12.55	0.2931	13.32	3.82
1982	3.6	2.8	12,633	-0.1	9.4	38,878	8.54	8.10	8.6	13.78	0.3029	7.20	4.07
1983	1.9	1.5	12,526	-0.8	7.9	37,419	11.11	30.13	5.3	14.26	0.3095	12.84	3.24
1984	-7.3	-8.8	11,110	-11.3	10.6	33,729	16.70	50.27	47.1	28.24	0.2334	-27.10	3.05
1985	-7.3	-7.0	10,086	-9.2	11.1	31,533	18.61	11.43	23.4	25.87	0.2346	-11.25	2.86
1986	3.4	4.2	10,205	1.2	11.1	31,399	20.39	9.56	-0.4	15.63	0.2370	8.08	2.57
1987	4.3	4.6	10,476	2.7	9.1	30,785	20.57	0.89	3.0	11.51	0.2370	8.82	2.59
1988	6.8	7.7	10,971	4.7	8.3	31,058	21.10	2.56	8.9	14.67	0.2483	12.56	2.76
1989	6.2	5.6	11,385	3.8	8.4	31,927	21.74	3.04	12.2	18.64	0.2744	14.06	2.61
1990	3.0	3.7	11,661	2.4	8.1	32,446	24.31	11.84	13.2	26.67	0.2790	3.67	2.44
1991	-0.6	0.4	11,456	-1.8	9.0	31,270	27.48	13.03	18.5	21.11	0.2781	-2.67	2.47
1992	0.3	1.3	11,382	-0.6	8.6	30,340	25.51	-7.15	8.6	16.02	0.2851	1.92	2.51
1993	2.1	2.8	11,151	-2.0	8.9	30,111	27.12	6.30	7.0	12.45	0.3258	15.82	2.73
1994	4.4	5.3	11,456	2.7	8.4	30,616	26.45	-2.47	8.3	12.71	0.3589	16.02	3.10
1995	4.7	4.9	11,733	2.4	8.4	31,269	25.70	-2.84	8.0	11.30	0.3995	15.95	3.32
1996	5.8	7.2	12,298	4.8	7.4	31,209	26.21	1.98	9.1	12.40	0.4058	6.81	3.36
1997	5.2	5.3	12,653	2.9	7.9	32,168	29.47	12.44	5.9	13.10	0.4398	15.08	3.50
1998	-0.5	0.1	12,388	-2.1	9.6	31,841	40.89	38.76	9.8	15.30	0.4291	-2.33	3.68
1999	3.2	3.6	12,561	1.4	9.4	31,635	39.09	-4.41	6.6	10.20	0.4567	12.7	3.95

Source: National Statistical Coordination Board.

Table 10.2a Balance of Payments

(Unit: US $ millions)

Item		1992	1993	1994	1995	1996	1997	1998	1999
I.	Current Account								
A.	Trade, Net	-1675	-3715	-3886	-4179	-4542	-5431	1111	6707
	(as % of GNP)	-3.1	-6.7	-5.9	-5.5	-5.2	-6.3	1.6	8.4
	Goods, Net	-4695	-6222	-7850	-8944	-11342	-11127	-28	4306
	(as % of GNP)	-8.7	-11.2	-11.9	-11.7	-13.1	-13	-0.04	5.4
	Exports	9824	11375	13483	17447	20543	25228	29496	35032
	Imports	14519	17597	21333	26391	31885	36355	29524	30726
	Services, Net	3020	2507	3964	4765	6800	5696	1139	2401
	Receipts	7443	7497	10550	14374	19006	22835	13917	12854
	Payments	4423	4990	6586	9609	12206	17139	12778	10453
B.	Transfers, Net	817	699	936	882	589	1080	435	481
	Inflow	826	746	1041	1147	1185	1670	758	645
	Outflow	9	47	105	265	596	590	323	164
	Current Account, Net	-858	-3016	-2950	-3297	-3953	-4351	1546	7188
	(as % of GNP)	-1.6	-5.5	-4.5	-4.3	-4.6	-5.1	2.3	9.0
II.	Capital and Financial Account								
A.	Medium and Long-Term Loans, Net	633	2455	1313	1276	2841	4824	2740	4716
	Availment	7432	5205	4369	3927	6540	7724	6025	9279
	Repayment	6799	2750	3056	2651	3699	2900	3285	4563
B.	Trading of Bonds I the Secondary Market						-37	-676	-1083	102
	Resale of Bonds						4148	3072	3307	4511
	Purchase of Bonds						4185	3748	4390	4409
C.	Investments, Net	737	812	1558	1609	3517	762	1672	1218
	Non-Res. Investment in the Phil	931	2135	2492	2944	3621	843	2016	1589
	Resident Investments Abroad	194	1323	934	1335	104	81	344	371
D.	Change in the NFA of KBs	289	299	674	564	4214	1188	-1330	-1836
E.	Purchase of Collaterral	469							
F.	Short-Term Capital, Net	660	148	1002	56	540	495	-1521	-3610
	Capital and Financial Account, Net	1850	2820	4547	3393	11075	6593	478	590
III.	Others								
A.	Monetization of Gold	130	113	154	177	198	105	118	198
B.	Revaluation of Adjustments	527	431	100	96	-203	-465	-22	82
	Others, Total	657	544	254	81	-5	-360	96	280
IV.	Net Unclassified Items	-157	-514	-49	454	-3010	-5245	-761	-4219
V.	Overall BOP Position	1492	-166	1802	631	4107	-3363	1359	3839
	(as % of GNP)	2.8	-0.3	2.7	0.8	4.8	-3.9	2.0	4.8

Source : Bangko Sentral ng Pilipinas (BSP).

Table 10.2b Foreign Investments

(Unit: US $ millions)

Item	1992	1993	1994	1995	1996	1997	1998	1999
Investments, Net	737	812	1558	1609	3517	762	1672	1218
A. Non-Resident Investments in the Phils.	931	2135	2492	2944	3621	843	2016	1589
Direct Investments	776	1238	1591	1459	1520	1249	1752	1077
Placements	776	1238	1591	1459	1520	1249	1752	1089
New Foreign Investments in the	234	547	930	1300	1074	1073	1631	1025
Reinvested Earnings	42	43	29	23	44	56	85	38
Technical Fees and Others								
Converted to Equity	41	5	36	22	0	0	0	26
Debt Conversion	269	193	2	0	0	0	0	0
Bond Conversion	0	0	45	46	277	114	36	0
Imports Converted into Investm	5	0	1	6	0	6	0	0
Others	185	450	548	62	125	0	0	0
Withdrawals								12
Portfolio Investments	155	897	901	1485	2101	-406	264	512
Placements	566	2257	2979	3861	6687	6947	4297	13186
Withdrawals	411	1360	2078	2376	4586	7353	4033	12674
B. Less: Resident Investments Abroad	194	1323	934	1335	104	81	344	371
Direct Investments	101	374	302	98	182	136	160	206
Placements	101	374	302	98	182	136	160	213
Residents' Investments Abroad	24	323	112	98	182	136	160	213
Others	77	51	190	0	0	0		
Withdrawals	0	0	0	0	0	0	0	7
Portfolio Investments, Net	93	949	632	1237	-78	-55	184	165
Placements	115	1061	1338	1864	119	184	184	185
Withdrawals	22	112	706	627	197	239	0	20
Residents' Withdrawal of Foreign								
Investments Abroad	22	112	706	627	197	239	0	20

Source : Bangko Sentral ng Pilipinas (BSP).

Table 10.3 GNP and GDP by Industrial Origin, 1980-1999

(Unit:as % of GDP)

INDUSTRY	1980	1981	1982	1983	1984	1985	1986	1987	1988	1989	1990	1991	1992	1993	1994	1995	1996	1997	1998	1999
I. AGRI.FISHERY,FORESTRY	23.5	23.5	22.9	21.7	23.2	24.6	24.6	24.4	23.6	22.9	22.3	22.7	22.8	22.8	22.4	21.5	21.1	20.7	19.4	21.1
a. Agriculture industry		20.9	20.8	19.7	21.3	23.0	22.9	22.4	21.9	21.5	21.3	22.1	22.2	22.3	22.0	21.3	20.9	20.6	19.3	20.0
b. Forestry		2.6	2.1	2.0	1.9	1.6	1.7	2.0	1.7	1.3	1.0	0.7	0.6	0.5	0.4	0.2	0.2	0.1	0.1	0.1
II. INDUSTRY SECTOR	40.5	41.0	40.5	40.4	38.6	35.1	34.7	34.6	35.2	35.6	35.5	34.7	34.4	34.3	34.7	35.4	35.6	35.9	35.5	34.5
a. Mining and Quarrying	1.5	1.5	1.4	1.4	1.5	2.1	2.1	1.8	1.8	1.6	1.5	1.5	1.6	1.6	1.4	1.3	1.2	1.2	1.2	1.1
b. Manufacturing	27.6	27.2	26.7	26.1	25.3	25.2	24.8	25.1	25.7	25.6	25.5	25.6	25.0	24.7	24.8	25.3	25.3	25.0	24.9	24.5
c. Construction	9.4	10.1	9.8	10.5	9.1	5.1	4.8	5.1	5.0	5.7	5.8	4.9	5.0	5.2	5.5	5.5	5.8	6.4	5.9	5.6
d. Elect,Gas and Water	2.0	2.3	2.7	2.4	2.7	2.8	3.0	2.6	2.7	2.7	2.6	2.7	2.7	2.8	3.0	3.2	3.3	3.3	3.5	3.4
III. SERVICE SECTOR	36.0	35.5	36.6	37.9	38.2	40.4	40.7	41.0	41.2	41.5	42.2	42.5	42.8	43.0	42.9	43.1	43.3	43.4	45.1	45.5
a. Trans., Comm. and Stor.	4.8	4.9	4.8	4.9	5.2	5.5	5.6	5.7	5.8	5.8	5.7	5.8	5.8	5.8	5.8	5.9	6.0	6.2	6.6	6.7
b. Trade	13.0	12.6	13.2	13.5	13.6	14.5	14.7	14.6	14.5	14.7	14.9	15.1	15.3	15.3	15.3	15.4	15.3	15.2	15.6	15.8
c. Finance	3.9	3.3	3.4	3.7	3.3	3.0	3.1	3.5	3.6	3.9	4.2	4.1	4.1	4.1	4.1	4.2	4.5	4.9	5.1	5.0
d. O. Dwellings and R. Estate	5.2	5.0	5.2	5.2	5.3	5.6	5.6	5.6	5.6	5.6	5.6	5.6	5.6	5.6	5.5	5.5	5.4	5.3	5.4	5.3
e. Private Services	4.9	5.4	5.6	6.4	6.4	6.8	6.8	6.8	6.9	6.8	6.8	6.9	6.9	6.9	6.9	6.9	6.9	6.8	7.2	7.4
f. Government Services	4.2	4.3	4.3	4.2	4.5	4.9	4.9	4.8	4.9	4.8	5.1	5.2	5.2	5.2	5.2	5.2	5.2	5.1	5.2	5.2
GROSS DOMESTIC PRODUCT	100.0	100.0	100.0	100.0	100.0	100.0	100.0	100.0	100.0	100.0	100.0	100.0	100.0	100.0	100.0	100.0	100.0	100.0	100.0	100.0
Net factor income from abroad	-0.2	-0.4	-1.1	-1.5	-3.1	-2.8	-2.1	-1.8	-0.9	-1.5	-0.8	0.1	1.1	1.7	2.6	2.8	4.1	4.3	4.8	5.2
GROSS NATIONAL PRODUCT	99.8	99.6	98.9	98.5	96.9	97.2	97.9	98.2	99.1	98.5	99.2	100.1	101.1	101.7	102.6	102.8	104.1	104.3	104.8	105.2

Source : National Statistics Coordiantion Board.

Table 10.4 GNP and GDP by Expenditure Shares, 1980-1999

(Unit:as % of GDP)

TYPE OF EXPENDITURE	1980	1981	1982	1983	1984	1985	1986	1987	1988	1989	1990	1991	1992	1993	1994	1995	1996	1997	1998	1999
1. Personal Consumption Expenditure	65.2	64.7	64.6	63.8	69.0	73.6	73.5	73.3	73.0	72.1	73.8	75.9	78.1	78.8	78.3	77.7	76.8	76.6	79.7	79.3
2. Government Consumption	8.2	7.7	8.0	7.5	7.1	7.6	7.4	7.4	7.6	7.6	7.9	7.8	7.7	8.0	8.1	8.2	8.1	7.8	7.9	8.1
3. Capital Formation	26.4	26.3	27.5	28.7	19.5	14.3	15.3	17.5	18.8	21.3	24.0	20.0	21.5	22.7	23.6	23.3	24.8	26.3	21.9	21.0
A. Fixed Capital	24.7	26.8	27.2	28.9	22.3	16.5	16.1	16.5	18.0	20.6	22.9	19.8	21.0	22.4	23.0	23.0	24.4	25.8	23.2	21.5
1. Construction	13.1	14.4	14.2	16.7	13.5	9.0	8.1	8.4	8.9	9.6	10.7	8.5	8.8	9.6	9.5	9.8	10.7	11.7	11.3	10.5
2. Durable Equipment	9.9	10.6	11.3	10.7	7.3	5.8	6.4	6.5	7.5	9.4	10.7	9.8	10.6	11.2	12.0	11.7	12.1	12.5	10.3	9.5
3. Breeding Stocks and Orchard Devt.	1.8	1.8	1.7	1.5	1.5	1.7	1.6	1.6	1.5	1.5	1.5	1.6	1.6	1.6	1.5	1.5	1.5	1.6	1.6	1.6
B. Changes in Stocks	1.7	-0.5	0.3	-0.2	-2.8	-2.1	-0.8	1.0	0.9	0.8	1.1	0.2	0.5	0.3	0.6	0.3	0.4	0.5	-1.3	0.6
4. Exports	25.4	26.9	23.2	23.5	26.5	24.0	27.1	27.8	29.8	30.6	30.2	32.3	33.6	34.9	40.1	42.9	46.8	52.3	47.1	40.8
5. Less : Imports	29.4	28.2	27.9	26.6	23.7	21.9	23.3	28.8	32.2	35.0	37.3	37.1	40.2	43.9	48.2	53.4	58.9	64.1	57.1	51.4
6. Statistical discrepancy	4.2	2.7	4.7	3.1	1.5	2.3	0.0	2.7	3.0	3.3	1.4	1.2	-0.6	-0.5	-1.9	1.3	2.5	1.0	0.5	2.3
GROSS DOMESTIC PRODUCT	100.0	100.0	100.0	100.0	100.0	100.0	100.0	100.0	100.0	100.0	100.0	100.0	100.0	100.0	100.0	100.0	100.0	100.0	100.0	100.0
Net factor income from abroad	-0.2	-0.4	-1.1	-1.5	-3.1	-2.8	-2.1	-1.8	-0.9	-1.5	-0.8	0.1	1.1	1.7	2.6	2.8	4.1	4.3	4.8	5.2
GROSS NATIONAL PRODUCT	99.8	99.6	98.9	98.5	96.9	97.2	97.9	98.2	99.1	98.5	99.2	100.1	101.1	101.7	102.6	102.8	104.1	104.3	104.8	105.2

Source : National Statistics Coordination Board.

Table 10.5 Value of Exports by Major Commodity Group

Commodity Group	in million US dollars				Percentage to total commodity exports							
	1996	1997	1998	1999	1992	1993	1994	1995	1996	1997	1998	1999
Agro-based Products	**2677**	**2707**	**2458**	**2132**	**22.86**	**20.28**	**18.40**	**17.35**	**13.03**	**10.73**	**8.33**	**6.09**
Petroleum Products	**272**	**258**	**129**	**216**	**1.53**	**1.20**	**0.98**	**0.98**	**1.32**	**1.02**	**0.44**	**0.62**
Manufactures	**17095**	**21462**	**25865**	**31305**	**74.29**	**76.74**	**78.73**	**79.49**	**83.22**	**85.07**	**87.69**	**89.36**
Elec and Elec Eqpt/Parts and Telecom	9988	13028	17156	21165	28.02	31.22	36.97	42.49	48.62	51.64	58.16	60.42
Garments	2423	2349	2356	2267	21.78	19.97	17.61	14.73	11.79	9.31	7.99	6.47
Textile Yarns/Fabrics	252	299	242	219	1.23	1.04	1.28	1.19	1.23	1.19	0.82	0.63
Footwear	170	194	147	86	1.47	1.48	1.56	1.19	0.83	0.77	0.50	0.25
Travel Goods and Handbags	121	174	182	154	0.54	0.47	0.56	0.63	0.59	0.69	0.62	0.44
Wood Manufactures	151	134	118	129	1.15	0.92	0.96	0.77	0.74	0.53	0.40	0.37
Furniture and Fixtures	293	322	324	353	1.84	1.78	1.78	1.58	1.43	1.28	1.10	1.01
Chemicals	353	383	339	294	2.73	2.30	2.27	1.97	1.72	1.52	1.15	0.84
Non-Metallic Mineral Manufactures	95	105	106	111	0.81	0.76	0.71	0.62	0.46	0.42	0.36	0.32
Machinery and Transport Equipment	1294	2685	3318	4951	2.93	3.19	3.48	4.25	6.30	10.64	11.25	14.13
Processed Food and Beverages	334	346	305	256	2.24	2.38	2.25	1.67	1.63	1.37	1.03	0.73
Iron and Steel	80	46	28	18	0.23	0.44	0.39	0.32	0.39	0.18	0.09	0.05
Baby Carr., toys, Games and Sporting Goods	224	203	169	157	1.52	1.48	1.41	1.32	1.09	0.80	0.57	0.45
Basketwork, Wickerwork and Other Articles of Plaiting Materials	101	93	85	84	1.35	1.16	0.99	0.72	0.49	0.37	0.29	0.24
Misc Manufactured Articles, n.e.s.	221	209	202	212	1.66	1.64	1.44	1.15	1.08	0.83	0.68	0.61
Others	995	892	785	849	4.77	6.49	5.07	4.89	4.84	3.54	2.66	2.42
Special Transactions	**117**	**287**	**311**	**436**	**0.33**	**0.33**	**0.55**	**0.62**	**0.57**	**1.14**	**1.05**	**1.24**
Re-Exports	**382**	**514**	**733**	**943**	**1.00**	**1.45**	**1.34**	**1.56**	**1.86**	**2.04**	**2.49**	**2.69**
Total Exports	**20543**	**25228**	**29496**	**35032**	**100**	**100**	**100**	**100**	**100**	**100**	**100**	**100**

Source : National Statistics Office (NSO).

Table 10.6 Selected Interest Rates, Exchange Rate, Gross Reserves

(Unit:weighted averages in percent per annum)

Period (end of period)	Exchange Rate	Treasury Bill Rates 91-day	Treasury Bill Rates 182-day	Treasury Bill Rates 364-day	Time Dep. Rate All Maturities	Time Dep. Rate S-T <360 d	Time Dep. Rate >360 d	Savings Deposit Rates 1	Bank Average Lending Rates 2	BSP RP rates (Lending) Overnight	BSP RRP rates (Borrowing) Overnight	Interbank Call Loan Rates	Gross International Reserves (in $ millions)
1990	24.31	23.4	25.2	26.1	24.7	20.6	19.7	10.9	24.3	15.9	16.8	14.8	1993
1991	27.48	21.4	22.5	23.9	22.5	18.5	18.6	11.0	23.5	13.0	14.0	15.7	4470
1992	25.51	16.1	17.0	18.0	17.0	14.1	14.0	10.6	19.4	16.7	23.8	16.7	5218
1993	27.12	12.3	13.1	14.1	13.1	10.3	11.0	8.3	14.6	34.2	13.2	13.7	5801
1994	26.42	13.6	13.7	14.0	13.8	10.7	12.0	8.0	15.0	17.5	12.7	13.4	6995
1995	25.71	11.3	12.5	13.4	12.5	9.3	10.7	8.0	14.6	14.5	11.2	12.1	7633
1996	26.21	12.4	12.9	13.4	13.0	11.5	9.9	8.0	14.8	14.4	12.9	12.6	11620
1997	29.47	13.1	13.0	13.6	13.3	11.2	11.4	9.1	16.2	17.0	15.0	17.9	
1998												13.8	
January	42.41	19.1	21.0	22.7	20.5	16.1	14.8	13.7	21.1	15.7	12.4	13.0	8531
February	40.36	17.8	19.1	20.6	19.0	15.8	15.6	12.5	20.0	15.1	13.1	13.5	9132
March	39.08	16.6	17.4	18.6	17.5	13.9	11.2	12.1	20.1	15.0	13.0	13.3	9237
April	39.98	15.2	16.7	17.7	16.4	12.1	8.7	12.1	18.1	15.1	13.0	13.2	10725
May	38.86	14.4	15.7	16.8	15.5	12.3	5.4	10.3	17.1	15.4	13.3	13.6	10733
June	42.09	14.0	15.4	16.8	15.3	11.6	12.4	10.1	16.0	15.1	13.1	13.2	10448
July	42.02	14.7	16.2	17.7	16.3	11.6	13.3	10.3	16.1	15.1	13.1	13.2	10273
August	43.87	14.1	15.1	16.8	15.3	11.3	12.5	10.2	15.2	17.1	16.7	15.8	9823
September	43.81	13.8	14.9	16.6	15.2	11.1	13.8	10.1	14.5	18.0	16.0	15.9	10503
October	40.83	13.5	14.6	15.7	14.8	11.3	13.5	9.9	14.5	15.9	13.9	14.0	10396
November	39.46	13.5	14.2	14.8	14.2	11.5	13.6	10.0	13.6	15.6	13.7	14.1	10388
December	39.06	13.4	13.9	14.3	13.8	11.0	12.2	10.0	14.8	15.4	13.4	13.9	10684
1999												10.8	
January	38.72	13.2	13.7	13.9	13.6	12.3	14.5	9.3	14.9	15.2	13.1	13.2	11551
February	39.10	12.7	13.0	13.2	13.0	11.7	14.3	8.9	12.4	14.5	12.5	12.7	12129
March	38.77	12.1	12.4	13.0	12.4	10.6	16.6	8.9	14.0	14.0	12.1	12.3	12832
April	38.02	10.9	11.1	11.4	11.1	8.6	16.6	8.3	12.1	13.8	11.0	11.1	13691
May	38.06	10.0	10.4	10.9	10.3	8.3	9.2	7.6	12.7	n.t.	10.0	10.1	13622
June	38.02	9.3	9.6	10.3	9.8	8.9	10.5	7.1	11.5	11.2	9.5	9.5	13712
July	38.25	8.4	8.6	9.2	8.7	8.0	7.9	6.8	10.4	11.0	9.0	9.1	13838
August	39.67	8.4	8.9	9.5	8.5	7.8	8.1	6.6	10.3	n.t.	9.0	9.0	14071
September	41.11	8.6	10.1	10.8	9.4	7.2	11.2	6.2	10.1	n.t.	9.0	8.8	14454
October	40.16	8.6	9.7	10.6	9.5	7.6	12.7	6.2	9.8	n.t.	9.0	8.8	14493
November	40.79	8.9	10.1	11.3	10.2	7.6	10.3	6.2	10.1	11.0	8.8	8.6	14629
December	40.31	8.9	10.1	11.3	10.3	8.3	13.0	6.5	12.9	11.8	8.8	8.7	14988
2000													
January	40.39	8.9	9.6	10.3	9.6	8.4	10.6	6.3	10.2	11.8	8.8	8.7	14648
February	40.85	8.8	9.6	10.5	9.6	8.0	10.8	n.a.	n.a.	n.t.	8.8	8.8	14478

Source : Bangko Sentral ng Pilipinas (BSP).

Table 10.7 Loans Outstanding of Commercial Banks*

(Unit: Peso millions)

	1990	1991	1992	1993	1994	1995	1996	1997	1998	1999
Classified by Economic Activity										
1. Agriculture, Fisheries and Forestry	26920	35159	38700	46092	49845	59603	63434	70705	62930	58859
2. Mining and Quarrying	6225	5569	6862	10767	5586	5711	9529	16231	20048	16466
3. Manufacturing	92516	89712	112702	142985	189458	253639	361556	424255	357455	382267
4. Electricity, Gas and Water	3169	3506	4047	10502	13199	16460	31369	42024	47284	53274
5. Construction	6394	6954	8239	13620	18020	24760	43132	51590	54972	53384
6. Wholesale and Retail Trade	34765	44378	53224	67994	95090	130568	180281	230765	210191	203177
7. Transportation, Storage and Communication	9030	9077	11063	16900	25988	44708	68557	101253	98636	91024
8. Fin. Inst., Real Estate and Bus. Service	40495	48267	65694	72308	99334	123944	244422	348477	347339	342673
9. Community, Social and Personal Services	20743	21454	26897	51662	46277	74868	117984	131485	149336	153104
Total	240255	264074	327430	432829	542796	737260	1120265	1416785	1348191	1354228

Note: * Peso and Foreign Accounts but excluding transactions of local banks' foreign offices.
Source: Commercial Banks Monthly Statements of Conditions.

Table 10.8 Foreign Currency Deposit Unit (FCDU) Loans by Borrower

(Unit: US $ millions)

End of Quarter	1993 Q4	1994 Q1	Q2	Q3	Q4	1995 Q1	Q2	Q3	Q4	1996 Q1	Q2	Q3	Q4	1997 Q1	Q2	Q3	Q4	1998 Q1	Q2	Q3	Q4	1999 Q1	Q2	Q3
Commodity Exporter	1109	1037	1267	1399	1716	1849	2221	2656	2986	3565	4536	5288	5868	6081	6006	5989	5171	4363	3833	3339	2940	2777	2879	2845
Service Exporter	44	33	52	70	56	62	50	96	108	178	198	245	286	288	301	390	351	334	346	308	304	271	269	262
Producers/Manufacturers	19	21	12	14	15	49	47	63	57	60	64	65	89	97	154	167	150	136	139	129	117	96	116	134
Oil Companies	492	432	490	588	539	614	341	284	400	423	487	514	449	378	419	451	402	247	159	118	304	215	271	302
Public Utilities	335	440	483	433	449	599	700	745	870	886	1141	1198	1485	1399	1454	1484	1615	1632	1637	1724	1814	1749	1753	1734
Others	16	83	94	104	321	247	317	618	614	1075	1313	1929	2401	2843	3586	3265	2713	2600	2493	2721	2443	2268	2079	1986
TOTAL	2015	2046	2398	2608	3096	3420	3676	4462	5035	6187	7739	9239	10578	11086	11920	11746	10402	9312	8607	8339	7922	7376	7367	7263

Source: MEDD, BSP.

Table 10.9 Total Foreign Exchange Liabilities

(Unit: end of period, US $ millions)

	1992	1993	1994	1995	1996	1997	1998	Mar	Jun	Sept.'99
By Type of Debt	32089	35535	38723	39367	41875	45433	47817	48636	48128	51172
Medium and Long-Term[a]	26833	30500	33526	34088	34668	36994	40632	41849	41591	44534
Short Term	5256	5035	5197	5279	7207	8439	7186	6787	6537	6638
Trade	4937	3495	3401	2674	4096	4032	2551	2367	1878	2091
Non-trade	319	1540	1796	2605	3111	4407	4634	4420	4659	4547
By Borrower	32089	35535	38723	39367	41875	45433	47817	48636	48128	51172
Banking System[b]	4709	3298	4143	5452	8632	10664	11215	10887	10705	10754
Bangko Sentral	2337	1288	855	1212	1415	2499	3437	3136	3196	3287
Commercial Banks	2372	2010	3288	4240	7217	8165	7778	7751	7509	7467
Government Banks[c]	924	1489	2308	2240	1838	2187	2368	2310	2488	2715
Private Banks	1448	521	980	2000	5379	5978	5410	5441	5021	4752
Foreign Banks	603	422	376	259	348	609	494	849	385	361
Domestic Banks	845	99	604	1741	5031	5369	4915	4592	4636	4391
Public and Private	27381	32236	34580	33915	33244	34768	36602	37748	37424	40418
Public	22406	26940	27721	26664	24132	22271	24506	25504	27952	27369
Public-NG and Others	22406	25293	26015	25172	22943	21393	23825	24917	24351	26701
CB - BOL		1647	1706	1492	1189	878	681	587	601	668
Private	4975	5296	6859	7251	9112	12497	12095	12244	12472	13049
of w/c: Red Clause Advances										
Export Advances	1053	1097	508	426	421	496	332	343	351	342
By Institutional Creditor	32089	35535	38723	39367	41875	45433	47817	48636	48128	51172
Banks	5368	4874	4689	5106	7415	8872	8584	8917	8579	8636
Other Financial Inst.	324	303	841	1239	958	1304	1088	1099	1017	1267
subtotal	5692	5177	5530	6345	8373	10176	9672	10016	9596	9903
Suppliers	2963	3185	3549	2587	2588	2359	1562	1596	1630	1699
Multilateral	8323	9202	9859	9617	8634	8638	10058	9739	9624	10115
Bilateral	11328	13369	15033	14393	13439	13307	14925	14904	14860	16224
Others	3783	4602	4752	6425	8841	10953	11599	12381	12417	13232

Note : a) Includes cumulative foreign exchange revaluation on US$ denominated multi-currency loans from World Bank and Asian Development Bank amounting to $817 million for December 1996 and $159 million for 1997.

b) Effective July 3, 1993, accounts of old CB were split between Bangko Sentral ng Pilipinas and Central Bank - Board of Liquidators.

c) Accounts of the Development Bank of the Philippines have been reclassified from public non-banking to banking sector liabilities starting 1996.

Source : MEDD, BSP.

Table 10.10 Non-Performing Loans (NPL), Loan Loss Provisions, Unprovisioned Non-Performing Loans and Total Loans of the Banking System*

(Unit: end-of-period; levels in Peso billions; ratios in %)

	Non-Performing Loans				Loan Loss Provisions				Unprovisioned Non-Perf. Loans				Total Loans			
	KBs	TBs	RBs	Total	KBs	TBs	RBs	Total	KBs	TBs	RBs	Total	KBs	TBs	RBs	Total
1980	12.2	0.4	1.3	13.9	2.3	0.0	0.1	2.4	9.9	0.4	1.2	11.5	111.6	6.5	4.7	122.8
1985	37.7	1.2	2.8	41.8	5.8	0.1	0.2	6.1	32.0	1.1	2.6	35.7	166.7	8.0	6.6	181.3
1990	19.4	1.7	2.8	23.9	12.7	0.3	0.4	13.4	6.7	1.4	2.4	10.5	270.8	23.4	9.7	303.9
1991	20.2	2.2	2.8	25.2	12.3	0.5	0.4	13.2	8.0	1.7	2.4	12.0	306.2	28.5	10.7	345.4
1992	22.5	2.7	3.1	28.3	12.5	0.6	0.5	13.5	10.0	2.1	2.6	14.8	366.8	34.6	12.7	414.1
1993	23.8	2.7	3.3	29.9	13.3	0.6	0.5	14.4	10.5	2.1	2.8	15.4	506.4	45.1	15.5	567.0
1994	25.1	5.5	3.5	34.0	12.0	2.0	0.6	14.6	13.1	3.5	2.9	19.4	637.2	65.7	19.1	722.0
1995	28.0	7.0	4.0	39.0	13.8	2.4	0.7	16.8	14.2	4.7	3.3	22.2	866.3	89.2	24.9	980.4
1996	34.2	9.5	4.7	48.4	15.1	3.3	0.7	19.1	19.1	6.2	4.0	29.3	1221.8	122.1	33.4	1377.3
1997																
March	42.3	9.9	5.1	57.3	16.9	3.0	0.7	20.6	25.4	6.8	4.4	36.6	1284.6	132.6	34.3	1451.5
Jun	47.9	11.3	5.4	64.5	18.5	3.1	0.7	22.3	29.3	8.2	4.7	42.2	1419.0	145.8	36.9	1601.7
Sep	59.4	14.9	5.9	80.2	21.5	3.2	0.7	25.5	37.9	11.7	5.2	54.8	1499.2	148.0	39.4	1686.6
Dec	72.2	14.9	6.3	93.4	34.8	4.4	0.8	39.9	37.5	10.5	5.5	53.5	1573.1	139.6	40.8	1753.6
1998																
March	112.6	18.8	6.8	138.2	39.3	4.8	0.9	45.0	73.3	14.0	6.0	93.2	1517.6	133.4	40.9	1691.9
Jun	142.7	22.5	7.4	172.6	43.8	5.2	0.9	50.0	99.0	17.2	6.5	122.6	1595.4	135.8	41.2	1772.3
Sep	175.1	22.3	7.6	205.0	49.2	5.8	1.0	56.0	125.9	16.5	6.6	149.1	1586.3	143.3	41.6	1771.1
Dec	160.0	21.3	7.8	189.1	61.3	6.3	1.2	68.8	98.7	15.0	6.5	120.2	1542.5	130.7	41.8	1715.0
1999																
March	195.6	21.5	8.2	225.4	67.7	6.5	1.4	75.6	127.9	15.0	6.9	149.8	1484.5	123.9	41.9	1650.3
Jun	197.3	21.0	8.2	226.5	71.5	6.6	1.4	79.5	125.7	14.5	6.9	147.1	1505.6	129.0	41.9	1676.5
Sep	208.6	N.A.	N.A.	N.A.	76.2	N.A.	N.A.	N.A.	132.4	N.A.	N.A.	N.A.	1557.1	N.A.	N.A.	N.A.
Dec	195.4	N.A.	N.A.	N.A.	91.0	N.A.	N.A.	N.A.	104.4	N.A.	N.A.	N.A.	1582.9	N.A.	N.A.	N.A.
2000																
Jan.	203.2	N.A.	N.A.	N.A.	94.0	N.A.	N.A.	N.A.	109.1	N.A.	N.A.	N.A.	1513.0	N.A.	N.A.	N.A.

Note :* Inclusive of Specialized Government Banks.
Source : BSP.

Table 10.11 Allowances for Probable Losses

(Unit: in % of loan amount)

Classification	Before 31/12/98	31/12/98	15/4/99
Loans especially mentioned	0	2.5	5
Substandard			
Collateralized	0	12.5	25
Uncollateralized	25	25	25
Doubtful	50	50	50
Loss	100	100	100

Table 10.12 Minimum Capital Requirement for Banks

(Unit: Pesos millions)

	Existing Requirement	Compliance Period 24/12/98	31/12/98	31/12/2000
Expanded Commercial Banks	3500	4500	4950	5400
Commercial Banks	1625	2000	2400	2800
Thrift Banks				
Within Metro Manila	200	250	325	400
Outside Metro Manila	40	40	52	64
Rural Banks				
Within Metro Manila	20	20	26	32
Cities of Cebu and Davao	10	10	13	16
1st, 2nd, 3rd class cities and 1st class municipalities	5	5	6.5	8
4th, 5th, 6th class cities and 2nd, 3rd, 4th class municipalities	3	3	3.9	4.8
5th, 6th class municipalities	2	2	2.6	3.2

11 India's Financial Sector Reforms: Progress and the Macroeconomic Constraints

PARTHA SEN

Introduction

Financial deregulation is proceeding at a feverish pace all over the world. Spurred on by the revolution in new information technology, new instruments are being offered which are pushing forward the frontiers of the financial sector while blurring the roles of existing financial institutions. Regulatory authorities are finding it difficult to cope with the easy international movement of capital as well as innovations creating instruments that are close substitutes for those that the authorities seek to control. In an era when state intervention in economic policy-making is deemed to be anachronistic, what should the role of the government be in regulating financial markets?

Issues of capital account convertibility and trade in services, which were not part of international negotiations in the past – even the very recent past – have come to occupy centre stage at the expense of traditional concerns with merchandise trade. Supporters of financial liberalisation draw parallels with trade in goods and gains in efficiency by equating the relevant marginal quantities, while opponents point to problems of aggregate risk of volatile capital flows and the attendant volatility of the prices of non-traded goods and assets. They remind us that problems of information are, after all, at the heart of the functioning of financial markets. Financial markets are, of course, fragile by their very nature.

The financial big bang projects which took place in some Asian economies provided an interim report on this debate. Why did the financial crises occur? Were international financial flows to blame? What were appropriate policy responses? What were the implications for corporate and, indeed, global governance? Tsurumi (1999) asks some questions and provides the outlines of some answers.

The Indian financial sector has experienced no big bang. Yet the experiences of other countries in Asia are very relevant to its future policy actions. There are obvious parallels in the way the financial sector has been regulated, especially with the Chinese experience as well as that of Indonesian banking. It must be remembered that because of the needs of colonialism, India was an early starter in developing financial institutions. It has had stock exchanges, banks etc., for over a century now. Even then, one can certainly say: "Almost all Asian developing countries lack efficient money markets, deep capital markets, an effective governance structure and an effective system for supervising and monitoring financial activities" [Tsurumi (1999)].

India is a relatively closed economy compared with the other countries included in this project. At the beginning of the 1990s, over forty years since independence, its share in world trade had fallen to about 0.5%.

Unlike the East and Southeast Asian economies, its capital account is still, by and large, closed. Unlike these countries, and unlike China, it has not been able to attract a very large volume of foreign direct investment (FDI). Even with the FDI it has attracted, there have been major gaps between approvals and actual investment. For instance, in 1997-98 and in the previous year, approvals amounted to about five times the actual flow [see Bajpai and Sachs (1999)]. I would like to take a brief look at FDI flows to the Indian economy, prior to a more detailed analysis of its financial system.

Over time, and in a controlled manner, India's capital account has been opened to foreign investors for FDI and to foreign institutional investors (FIIs) for portfolio investments. India attracted $149 billion in FDI in the fiscal year 1998-99, representing 2.2% of all FDI flows to developing countries. Mauritius, the USA and South Korea are the three largest sources of FDI flows to India. FIIs can invest in listed securities, and are given preferential tax treatment. India's relative success (or rather the lack of it) in attracting portfolio capital is summarised in Table 11.1. Since 1992, Indian companies have been allowed to raise capital through global depository receipts (GDR) and external commercial borrowings (ECB). Initially, there were restrictions on their use and terms, but these have been liberalised progressively (for instance end-use restrictions have been removed except for use in real estate or the stock markets).

In the wake of the foreign exchange crisis in 1990-91 (discussed below), foreign currency deposits in commercial banks were encouraged. But over time the returns were brought into line with international rates, and the importance of these deposits has declined. In the last financial year (1998-99), after India conducted its nuclear tests and sanctions were imposed by the U.S., Japan and other countries, the Government raised

$4.2 billion by issuing the so-called Resurgent India Bonds. The interest on dollar denominated bonds was 7.75% per annum – about 4% in excess of LIBOR. This is measure of the risk premium on India's international borrowing.

Table 11.1 FII Net Investment in India as a Percent of Portfolio Investment in Developing Countries

(Unit: US$ millions)

Item	1994	1995	1996	1997
Portfolio investment in India	5,348	1,361	4,579	2,816
Net portfolio invetsment in developing countires	85,700	22,200	52,700	55,500
India's share in developing countires	6.2	6.1	8.7	5.1

Source: Economic Survey (1998-99).

In this paper I will first, in Section I, briefly discuss the evolution of the Indian financial system since independence (in 1947) with an analysis of the fiscal and monetary policies in place. In section II, I will discuss the consequences of the financial sector reforms in the 1990s, especially their effects on the banking sector and the capital markets. Finally in section III, I will discuss the government's overall budgetary position and the implications for the financial markets. India's Central Bank – the Reserve Bank of India (RBI) has the unenviable task of trying to liberalise the financial sector while operating under political constraints. Its monetary and exchange rate policies should be seen in that context. I hope to bring out clearly the underlying trends of the economy, showing that the financial sector is very fragile.

From 1947 To 1990

Overview

Any study of the financial institutions in India today must cover the events of at least the last thirty years. Before 1955, all the commercial banks in India were privately owned. That year the Government took over the Imperial Bank and renamed it the State Bank of India. It was in 1969 that the then Prime Minister, Indira Gandhi, nationalised 14 major commercial banks.[1] Over the next eight years – including the two years from 1975 to 1977 – when all civil liberties were suspended in a state of internal emergency – she took other populist measures. From 1967 to 1989, with a break between 1977 and 1980, either Mrs. Gandhi or her son Rajiv, ruled India as Prime Minister.

The 1970s were a decade of oil price increases, which India weathered better (relatively speaking) than most developing countries, thanks to remittances by Indian expatriates in the Gulf countries. In the 1980s, India saw good growth performance accompanied by deteriorating macroeconomic and financial statistics. This was a decade of populism and of the postponement of hard decisions. The happy times were not to last long. The populist measures had disastrous consequences for the financial system. Even ten years after the introduction of economic reforms, the government is still finding it difficult to jettison its populist habit.

In 1990-91, a balance of payments crisis erupted. The Government of India had to seek assistance from the IMF. With the blessings of the IMF and the World Bank and under the stewardship of the then Finance Minister, Manmohan Singh, India embarked on a rather gingerly journey on the path of economic liberalisation – a transition that has been described as one from being a "backward center" to a "progressive periphery".[2] Since that date, much progress has been made to restore viability to the financial system. In certain sectors, the turnaround has been amazing. But given the magnitude of the problem, it has not been sufficient. Again given the magnitude of the problem it is easy to understand why successive governments have not done more. It is important to remember that since 1989, India's governments either have had a wafer-thin majority in Parliament, or none at all. To expect coalition governments to address long term issues when their term in office is uncertain is being too optimistic. But as the analysis below will show, this has had its costs. Any attempt at further liberalisation in specific areas, such as capital account convertibility, without remedying the malaise afflicting the Indian financial system, could be a recipe for disaster. Fortunately, we have the experience of a variety of liberalisation programmes – both failures and successes – in Latin America and Asia to learn from.

As noted above, India embarked on its liberalisation experiment following a major crisis at the beginning of the 1990s. Industry, foreign trade and the financial system were unshackled, albeit to different degrees. In the macroeconomic literature on developing countries, the term "financial repression" denotes a situation where the government keeps the rate of interest on deposits low and uses private savings to finance its deficits. The Indian financial system from the 1970s (up to the end of the 1980s) fits this picture perfectly. Over the last quarter century, the Indian financial sector was probably one of the most controlled regimes in the world. This experience showed that while efficiency was sacrificed there were very few gains in terms of a more equitable distribution of income and assets. Vested interests had hijacked the economy using populist slogans. As liberalization took place, at a slow pace, we came to realize that control and regulation are not synonymous.

Macroeconomic Policy Until 1990

Fiscal Policy In the process of development, it was believed that the government should finance capital expenditures by running revenue surpluses and if necessary by borrowing (either from the Central Bank or the public). Monetary policy was expected to be used to finance deficits, though it was important to keep an eye on inflationary developments. India's monetary policy has always been passive *vis-à-vis* fiscal policy – probably this was true the world over during this period. We shall see below that there have been attempts recently to give the Reserve Bank of India some independence.

The crisis in 1990-91 forced a liberalisation of the financial markets. Unfortunately, progress in this area has not matched expectations. A combination of an unsustainable budget deficit (due to *inter alia* high interest payments and high current consumption) and an attempt to keep the nominal exchange rate fixed, is not the ideal environment in which to contemplate interest rate deregulation and capital account convertibility.

Table 11.2 India's Macroeconomic History

(Unit: %)

	1950s	1960s	1970s	1980s	1991	1992	1993	1994	1995	1996	1997
Fiscal Deficit/GDP a)	2.8	4.5	4.0	7.2	7.7	5.4	5.2	6.9	5.6	4.9	4.7
Domestic Public Debt/GDP	28.2	31.4	31.0	44.2	52.8	51.5	50.9	53.2	51.1	50.5	48.7
Primary Deficit/GDP	2.5	4.3	3.7	6.1	4.3	1.6	1.3	2.9	1.4	0.9	0.4
Interest Rate b)	3.2	4.5	5.9	9.9	11.4	11.8	12.5	12.6	11.9	13.7	13.7
Interest Payments/Revenue Receipts	17.9	17.8	17.5	26.6	39.1	40.3	41.9	48.7	48.4	45.4	44.7
Money Supply(Growth)	1.1	6.2	17.6	17.2	15.1	19.3	15.7	18.4	22.3	13.7	15.6
Inflation Rate	1.8	6.4	8.9	8.0	10.3	13.7	10.0	8.3	10.9	7.8	6.4
Real Growth Rate	3.3	4.0	2.9	5.9	5.4	0.8	5.3	6.0	7.2	7.1	6.8

Notes: a) Refers to revised GDP series from 1991.
b) Relates to weighted average interest rate on Central Government dated securities.
Sources: Pillai *et al*. (1997). *Economic Survey* (1998-99).

A summary of trends in the various fiscal and monetary variables is given in Table 11.2. The fiscal variables tell a sorry tale of lack of discipline. The improvement in the fiscal deficit to GDP ratio in the 1990s is partly due to a new GDP series. The Central and the State governments ran revenue surpluses until the 1980s. From a mere 0.4% of GDP in 1980-81, the revenue deficit had risen to 4.5%. The revenue accounts of the (i.e., the provinces) turned into deficits for the first time in 1986-87. By 1996-97 these had risen to 1.2% of GDP [Pillai, *et. al.* (1997)]. The estimates for the revenue deficit for the Central and State governments for fiscal year 1998-99 are expected to be 2.7% and 1% of GDP, respectively [*Economic Survey* (1998-99)].

Four other features of the Government's finances should be mentioned here. The first is the growth of subsidies. Explicit (as opposed to hidden) subsidies have grown at an average compound growth rate of 20% per annum since the beginning of the 1970s – as a consequence of Indira Gandhi's populist politics. Successive governments have found it impossible to dismantle this. Second, capital expenditures have declined from about 7.5% of GDP in the 1970s to 5% in the 1990s. There is widespread concern about the deteriorating quality of infrastructure, but limited action is possible to remedy this. With the government uncertain about how to proceed forward, private initiative has also not been forthcoming to fill the gap. Third, interest payments increased from 1.6% of GDP in the 1970s to about 4.6% in the mid-1990s (or from about a fifth of the Central Government's revenues to about 45% of its revenues). Overall borrowing levels of the Central government reached 8.5% of GDP in the 1980s. It is expected to be around 7% of GDP this year – although as mentioned above the new GDP series may show it as being slightly lower. Finally, it must be pointed out that government borrowing figures in India are calculated after taking into account the proceeds from the sales of government-owned companies [or public sector undertakings (PSUs) as they called in India].

The evolution of public debt in India and the average interest paid on this debt can also be seen from Table 11.2. From a value of 26.4% in 1951, the debt/GDP ratio reached a level of 52.4% in 1990. The weighted interest rates on Government securities rose, from a range of 3-4% in the 1950s to about 11.5% in 1990. The (*ex-post*) real interest rates were very low, usually negative, in a financially repressed regime. This, among other factors, had a very distorting effect on the Indian banks, as we shall see below.

Monetary Policy The average annual growth rate of the broad money stock (M3) – which is the RBI's preferred monetary target – in India between 1951-52 to 1996-97 was 13.4%, while GDP grew at 4.3%. The average inflation rate (of the wholesale price index (WPI)) was 6.8% and the growth rate of bank credit was 14.7%. It was from the 1980s that the growth rate of credit fell below that of the broad money stock [Mohanty *et al.* (1997)].

Before the nationalisation of the fourteen commercial banks in 1969, the RBI was trying to streamline the banking system. This consolidation saw a reduction in the number of banks from 640 in December 1947 to 387 in December 1957.[3]

The RBI was also instrumental in setting up the various term finance institutions e.g., Industrial Finance Corporation of India (IFCI), Industrial Credit and Investment Corporation of India (ICICI) and Industrial Development Bank of India (IDBI), as well as India's first mutual fund – the Unit Trust of India (UTI) in 1964.[4]

Turning to the instruments of monetary policy, we see that the Bank Rate (at which the Reserve Bank of India provided funds) lost its prominent position in the 1960s with increased emphasis being placed on the Cash Reserve Ratio (CRR) and the Statutory Liquidity Ratio (SLR); the latter forced the commercial banks to hold government debt. But even these proved inadequate in meeting the fiscal appetite of the government. Automatic monetisation was resorted to, through the issue of ad hoc treasury bills at low interest rates – a situation that continued until 1997. The maturity periods of securities and the interest rates came to reflect "essentially the perceptions of the issuer (i.e., the Government)".[5] The CRR then became the major tool of monetary policy – from 3% in 1962, it reached 25% in 1991-92. Given that this was a high tax on the banks, the interest rate on reserves was also raised progressively until it reached 10.5%.

Financial Markets up to 1990

Capital Markets The first quarter of a century after independence (1947-1972) was a quiet period for the capital markets.[6] As noted above, it saw the establishment of development financial institutions such as the IFCI, ICICI, IDBI and UTI. Foreign owned companies raised funds in London and, in India, a system known as the managing agency system acted as a surrogate for the capital market.

Following the introduction of the Foreign Exchange Regulation Act (FERA) of 1973, many foreign owned firms, in a bid to dilute their stake to the 40% required by law, offered large volumes of shares in the market. The response to these equity offers was good. Encouraged by this, many public limited companies began to approach the primary market with new issues. Almost Rs. ten billion were raised through new issues in this decade. This phase continued until 1980.

The 1980s saw the appearance of debentures in the primary market. Of the Rs.233.6 billion worth of capital issues in this decade, two-thirds were via debentures. Many public sector enterprises borrowed large sums of the money from the public. This was a period of widening and deepening of the market, with the emergence of the Security and Exchanges Board of India (SEBI), and credit rating agencies such as CRISIL and ICRA [Misra (1997)].

Figures on the intermediation of savings through the primary market and the banking system are given in Table 11.3. As can readily be seen, it is only in the 1990s that the primary market became relatively important.

The insurance industry, which was once totally government-owned, is now set to accept the entry of foreign players. However, I will not discuss this sector. A good summary of the Indian insurance industry can be found in Ranade and Ahuja (1999).

Table 11.3 Asset Intermediation by Banks and Capital Market

			(Unit: Rupees billions)
Period	Incremental Aggregate Deposits of Scheduled Commercial Banks	Total Mobilisation in Primary Market	(3) as a % of (2)
(1)	(2)	(3)	(4)
1970-71 to 1979-80	267.3	8.9	3.4
1980-81 to 1989-90	1352.0	306.6	22.7
1990-91 to 1995-96	2668.6	1505.0	56.4

Source: B. M. Misra. *op.cit.*

Banking   Before turning to a detailed analysis of the banking sector in India, I will present a short overview of this sector to emphasize its pivotal role in the financial system.

First, banks account for two thirds of total assets of all financial institutions. Second, at the time of independence, banks were almost absent in the rural areas where the overwhelming majority of India's population lived. In 1951, 92.8% of the debt of rural households was owed to non-institutional lenders. In 1981, this had fallen to 38.8%. Third, the gross saving ratio as a proportion of GDP rose from 10.4% to 25.6%, with bank deposits constituting the bulk of it. Finally, the share of borrowing from banks as a proportion of total borrowing of the private corporate sector has come down from 62.7% in 1968-69 to 32% in 1992-93. The bulk of this decline is attributable to a switch from banks to capital markets among medium and large firms.

However, this overview conceals the mess which in reality the Indian banking system is in. As a succinct summary of the banking system's performance, one can say that it has been quite successful in raising resources – see Table 11.4 (which shows the branch expansion of government-owned banks) – but very unsuccessful in allocating these resources efficiently (even in terms of their own objectives) (see Table 11.5). The growth of the banking system has been quite spectacular. From 1951 to 1996, the number of branches of commercial banks increased from 4,151 to 63,092, population per branch came down from 87,000 to 15,000, and bank deposits as a proportion of GDP rose from 10.5% to 43.2%.

Table 11.4 Branch Expansion of Public Sector Banks and Other Commercial Banks

(Unit: Number)

Bank Group	as on June 30			Increase between 30/6/69 and 30/6/98	Rural branches as on 30/6/98	% age of Rural branches as on 30/6/98 [6/4]
	1969	1994	1998			
1	2	3	4	5	6	7
A. State Bank of India & Associates	2,462	12,676	13,106	10,644	5,507	42.0%
B. Nationalised Bank	4,553	30,405	31,853	27,300	13,913	43.7%
C. Regional Rural Banks	-	14,530	14,420	14,420	12,307	85.3%
Total of Public Sector Banks (A-C)	7,015	57,611	59,379	52,364	31,727	53.4%
D. Other Inidan Scheduled Commercial Banks	900	3,987	4,710	3,810	1,135	24.1%
E. Foreign Banks	130	146	182	52	0	0.0%
All Scheduled Banks (A-E)	8,045	61,744	64,271	56,226	32,862	51.1%
F. Non-scheduled Banks	217	48	9	-208	3	33.3%
All Commercial Banks (A-F)	8,262	61,792	64,280	56,018	32,865	51.1%

Source: *Economic Survey*(1998-99).

Table 11.5 Distribution of Gross NPAs of Public Sector Banks in 1997-1998

(Unit: %)

Bank Group	Priority Sector	Non-Priority Sector	Public Sector
1. SBI & Associates	48.1 (50.4)	47.6 (43.8)	4.3 (5.7)
2. Nationalised Banks	45.5 (46.3)	52.2 (51.5)	2.3 (2.2)
3. Public Sector Banks (1+2)	46.4 (47.7)	50.6 (49.0)	3.0 (3.3)

Notes: Figures in brackets are for 1996-97.
Figures may not add upto 100 due to rounding.
Source: *Economic Survey* (1989-99).

In the post-nationalization phase, the government-owned banks accounted for about 85 to 90% of the deposits of the banking industry. The figures for disbursement of credit are similar. Recently, some new private commercial banks have started operations, and restrictions on the expansion of branches of existing banks have been liberalised. But even today, loans account for just over 50% of banks' assets, the rest being held as government securities – SLR (35%) – and cash reserve ratio CRR (11%).

Loans Policy

(1) Administered Interest Rates and Cross-subsidisation. Ceiling rates on deposits and advances were in place for about three decades from the mid-1960s to early 1990s. Priority sector interest rates were kept low and non-priority sectors had to subsidise them. The system became clogged with red tape, with interest stipulations by sector, region and programme. From September 1990, only two sizes of loans had rates prescribed for them. Larger loans could have rates fixed bilaterally by negotiation between the borrower and the bank. This liberalisation has caused interest rates to move up which has caused some worry about their output effects as well as the sustainability of deficits.

(2) Directed Credit. One of the pillars of the credit policy regime up to the 1980s, and which continues to date, is the policy of directed credit. It began in 1974 when banks were directed to allocate a third of their lending to priority sectors consisting of (mainly) agriculture and small-scale industry. This target was raised to 40% of bank credit by 1985 and the share of agriculture was 18% of bank credit.

The results of these policies were dismal according to almost any yardstick. It is notable that these were quantitative targets, and therefore the credit worthiness of the borrower would take a back seat in attaining the targets. And if the reason for putting these targets in place was to make credit available to those who would otherwise not get it, this certainly did not happen. For instance, the Integrated Rural Development Project (IRDP), launched 1979, sought to raise individuals' incomes above a set poverty line by getting the targeted population to invest in assets. Half of the transfer was a grant from the government and the other half a (non-collaterised) bank loan. Studies such as Dreze (1990) show that targeted groups included rich households and not poor households, as intended.

The policy of directed financial credit to the agricultural sector was not viable either. "Commercial banks have met directed credit targets but at the cost of cross-subsidies and bad debts" [Joshi and Little (1996)]. Loan recovery was also extremely poor in agriculture. The share of bank credits held by agriculture increased from 2.2% at the time of nationalisation to 17% before the start of reforms in the banking sector in 1990, and fell back to about 12% in 1996. In the meantime, the share of agriculture in output fell from about 48% to 28%. The share of priority sectors rose from 11% to 33% in the 28-year period. The recovery of loans made by IRDP was a dismal 30% at the end of 1996, and for agricultural loans it was 60%. The industrial over-dues scenario was better, but bank credit to "sick" industries increased from 6.1% in 1980 to 14.4% in 1993. The proportion of over-dues as a proportion of credit was 21.4% in 1993.

The record of directed lending to small-scale industry has also been dismal. The proportion of lending to over-dues was higher in the non-targeted sectors. Also, the proportion of credit to "sick" units was higher in small-scale in comparison with medium and large industry.

Overall, there is evidence that this aspect of government policy has been responsible for the poor balance sheets of banks, while at the same time failing to achieve the much-touted equity. Policies have been badly formulated and/or the rich have willfully misused these schemes by getting credit using low interest rates loans, and then not repaying them.

(3) Profitability. The cost of deposits rose from 3.4% in 1970 to 8% in 1989 and fell to 6.9% in 1996. Returns on loans for the corresponding periods, in percentage terms, were 7.2, 12.8 and 12.3, while the return on investments was respectively 3.5, 4.2 and 11.2 (again in %). Net interest income as a proportion of total assets rose from 2.7% to 2.9% and to 3.2% in the corresponding periods.

Reform of the Financial System

Banking

Two committees set up by the RBI have prompted some reforms in the banking system. The first in 1985, known as the Chakravarty Committee,[7] wanted to break the Government's ability to corner banks' funds. It recommended paying interest rates which reflected market conditions. This recommendation has been implemented in dribs and drabs. Interest rates on government bonds were raised and some new instruments offered – e.g., a 182-day treasury bill, sold by auction and non-rediscountable by the RBI, was launched in 1986.

The recommendation to automatically meet the governments needs through SLRs was not implemented until the Narasimham Committee (1991)[8] proposed it as a part of a bid to make the banking system more competitive, and more importantly, more transparent. This committee recommended that interest rates be deregulated (gradually), that the SLR be reduced from 38.5 to 25% in stages, and that the RBI pay higher interest on CRR, which was 15% at the time, with an incremental 10% in 1991. This ratio is currently 11%. The CRR will remain a major tool of monetary policy until open market operations come to play a bigger role. Government-owned banks were allowed to raise equity from the capital market, borrowing by the government at market (related) interest rates, allowing entry of private commercial banks and help banks to attain the Basle norms (of the BIS) for capitalisation.

The accounting rules in the nationalised banks prior to this were designed to conceal any problems. It was "accrual", rather than cash received, that constituted income. It follows that provisioning norms were also soft. It is a small wonder then that at the start of the liberalisation process, 24% of the advances of the public sector banks were non-performing and only 15 of the 28 banks had positive net profits.

Following the Narasimham Committee's recommendations, income was no longer calculated on an accrual basis. If interest had not been paid on a loan for 180 days, it was classified as sub-standard and required a provisioning of 10%. If the loan had not received interest for a period from 180 days to two years, it was classified as doubtful and carried a 20 to 50% provisioning. A loan which has not received interest for over two years or had been certified lost by an external auditor had 100% provisioning. These norms have been further tightened: starting this financial year (1999-2000), the upper limit of a loan classified as doubtful has been lowered from two years to·18 months.

The Committee also asked the banks to adopt the Basle Accord capital adequacy standards, requiring banks to have a ratio of capital to risk-adjusted assets of 8% by March 1996. The Government, in the 1999-2000 budget, is seeking to increase the capital to risk-adjusted assets ratio (CRAR) of banks to 10% in two phases, with the immediate implementation of 1% increase. The Government has introduced other safety norms, such as giving government securities a risk weight of 2.5%, foreign exchange open positions 100%, and standard assets 0.2%.

Seven of the 26 publicly-owned banks did not meet the 8% capital adequacy ratio in 1995-96. But of the 15 banks, for which figures were available in 1995-96, only two had the non-performing assets (NPAs) as a proportion of net advances in excess of 10% (with one – the State Bank of Hyderabad – hovering at 9.94%). By this year, 26 of the 27 government-owned banks had CRARs in excess of 8%, and 19 had figures in excess of 10%. But this healthy picture is primarily due to a massive recapitalisation from the budget, which so far has amounted to over Rs.200 billion.

What was to be done with NPAs of banks? Liquidating banks was not an option any government would countenance – the banks were "too big to fail". In any case the powerful bank unions would veto it. As a result, the recapitalisation package to restore the banks' net worth was charged to the taxpayers. The setting up of an Asset Reconstruction Fund (ARF) to take over the banks' NPAs as recommended by the Narasimham Committee did not look very promising initially, but now it looks like it is taking off: a task-force has submitted its report on this. The setting up of an ARF is related to the issue of the privatisation of banks, as discussed below. If bad loans involve bank-client specific information, then handing them over to a new body would mean diluting the information content. But if the bad loans are due to theft under benign public ownership and the "too-big-to-fail" criterion, then an ARF is a good idea. Some Debt Recovery Tribunals have also been set up in the major metropolitan areas.

In 1990, before the Narasimham Committee's report, the lending policy of banks was freed of the many restraints imposed on it. Except for lending to priority sectors – agriculture, small-scale industry, exports and small transport operators – banks were given the freedom to determine their lending rates on loans over Rs.200,000, subject to a minimum lending rate. There were five slabs of rates below that amount. This was progressively relaxed – now banks fix their own prime lending rates and the maximum spreads over these. The five slabs for small loans have also been reduced to just two. The banks must ensure that their lending policies are such that the history of the NPAs does not repeat itself. At the present, one cannot be very sanguine about this – the banks are still required to lend to the priority sectors and loan recovery rates there are still very low e.g., in agriculture it is still less than two-thirds [*Economic Survey* (1998-99)].

The RBI showed more caution toward deposit rates, and rightly in the light of international experience in financial liberalisation. These rates were liberalised at a time when capital inflows were sizeable, and the RBI chose not to sterilise them. Initially, with the exception of those with maturities between 46 days and three years, banks were allowed to fix the interest rates on deposits. The upper limit for which a maximum rate is fixed has been brought down to one year. All money market rates have been completely freed.

Ad hoc treasury bills, through which the government deficits were financed automatically, have been phased out and an advance system of ways and means has been put in place. This system allows temporary mismatches in government receipts and payments. Excess borrowing attracts high rates of interest by the RBI.

Since April 1992, dated securities to finance government borrowing have been sold through auctions. Open market operations have gained some momentum, but the market lacks depth; banks and other financial institutions are the major players and have "unidirectional perceptions about liquidity".[9] Now that the FIIs are allowed to buy government securities, this may change. A system of satellite dealers has also been set up. Finally, after decades, the Bank Rate has again become a signal of the RBI's policy stance.

The Narasimham Committee allowed the entry of new banks, both domestic and foreign. The branch expansion policy of domestically-owned banks was considerably liberalised – financially sound domestic banks can now open branches without the permission of the RBI. There has been an attempt to ensure equal treatment for domestic and foreign banks, e.g., even foreign banks are now required to make loans to the priority sector (32%), whereas previously their only obligation was to lend to exporters (10%).

While the growth of deposits and advances for all banks has fallen after liberalisation, reflecting the appearance of other instruments for savers, domestic private banks as a group (compared to government-owned and foreign banks) have done remarkably well in this period. Lending by government-owned banks has fallen in spite of lower CRR and SLR through increased holdings of government securities with their market rates of return, and also in response to the more stringent prudential norms; when banks do not need to make profits they can be excessively risk-averse. A shortfall of priority sector lending could also be seen in such risk aversion. Non-interest income has risen for all domestic banks in the post-liberalisation phase, while it has fallen for the foreign banks.[10]

The overall evidence is that the effect of liberalisation policies has increased competition in the banking sector, but that the oligopolistic structure is far from shaking. One should note a view put forward by Caprio and Summers (1995) that entry reduces the franchise value of a bank license by reducing profits. If profits fall, the banking system as a whole tends to make more risky investments to recoup lost profits. If the franchise value is high, then banks follow more sound lending policies. In India, this is not a danger for the banking system as a whole, but may be true for the relatively weak banks.

Sarkar and Aggarwal (1997) provide evidence that in the 1990s, the fall in the relative share of government-owned banks in total advances and deposits has been faster (about 5 and 8% for deposits and lending, respectively) than in the period 1980 to 1991-92, when their share in deposits and advances fell by about 2%. They also show that the four-bank concentration ratio for deposits and advances fell by about 4% in the three years following the Narasimham Committee's report.[11]

The initial data for changes in spreads do not seem to indicate increased competitiveness. The behaviour of the public sector banks has not changed very much in terms of increased competition, but the data here should be treated with caution because of the continuing (and hence sequential) deregulation and cyclical changes in loan demand.

Privatisation of Banks? The Narasimham Committee tried to herald in more competitiveness and efficiency in the financial system. One crucial issue that it has failed to address is the ownership of the government-owned banks. It had suggested a policy of diluting government control and granting autonomy, rather than outright privatization. In its words, it took the view that the "issues of competitive efficiency and profitability are ownership neutral".

It is true that the removal of shackles on entry and branch expansion by private banks, both domestic and foreign, has provided some competition to the established government-owned banks. However, they still account for over 80% of deposits and lending in the banking system as whole. They continue to behave in an oligopolistic manner. And of course, their commercial practices have not changed significantly. The government, having decided not to give autonomy to these banks, has set aside vast sums of money for their recapitalisation.[12] There is a real danger here that a one-time improvement in balance sheets will be eroded very quickly by their "business-as-usual" policies.

The fragility of financial systems all over the world has given rise to deposit insurance. However, deposit insurance has been criticised for the moral hazard that it entails. Government ownership and recapitalisation, in the absence of shake-ups in the way the banks function, is an invitation for repeated unscrupulous deals. This is especially true when these banks have nothing to fear in terms of competition from private banks, whose share of the market is small, and who have inadequate branch networks.

It is not true that if the government-owned banks were privatised, they would fail to respond to social needs. In fact, the government owned banks' performance in this sphere has been very patchy. Moreover, directed credit policies could be part of the regulatory framework. Government-ownership and the needs of "society" are not identical. Public sector unions, the bureaucracy and politicians have combined vested interests in the status quo. There are numerous problems which may arise, as can be seen from the experiences of other economies, but if India's banks have to make profits, privatisation is the only way.

Capital Markets

An analysis of the capital markets in India since the liberalisation period shows some problems. In the last decade, the stock market has swung from what seemed to be an unstoppable rise to an extended period of dormancy following a major scandal which broke in 1992 and involved a large number of banks. For instance, the market capitalisation to GDP ratio, which remained (well) under 10% in the first 40 years since independence, rose to 53.3% in 1991-92 because of the boom in share prices associated with the securities scam. Following the burst of the bubble, the figure stood at 32.4% in the next year. In 1995-96 it stood at 58.7%, with the revival being primarily due to the offer of shares by public sector companies following a disinvestment decision by the Government.[13] It was around 35% at the end of 1998 and has risen considerably this year following the recent surge in stock prices.[14]

The need for the development of a capital market where investors are protected will entail the establishment of a regulatory authority with statutory powers. The Securities and Exchange Board of India (SEBI) was set up in 1988, and given statutory powers in 1992. In the primary equity market, the Capital Issues (Control) Act of 1947 was repealed in May 1992. Under this Act, the Controller of Capital Issues had the power to decide both the amount and pricing of issues. Repeated cases of price-rigging by companies in connivance with merchant banks and/or brokers show that the SEBI has its work cut out for it. India's secondary market for equity has attracted epithets like "a snake-pit".[15] Some progress has been made in introducing screen-based trading through the establishment of the National Stock Exchange (NSE), though in the face of strong opposition from the older Bombay Stock Exchange (BSE), which despite its share of over 40% in the total turnover in all the exchanges, is "well known for its murky practices".[16] By March 1995, the BSE had gone on-line, followed by all significant stock exchanges. The SEBI has also initiated the process of setting up depositories which, in addition to reducing settlement time and risks, will curtail the powers of dishonest company managers. The National Security Clearing Corporation has, from July 1996, started guaranteeing all trades on the NSE. The National Securities Depository was inaugurated in November 1996, but trading has not shifted to electronic settlement yet – the proportion of dematerialised securities has not yet grown "large" enough.[17] India's stock exchanges have the largest number of listed companies in the world – 9,730 in March 1996, compared with 2,263 in Japan and 7,671 in the USA – but this fact "partly reflects liberal listing requirements" [Misra (1997)]. Recently, the paid-up capital required for listing has been raised substantially to make listing more difficult.

Turning to debt markets, there was no primary auction market for government debt in the past because of SLR and administered interest rates. Firms financed investment by borrowing, with inventory investment coming from banks, and term borrowing coming from institutions specialising in development finance, e.g., the ICICI, IDBI, etc. The growth of a secondary debt market would probably have to wait for the banks' balance sheets to improve and, as mentioned above, for players with heterogeneous views to appear on the scene. In the debt market, as in the equity market, a proper regulatory authority is needed, together with simplified of rules. Some progress has been made in this respect: almost half of the government debt is market-to-market and a reasonable yield curve is evident.

In the first five years following liberalisation, in spite of the ups and downs in the stock market, Rs.986 billion were raised from the primary market, with equity accounting for close to 60%. Another Rs.520 billion were mobilised through private placement.[18]

This represents a quantum leap over what the markets had raised in previous decades.[19] The number of investors now is close to 20 million, or the equivalent of about 2% of the population. This figure has almost doubled since the beginning of the 1990s. Cumulative net investment by the FIIs since they were allowed into the country has grown over ten fold in five years, from $827 million in 1993 to $8.7 billion in December 1998. This, however, is down from $9.3 billion in March 1997, as a result of the uncertainties associated with the Asian crisis and India's nuclear tests.

Macroeconomic Options

Where do we go from here? India, which escaped the effects of the East and Southeast Asian crisis by keeping its capital account relatively closed, cannot really rejoice when looking at its overall economic situation. Apart from the fact that real growth has been very slow, we see a potentially bigger problem and a deterrent to future growth in the financial sector. We saw earlier that since the nationalisation of banks in 1969, and especially in the 1980s, the banks' balance sheets were made into repositories of government borrowing instruments on very easy terms. On top of this, bank lending was politically directed. Much progress has been made in making the financial system viable and competitive. A lot remains to be done.

The twin dangers of an inadequately prepared banking system and a profligate government persist. The latter poses the bigger macroeconomic problem and deserves more detailed analysis than can be provided here. The large budget (both revenue and fiscal) deficits, in textbook fashion, raise real interest rates and cause real appreciation. The rising interest rates hamper domestic capital formation, but may encourage some savings on the part of households. The real appreciation makes the current account deficit burgeon. Over the last three years, as the result of a slowdown in growth, the full impact of the rising interest rates and appreciation have not been visible – credit demand and imports have been low. The government has borrowed to finance current consumption, crowding out private consumption and investment. The effect of the deficit on interest payments at market-determined rates of interest have the potential to cause another financial crisis of the type witnessed in 1991. Under a liberalised financial regime, high CRR and SLR cannot be used to force financial institutions to hold government debt.

Moreover, private savings have not responded as expected to rising interest rates, for a variety of possible reasons, e.g.; the liberalization of the external sector, which has made new consumer goods available, and past credit, because banks, in addition to the traditional Non-Banking Financial Companies (NBFCs) are engaged in the hire-purchase business. What should be the stance of monetary (and exchange rate) policy? Inflation, as measured by the wholesale price index (WPI) is quite low, whereas the consumer price inflation is higher – around 15%. The RBI is really caught in a bind. If it monetises the debt, then inflation will raise its head. On the other hand, the level of debt is fast reaching (and many analysts would argue has already reached) unsustainable levels [see Rajaraman and Mukhopadhyaya (1998) for details].

On the issue of exchange rate management, the RBI is unsure of what to do. The Indian rupee is convertible on the current account, but not so on the capital account. But over the last decade, foreign institutional investors (FIIs) have entered in a relatively (relative to the domestic financial sector, that is) big way. For them, the expected future path of the exchange rate is important. This is also true for Indian firms, who can raise capital through ECBs and GDRs.

The nominal exchange rate (against the US dollar) has remained stable, except on two occasions, when in each case the depreciation was around 12%. The real exchange rate has appreciated steadily except, on the two occasions, when it depreciated, standing at 77.5 in December 1998 compared to the base year 1990.[20]

The RBI should, in my view, follow a policy of gradual depreciation. I would like to emphasise that I am not proposing a Latin American-type tablita-type scheme, where the exchange rate was used as an anti-inflation device. This resulted in real appreciation which, in turn, caused the (anti-inflationary) policies to be abandoned [see Calvo and Vegh (1999)]. I am suggesting rather that the nominal exchange rate path be used to accommodate the inflationary pressures in the economy. The problem of maintaining a more or less fixed rate in the face of pressure as corrective pressures build up, is like all vulnerable price-fixing schemes in that it gives rise to a one-way wager against the Central Bank. This is one lesson that the Indian authorities could learn from the Asian crisis.

In conclusion one can only say that fiscal consolidation and the continuation of banking sector reforms must constitute the core of the government's financial and macroeconomic policies. There are sensible monetary policy and exchange rate policy options that can be followed once these have been achieved.

Notes

1 Each of these had deposits of over Rs.500 million. In 1980, six more banks with deposits of more than Rs.two billion each were nationalized.
2 Esho (1999), p. 39.
3 Mohanty *et al.* (1997), p.236.
4 Since the UTI was set up by an Act of Parliament, there is some conflict now about it being subject to SEBI guidelines. This became a burning issue once its premier scheme US 64 faced major redemptions. SEBI has been less than successful in getting UTI to be as transparent as it would like the other (later) mutual funds to be.
5 Mohanty *et al.* (1997), p.239.
6 Misra (1997) is a good introduction. The historical figures below are taken from that paper, as in Table 11.3.
7 It was formally called the Committee to Review the Working of the Monetary System.
8 It was formally called the Committee on the Financial System.
9 Mohanty *et al.* (1997), p.250.
10 See Sarkar and Aggarwal (1997), pp.99-200 and pp.205-206 (especially Table 7) for details.
11 Deposits went from 43.3% to 39.5% and loans from 46.6% to 41.2% [Sarkar and Aggarwal (1997), p.207].
12 Sarkar and Aggarwal (1997) look at various efficiency indicators – operating costs as a proportion of working funds and staff expenditure as a proportion of working funds – and find that the public sector banks have not effected any significant increases in efficiency [Sarkar and Aggarwal (1997), pp.208-209].
13 Misra (1997), p. 368.
14 Between April 1998 and November 1998, the All-India capitalisation figure had fallen by 23% [*Economic Survey* (1998-99) p.58].
15 Joshi and Little (1996), p.156.
16 Joshi and Little (1996), p.156.
17 Dematerialised trading is, however, moving forward very quickly. Between December 1996 and December 1998. The number of shares so traded increased from Rs. eight million to Rs. five billion, while the value increased from Rs. two billion to Rs.702 billion [*Economic Survey* (1998-99), p.56].
18 Misra (1997), pp.358-359.
19 See also Table 11.3 above.
20 This is the ten-county REER index. See *Economic Survey* (1998-99), p.S-80.

References

Ajit, D. and R.D. Bangar (1997), 'Banks in Financial Intermediation – Performance and Key Issues', *Reserve Bank of India Occasional Papers*, Vol.18, pp.303-341.
Bajpai, N., and J.D.Sachs (1999), 'Fiscal Policy in India's Reforms', in Sachs, Varshney and Bajpai (1999), pp.81-120.
Calvo, G.A. and C.Vegh (1999), 'Inflation Stabilisation and BOP Crises in Developing Countries', *National Bureau of Economic Research Working Paper*, No. 6925.
Caprio, G. and L. Summers (1995), 'Finance and its Reform: Beyond *Laissez Faire*', *World Bank Research Paper*, No.1171.

Dreze, J. (1990), 'Poverty in India and the IRDP Delusion', *Economic and Political Weekly*, A95-A104.

Esho, H. (1999), 'India's New Economic Policy and the Japanese Response', *Journal of International Economic Studies*, No.13, pp.39-57.

Government of India (1991), *Report of the Committee on the Financial System* (Chairman: M. Narasimham), Ministry of Finance, New Delhi.

Joshi, V. and I.M.D. Little (1995), *India's Economic Reforms 1991-2001*, Oxford University Press, Oxford U.K.

Misra, B.M. (1997), 'Fifty Years of Indian Capital Markets: 1947-1997', *Reserve Bank of India Occasional Papers*, Vol.18, pp.351-383.

Mohanty, D., A.Sardar and A.Prasad (1997), 'Monetary Developments and Policy in India', *Reserve Bank of India Occasional Papers* Vol.18, pp.225-277.

Parikh, K. (ed.) (1997), *India Development Report*, Oxford University Press, New Delhi.

Parikh, K. (ed.) (1999), *India Development Report*, Oxford University Press, New Delhi.

Pillai, S.M., S. Chatterjee, B. Singh, S. Das and A. Gupta (1997), 'Fiscal Policy: Issues and Perspectives', *Reserve Bank of India Occasional Papers*, Vol.18, pp.187-221.

Rajaraman, I. and A. Mukhopadhyay (1998), 'Sustainability of Public Domestic Debt in India', *National Institute of Public Finance and Policy*, New Delhi.

Ranade, A. and R. Ahuja (1999), 'Insurance Liberalisation', in Parikh (1999).

Reserve Bank of India (1985), *Report of the Committee to Review the Working of the Monetary System* (Chairman: S. Chakravarty), Bombay.

Sachs, J.D., A.Varshney and N.Bajpai (1999), *India in the Era of Reforms*, Oxford University Press, New Delhi.

Sarkar, J. and P. Aggarwal (1997), 'Banking: The Challenges of Deregulation', in Parikh (1997), pp.197-217.

Shah A. and S. Thomas (1997), 'Securities Markets: Towards Greater Efficiency', in Parikh (1997), pp.167-192.

Tsurumi, M. (1999), 'Financial Big Bang in Asia', Hosei University Symposium on Financial Big Bang in Asia.

12 Conclusion: Financial Big Bang in Asia

MASAYOSHI TSURUMI

Under the Financial Big Bang, far-reaching financial system reform is being carried out in Asia. There were two possible ways to escape from the crisis. One was to re-introduce financial regulation. A typical example of this was Malaysia, which suddenly introduced capital controls in September 1998. Almost all of the other economies involved in the crisis took the reverse policy of going further forward with financial reform toward liberalization. The reform has been so rapid and radical that it can be called a 'Financial Big Bang'. But it is actually the third upsurge of financial liberalization in Asia. The development of liberalization in the region can be described as follows.

The first wave of financial liberalization started in the 1970s. It was an inevitable policy, devised to deal with the high inflation rates which prevailed during that decade. The well-regulated postwar financial system was shaken to its very foundations by the fierce inflation that peaked during the 1973 and 1979 oil crises. Once inflation accelerates, the real interest rate falls into minus levels, disturbing the real economy. Financial liberalization began with deposit interest rates in the developed countries. The pressure extended not only to the advanced economies but to the developing ones as well. And further, the McKinnon-Show hypothesis of a "financial repression" began to exert pressure toward financial liberalization in the developing economies. Singapore, Malaysia, and the Philippines liberalized their interest rates earlier than other Asian countries. In many of the developing economies, the pressure for financial liberalization was still weak, however, due to their low levels of financial assets. It ended in mere buds in Korea, Taiwan, Thailand, and Indonesia, while Malaysia back-pedaled toward re-regulation once more after liberalizing.

The second wave of the financial liberalization was a full-scale one, executed since 1985. It followed a policy change toward an export-oriented, foreign capital-dependent strategy of economic development. The change was based mainly on the developing economies' severe experiences of foreign debt crises or domestic financial crises in the beginning of the 1980s.

At that time, many of the Asian economies discarded the then-prevailing policy set of import-substitution, big government, and broad intervention, adopting instead policies based on private capital and an open economy. The first prominent feature of that wave was its extent. It spread from a small number of economies to many of the Asian economies. Korea, Taiwan, Thailand, and Indonesia accelerated their financial liberalization, following in the footsteps of Hong Kong, Singapore, and the Philippines. Second, its scope was larger, involving interest rates, business areas, strengthening competition, the promotion of capital markets, and capital transactions.

The new wave of financial liberalization in the Asian developing economies since 1985 joined with and accelerated the torrent of financial globalization in the advanced economies. The rapid liberalization caused disorder in the financial systems in the Asian economies, leading to the crisis. With the crisis, the wave of liberalization suddenly stopped. In the end, though, the crisis did not disturb the reform but rather promoted it. This led to the third wave, namely the Financial Big Bang in Asia. The point was to overcome the defects of the financial system in Asia, and to build a more competitive, stable and competent system in the face of financial globalization. It consisted of three consecutive small waves: the big bang plans in Japan and Korea, the IMF-led reform, and the reforms in the NIES taken as reaction.

The starting point was the blueprints for Financial Big Bangs formulated in 1996 independently by the governments of Japan and Korea. They were intended as plans to break out of political and economic deadlock caused by financial trouble. The purpose was to restructure the financial system toward a freer and fairer one able to withstand global competition. They covered much larger scopes than the original "Financial Big Bang" in the United Kingdom, which focused only on security market reform. They involved interest rates, business areas, security markets, and foreign capital transactions. Though they were relatively radical reforms for gradualism-oriented Japan and Korea, at the beginning only vague results were expected.

The wave of reform in Asia following the outbreak of the crisis has gone much further than the "Financial Big Bang" plans in Japan and Korea. The initiative behind reform shifted from voluntary movements to IMF conditionalities. IMF pushed the countries to carry out structural reforms of their economic or financial systems in exchange for the provision of international liquidity. They were radical restructurings, based on

Anglo-Saxon ideas. Following the Philippines, Thailand, Korea, and Indonesia have executed radical reforms of their financial systems according to IMF programs. The reform in Korea went much farther than the "Financial Big Bang" plan, while Thailand and Indonesia also carried out radical reforms, even though the pace of the reform was slowed by domestic political struggles.

The second wave caused another wave of reaction. Now the wave of Asian financial reform is entering a new stage. NIES such as Singapore and Hong Kong also are setting up plans to reform their financial systems after the crisis. These economies were a driving force of the high economic development in Asia, and were not influenced heavily by the financial crisis. Their purpose rather is to make their local financial markets robust enough to be able to compete with global financial institutions. As Korea, Japan, and the other Asian economies which had been involved in the crisis started to radically modernize their financial systems, these NIES, whose financial systems had for the most part escaped the crisis, feared that they might lose their competitive edge and fall behind in the Asian market. They had to make moves to maintain their leading positions in the Asian financial market. In 1998 Singapore, for example, launched a financial reform plan, removing the strict regulation that had long separated domestic trading from overseas trading. Singapore decided to transform it domestic market from an over-regulated or over-protected one to a free one, under an "implicit government insurance". This was the "Financial Big Bang" in Singapore.

In short, the three waves of Japan and Korea, IMF, and NIES occurred successively, with some overlap. As a result, the Asian financial market is entering the new stage, called the "Financial Big Bang in Asia". The new changes are as follows.

The first is a shift to floating foreign exchange rate systems. Before the outbreak of the crisis, the foreign exchange rate systems in almost all the Asian economies had been gradually liberalized to somewhere between Japan's floating system and Hong Kong's fixed rate (currency board) system. The foreign exchange rate, however, was somewhat inflexible in many economies because the government placed importance on it as an anchor of macro-economic policy. As currency speculators attacked these economies in 1997, focusing on this point, almost all the economies shifted to a floating system. Only China, Hong Kong with its currency board system, and Malaysia following the reintroduction of capital controls still have fixed rate systems.

The second change is the removal of implicit government guarantees. Financial authorities in nearly all Asian economies had traditionally offered government guarantees to banks in order to maintain market stability. The crisis forced these governments to change the implicit government guarantees to explicit ones. State bank guarantees are shifting from full guarantees to limited ones based on a state deposit insurance scheme. Under this system, the government limits its guarantee to small-denominated depositors, and not to other parties such as stockholders, lenders and so on. This change may constrain the development of moral hazard from full-scale to limited scale one. The authorities in many economies such as Japan, Korea, Thailand, and Indonesia forcefully liquidated many insolvent banks or financial institutions during the crisis. This indicates that the implicit government guarantee system has collapsed.

The third change is the liberalization of exit policies. Free entry and exit is very important to ensure sound banking management. It can constrain moral hazard. During the crisis, authorities in many economies forced insolvent banks or financial institutions to liquidate instead of bailing them out. The door has been opened for banks to exit the market. The problem is for the authority to establish new rules for bank exits from the market. The point is to clarify a principle and a procedure on making choices on how to treat a bank in crisis: whether to choose a close-down, a liquidation, a merger with a sound bank, or a bailout, for example. In this regard, large amendments to bankruptcy laws and labor protection laws have been made in Korea, Indonesia, and other countries.

The fourth change is further liberalization on entry into financial markets. Many foreign institutions entered into the local markets using M&As in the process of restructuring ailing local banks in Japan, Korea, Thailand, and Indonesia. Eventually, the presence of foreign banks in these local markets became much larger in these economies than in the pre-crisis period. Singapore launched a reform plan to remove regulations separating the domestic market and the offshore market, while Malaysia maintains strict regulations on foreign bank's entry into the domestic market.

The fifth change is the introduction of prudential bank management policies. The tough competition for survival during the crisis forced risk-insensitive managements in the banking business under government guarantees to become more autonomous and prudent. Financial authorities have taken some measures, as follows. First, they have injected public funds to liquidate the huge non-performing loans accumulated in financial institutions. Second, they have introduced income recognition rules and accounting rules to clarify when a bank falls into insolvency. Third, they have strengthened shock-absorbing functions against financial crises, by strengthening rules on provisions for possible losses such as loan losses and payment troubles in financial institutions. Fourth, they have strengthened the authority's supervisory system through the introduction of the BIS risk-base ratio of owner's equity and early warning - prompt collective action system. New supervisory systems have finally been introduced and started to work in the Asian economies.

The sixth change has been the development of capital markets. In many of the Asian economies, with the exception of Malaysia, the financial systems are based mainly on banking rather than on security markets, which are still underdeveloped. This bank-dominated financial structure concentrated stress arising from mismatches in term-structure between short-term banking business and development finance onto the banking sector. Because of the lack of security markets as alternative means of fund-raising, it was difficult for enterprises to evade the negative effects of credit crunches resulted from banking crises. This made it easy from crises to spread from the banking sector to the real sector. Based on these lessons, Asian governments have taken various measures after the crisis to promote the development of security markets, especially bond markets. Singapore, Thailand, Malaysia, and Hong Kong are now competing to carry out broad reforms covering stock exchanges, primary markets, and secondary markets.

The seventh change is a reform of the privileged, oligopolistic structure of the economy. Although the IMF's structural adjustment policies may have aggravated the regional liquidity crisis in the short run, they made big steps in the long run to reform distorted economic structures in Korea, Thailand, and Indonesia. For example, a custom of inside-guarantee in a group and privileged interests between politicians, bureaucrats, and businessmen have been corrected, while a fair trade act has been introduced.

In short, financial system reforms have been carrying out in Asia, which driven by new entry of foreign capitals. That could be called "Financial Big Bang in Asia".

The 1997 Asian financial crisis can be attributed mainly to an institutional mismatch between factors on three levels: regional movements of short-term capital, rapid financial liberalization, and excessively-regulated (protected) financial systems. These factors were not shared only by the East Asian developing economies, but also by Japan, which was involved in the crisis. For the East Asian developing economies it meant the failure of the export-oriented development strategy, which depended heavily on foreign capital, that they had adopted since the middle of 1980s. The strategy might have been very effective for underdeveloped economies hoping to accomplish high economic growth. However, it was accompanied by rapid financial liberalization in the absence of the development of robust domestic financial markets which could resist volatile and huge movements of short-term capital. This institutional mismatch caused an asset bubble or over-investment and the consequent financial crisis.

In order to prevent a recurrence of the financial crisis, the East Asian economies need to correct this institutional mismatch. There are two ways to do this: a closed policy or an open policy. The first would involve the reintroduction of regulations on capital transactions so as to shut the domestic market from volatile movements of short-term capital. The second would be to restructure the domestic financial system into a more robust one by moving forward with further financial liberalization. All the East Asian economies involved in the crisis, with the sole exception of Malaysia, have adopted the second route. Many scholars, including IMF researchers, have approved of Malaysia's reintroduction of capital controls as an effective measure against the financial crisis in terms of a short-term stability. This book, however, focuses on log-term strategies centered on an efficient, stable financial system rather than on short-term patchwork measures. A consensus on this matter seems to have already been reached in the East Asian economies. Not only Thailand, Korea, and Indonesia, with the IMF's intervention, but also Japan, Taiwan, and Singapore without its intervention, are now competing on the second course. The driving force of this new wave has been the many foreign financial institutions which have entered into the local markets through M&As. The foreign banks have put down their roots so deeply and broadly into the local markets that they have considerable influence on the direction of local financial reform.

A new wave is surging through East Asia, under the name of the Financial Big Bang in Asia. The financial authorities have suspended their implicit government guarantees, strengthened market competition, and introduced prudential bank supervision based on the BIS risk base equity ratio and state deposit insurance schemes. It is undeniable that the financial systems in the East Asian economies have been modernized after the crisis.

The issue is to establish an efficient, stable financial system in order to prevent a recurrence of the financial crisis in Asia. In this regard, there are not necessarily any problem with either of the above-mentioned routes. The problem of the first is whether or not a closed economy isolated from international capital inflows could still maintain high economic growth. On the other hand, the problem with the second is whether or not it is possible to establish a financial system robust enough to withstand volatile movements of foreign capital. Nearly all the East Asian economies, with the exception of Malaysia, are carrying out financial system reform based on the second, open policy, and they may not yet have settled various problems. It is unclear whether such open policies will be able to prevent the recurrence of asset bubbles or over-investment when huge amounts of short-term foreign capital accumulate in the local market. This issue has not yet been verified even in the advanced economies. It appears that financial authorities in the advanced economies do not yet possess a set of effective measures to prevent the recurrence of asset bubbles and financial crises. In recent years they have developed a succession of preventive measures to replace the strict regulation of the past, ranging from the BIS risk base equity ratio and early warning schemes, to new management techniques for risk control such as a value-at-risk method. However there are no certain methods yet against crises under open policies.

Second, financial systems in the developing economies suffer from another weakness, namely the lack of sophisticated, mature markets. The East Asian economies have begun to reform their financial systems, through the introduction of prudential management, the development of security markets, and the modernization of business groups, etc. However, these reforms will take a long time to accomplish. The reason for this is that the East Asian economies are inclined to maintain well-regulated financial systems, based considerably on interdependent relationships between the government, banks, and business groups. Systems of this type met the need of developing economies to carry out economic development in an efficient way. In addition, however, such systems maintained an "implicit contract" relationship that is a peculiar and traditional social relationship in East Asian economic societies. It may prove difficult to change such traditional social relationships in a short time. The potential of the Financial Big Bang in the East Asian economies will be decided by a battle between drastic system reform based on the Anglo-Saxon model, and the "implicit contract" relationship that is so deeply imbedded in society. In the end, a new financial system is bound to emerge in the East Asian economies.

Reference

Asiamoney (1999a), 'Guide to Asian Currency Bond Markets 1999', May.
Asiamoney (1999b), 'Hong Kong's Big Bang: Too Much of a Good Thing', June.
Emery, Robert F (1997), *The Bond Markets of Developing East Asia*, Westview Press, Oxford.
Hancock, Phil and Greg Tower (1995), 'Accounting Regulation in East Asia', in Ky Cao (ed.), *The Changing Capital Markets of East Asia*, Chapter 9, Routledge.
Heij, Gitte (1995), 'Tax Regimes in East Asia: A Comparative Review', in Ky Cao (ed.), *The Changing Capital Markets of East Asia*, Chapter 8, Routledge.
Huar, Tan Chwee (2000), *Financial Sourcebook for Southeast Asia and Hong Kong*, Singapore University Press.
World Bank (1995), *The Emerging Asian Bond Market*, The World Bank.

Index

Obstfeld('s) model
(*see* second generation model)
off-exchange trades (trading) 48, 51
offshore market 21, 182, 204, 314
oil crises 311
oligopolistic 21, 304-305, 315
on-the-spot trading 147
overborrowing 66, 255, 258, 270
over-investment 2, 5, 14-20, 24, 27-28, 31,
65, 273, 315-316
over-lending 15, 270, 272
overseas Chinese 89
over-the-counter 99, 144, 148, 161-162,
171

Paris club 30
pay-off 51
People's Bank of China 137-138, 141,
145-146, 148
Plaza Accord 248
portfolio investment 7-12, 32, 81, 92,
100-102, 173, 235, 244-245, 259-
260, 271-272, 292-293
primary markets 95, 149, 164, 297-298,
307, 315
priority sector loan 297, 300-301
privatization 23-24, 63, 230, 234-235, 237,
254, 303-305
prompt corrective action 51, 314
prudential norm/scheme
(*see* prudential regulation)
prudential regulation 26, 74, 110, 185, 231,
238, 240, 243-245, 270, 272, 276,
304

regional liquidity crisis (crises) 2-3, 5-6,
11, 27, 33, 315
reschedule 30-31, 218
Reserve Bank of India (RBI) 293, 296-297,
301, 303-304, 308
resource allocation 33, 156, 168, 181
risk premium 123, 257, 293
risk-asset ratio/risk-adjusted assets ratio,
etc., (*see* capital adequacy ratio)
risk-averse(aversion) 304
risk-taking 44

safety-net 34, 53, 273, 277
second generation model 4-5, 28, 125
secondary market 44-45, 97, 143, 149,
159-160, 164, 306, 315
Securities and Exchange Council 44, 171

Securities Committee of the State Council
(SCSC) 148
securities scam 305
Securities Supervision and Administration
Commission (SSAC) 148, 158-160
Securities Supervision and Regulation
Commission 141
securitization 28, 41, 96-97, 102
Security and Exchanges Board of India
(SEBI) 298, 306
self-fulfilling 4-5, 14, 28
self-fulfilling speculation model
(*see* second generation model)
Shanghai Stock Exchange 140, 144-145,
148-150
Shenzhen Stock Exchange 140, 144-145,
148-150
short-term capital flows 81, 178, 181, 242,
275
short-term debt 11-14, 32-33, 167, 173,
186n, 258
sovereign debt 9, 30
speculation 4-5 14, 28, 37, 51, 95, 114,
119-121, 125, 149-150, 161, 164,
207, 234-235, 243, 260, 262-263,
271, 273, 275
sterilization 103, 210, 270
Stock Exchange of Thailand (SET) 172,
175
stock market booms 17, 117, 176-177
supervision (supervising) 1, 53-54, 67, 74,
82, 85, 96, 102, 117, 136, 141, 145,
148-151, 156, 158-161, 171, 185,
215-217, 220, 231, 233, 238,
243- 244, 265, 276, 292
swap 77, 182, 207
systemic risk 37, 48-49, 55, 231

Tablita 308
Taiwan International Mercantile Exchange
(TAIMEX) 101
third generation model 5-6, 9, 11, 13
Tobin tax 33, 208
Tokyo Stock Exchange 41

Treasury Bill 248, 252, 260, 263, 297, 301,
303
triple crises 5-6, 11, 13
21st century type financial crisis 2
twin crises (*see* third generation model)

universal banking 98, 104, 171